Made in America

Bill Bryson was born in Des Moines, Iowa, in 1951. He settled in England in 1977 and now lives in North Yorkshire with his English wife and four children. His other books include *Mother Tongue, The Lost Continent* and *Neither Here Nor There*.

Also by Bill Bryson

The Lost Continent
Mother Tongue
Neither Here Nor There*

available from Minerva

BILL BRYSON

Made in America

Illustrations by Bruce McCall

Minerva

A Minerva Paperback

MADE IN AMERICA

First published in Great Britain 1994
by Martin Secker & Warburg Limited
This Minerva edition published 1995
by Mandarin Paperbacks
an imprint of Reed Consumer Books Limited
Michelin House, 81 Fulham Road, London SW3 6RB
and Auckland, Melbourne, Singapore and Toronto

Reprinted 1995 (three times)

Copyright © 1994 by Bill Bryson
Illustrations copyright © by Bruce McCall

The author has asserted his moral rights

A CIP catalogue record for this title
is available from the British Library
ISBN 0 7493 9654 7

Printed and bound in Great Britain
by Cox & Wyman Ltd, Reading, Berkshire

To David, Felicity, Catherine and Sam

Contents

List of Illustrations

Acknowledgements

Among the many people to whom I am indebted for assistance and encouragement during the preparation of this book, I would like especially to thank Maria Guarnaschelli, Geoff Mulligan, Max Eilenberg, Carol Heaton, Dan Franklin, Andrew Franklin, John Price, Erla Zwingle, Karen Voelkening, Oliver Salzmann, Hobie and Lois Morris, Heidi Du Belt, James Mansley, Samuel H. Beamesderfer, Bonita Lousie Billman, Dr John L. Sommer, Allan M. Siegal, Bruce Corson, and the staffs of the Drake University Library in Des Moines and the National Geographic Society Library in Washington. Above all, and as ever, my infinite, heartfelt thanks and admiration to my wife, Cynthia.

Introduction

In the 1940s, a British traveller to Anholt, a small island fifty miles out in the Kattegat strait between Denmark and Sweden, noticed that the island children sang a piece of doggerel that was clearly nonsense to them. It went:

Jeck og Jill
Vent op de hill
Og Jell kom tombling after.

The ditty, it turned out, had been brought to the island by occupying British soldiers during the Napoleonic wars, and had been handed down from generation to generation of children for 130 years, even though the words meant nothing to them.

In London, this small discovery was received with interest by a couple named Peter and Iona Opie. The Opies had dedicated their lives to the scholarly pursuit of nursery rhymes. No one had put more effort into investigating the history and distribution of these durable but largely uncelebrated components of childhood life. Something that had long puzzled the Opies was the curious fate of a rhyme called 'Brow Bender'. Once as popular as 'Humpty Dumpty' and 'Hickory Dickory Dock', it was routinely included in children's nursery books up until the late eighteenth century, but then it quietly and mysteriously vanished. It had not been recorded in print anywhere since 1788. Then one night as the Opies' nanny was tucking their children in to bed, they overheard her reciting a nursery rhyme to them. It was, as you will have guessed, 'Brow Bender', exactly as set down in the 1788 version and with five lines never before recorded.

Now what, you may reasonably ask, does any of this have to do with a book on the history and development of the English language in America? I bring it up for two reasons. First, to make the point that it is often the little, unnoticed things that are most revealing about the history and nature of language. Nursery rhymes, for example, are fastidiously resistant to change. Even when they make no sense, as in the case of 'Jack and Jill' with children on an isolated Danish isle, they are generally passed from generation to generation with solemn precision, like a treasured incantation. Because of this, they are often among the longest-surviving features of any language. 'Eenie, meenie, minie, mo' is based on a counting system that predates the Roman occupation of Britain, and that may even be pre-Celtic. If so, it is one of our few surviving links with the very distant past. It not only gives us a fragmentary image of how children were being amused at the time that Stonehenge was built, but tells us something about how their elders counted and thought and ordered their speech. Little things, in short, are worth looking at.

The second point is that songs, words, phrases, ditties – any feature of language at all – can survive for long periods without anyone particularly noticing, as the Opies discovered with 'Brow Bender'. That a word or phrase hasn't been recorded tells us only that it hasn't been recorded, not that it hasn't existed. The inhabitants of England in the age of Chaucer commonly used an expression, *to be in hide and hair*, meaning to be lost or beyond discovery. But then it disappears from the written record for four hundred years before resurfacing, suddenly and unexpectedly, in America in 1857 as *neither hide nor hair*. It is clearly unlikely that the phrase went into a linguistic coma for four centuries. So who was quietly preserving it for four hundred years, and why did it so abruptly return to prominence in the sixth decade of the nineteenth century in a country two thousand miles away?

Why, come to that, did the Americans save such good old English words as *skedaddle* and *chitterlings* and *chore*, but not *fortnight* or *heath*? Why did they keep the irregular British pronunciations in words like *colonel* and *hearth*, but go our own way with *lieutenant* and *schedule* and *clerk*? Why in short is American English the way it is?

This is, it seems to me, a profoundly worthwhile and fascinating question, and yet until relatively recent times it is one that hardly anyone thought to ask. Until well into this century serious studies of American speech were left almost entirely to amateurs – people like the heroic Richard Harwood Thornton, an English-born lawyer who devoted years of his spare time to poring through books, journals and manuscripts from the earliest colonial period in search of the first appearances of hundreds of American terms. In 1912 he produced the two-volume *American Glossary*. It was a work of invaluable scholarship, yet he could not find a single American publisher prepared to take it on. Eventually, to the shame of American scholarship, it was published in London.

Not until the 1920s and '30s, with the successive publications of H. L. Mencken's incomparable *The American Language*, George Philip Krapp's *The English Language in America*, and Sir William Craigie and James R. Hulbert's *Dictionary of American English on Historical Principles*, did America at last get books that seriously addressed the question of its language. But by then the inspiration behind many hundreds of American expressions had passed into the realms of the unknowable, so that now no one can say why Americans *paint the town red*, *talk turkey*, *take a powder* or hit practice flies with a *fungo bat*.

This book is a modest attempt to examine how and why American speech came to be the way it is. It is not, I hope, a conventional history of the American language. Much of it is unashamedly discursive. You could be excused for wondering what Mrs Stuyvesant Fish's running over her servant three times in succession with her car has to do with the history and development of the English language in the United States, or how James Gordon Bennett's lifelong habit of yanking the cloths from every table he passed in a restaurant connects to the linguistic development of the American people. I would argue that unless we understand the social context in which words were formed – unless we can appreciate what a bewildering novelty the car was to those who first encountered it, or how dangerously extravagant and out of touch with the masses a turn-of-the-century business person could be – we cannot begin to appreciate the richness and vitality of the words that make American speech.

Oh, and I've included them for a third reason: because I thought they were interesting and hoped you might enjoy them. One of the small agonies of researching a book like this is that you come across stories that have no pressing relevance to the topic and must be let lie. I call them Ray Buduick stories. I came across Ray Buduick when I was thumbing through a 1941 volume of *Time* magazines looking for something else altogether. It happened that one day in that year Buduick decided, as he often did, to take his light aircraft up for an early Sunday morning spin. Nothing remarkable in that, except that Buduick lived in Honolulu and that this particular morning happened to be 7 December 1941. As he headed out over Pearl Harbour, Buduick was taken aback, to say the least, to find the western skies dense with Japanese Zeros, all bearing down on him. The Japanese raked his plane with fire and Buduick, presumably issuing utterances along the lines of 'Golly Moses!', banked sharply and cleared off. Miraculously he managed to land his plane safely in the midst of the greatest airborne attack yet seen in history, and lived to tell the tale, and in so doing became the first American to engage the Japanese in combat, however inadvertently.

Of course, this has nothing at all to do with the American language. But everything else that follows does. Honestly.

Founding Fathers' Day, Plymouth Rock

I

The Mayflower and Before

I

The image of the spiritual founding of America that generations of Americans have grown up with was created, oddly enough, by a poet of limited talents (to put it in the most magnanimous possible way) who lived two centuries after the event in a country three thousand miles away. Her name was Felicia Dorothea Hemans and she was not American but Welsh. Indeed, she had never been to America and appears to have known next to nothing about the country. It just happened that one day in 1826 her local grocer in north Wales wrapped her purchases in a sheet of two-year-old newspaper from Massachusetts, and her eye was caught by a small article about a founders' day celebration in Plymouth. It was very probably the first she had heard of the *Mayflower* or the Pilgrims, but inspired as only a mediocre poet can be, she dashed off a poem, 'The Landing of the Pilgrim Fathers (in New England)', which begins:

> The breaking waves dashed high
> On a stern and rock-bound coast,
> And the woods, against a stormy sky,
> Their giant branches toss'd
>
> And the heavy night hung dark
> The hills and water o'er,
> When a band of exiles moor'd their bark
> On the wild New England shore . . .

and continues in a vigorously grandiloquent, indeterminately

3

rhyming vein for a further eight stanzas. Although the poem was replete with errors – the *Mayflower* was not a bark, it was not night when they moored, Plymouth was not 'where first they trod' but in fact their fourth landing site – it became an instant classic, and formed the essential image of the *Mayflower* landing that most Americans carry with them to this day.*

The one thing the Pilgrims certainly didn't do was step ashore on Plymouth Rock. Quite apart from the consideration that it may have stood well above the high-water mark in 1620, no prudent mariner would try to bring a ship alongside a boulder on a heaving December sea when a sheltered inlet beckoned from near by. Indeed, it is doubtful that the Pilgrims even noticed Plymouth Rock. No mention of the rock is found among any of the surviving documents and letters of the age, and it doesn't make its first recorded appearance until 1715, almost a century later.[1] Not until about the time Ms Hemans wrote her swooping epic did Plymouth Rock become indelibly associated with the landing of the Pilgrims.

Wherever they first trod, we can assume that the 102 Pilgrims stepped from their storm-tossed little ship with unsteady legs and huge relief. They had just spent nine and a half damp and perilous weeks at sea, crammed together on a creaking vessel about the size of a modern double-decker bus. The crew, with the customary graciousness of sailors, referred to them as *puke stockings*, on account of their apparently boundless ability to spatter the latter with the former, though in fact they had handled the experience reasonably well.[2] Only one passenger had died en route, and two had been added through births (one of whom revelled ever after in the exuberant name of Oceanus Hopkins).

They called themselves *Saints*. Those members of the party who were not Saints they called *Strangers*. *Pilgrims*, in reference to these early voyagers, would not become common for another two hundred years. Nor, strictly speaking, is it correct to call them *Puritans*. They were *Separatists*, so called because they had left the Church of England. *Puritans* were those who remained in the Anglican Church but wished to purify it. They would not arrive in

---

* Mrs Hemans' other principal contribution to posterity was the poem 'Casabianca', now remembered chiefly for its opening line: 'The boy stood on the burning deck.'

America for another decade, but when they did they would quickly eclipse, and eventually absorb, this little original colony.

It would be difficult to imagine a group of people more ill-suited to a life in the wilderness. They packed as if they had misunderstood the purpose of the trip. They found room for sundials and candle snuffers, a drum, a trumpet, and a complete history of Turkey. One William Mullins packed 126 pairs of shoes and 13 pairs of boots. Yet between them they failed to bring a single cow or horse or plough or fishing line. Among the professions represented on the *Mayflower*'s manifest were two tailors, a printer, several merchants, a silk worker, a shopkeeper and a hatter – occupations whose importance is not immediately evident when one thinks of surviving in a hostile environment.[3] Their military commander, Miles Standish, was so diminutive of stature that he was known to all as 'Captain Shrimpe'[4] – hardly a figure to inspire awe in the savage natives whom they confidently expected to encounter. With the uncertain exception of the little captain, probably none in the party had ever tried to bring down a wild animal. Hunting in seventeenth-century Europe was a sport reserved for the aristocracy. Even those who labelled themselves farmers generally had scant practical knowledge of husbandry, since *farmer* in the 1600s, and for some time afterwards, signified an owner of land rather than one who worked it.

They were, in short, dangerously unprepared for the rigours ahead, and they demonstrated their manifest incompetence in the most dramatic possible way: by dying in droves. Six expired in the first two weeks, eight the next month, seventeen more in February, a further thirteen in March. By April, when the *Mayflower* set sail back to England*, just fifty-four people, nearly half of them children, were left to begin the long work of turning this tenuous toehold into a self-sustaining colony.[5]

At this remove, it is difficult to conceive just how alone this small,

---

* The *Mayflower*, like Plymouth Rock, appears to have made no sentimental impression on the colonists. Not once in *Of Plimouth Plantation*, William Bradford's history of the colony, did he mention the ship by name. Just three years after its epochal crossing, the *Mayflower* was unceremoniously broken up and sold for salvage. According to several accounts, it ended up being made into a barn that still stands in the village of Jordans, Buckinghamshire, about twenty miles from London. Coincidentally, almost in its shadow is the grave of William Penn, the founder of Pennsylvania.

hapless band of adventurers was. Their nearest kindred neighbours – at Jamestown in Virginia and at a small and now all but forgotten colony at Cupers (now Cupids) Cove in Newfoundland* – were five hundred miles off in opposite directions. At their back stood a hostile ocean, and before them lay an inconceivably vast and unknown continent of 'wild and savage hue', in William Bradford's uneasy words. They were about as far from the comforts of civilization as anyone had ever been (certainly as far as anyone had ever been without a fishing line).

For two months they tried to make contact with the natives, but every time they spotted any, the Indians ran off. Then one day in February a young brave of friendly mien approached a party of Pilgrims on a beach. His name was Samoset and he was a stranger in the region himself, but he had a friend named Tisquantum from the local Wampanoag tribe, to whom he introduced them. Samoset and Tisquantum became the Pilgrims' fast friends. They showed them how to plant corn and catch wildfowl and helped them to establish friendly relations with the local *sachem*, or chief. Before long, as every schoolchild knows, the Pilgrims were thriving, and Indians and settlers were sitting down to a cordial Thanksgiving feast. Life was grand.

A question that naturally arises is *how* they managed this. Algonquian, the language of the eastern tribes, is an extraordinarily complex and agglomerative tongue (or more accurately family of tongues), full of formidable consonant clusters that are all but unpronounceable to the untutored, as we can see from the first primer of Algonquian speech prepared some twenty years later by Roger Williams in Connecticut (a feat of scholarship deserving of far wider fame, incidentally). Try saying the following and you may get some idea of the challenge:

Nquitpausuckowashâwmen – There are a hundred of us.
Chénock wonck cuppee-yeâumen? – When will you return?

* Founded in 1610, this small colony was abandoned in the 1630s, though it was soon replaced by other British settlements on the island. Because of their isolation, Newfoundlanders created a peculiarly colourful patois blending new coinages and old English dialectal words that now exist nowhere else: *diddies* for a nightmare, *nunny-bag* for a kind of knapsack, *cocksiddle* for a somersault, *rushing the waddock* for the game of rugby. They continue to employ many odd pronunciations. *Chitterlings*, for instance, is pronounced 'chistlings'. The one word that Newfoundland has given the world is *penguin*. No one has any idea what inspired it.

Tashúckqunne cummauchenaûmis – How long have you been sick?
Ntannetéimmin – I will be going.[6]

Clearly this was not a language you could pick up in a weekend,
and the Pilgrims were hardly gifted linguists. They weren't even
comfortable with Tisquantum's name; they called him Squanto.
The answer, surprisingly glossed over by most history books, is
that the Pilgrims didn't have to learn Algonquian for the happy and
convenient reason that Samoset and Squanto spoke English.
Samoset spoke it only a little, but Squanto spoke English with total
assurance (and Spanish into the bargain).

That a straggly band of English settlers could in 1620 cross a vast
ocean and find a pair of Indians able to welcome them in their own
tongue seems little short of miraculous. It was certainly lucky – the
Pilgrims would very probably have perished or been slaughtered
without them – but not as wildly improbable as it at first seems. The
fact is that in 1620 the New World wasn't really so new at all.

II

No one knows who the first European visitors to the New World
were. The credit generally goes to the Vikings, who reached the
New World in about AD 1000, but there are grounds to suppose
that others may have been there even earlier. An ancient Latin text,
the *Navigatio Sancti Brendani Abbatis* (*The Voyage of St.
Brendan the Abbot*), recounts with persuasive detail a seven-year
trip to the New World made by this Irish saint and a band of
acolytes some four centuries before the Vikings – and this on the
advice of another Irishman who claimed to have been there earlier
still.

Even the Vikings didn't think themselves the first. Their sagas
record that when they first arrived in the New World they were
chased from the beach by a group of wild white people. They
subsequently heard stories from natives of a settlement of
Caucasians who 'wore white garments and . . . carried poles before
them to which rags were attached'[7] – precisely how an Irish
religious procession would have looked to the uninitiated.
(Intriguingly, five centuries later Columbus's men would hear a
similar story in the Caribbean.) Whether by Irish or Vikings – or

Italians or Welsh or Bretons or any of the other many groups for whom credit has been sought – crossing the Atlantic in the Middle Ages was not quite as daring a feat as it would at first appear, even allowing for the fact that it was done in small, open boats. The North Atlantic is conveniently scattered with islands that could serve as stepping-stones – the Shetland Islands, Faeroes, Iceland, Greenland and Baffin. It would be possible to sail from Scandinavia to Canada without once crossing more than 250 miles of open sea. We know beyond doubt that Greenland – and thus, technically, North America – was discovered in 982 by one Eric the Red, father of Leif Ericson (or Leif Eiríksson), and that he and his followers began settling it in 986. Anyone who has ever flown over the frozen wastes of Greenland could be excused for wondering what they saw in the place. But in fact Greenland's southern fringes are further south than Oslo and offer an area of grassy lowlands as big as the whole of Britain.[8] Certainly it suited the Vikings. For nearly five hundred years they kept a thriving colony there, which at its peak boasted sixteen churches, two monasteries, some 300 farms and a population of 4,000. But the one thing Greenland lacked was wood with which to build new ships and repair old ones – a somewhat vital consideration for a seagoing people. Iceland, the nearest land mass to the east, was known to be barren. The most natural thing would be to head west to see what was out there. In about 1000, according to the sagas, Leif Ericson did just that. His expedition discovered a new land mass, probably Baffin Island, far up in northern Canada, over a thousand miles north of the present-day United States, and many other places, most notably the region they called Vinland.

Vinland is one of history's more tantalizing posers. No one knows where it was. By careful readings of the sagas and calculations of Viking sailing times, various scholars have put Vinland all over the place – on Newfoundland or Nova Scotia, in Massachusetts or even as far south as Virginia. A Norwegian scholar named Helge Ingstad claimed in 1964 to have found Vinland at a place called L'Anse au Meadow in Newfoundland. Others suggest that the artefacts Ingstad found were not of Viking origin at all, but merely the detritus of later French colonists.[9] No one knows. The name is no help. According to the sagas, the Vikings called it Vinland because of the grape-vines they found growing in profusion there. The problem is that no place within a thousand miles of where they must have been could possibly have supported grapes. One possible explanation is that Vinland was a mistranslation. *Vinber*, the Viking word for grapes, could be used to describe many other fruits – cranberries, gooseberries and red currants, among them – that might have been found at these northern latitudes. Another possibility is that Vinland was merely a bit of deft propaganda, designed to encourage settlement. These were after all the people who thought up the name Greenland.

The Vikings made at least three attempts to build permanent settlements in Vinland, the last in 1013, before finally giving up. Or possibly not. What is known beyond doubt is that sometime after 1408 the Vikings abruptly disappeared from Greenland. Where they went or what became of them is unknown.[10] The tempting presumption is that they found a more congenial life in North America.

There is certainly an abundance of inexplicable clues. Consider the matter of lacrosse, a game long popular with Indians across wide tracts of North America. Interestingly, the rules of lacrosse are uncannily like those of a game played by the Vikings, including one feature – the use of paired team-mates who may not be helped or impeded by other players – so unusual, in the words of one anthropologist, 'as to make the probability of independent origin vanishingly small'. Then there were the Haneragmiuts, a tribe of Inuits living high above the Arctic Circle on Victoria Island in northern Canada, a place so remote that its inhabitants were not known to the outside world until early this century. Yet several members of the tribe not only looked unsettlingly European but were found to be carrying indubitably European genes.[11] No one has ever provided a remotely satisfactory explanation of how this could be. Or consider the case of Olof and Edward Ohman, father and son respectively, who in 1888 were digging up tree stumps on their farm near Kensington, Minnesota, when they came upon a large stone slab covered with runic inscriptions, which appear to describe how a party of thirty Vikings had returned to that spot after an exploratory survey to find the ten men they had left behind 'red with blood and dead'. The inscriptions have been dated to 1363. The one problem is how to explain why a party of weary explorers, facing the prospect of renewed attack by hostile natives, would take the time to make elaborate carvings on a rock deep in the American wilderness, thousands of miles from where anyone they knew would be able to read it. Still, if a hoax, it was executed with unusual skill and verisimilitude.

All this is by way of making the point that word of the existence of a land beyond the Ocean Sea, as the Atlantic was then known, was filtering back to Europeans long before Columbus made his epic voyage. The Vikings did not operate in isolation. They settled all over Europe and their exploits were widely known. They even left a map – the famous Vinland map – which is known to have been circulating in Europe by the fourteenth century. We don't positively know that Columbus was aware of this map, but we do know that the course he set appeared to be making a beeline for the mythical island of Antilla, which featured on it.

Columbus never found Antilla or anything else he was looking for. His epochal voyage of 1492 was almost the last thing – indeed almost the only thing – that went right in his life. Within eight years, he would find himself summarily relieved of his post as Admiral of the Ocean Sea, returned to Spain in chains and allowed to sink into such profound obscurity that even now we don't know for sure where he is buried. To achieve such a precipitous fall in less than a decade required an unusual measure of incompetence and arrogance. Columbus had both.

He spent most of those eight years bouncing around the islands of the Caribbean and coasts of South America without ever having any real idea of where he was or what he was doing. He always thought that *Cipangu*, or Japan, was somewhere near by and never divined that Cuba was an island. To his dying day he insisted that it was part of the Asian mainland (though there is some indication that he may have had his own doubts since he made his men swear under oath that it was Asia or have their tongues cut out). His geographic imprecision is most enduringly preserved in the name he gave to the natives: *Indios*, which of course has come down to us as *Indians*. He cost the Spanish crown a fortune and gave in return little but broken promises. And throughout he behaved with the kind of impudence – demanding to be made hereditary Admiral of the Ocean Sea, as well as Viceroy and Governor of the lands that he conquered, and to be granted one-tenth of whatever wealth his enterprises generated – that all but invited his eventual downfall.

In this he was not alone. Many other New World explorers met misfortune in one way or another. Juan Díaz de Solís and Giovanni da Verrazano were eaten by natives. Balboa, after discovering the Pacific, was executed on trumped-up charges, betrayed by his colleague Francisco Pizarro, who in his turn ended up murdered by rivals. Hernando de Soto marched an army pointlessly all over the south-western US for four years until he caught a fever and died. Scores of adventurers, enticed by tales of fabulous cities – Quivira, Bimini, the City of the Caesars and Eldorado ('the gilded one') – went looking for wealth, eternal youth, or a shortcut to the Orient and mostly found misery. Their fruitless searches live on, sometimes unexpectedly, in the names on the landscape. California commemorates a Queen Califía, unspeakably rich but unfortunately non-existent. The Amazon is named for a tribe of one-breasted women. Brazil and the Antilles recall fabulous, but also fictitious, islands.

Further north the English fared little better. Sir Humphrey Gilbert perished in a storm off the Azores in 1583 after trying unsuccessfully to found a colony on Newfoundland. His half-brother Sir Walter Raleigh attempted to establish a settlement in Virginia and lost a fortune, and eventually his head, in the effort. Henry Hudson pushed his crew a little too far while looking for a north-west passage and found himself, Bligh-like, being put to sea in a little boat, never to be seen again. The endearingly hopeless Martin Frobisher explored the Arctic region of Canada, found what he thought was gold and carried 1,500 tons of it home on a dangerously overloaded boat only to be informed that it was worthless iron pyrite. Undaunted, Frobisher returned to Canada, found another source of gold, carted 1,300 tons of it back and was informed, no doubt with a certain weariness on the part of the royal assayer, that it was the same stuff. After that, we hear no more of Martin Frobisher.

It is interesting to speculate what these daring adventurers would think if they knew how whimsically we commemorate them today. Would Giovanni da Verrazano think being eaten by cannibals a reasonable price to pay for having his name attached to a toll bridge between Brooklyn and Staten Island? I suspect not. De Soto found transient fame in the name of an automobile, Frobisher in a distant icy bay, Raleigh in a city in North Carolina, a brand of cigarettes and a type of bicycle, Hudson in several waterways and a chain of department stores. On balance, Columbus, with a university, two state capitals, a country in South America, a province in Canada and high schools almost without number, among a great deal else, came out of it pretty well. But in terms of linguistic immortality no one got more mileage from less activity than a shadowy Italian-born businessman named Amerigo Vespucci.

A Florentine who had moved to Seville where he ran a ship supply business (one of his customers was his compatriot Christopher Columbus), Vespucci seemed destined for obscurity. How two continents came to be named in his honour required an unlikely measure of coincidence and error. Vespucci did make some voyages to the New World (authorities differ on whether it was three or four), but always as a passenger or lowly officer. He was not, by any means, an accomplished seaman. Yet in 1504–5, there began circulating in Florence letters of unknown authorship, collected under the title *Nuovo Mundo* (*New World*), which stated that Vespucci had not only been captain of these voyages but had discovered the New World.

The mistake would probably have gone no further except that an instructor at a small college in eastern France named Martin Waldseemüller was working on a revised edition of Ptolemy and decided to freshen it up with a new map of the world. In the course of his research he came upon the Florentine letters and, impressed with their spurious account of Vespucci's exploits, named the continent in his honour. (It wasn't quite as straightforward as that: first he translated *Amerigo* into the Latin *Americus* and then transformed that into its feminine form, *America*, on the ground that *Asia* and *Europe* were feminine. He also considered the name *Amerige*.) Even so it wasn't until forty years later that people began to refer to the New World as America, and then they meant by it only South America.

Vespucci did have one possible, if slightly marginal, claim to fame. He is thought to have been the brother of Simonetta Vespucci, the model for Venus in the famous painting by Botticelli.[12]

Since neither Columbus nor Vespucci ever set foot on the land mass that became the United States, it would be more aptly named for Giovanni Caboto, an Italian mariner better known to history by his Anglicized name of John Cabot. Sailing from Bristol in 1495, Cabot 'discovered' Newfoundland and possibly Nova Scotia and a number of smaller islands, and in the process became the first known European to visit North America, though in fact he more probably was merely following fishing fleets that were trawling the Grand Banks already. What is certain is that in 1475, because of war in Europe, British fisherman lost access to the traditional fishing grounds off Iceland. Yet British cod stocks did not fall, and in 1490 (two years before Columbus sailed) when Iceland offered the British fishermen the chance to come back, they declined. The presumption is that they had discovered the cod-rich waters off Newfoundland and didn't want anyone else to know about them.[13]

Whether Cabot inspired the fishermen or they him, by the early 1500s the Atlantic was thick with English vessels. A few came to prey on Spanish treasure ships, made sluggish and vulnerable by the weight of gold and silver they were carrying back to the Old World. Remarkably good money could be made from this.* On a single voyage Sir Francis Drake returned to England with booty worth $60 million in today's money.[14] On the same voyage, Drake briefly put ashore in what is now Virginia, claimed it for the crown and called it *New Albion*.[15]

To give the claim weight, and to provide a supply base for privateers, Queen Elizabeth I decided it might be an idea to establish a colony. She gave the task to Sir Walter Raleigh. The result was the ill-fated 'lost colony' of Roanoke, whose 114 members were put ashore just south of Albemarle Sound in what is now North Carolina in 1587. From that original colony sprang seven names that still feature on the landscape: *Roanoke* (which has the distinction of being the first Indian word borrowed by

---

* Spain was preyed on not only by sailors from rival nations, but also by mutineer sailors of her own. These latter were called *buccaneers* because after fleeing their Spanish masters they would sustain themselves by smoking the flesh of wild hogs on a wooden frame called a *boucan*, until they could capture a becalmed ship and make it their own.

English settlers), *Cape Fear, Cape Hatteras*, the *Chowan* and *Neuse* rivers, *Chesapeake* and *Virginia*.[16] (Previously Virginia had been called *Windgancon*, meaning 'what gay clothes you wear' — apparently what the locals had replied when an early reconnoitring party had asked them what they called the place.) But that alas was about all the colony achieved. Because of the war with Spain, no English ship was able to return for three years. When at last a relief ship called, it found the colony deserted. For years afterwards, visitors would occasionally spot a blond-haired Indian child, and the neighbouring Croatoan tribe was eventually discovered to have incorporated several words of Elizabethan English into its own tongue, but no firmer evidence of the colony's fate was ever found.

Other settlements followed, among them the now forgotten Popham Colony, formed in 1610 in what is now Maine, but abandoned after two years, and the rather more durable but none the less ever-precarious colony of Jamestown, founded in Virginia in 1607.

Mostly, however, what drew the English to the New World was the fishing, especially along the almost unimaginably bounteous waters off the north-east coast of North America. For at least 120 years before the *Mayflower* set sail European fishing fleets had been an increasingly common sight along the eastern seaboard. Often the fleets would put ashore to dry fish, replenish stocks of food and water, or occasionally wait out a harsh winter. As many as a thousand fishermen at a time would gather on the beaches. It was from such groups that Samoset had learned his few words of English.

As a result, by 1620 there was scarcely a bay in New England and eastern Canada that didn't bear some relic of their passing. The Pilgrims themselves soon came upon an old cast-iron cooking pot, obviously of European origin, and while plundering some Indian graves (an act of crass injudiciousness, all but inviting their massacre) they uncovered the body of a blond-haired man, 'possibly a Frenchman who had died in captivity'.[17]

New England may have been a new world to the Pilgrims, but it was hardly terra incognita. Much of the land around them had already been mapped. Eighteen years earlier, Bartholomew Gosnold and a party described as '24 gentlemen and eight sailors' had camped for a few months on nearby Cuttyhunk Island and left behind many names, two of which endure: *Cape Cod* and the romantically mysterious *Martha's Vineyard* (mysterious because we don't know who Martha was).

Seven years before, John Smith, passing by on a whaling expedition, had remapped the region, diligently taking heed of the names the Indians themselves used. He added just one name of his own devising: *New England*. (Previously the region had been called *Norumbega* on most maps. No one now has any clear idea why.) But in a consummate display of brown-nosing, upon his return to England Smith presented his map to Charles Stuart, the sixteen-year-old heir apparent, along with a note 'humbly intreating' his Highness 'to change their barbarous names for such English, as posterity might say Prince Charles was their Godfather.' The young prince fell to the task with relish. He struck out most of the Indian names that Smith had so carefully transcribed and replaced them with a whimsical mix that honoured himself and his family, or that simply took his fancy. Among his creations were *Cape Elizabeth, Cape Anne*, the *Charles River* and *Plymouth*. In consequence when the Pilgrims landed at Plymouth one of the few tasks they didn't have to manage was thinking up names for the landmarks all around them. They were already named.

Sometimes the early explorers took Indians back to Europe with them. Such had been the fate of the heroic Squanto, whose life story reads like an implausible picaresque novel. He had been picked up by a seafarer named George Weymouth in 1605 and carried off – whether voluntarily or not is unknown – to England. There he had spent nine years working at various jobs before returning to the New World as interpreter for John Smith on his voyage of 1613. As reward for his help, Smith gave Squanto his liberty. But no sooner had Squanto been reunited with his tribe than he and nineteen of his fellows were kidnapped by another Englishman, who carried them off to Málaga, and sold them as slaves. Squanto worked as a house servant in Spain before somehow managing to escape to England, where he worked for a time for a merchant in the City of London before finally, in 1619, returning to the New World on yet another exploratory expedition of the New England coast.[18] Altogether he had been away for nearly fifteen years, and he returned to find that only a short while before his tribe had been wiped out by a plague – almost certainly smallpox introduced by visiting sailors.

Thus Squanto had certain grounds to be disgruntled. Not only had Europeans inadvertently exterminated his tribe, but twice had carried him off and once sold him into slavery. Fortunately for the Pilgrims, Squanto was of a forgiving nature. Having spent the greater part of his adult life among the English, he may well have felt more comfortable among Britons than among his own people. In any case, he settled with them and for the next year, until he died of a sudden fever, served as their faithful teacher, interpreter, ambassador and friend. Thanks to him, the future of English in the New World was assured.

The question of what kind of English it was, and would become, lies at the heart of what follows.

2

Becoming Americans

> We whofe names are underwritten, the loyal subjects of our
> dread fovereigne Lord, King James, by ye grace of God, of
> Great Britaine, France and Ireland, King, defender of ye
> faith, etc., haveing undertaken for ye glory of God and
> advancement of ye Christian faith, and honour of our King
> and countrie, a voyage to plant ye firft Colonie in ye
> Northerne parts of Virginia, doe by thefe presents folemnly,
> and mutualy . . . covenant and combine ourfelves togeather
> into a civil body politick for our better ordering and
> prefervation and furtherance of ye end aforefaid. . . .

So begins the *Mayflower Compact*, written in 1620 shortly before
the Mayflower Pilgrims stepped ashore. The passage, I need hardly
point out, contains some differences from modern English. We no
longer use *f* interchangeably with *s*, or *ye* for *the*.* A few spellings –
Britaine, togeather, Northerne – clearly vary from modern practice, but generally only slightly and not enough to confuse us,
whereas only a generation before we would find far greater
irregularities (for example, *gelousie, conseil, audacite, wiche,
loware* for *jealousy, council, audacity, which* and *lower*). We
would not nowadays refer to a 'dread sovereign', and if we did we
would not mean by it one to be held in awe. But allowing for these
few anachronisms, the passage is clear, recognizable, wholly
accessible English.

---

* And that, incidentally, is all *ye* ever was – another way of writing *the*. It was a
convenience for scribes and printers, a device that made it easier to justify lines. It was
not pronounced 'yee'.

Were we, however, somehow to be transported to the Plymouth colony of 1620 and allowed to eavesdrop on the conversations of those who drew up and signed the *Mayflower Compact*, we would almost certainly be astonished at how different – how frequently incomprehensible – much of their spoken language would be to us. Though it would be clearly identifiable as English, it would be a variety of English unlike any we had heard before. Among the differences that would most immediately strike us:

- *Kn-*, which was always sounded in Middle English, was at the time of the Pilgrims going through a transitional phase in which it was commonly pronounced *tn*. Where the Pilgrims' parents or grandparents would have pronounced *knee* as 'kuh-nee,' they themselves would have been more likely to say 't'nee.'
- The interior *gh* in words like *night* and *light* had been silent for about a generation, but on or near the end of words – in *laugh, nought, enough, plough* – it was still sometimes pronounced, sometimes left silent and sometimes given an *f* sound.
- There was no sound equivalent to the *ah* in the modern *father* and *calm*. *Father* would have rhymed with the present-day *gather* and *calm* with *ram*.
- *Was* was pronounced not 'woz' but 'wass', and remained so, in some circles at least, long enough for Byron to rhyme it with *pass*. Conversely, *kiss* was often rhymed with *is*.
- *War* rhymed with *car* or *care*. It didn't gain its modern pronunciation until sometime after the turn of the nineteenth century.[1]
- *Home* was commonly spelled 'whome' and pronounced, by at least some speakers, as it was spelled, with a distinct *wh-* sound.
- The various *o* and *u* sounds were, to put it mildly, confused and unsettled. Many people rhymed *cut* with *put*, *plough* with *screw*, *book* with *moon*, *blood* with *load*. Dryden, as late as the second half of the seventeenth century, made no distinction between *flood, mood* and *good*, though quite how he intended them to be pronounced is anybody's guess. The vicissitudes of the wandering *oo* sound are evident both in its multiplicity of modern pronunciations (for example, *flood, wood, mood*) and the number of such words in which the pronunciation is not fixed even now, notably *roof, soot* and *hoof*.

- *Oi* was sounded with a long *i*, so that *coin'd* sounded like *kind* and *voice* like *vice*. The modern *oi* sound was sometimes heard, but was considered a mark of vulgarity until about the time of the American Revolution.

- Words that now have a short *e* were often pronounced and sometimes spelled with a short *i*. Shakespeare commonly wrote 'bin' for *been*, and as late as the tail-end of the eighteenth century Benjamin Franklin was defending a short *i* pronunciation for *get, yet, steady, chest, kettle* and the second syllable of *instead*[2] – though by this time he was fighting a losing battle.

- Speech was in general much broader, with stresses and a greater rounding of *r*s. A word like *never* would have been pronounced more like 'nev-*arrr*'.[3] Interior vowels and consonants were more frequently suppressed, so that *nimbly* became 'nimly', *fault* and *salt* became 'faut' and 'saut', *somewhat* was 'summat'. Other letter combinations were pronounced in ways strikingly at variance with their modern forms. In his *Special Help to Orthographie or the True-writing of English* (1643), a popular book of the day, Richard Hodges listed the following pairs of words as being 'so neer alike in sound ... that they are sometimes taken one for another': *ream* and *realm*, *shoot* and *suit*, *room* and *Rome*, *were* and *wear*, *poles* and *Paul's*, *flea* and *flay*, *eat* and *ate*, *copies* and *coppice*, *person* and *parson*, *Easter* and *Hester*, *Pierce* and *parse*, *least* and *lest*. The spellings – and misspellings – of names in the earliest records of towns like Plymouth and Dedham give us some idea of how much more fluid early colonial pronunciation was. These show a man named Parson sometimes referred to as *Passon* and sometimes as *Passen*; a Barsham as *Barsum* or *Bassum*; a Garfield as *Garfill*; a Parkhurst as *Parkis*; a Holmes as *Holums*; a Pickering as *Pickram*; a St John as *Senchion*; a Seymour as *Seamer*; and many others.[4]

- Differences in idiom abounded, notably with the use of definite and indefinite articles. As Baugh and Cable note, Shakespeare commonly discarded articles where we would think them necessary – 'creeping like snail', 'with as big heart as thou' and so on – but at the same time he employed them where we would not, so that where we say 'at length' and 'at last', he wrote 'at the length' and 'at the last'. The preposition *of* was also much more freely employed. Shakespeare used it in many places where we would require another: 'it was well done of [by] you', 'I brought him up of [from] a puppy', 'I have no mind of [for] feasting', 'That did but show thee of [as] a fool', and so on.[5] One relic of this practice survives in American English in the way we tell time. Where Americans commonly say that it is 'ten of three' or 'twenty of four', the British only say 'ten to' or 'twenty to'.

- *Er* and *ear* combinations were frequently, if not invariably, pronounced 'ar', so that *convert* became 'convart', *heard* was 'hard' (though also 'heerd'), and *serve* was 'sarve'. *Merchant* was pronounced and often spelled 'marchant'. The British preserve the practice in several words today – as with *clerk* and *derby*, for instance – but in America the custom was long ago abandoned but for a few well-established exceptions like *heart, hearth* and *sergeant*, or else the spelling was amended, as with making *sherds* into *shards* or *Hertford*, Connecticut, into *Hartford*.

- Generally, words containing *ea* combinations – *tea, meat, deal* and so on –were pronounced with a long *ā* sound (and of course many still are: *great, break, steak,* for instance), so that, for example, *meal* and *mail* were homonyms. The modern *ee* pronunciation was just emerging, so that Shakespeare could, as his whim took him, rhyme *please* with either *grace* or *knees*. Among more conservative users the old style persisted well into the eighteenth century, as in the well-known lines by the poet William Cowper:

> I am monarch of all I survey. . .
> From the centre all round to the sea.

Different as this English was from modern English, it was nearly as different again from the English spoken only a generation or two before in the mid-1500s. In countless ways, the language of the Pilgrims was strikingly more advanced, less visibly rooted in the conventions and inflections of Middle English, than that of their grandparents or even parents.

The old practice of making plurals by adding *-n* was rapidly giving way to the newer convention of adding *-s*, so that by 1620 most people were saying *knees* instead of *kneen, houses* instead of *housen, fleas* instead of *flean*. The transition was by no means complete at the time of the Pilgrims – we can find *eyen* for *eyes* and *shoon* for *shoes* in Shakespeare – and indeed survives yet in a few words, notably *children*, *brethren* and *oxen*, but the process was well under way.

A similar transformation was happening with the terminal *-th* on verbs like *maketh*, *leadeth* and *runneth*, which also were increasingly being given an *-s* ending in the modern way. Shakespeare used *-s* terminations almost exclusively except for *hath* and *doth*.* Only the most conservative works, such as the King James Bible of 1611, which contains no *-s* forms, stayed faithful to the old pattern. Interestingly, it appears that by the early seventeenth century even when the word was spelled with a *-th* termination it was pronounced as if spelled with an *-s*. In other words, people wrote 'hath' but said 'has', saw 'doth' but thought 'does', read 'goeth' as 'goes'. The practice is well illustrated in Hodges' *Special Help to Orthographie*, which lists as homophones such seemingly odd bedfellows as *weights* and *waiteth*, *cox* and *cocketh*, *rights* and *righteth*, *rose* and *roweth*.

At the same time, endings in *-ed* were beginning to be blurred. Before the Elizabethan age, an *-ed* ending was accorded its full phonetic value, a practice we preserve in a few words like *beloved* and *blessed*. But by the time of the Pilgrims the modern habit of eliding the ending (except after *t* and *d*) was taking over. For nearly two hundred years, the truncated pronunciation was indicated in writing with an apostrophe – *drown'd*, *frown'd*, *weav'd* and so on. Not until the end of the eighteenth century would the elided pronunciation become so general as to render this spelling distinction unnecessary.

The median *t* in *Christmas*, *soften* and *hasten* and other such words was beginning to disappear (though it has been reintroduced by many people in *often*). Just coming into vogue, too, was the *sh* sound of *ocean*, *creation*, *passion* and *sugar*. Previously such words

---

* Why the *-s* termination rose to prominence is something of a mystery. It came from northern England, a region that had, and still has, many dialectal differences from the more populous south, none other of which has ever had the slightest influence on the speech of London and its environs. Why the inhabitants of southern England suddenly began to show a special regard for the form in the late sixteenth century is unknown.

had been pronounced as sibilants, as many Britons still say 'tiss-you' and 'iss-you' for *tissue* and *issue*.

The early colonists were among the first to use the new word *good-bye*, contracted from *God be with you* and still at that time often spelled 'Godbwye', and were among the first to employ the more democratic forms *ye* and *you* in preference to the traditional *thee*, *thy* and *thou*, though many drifted uncertainly between the forms, as Shakespeare himself did, even sometimes in adjoining sentences, as in *1 Henry IV*: 'I love thee infinitely. But hark you, Kate.'*

They were also among the first to make use of the newly minted letter *j*. Previously *i* had served this purpose, so that Chaucer, for instance, wrote *ientyl* and *ioye* for *gentle* and *joy*. At first, *j* was employed simply as a variant of *i*, as *f* was a variant for *s*. Gradually *j* took on its modern *juh* sound, a role previously filled by *g* (and hence the occasional freedom in English to choose between the two letters, as with *jibe* and *gibe*).

In terms of language, the Pilgrims could scarcely have chosen a more exciting time to come. Perhaps no other period in history has been more linguistically diverse and dynamic, more accommodating to verbal invention, than that into which they were born. It was after all the age of Shakespeare, Marlowe, Lyly, Spenser, Donne, Ben Jonson, Francis Bacon, Sir Walter Raleigh, Elizabeth I. As Mary Helen Dohan has put it: 'Had the first settlers left England earlier or later, had they learned their speechways and their attitudes, linguistic and otherwise, in a different time, our language – like our nation –would be a different thing.'[6]

Just in the century or so that preceded the Pilgrims' arrival in the New World, English gained 10,000 additional words, about half of them sufficiently useful as to be with us still. Shakespeare alone created some 2,000 – *reclusive, gloomy, barefaced, radiance, dwindle, countless, gust, leapfrog, frugal, summit*, to name but a

---

* This *ye*, it should be noted, is etymologically distinct from the *ye* used as an alternative for *the*. As a pronoun *ye* was used for one person and *you* for more than one. Gradually this useful distinction fell out of use and *you* became the invariable form. But we kept the odd practice of associating it with a plural verb, which is why we address a single person with 'you are' when logically we ought to say 'you is'. In fact, until about 1760 'you is' and 'you was' were wholly unexceptionable.

few – but he was by no means alone in this unparalleled outpouring.

A bare sampling of words that entered English around the time of the Pilgrims gives some hint (another Shakespeare coinage, incidentally) of the lexical vitality of the age: *alternative* (1590); *incapable* (1591); *noose* (1600); *nomination* (1601); *fairy, surrogate* and *sophisticated* (1603); *option* (1604); *creak*, in the sense of a noise, and *susceptible* (1605); *coarse*, in the sense of being rough (as opposed to natural), and *castigate* (1607); *obscenity* (1608); *tact* (1609); *commitment, slope, recrimination* and *gothic* (1611); *coalition* (1612); *freeze*, in a metaphoric sense (1613); *nonsense* (1614); *cult, boulder* and *crazy*, in the sense of insanity (1617); *customer* (1621); *inexperienced* (1626).

If the Pilgrims were aware of this linguistic ferment into which they had been born, they gave little sign of it. Nowhere in any surviving colonial writings of the seventeenth century is there a single reference to Shakespeare or even the Puritans' own revered Milton. And in some significant ways their language is curiously unlike that of Shakespeare. They did not employ the construction 'methinks', for instance. Nor did they show any particular inclination to engage in the new fashion of turning nouns into verbs, a practice that gave the age such perennially useful innovations as *to gossip* (1590), *to fuel* (1592), *to attest* (1596), *to inch* (1599), *to preside* (1611), *to surround* (1616), *to hurt* (1662) and several score others, many of which (*to happy, to property, to malice*) didn't last.

Though they were by no means linguistic innovators, the peculiar circumstances in which they found themselves forced the first colonists to begin tinkering with their vocabulary almost from the first day. As early as 1622, they were using *pond*, which in England designated a small artificial pool, to describe large and wholly natural bodies of water, as in *Walden Pond*. *Creek* in England described an inlet of the sea; in America it came to signify a stream. For reasons that have never, so far as I can tell, been properly investigated, the colonials quickly discarded many seemingly useful English topographic words – *hurst, mere, mead, heath, moor, marsh* and (except in New England) *brook*, and began coming up with new ones, like *swamp* (first recorded in John Smith's *Generall Historie of Virginia* in 1626),[7] *ravine, hollow,*

23

range (for an open piece of ground) and *bluff*. Often these were borrowed from other languages. *Bluff*, which has the distinction of being the first word attacked by the British as a misguided and obviously unnecessary Americanism, was probably borrowed from the Dutch *blaf*, meaning a flat board. *Swamp* appears to come from the German *zwamp*, and *ravine*, first recorded in 1781 in the diaries of George Washington though almost certainly used much earlier, is from the French.

Oddly, considering the extremities of the American climate, weather words were slow in arising. *Snowstorm*, the first meteorological Americanism, is not recorded before 1771 and no one appears to have noticed a *tornado* before 1804. In between came *cold snap* in 1776, and that about exhausts America's contribution to the world of weather terms in its first two hundred years. *Blizzard*, a word without which any description of a northern American winter would seem incomplete, did not in fact come to describe a heavy snowstorm until as late as 1870, when a newspaper editor in Estherville, Iowa, applied it to a particularly fierce spring snow. The word, of unknown origin, had been coined in America some fifty years earlier, but previously had denoted a blow or series of blows, as from fists or guns.

Where they could, however, the first colonists stuck doggedly to the words of the Old World. They preserved words with the diligence of archivists. Scores, perhaps hundreds, of English terms that would later perish from neglect in their homeland live on in America thanks to the essentially conservative nature of the early colonists. *Fall* for *autumn* is perhaps the best known. It was a relatively new word at the time of the Pilgrims – its first use in England was recorded in 1545 – but it remained in common use in England until as late as the second half of the nineteenth century. Why it died out there when it did is unknown. The list of words preserved in America is practically endless. Among them: *cabin* in the sense of a humble dwelling, *bug* for any kind of insect, *hog* for a pig, *deck* as in a pack of cards and *jack* for a knave within the deck, *raise* for rear, *junk* for rubbish, *mad* in the sense of angry rather than unhinged, *bushel* as a common unit of measurement, *closet* for cupboard, *adze*, *attic*, *jeer* and *hatchet*, *stocks* as in stocks and bonds, *cross-purposes*, *livestock*, *gap* and (principally in New England) *notch* for a pass through hills, *gully* for a ravine, *rooster* for the male fowl, *slick* as a variant of *sleek*, *zero* for nought, *back and forth* (instead of *backwards and forwards*), *plumb* in the sense of utter or complete, *noon** in favour of *midday*, *molasses* for treacle, *cesspool*, *home-spun*, *din*, *trash*, *talented*, *chore*, *mayhem*, *maybe*, *copious*, and so on. And that is just a bare sampling.

The first colonists also brought with them many regional terms, little known outside their private corners of Britain, which prospered on American soil and have often since spread to the wider English-speaking world: *drool*, *teeter*, *hub*, *swamp*, *squirt* (as a term descriptive of a person), *spool* (for thread), *to wilt*, *cater-cornered*, *skedaddle* (a north British dialect word meaning to spill something noisy, such as a bag of coal), *gumption*, *chump* (an Essex word meaning a lump of wood and now preserved in the expression 'off your chump'),[8] *scalawag*, *dander* (as in *to get one's dander up*), *chitterlings*, *chipper*, *chisel* in the sense of to cheat, and *skulduggery*. The last named has nothing to do with skulls which is why it is spelled with one *l*. It comes from the Scottish *sculdudrie*, a word denoting fornication. *Chitterlings, or chitlins*, for the small intestines of the pig, was unknown outside Hampshire until nourished to wider glory in the New World.[9] That it evolved in some quarters of America into *kettlings* suggests that the *ch-* may have been pronounced by at least some people with the hard *k* of *chaos* or *chorus*.

And of course they brought many words with them that have not survived in either America or Britain, to the lexical impoverishment of both: *flight* for a dusting of snow, *fribble* for a frivolous person, *bossloper* for a hermit, *spong* for a parcel of land, *bantling* for an infant, *sooterkin* for a sweetheart, *gurnet* for a protective sandbar, and the much-missed *slobberchops* for a messy eater.

Everywhere they turned in their new-found land, the early colonists were confronted with objects that they had never seen

---

* *Noon* is a small oddity. It comes from the Old English word *nones*, meaning the ninth hour of daylight, or 3 p.m., when prayers were commonly said. It changed to 12 p.m. in the Middle Ages when the time of prayers changed to midday. But in Britain for a time it represented either of the twelfth hours, which explains references in older texts to 'the noon of midnight' and the like.

before, from the mosquito (at first spelled *mosketoe* or *musketto*) to the persimmon to poison ivy, or 'poysoned weed' as they called it. At first, no doubt overwhelmed by the wealth of unfamiliar life in their new Eden, they made no distinction between pumpkins and squashes or between the walnut and pecan trees. They misnamed plants and animals. *Bay, laurel, beech, walnut, hemlock*, the *robin* (actually a thrush), *blackbird, hedgehog, lark, swallow* and *marsh hen* all signify different species in America from those of England.[10] The American rabbit is actually a hare. (That the first colonists couldn't tell the difference offers some testimony to their incompetence in the wild.) Often they took the simplest route and gave the new creatures names imitative of the sounds they made – *bob white, whippoorwill, katydid* – and when that proved impractical they fell back on the useful, and eventually distinctively American, expedient of forming a new compound from two older words.

Colonial American English positively teems with such constructions: *jointworm, glowworm, eggplant, canvasback, copperhead, rattlesnake, bluegrass, backtrack, bobcat, catfish, bluejay, bullfrog, sapsucker, timberland, underbrush, cookbook, frostbite, hillside* (at first sometimes called a *sidehill*), plus such later additions as *tightwad, sidewalk, cheapskate, sharecropper, skyscraper, rubberneck, drugstore, barbershop, hangover, rubdown, blowout* and others almost without number. These new terms had the virtues of directness and instant comprehensibility – useful qualities in a land whose populace included increasingly large numbers of non-native speakers – which their British counterparts often lacked. *Frostbite* is clearly more descriptive than *chilblains*, *sidewalk* than *pavement*, *eggplant* than *aubergine*, *doghouse* than *kennel*, *bedspread* than *counterpane*, whatever the English might say.

One creature that very much featured in the lives of the earliest colonists was the passenger pigeon. The name comes from an earlier sense of passenger as one that passes by, and passenger pigeons certainly did that in almost inconceivably vast numbers. One early observer estimated a passing flock as being a mile wide and 240 miles long. They literally darkened the sky. At the time of the *Mayflower* landing there were perhaps nine billion passenger pigeons in North America, more than twice the number of all the birds found on the continent today. With such numbers they were absurdly easy to hunt. One account from 1770 reported that a hunter brought down 125 with a single shot from a blunderbuss. Some people ate them, but most were fed to pigs. Millions more were slaughtered for the sport of it. By 1800 their numbers had been roughly halved and by 1900 they were all but gone. On 1 September 1914 the last one died at Cincinnati Zoo.

The first colonists were not, however, troubled by several other creatures that would one day plague the New World. One was the common house rat. It wouldn't reach Europe for another century (emigrating there abruptly and in huge numbers from Siberia for reasons that have never been explained) and did not make its first recorded appearance in America until 1775, in Boston. (Such was its adaptability that, by the time of the 1849 gold rush, early arrivals to California found the house rat waiting for them. By the 1960s there were an estimated one hundred million house rats in America.) Many other now common animals, among them the house mouse and the common pigeon, were also yet to make their first trip across the ocean.

For certain species we know with some precision when they arrived, most notoriously with that airborne irritant the starling, which was brought to America by one Eugene Schieffelin, a wealthy German emigrant who had the odd, and in the case of starlings regrettable, idea that he should introduce to the American landscape all the birds mentioned in the writings of Shakespeare. Most of the species he introduced failed to prosper, but the forty pairs of starlings he released in New York's Central Park in the spring of 1890, augmented by twenty more pairs the following spring, so thrived that within less than a century they had become the most abundant bird species in America, and one of its greatest pests. The common house sparrow (actually not a sparrow at all but an African weaverbird) was in similar fashion introduced to the New World in 1851 or 1852 by the president of the Natural History Society of Brooklyn, and the carp by the secretary of the Smithsonian Institution in the 1870s.[11] That there were not greater ecological disasters from such well-meaning but often misguided introductions is a wonder for which we may all be grateful.

Partly from lack of daily contact with the British, partly from conditions peculiar to American life, and partly perhaps from whim, American English soon began wandering off in new directions. As early as 1682, Americans were calling folding money *bills* rather than *notes*. By 1751, *bureau* had lost its English meaning of a writing desk and come to mean a chest of drawers. *Barn* in Britain was and generally still is a storehouse for grain, but in America it took on the wider sense of being a general-purpose farm building. By 1780 *avenue* was being used to designate any wide street in America; in Britain it implied a line of trees – indeed, it still does to the extent that many British towns have streets called Avenue Road, which sounds comically redundant to American ears. Other words for which Americans gradually enlarged the meanings include *apartment, pie, store, closet, pavement* and *block*. *Block* in late eighteenth-century America described a group of buildings having a similar appearance – what the British call a *terrace* – then came to mean a collection of adjoining lots and finally, by 1823, was being used in its modern sense to designate an urban rectangle bounded by streets.[12]

But the handiest, if not always the simplest, way of filling voids in the American lexicon was to ask the local Indians what words they used. At the time of the first colonists there were perhaps fifty million Indians in the New World (though other estimates have put the figure as high as one hundred million and as low as eight million). Most lived in Mexico and the Andes. The whole of North America had perhaps no more than two million inhabitants. The Indians of North America are generally broken down into six geographic, rather than linguistic or cultural, families: those from the plains (among them the Blackfoot, Cheyenne and Pawnee), eastern woodlands (the Algonquian family and Iroquois confederacy), south-west (Apache, Navaho, Pueblo), north-west coast (Haida, Modoc, Tsimshian), plateau (Paiute, Nez Percé), and northern (Kutchin, Naskapi). Within these groups considerable variety was to be found. Among the plains Indians, the Omaha and Pawnee were settled farmers, while the Cheyenne and Commanches were nomadic hunters. There was also considerable movement: the Blackfoot and Cheyenne, for example, began as eastern seaboard Indians, members of the Algonquian family, before pushing west into the plains.

Despite, or perhaps because of, the relative paucity of inhabitants in North America, the variety of languages spoken on the continent was particularly rich, with as many as 500 altogether.

Put another way, the Indians of North America accounted for only 5 per cent of the population of the New World, but perhaps as much as a quarter of its tongues. Many of these languages – Puyallup, Tupi, Assinboin, Hidatsa, Bella Coola – were spoken by only a relative handful of people. Even among related tribes the linguistic chasm could be considerable. As the historian Charlton Laird has put it: 'The known native languages of California alone show greater linguistic variety than all the known languages of the continent of Europe.'[13]

Almost all of the Indian terms taken directly into English by the first colonists come from the two eastern families: the Iroquois confederacy, whose members included the Mohawk, Cherokee, Oneida, Seneca, Delaware and Huron tribes, and the even larger Algonquian group, which included Algonquin, Arapaho, Cree, Delaware, Illinois, Kickapoo, Narragansett, Ojibwa, Penobscot, Pequot and Sac and Fox, among many others. But here, too, there was huge variability, so that to the Delaware Indians the river was the Susquehanna, while to the neighbouring Hurons it was the Kanastoge (or Conestoga).

The early colonists began borrowing words from the Indians almost from the moment of first contact. *Moose* and *papoose* were taken into English as early as 1603. *Raccoon* is first recorded in 1608, *caribou* and *opossum* in 1610, *moccasin* and *tomahawk* in 1612, *hickory* in 1618, *powwow* in 1624, *wigwam* in 1628.[14] Altogether, the Indians provided some 150 terms to the early colonists. Another 150 came later, often after being filtered through intermediate sources. *Toboggan*, for instance, entered English by way of Canadian French. *Hammock, maize* and *barbecue* reached the continent via Spanish from the Caribbean.

Occasionally Indian terms could be adapted fairly simply. The Algonquian *seganku* became without too much difficulty *skunk*. *Wuchak* settled into English almost inevitably as *woodchuck* (despite the tongue-twister, no woodchuck ever chucked wood). *Wampumpeag* became *wampum*. The use of *neck* in the northern colonies was clearly influenced by the Algonquian *naiack*, meaning a point or corner, and from which comes the expression *that neck of the woods*. Similarly the preponderance of *capes* in New England is at least partly due to the existence of an Algonquian word, *kepan*, meaning 'a closed-up passage'.[15]

Most Indian terms, however, were not so amenable to simple transliteration. Many had to be brusquely and repeatedly pummelled into shape, like a recalcitrant pillow, before any English speaker could feel comfortable with them. John Smith's first attempt at transcribing the Algonquian word for a tribal leader came out as *cawcawwassoughes*. Realizing that this was not remotely satisfactory he modified it to a still somewhat hopeful *coucorouse*. It took a later generation to simplify it further to the form we know today: *caucus*.[16] *Raccoon* was no less challenging. Smith tried *raugroughcum* and *rahaugcum* in the same volume, then later made it *rarowcun*, and subsequent chroniclers attempted many other forms – *aracoune* and *rockoon*, among them – before finally finding phonetic comfort with *rackoone*.[17] *Misickquatash* evolved into *sacatash* and eventually *succotash*. *Askutasquash* became *isquontersquash* and finally *squash*. *Pawcohiccora* became *pohickery* and then *hickory*.

Tribal names, too, required modification. *Cherokee* was really *Tsalaki*. *Algonquin* emerged from *Algoumequins*. *Irinakhoiw* yielded *Iroquois*. *Choctaw* was variously rendered as *Chaqueta*, *Shacktau* and *Choktah* before settling into its modern form. Even the seemingly straightforward *Mohawk* has as many as 142 recorded spellings.*

Occasionally the colonists gave up. For a time they referred to an edible cactus by its Indian name, *metaquesunauk*, but eventually abandoned the fight and called it a *prickly pear*.[18] Success depended largely on the phonetic accessibility of the nearest contact tribe. Those who encountered the Ojibwa Indians found their dialect so deeply impenetrable that they couldn't even agree on the tribe's name. Some said *Ojibwa*, others *Chippewa*. By whatever name, the tribe employed consonant clusters of such a confounding density – *mtik, pskikye, kchimkwa*, to name but

---

* At least the English colonists made some attempt to honour the Indian names. The French and Spanish appeared scarcely to notice what names the tribes used. The French ignored the name *Chopunnish*, the name used by a tribe of the Pacific northwest, and instead called the people the *Nez Percé*, 'pierced nose', for their habit of wearing sea-shells in their nostrils. They performed a similar disservice with Siwash, which is actually just a modified form of the French *sauvage*, or *savage*, and with *Gros Ventre* (French for 'big belly'). The Spanish, meanwhile, ignored the comely, lilting name *Ha-no-o-shatch* ('children of the sun') and called this south-western tribe the Pueblos, 'people'.

three[19] – as to convince the new colonists to leave their tongue in peace.

Often, as might be expected, the colonists misunderstood the Indian terms and misapplied them. To the natives, *pawcohiccora* signified not the tree but the food made from its nuts. *Pakan* or *paccan* was an Algonquian word for any hard-shelled nut. The colonists made it *pecan* (after toying with such variants as *pekaun* and *pecaun*) and with uncharacteristic specificity reserved it for the produce of the tree known to science as the *Carya illinoensis*.

Despite the difficulties, the first colonists were perennially fascinated by the Indian tongues, partly no doubt because they were exotic, but also because they had a beauty that was irresistible. As William Penn wrote: 'I know not a language spoken in Europe, that hath words of more sweetness or greatness, in accent or emphasis, than theirs.'[20] And he was right. You have only to list a handful of Indian place names – *Mississippi, Susquehanna, Rappahannock* – to see that the Indians found a poetry in the American landscape that has all too often eluded those who displaced them.

If the early American colonists treated the Indians' languages with respect, they did not always show such scruples with the Indians themselves. From the outset they often treated the natives badly, albeit sometimes unwittingly. One of the first acts of the *Mayflower* Pilgrims, as we have seen, was to plunder Indian graves. (One wonders how the Pilgrims would have felt had they found Indians picking through the graves in an English churchyard.) Confused and easily frightened, the early colonists often attacked friendly tribes, mistaking them for hostile ones. Even when they knew the tribes to be friendly, they sometimes took hostages in the decidedly perverted belief that this would keep them respectful.

When circumstances were deemed to warrant it, they did not hesitate to impose a quite shocking severity, as a note from soldiers to the governor of the Massachusetts Bay Colony during King Philip's War reminds us: 'This aforesaid Indian was ordered to be tourne to peeces by dogs, and she was so dealt with.'[21] Indeed, early accounts of American encounters with Indians tell us as much about colonial violence as about seventeenth-century orthography. Here, for instance, is William Bradford describing a surprise attack on a Pequot village in his *History of Plimouth Plantation*. The victims, it may be noted, were mostly women and children: 'Those that scaped the fire were slaine with the sword; some hewed to peeces, others rune throw with rapiers, so as they were quickly dispatchte . . . It was a fearful sight to see them thus frying in the fyre . . . and horrible was the styncke and sente there of, but the victory seemed a sweete sacrifice.'[22] In 1675 in Virginia, John Washington, an ancestor of George, was involved in a not untypical incident in which the Indians were invited to settle a dispute by sending their leaders to a powwow. They sent five chiefs to parley and when things did not go to the European settlers' satisfaction, the chiefs were taken away and killed. Even the most faithful Indians were treated as expendable. When John Smith was confronted by hostile savages in Virginia in 1608 his first action was to shield himself behind his native guide.

In the circumstances, it is little wonder that the Indians began to view their new rivals for the land with a certain suspicion and to withdraw their goodwill. This was a particular blow to the Virginia colonists – or 'planters', as they were somewhat hopefully called – who were as helpless at fending for themselves as the *Mayflower* Pilgrims would prove to be a decade later. In the winter of 1609–10, they underwent what came to be known as the 'starving time', during which brief period the number of Virginia colonists fell from five hundred to about sixty. When Sir Thomas Gates arrived to take over as the new governor the following spring, he found 'the portes open, the gates from the hinges, the church ruined and unfrequented, empty howses (whose owners untimely death had taken newly from them) rent up and burnt, the living not able, as they pretended, to step into the woodes to gather other fire-wood; and, it is true, the Indian as fast killing without as the famine and pestilence within.'[23]

Fresh colonists were constantly dispatched from England, but between the perils of the Indians without and the famine and pestilence within, they perished almost as fast as they could be replaced. Between December 1606 and February 1625, Virginia received 7,289 immigrants and buried 6,040 of them. Most barely had time to settle in. Of the 3,500 immigrants who arrived in the three years 1619–21, 3,000 were dead at the end of the period. To go to Virginia was effectively to commit suicide.

For those who survived, life was a succession of terrors and discomforts, from hunger and homesickness to the dread possibility of being tomahawked in one's bed. As the colonist Richard Frethorne wrote with a touch of forgivable histrionics: 'I thought no head had been able to hold so much water as hath and doth dailie flow from mine eyes.' He was dead within the year.[24]

At least he was spared the messy end that awaited many of those who survived him. On Good Friday, 1622, during a period of amity between the colonists and native Americans, the Indian chief Opechancanough sent delegations of his tribes to the newly planted Virginia settlements of Kecoughtan, Henricus (also called Henrico or Henricopolis) and Charles City and their neighbouring farms. It was presented as a goodwill visit – some of the Indians even 'sate down at Breakfast', as one appalled colonial wrote afterwards –but upon a given signal, the Indians seized whatever implements happened to come to hand and murdered every man, woman and child they could catch, 350 in all, or about a third of Virginia's total population.[25]

Twenty-two years later, in 1644, the same chief did the same thing, killing about the same number of people. But by this time the 350 deaths represented less than a twentieth of Virginia's English inhabitants, and Opechancanough's incursion was more a brutal annoyance than a catastrophe. Something clearly had changed in the interim. What it was can be summed up in a single word: *tobacco*. To the Indians of Virginia this agreeable plant was not tobacco, but *uppówoc*. *Tobacco* was a Spanish word, taken from the Arabic *tabāq*, signifying any euphoria-inducing herb. The first mention of tobacco in English was in 1565 after a visit by John Hawkins to a short-lived French outpost in Florida. With a trace of bemusement, and an uncertain mastery of the expository sentence, he reported that the French had 'a kind of herb dried, who with a cane and an earthen cup on the end, with fire, – doe suck through the cane the smoke thereof'.[26] Despite Hawkins's apparent dubiousness about just how much pleasure this sort of thing could bring, he carried some tobacco back to England with him, where it quickly caught on in a big way. At first the practice was called 'drinking' it, before it occurred to anyone that *smoking* might be a more apt term. Wonderful powers were ascribed to it. Tobacco was believed to be both a potent aphrodisiac and a marvellously versatile medicine, which 'purgeth superfluous phlegm and other gross humours, and openeth all the pores and passages of the body'.[27] Before long, it was all the rage and people simply couldn't get enough of it.

The Jamestown colonists began planting it in the second decade of the seventeenth century and found to their joy that it grew nearly as well as poison ivy. Suddenly fortunes were to be made in Virginia. People began to flock to the colony in numbers the Indians couldn't cope with. Virginia's future was secure, and almost entirely because of an addictive plant.

In the mean time, the persecution of Puritans in Britain made New England a much less lonely spot. During the years 1629–40, 80,000 Puritans fled the Old World for the New. Only some 20,000 went to New England. A similar number settled in the Caribbean, in places like Barbados and St Kitts. Some formed a new, and now almost wholly forgotten, colony on Old Providence Island along Nicaragua's Mosquito Coast. The West Indies were for a long time the most populous part of the New World. By 1700 Barbados had almost a third more English-speaking inhabitants than Virginia and more than twice as many as New York. None the less, enough Britons settled in Massachusetts to secure its future beyond doubt. By the beginning of the eighteenth century it had a population of 80,000. Its wealth, too, had an unseemly side. As early as 1643, just twenty-two years after the Pilgrim Fathers first planted their feet on American soil with a view to making the world a better, more godly place, New England entrepreneurs were busily engaged in an enterprise that would make them very rich indeed: the slave trade.

Such was the outflow of immigrants in the seventeenth century that by 1700 the British government had grown alarmed by the exodus of sturdy, industrious people and effectively cut off the supply, apart from regular boatloads of transported felons (among them the fictional Moll Flanders).* Convicts apart, very few true Englishmen or women emigrated to America after 1700. None the less, in the first half of the century the population of the colonies

---

* Not all of them made it. In the late seventeenth century one Thomas Benson secured a contract to transport convicts to the southern colonies of America, but quickly realized it was far simpler and more lucrative to dump them on Lundy, just off the north Devon coast. When he was at last caught, he claimed to have fulfilled his contract because he had taken them 'overseas'. The magistrates were not persuaded and fined him £7,872. The fate of the stranded convicts is unknown.

quadrupled. It achieved this apparent paradox by drawing large numbers of people from other New World colonies – Carolina, for instance, was founded in 1669 by only about a hundred people from England; the rest were planters from Barbados[28] – and from an influx of non-English peoples: Germans, French and most especially Scots-Irish from Ulster, of whom possibly as many as 250,000 arrived just in the middle fifty years of the eighteenth century.[29] All of this contributed significantly to America's long, slow drift away from the standard, London-based branch of English.

Sprinkled among this motley assemblage of new arrivals were increasing numbers of black Africans. Blacks had begun arriving in Virginia as early as 1619 – thus easily predating the oldest New England families – but not until late in the century did their usefulness as field workers and household servants become overwhelmingly evident. Though their removal to America was involuntary, they were at first regarded as servants, with the same rights of eventual earned freedom as indentured whites. The irony is that all these early menials, white and black alike, were called *slaves*, the term having temporarily lost its sense of permanent involuntary servitude. Servants were called *indentured*, incidentally, because their contract was indented, or folded, along an irregular line and torn in two, master and servant each keeping one half.[30]

Gradually, out of this inchoate mass a country began to emerge – loosely structured, governed from abroad, populated by an unlikely mix of refugees, idealists, slaves and convicts, but a country none the less. By the fourth decade of the eighteenth century the British were feeling sufficiently confident of their standing in the New World to begin looking for an excuse to throw their weight around a little. In 1739, the Spanish gave it to them when they made manifest their long and wholly understandable exasperation with British privateers by cutting off the ear of an English smuggler named Edward Jenkins. Never mind that Jenkins was little more than a common criminal. The British responded by launching possibly the only interesting-sounding conflict in history, the War of Jenkins' Ear.

The war was in fact pretty dull, but it did have a couple of interesting linguistic spin-offs. One came with the introduction of a daily ration of rum and water for the sailors on the instructions of the commander of the fleet, Edward Vernon. Vernon's nickname was Old Grog – no one seems to know why – and the drink, as you will doubtless have guessed, was soon called *grog*. (And those who drank too much of it would perforce become *groggy*.) Vernon was by all accounts an inspiring figure, and was greatly loved by his men. One of his colonial officers, Lawrence Washington, half-brother of George, was so taken with the admiral that he named his Virginia plantation Mount Vernon in his honour.

However – and here we come to the point of all this – the euphonious if largely forgotten War of Jenkins' Ear marked a telling semantic transition. It was then for the first time that the British began to refer to their colonial cousins as *Americans*, rather than as *provincials* or *colonials*. *American* had been recorded as early as 1578, but previously had been applied only to the native Indians. No one realized it yet, but a new nation had begun.

3

A 'Democratical Phrenzy': America in the Age of Revolution

I

When dawn broke on that epochal year 1776 – a year that would also see the publication of Adam Smith's *Wealth of Nations* and the first volume of Edward Gibbon's *Decline and Fall of the Roman Empire* – America's war with its British masters was already, in a sense, several years old. The much despised Stamp Act was eleven years in the past. It was nearly three years since the Boston Tea Party (which wouldn't in fact generally be called that for another half-century) and six since the infamous, if widely misreported, Boston Massacre. It had been nine months since some unknown soul had stood at Concord green and fired, in Emerson's memorable phrase, 'the shot heard round the world', and not much less since the bloody, curiously misnamed Battle of Bunker Hill, which did not take place on Bunker Hill at all (or Bunker's Hill as it was then more commonly called). Though the battle was intended to take place on Bunker Hill (these matters being rather more formally arranged in the eighteenth century), for reasons unknown colonial troops under Col. William Prescott fortified the wrong hill, the neighbouring Breed's Hill, and it was there that the first pitched battle of America's war for independence was fought. To complicate matters, Breed's Hill was often thereafter referred to as Bunker Hill. At any rate, and by any measure, in January 1776 Britain and a significant portion of its American colonies were at war.

We might reasonably ask why. In 1776 Americans already were 'the freest people in the world', as Samuel Eliot Morison has noted.[1] Most Americans enjoyed economic mobility, the right to vote for their own local representatives, a free press and the benefits of what one English contemporary tellingly called a 'most disgusting equality'. They ate better, were more comfortably housed and on the whole were probably better educated than their British cousins. (In Massachusetts, for instance, the literacy rate was at least double that of Britain.)[2] The Revolution when it came would not be to secure America's freedom, but to preserve it.

What the colonists did lack were seats in Parliament. They resented – not unreasonably, it seems to us today – being required to pay taxes to the mother country when they were denied a voice in the House of Commons. To the British such a notion was overambitious, if not actually preposterous, since most Britons did not themselves enjoy such a lavish franchise. Only about one Briton in twenty had the right to vote and even some large thriving cities such as Liverpool and Manchester had no directly elected Member of Parliament. Why should mere colonists, the semi-British, be accorded greater electoral privilege than those reared on British soil?

Nor, it should be noted, were the taxes levied on the colonists by any stretch onerous or unreasonable. The principal aim of the stamp duties and other revenue-raising measures was to fund the protection of the colonies. It was hardly beyond the bounds of reasonableness to expect the colonists to make a contribution towards the cost of their own defence. In the 1760s, it was estimated, the average American paid about sixpence a year in tax. The average Briton paid twenty-five shillings – fifty times as much. And in any case, Americans seldom actually paid their taxes. The hated Townshend duties raised just £295 in revenue in their first year and cost £170,000 to implement. The equally reviled Stamp Act duties were never collected at all.

None the less, as every schoolchild knows, throughout the 1770s America rang with the cry 'Taxation without representation is tyranny.' Actually, not. James Otis, to whom the phrase is commonly attributed, appears never to have said any such thing – or at least if he did no one at the time noticed. The famous words weren't ascribed to him until 1820, nearly forty years after he died.[3]

The American Revolution was in fact an age drowning in myths. Many of the expressions that are proudly associated with the struggle for independence were in fact never uttered. Patrick Henry almost certainly didn't issue the defiant cry 'If this be treason, make the most of it' or any of the other deathless remarks confidently attributed to him in the Virginia House of Burgesses in May 1765. The clerk of the convention made no notes of Henry's speech, and none of those present gave any hint in their correspondence that Henry's remarks had been particularly electrifying that day. According to the one surviving eyewitness account – written by a French hydrologist who just happened to be present, and found quite by chance in the archives of the National Hydrological Institute of France in 1921 – Henry *did* make some intemperate remarks, but, far from being defiant, he immediately apologized to the House of Burgesses if 'the heat of passion might have lead [*sic*] him to have said something more than he intended' and timidly professed undying loyalty to the king – not quite the show of thrust-jawed challenge portrayed in countless school books.[4]

If Henry did engage in a little nervous back-pedalling, we should not be altogether surprised. He was the junior member of the house; he had taken his seat only nine days earlier. His brave and eloquent challenge to monarchy appears to have been invented from whole cloth forty-one years later, seventeen years after Henry died, by a priggish biographer named William Wirt, who had never met, seen or heard him. Thomas Jefferson, who *was* there, made no comment about the accuracy or otherwise of Wirt's account of events on that day, but he did freely offer the opinion that Wirt's effort was 'a poor book, written in bad taste, and gives an imperfect idea of Patrick Henry'. Nor, while we are at it, is there any evidence that Henry ever uttered the other famous remark attributed to him: 'I know not what course others may take; but as for me, give me liberty or give me death.' Indeed, there is no evidence that Henry ever said anything of substance or found space in his head for a single original thought. He was a country bumpkin, unread, poorly educated and famously indolent. His turn of phrase was comically provincial and frequently ungrammatical. He did, it is true, have certain oratorical powers, but these appeared to owe more to a gift for hypnotic sonorosity than to any command of thought or language. His style of speech was a kind of verbal sleight of hand that, in the words of one contemporary, 'baffled all description'. Jefferson once bemusedly recalled: 'When he had spoken in opposition to my opinion, had produced a great effect, and I myself been highly delighted and moved, I have asked myself when it ceased, "What the Devil has he said," and could never answer the enquiry.'[5]

Even those events that did unquestionably take place have often been distorted by history to show the colonials in a more favourable light. The classic example is the Boston Massacre, or the 'Bloody Massacre Perpetrated in King Street, Boston', as it was provocatively called in Paul Revere's famous engraving. Revere's rendition shows the British Redcoats, or *lobsterbacks* as they were more dismissively known, taking careful aim in broad daylight at a small, startled gathering of colonials, as if blithely executing midday shoppers. It wasn't quite like that. Five colonials did lose their lives in the incident, but it happened at night, amid great confusion, and after considerable provocation in which twenty British soldiers were repeatedly taunted, jostled, pelted with stones and other missiles and generally menaced by a drunken, ugly and very much larger mob. By the standards of the day, the British troops were eminently justified in replying with fire. John Adams, at any rate, had no hesitation in defending the soldiers in court (and securing the acquittal of all but two; the convicted pair had their thumbs branded, a light punishment indeed in a murder trial). It was his more hotheaded cousin, Sam Adams, who with the help of Paul Revere's artwork turned the incident into effective propaganda and popularized the expression Boston Massacre.

For almost a century afterwards, Paul Revere was known in America, in so far as he was known at all, not for his midnight ride but as the maker of that engraving. It wasn't until Henry Wadsworth Longfellow wrote his romanticized and hugely inaccurate* poem 'Paul Revere's Ride' (from *Tales of a Wayside Inn*) in 1863 that Revere became known as anything other than an engraver and silversmith.

---

* Among the inaccuracies, Revere didn't hang the lanterns in the old North Church, because it wasn't called that until later; at the time of the Revolution it was Christchurch; he made two rides, not one; and he never made it to Concord, as Longfellow has it, but in fact was arrested along the way. As a historian Longfellow was decidedly hopeless, but as a creator of catch phrases he was in the first rank. Among those that live with us yet: 'Footprints on the sands of time', 'This is the forest primeval', 'Into each life some rain must fall', 'ships that pass in the night', and 'I shot an arrow into the air/It fell to earth, I know not where.'

Perhaps the most singular instance of historical manipulation is that concerning Betsy Ross and the creation of the first American flag. The traditional story – recorded with solemnity in this author's school books in the 1950s – is that George Washington entered Mrs Ross's upholstery shop in Philadelphia in 1776, showed her a rough sketch of a flag and asked her to whip up something suitable for a new nation. The story was not first voiced until ninety-six years after the supposed event when one of her grandchildren presented the tale to a historical society in Pennsylvania. It has never been substantiated.[6] However, as a little thought should tell us, in 1776 George Washington had rather more pressing matters to engage his attention than hunting down a seamstress for a national flag. In any case, at the time of the story, America was still flying the Grand Union flag, a banner that had alternating red and white stripes in the manner of the modern American flag, but contained a Union Jack where the stars now go. Not until June 1777 did Congress replace the Union Jack with stars. But even then, such were the emotional ties to Britain, many flag makers arranged the stars in a Union Jack pattern.

The upshot is that in early January 1776 – despite the Boston Tea Party, the battles of Concord and Bunker Hill, the revolt over the Townshend Acts and all the other manifestations of popular discontent – Americans were not merely reluctant to part with Britain, but most had never even dreamed of such a thing. Until well after the Revolution had started Washington and his officers were continuing the nightly tradition of toasting the mother country (if not the monarch himself) and the Continental Congress was professing an earnest – we might almost say slavish – loyalty, insisting, even as it was taking up arms, that 'we mean not to dissolve the union which has so long and happily subsisted between us', and professing a readiness to 'cheerfully bleed in defense of our Sovereign in a righteous cause'. Their argument, they repeatedly assured themselves, was not with Britain but with George III. (The Declaration of Independence, it is worth noting, indicted only 'the present King of Great Britain'.) As the historian Bernard Bailyn has put it: 'It is not much of an exaggeration to say that one had to be a fool or a fanatic in early January 1776 to advocate American independence.'[7]

Fortunately there existed a man who was a little of both. He had been born Thomas Pain, though upon arrival in America he whimsically changed the spelling to Paine, and he was about as unlikely a figure to change the course of history as you could imagine. A tumbledown drunk, coarse of manner, blotchy-faced and almost wholly lacking in acquaintance with the virtues of soap and water – 'so neglectful in his person that he is generally the most abominably dirty being upon the face of the earth', in the words of one contemporary – he had been a failure at every trade he had ever attempted, and he had attempted many, from corset-making to tax collecting before finally, at the age of thirty-eight, abandoning his native shores and his second wife and coming to America.

However, Paine could write with extraordinary grace and power, and at a time of immense emotional confusion in America, he was possessed of an unusually clear and burning sense of America's destiny. In January 1776, less than two years after he had arrived in the colonies, he anonymously published a slender pamphlet that he called (at the suggestion of his friend and mentor Benjamin Rush) *Common Sense*. To say that it was a sensation merely hints at its impact. Sales were like nothing that had been seen before in the New World: 100,000 copies were sold in the first two months, 400,000 copies overall – this in a country with just three million inhabitants. It was the greatest best-seller America has ever seen, and it didn't make Paine a penny. He assigned the copyright to the Continental Congress, and thus not only galvanized America into revolution but materially helped to fund it.

Common Sense was a breathtakingly pugnacious tract. Writers did not normally refer to the king as 'a sottish, stupid, stubborn, worthless, brutish man' and 'the royal brute of England' or accuse him of sleeping with 'blood upon his soul'.[8] Above all Paine argued forcefully and unequivocally for independence: 'Everything that is right or reasonable pleads for separation. The blood of the slain, the weeping voice of nature cries, "Tis time to part." ' He was one of the first writers to employ *republic* with a positive connotation and helped to give *revolution* its modern sense, rather than to describe the movements of celestial spheres. And he did it all in language that anyone who could read could understand.

Jefferson freely acknowledged that his own prose style in the Declaration of Independence was indebted to Paine, whose 'ease and familiarity of style' he thought unrivalled. Others were less convinced. Benjamin Franklin believed Paine's writing lacked dignity. Gouverneur Morris dismissed him as 'a mere adventurer'. John Adams, never short of an acid comment, called *Common Sense* 'a poor, ignorant, malicious, short-sighted, crapulous mass', and likened Paine to a common criminal. But the book had the desired effect.

Paine's value was not as an originator of ideas, but as a communicator of them. He was a consummate sloganeer. In *Common Sense* and a flurry of following works, he showered the world with ringing phrases that live on yet: 'the Age of Reason'; 'the Rights of Man'; 'That government is best which governs least'; 'These are the times that try men's souls'; 'The summer soldier and the sunshine patriot'. Less poetically but no less memorably, he was the first to refer to 'the United States of America'. Previously even the boldest patriot had spoken of the 'United Colonies'. Under Paine's influence Americans became seized with what one British onlooker uneasily termed 'a Democratical phrenzy'.[9]

It is easy to forget that those who started the Revolution did not think of themselves as Americans in anything like the way they do today. They were British and proud of it. To them, *American* was more a descriptive term than an emotional one. Their primary attachment was to their colony. When Jefferson wrote to a friend that he longed 'to return to my own country', he meant Virginia.[10] In 1765 Christopher Gadsden of South Carolina lamented: 'There ought to be no New England men, no New York, etc., known on the Continent, but all of us Americans.'[11] That he felt it necessary to articulate the sentiment is revealing.

Their exposure to other colonies was often strikingly limited. John Adams, for one, had never left his home colony. In 1776 Philadelphia was the second largest city in the English-speaking world, but more of the delegates to the second Continental Congress had been to London than to Pennsylvania. Despite the interposition of two thousand miles of ocean, London remained the effective centre of American culture and politics. As Garry Wills has noted: 'Till almost the eve of the Revolution, resistance to imperial policy was better schemed at in London than in the colonies ... London [was] where policy was made and colonial protests directed, where colonial agents were located and a community of Americans from the whole continent resided.'[12]

In Philadelphia, they convened in a spirit of excitement mixed with high caution. Though they came from similar backgrounds – nine of Virginia's twelve delegates were related by blood or marriage[13] – they were wary of each other, and not without reason. They were engaged in treason and anyone who betrayed them would have much to gain. The step they were taking was radical and irreversible, and the consequences terrifying. The penalty for treason was to be hanged, cut down while still alive, disembowelled and forced to watch your organs burned before your eyes, then beheaded and quartered.[14] Widows would be deprived of their estates and children subjected to a life of opprobrium. Benjamin Franklin was no more than half jesting when he quipped to his fellow delegates – and here at last we have a remark that appears actually to have been uttered – 'We must all hang together or assuredly we shall all hang separately.' (Yet Franklin, thanks to his close ties with England and his initial support for the Stamp Act, was held by many of his fellows to be one of the most suspect of the lot.)

So what did they sound like, these new Americans? Had they by 1776 adopted a distinctive American accent? Did Jefferson speak with a southern drawl and Adams with the pinched nasal tones of a New Englander, or did they sound like the Englishmen they still loosely felt themselves to be? The evidence is tantalizingly ambiguous. Certainly regional differences were evident in America in 1776 and had been for some time. As early as 1720, visitors to New England were speaking of a 'New England twang', which bore a noticeable resemblance to the 'Norfolk whine' of England. In much the same way, visitors to the South sometimes remarked on the resemblance of speech there to the Sussex accent. Some detected quite specific differences. One observer in 1780 claimed that natives of the neighbouring towns of Easthampton and Southampton on Long Island could be distinguished in an instant by their peculiarities of speech. Much the same claim was sometimes made for proximate communities in Virginia.

The evidence suggests that in 1776 southerners would have been struck by the New England habit of saying 'kee-yow' and 'nee-yow' for *cow* and *now*, for saying 'marcy' for *mercy*, 'crap' for *crop* and 'drap' for *drop*. (This last variation, incidentally, accounts for our pair of words *strap* and *strop*.) Northerners would have regarded as curious the southern habit of saying 'holp' for *help*, for rhyming *wound* in the sense of an injury with *swooned* – New Englanders rhymed it with *crowned* – and for using *y'all* for a collective sense of *you* (a practice that had been a distinguishing feature of southern speech since the 1600s).

In his much-praised book *Albion's Seed*, David Hackett Fischer carefully argues that regional accents – indeed discrete regional cultures – were well in place in America by the time of the Revolution. He points out that American colonists came in four distinct waves: Puritans from eastern England to New England in 1629–40, a mix of élite royalists and indentured servants to Virginia in 1642–75, groups from the north Midlands and Wales to the Delaware Valley beginning in about 1675, and a great mass from the Scottish borders and Northern Ireland to Appalachia in 1718–75. 'By the year 1775 these four cultures were fully established in British America. They spoke distinctive dialects of English, built their houses in diverse ways, and had different methods of doing much of the ordinary business of life.'[15]

By assembling in America in enclaves that reflected their geographic origins, the four main waves of immigrants thus managed to preserve distinctive regional identities. That is why, for instance, horses in New England (as in East Anglia) neigh, while those in the middle states of America (and the Midlands of England) whinny.[16] Noting that many words became associated early on with the speech of Virginia – *afeared, howdy, catercorner, innards, traipse, woebegone, bide* and *tarry* for stay awhile, *tote* for carry, *disremember* for forget, *pekid* for being pale or unwell – Fischer says: 'Virtually all peculiarities of grammar, syntax, vocabulary and pronunciation which have been noted as typical of Virginia were recorded in the [southern England] counties of Sussex, Surrey, Hampshire, Dorset, Wiltshire, Somerset, Oxford, Gloucester, Warwick or Worcester.'[17] They may indeed have been recorded there – it would be surprising if they were not – but in fact at least some of the words he uses to support his thesis (for instance, *poorly* for being unwell and *right good* for something meritorious or agreeable) were primarily northern expressions.

Neat though it is, Fischer's argument presents two problems. First, with the exception of the final wave of immigrants from the Scottish borders and Ulster, the geographic background of colonial immigrants was nothing like as uniform as Fischer implies. The Puritan movement may have had its base in East Anglia – and this clearly accounts for the preponderance of East Anglian place-names in Massachusetts and Connecticut – but its followers came from every corner of England. The *Mayflower* manifest alone shows passengers hailing from Yorkshire, Devon, Lincolnshire, Westmorland and many other counties linguistically distinct from East Anglia. Equally, an indentured servant was as likely to come from Lanarkshire or Wales or Cornwall as from London. George Washington's forebears emigrated to America from Northumbria and settled in Virginia. Benjamin Franklin's came from a town just a dozen miles away, but settled in Boston. Throughout the colonial period, immigrants came from all over and settled all over. And once settled in the New World, significant numbers of them moved on – for example, Franklin transplanted himself from Boston to Philadelphia, Alexander Hamilton from the West Indies to New York.

The second problem with Fischer's thesis is that many contemporary accounts do not bear it out. Surprise at the uniformity of American speech is found again and again in letters and journals throughout the eighteenth century and into the nineteenth. In 1770 one William Eddis found it a cause of wonder that 'the language of the immediate descendants of such a promiscuous ancestry is perfectly uniform and unadulterated; nor has it borrowed any provincial, or national accent, from its British or foreign parentage.'[18] Another observer stated flatly: 'There is no dialect in all North America.'[19] John Pickering, president of the American Academy of Arts and Sciences and arguably the leading authority on American speech of his day, thought America was marked not by the variety of its speech but by its consistency. One could find 'a greater difference in dialect between one county and another in Britain than there is between one state and another in America', he contended, and attributed this to 'the frequent removal of people from one part of our country to another'. He cited his own New Jersey as a particular example: 'People from all the other states are constantly moving into and out of this state so that there is little peculiarity of manner.'[20]

This isn't to say that there *weren't* distinctive regional varieties of speech in America by the time of the Revolution, merely that they appear not to have been as fixed, evident and susceptible to generalization as we might sometimes be led to believe.

Even less certain is the question of the degree to which American speech had by 1776 become noticeably different from that of Britain. Flexner states that at least as early as 1720 Americans were aware that their language 'differed seriously' from that of England.[21] In 1756, Samuel Johnson referred without hesitation to an 'American dialect', and a popular American play of the day, *The Politician Out-Witted,* instructed the actors to render British speech as 'effeminate cries',[22] suggesting that differences in cadence and resonance, if not necessarily of pronunciation, were already evident. On the other hand, Krapp notes that visitors to Boston at the time of the Revolution commonly remarked that the accent of the people there was almost indistinguishable from the English of England.[23]

What is certain is that Britons and Americans alike sounded quite different from Britons and Americans of today, and in a multitude of ways. Both would have dropped the *w* sound in *backward, Edward* and *somewhat*, but preserved it in *sword*. They would not have pronounced the *c* in *verdict* or *predict* or the *l* in *vault, fault* and *soldier*. Words like *author* and *anthem* would have been pronounced with a hard *t*, as in *orator*, or even sometimes a *d*. *Fathoms*, for instance, was often spelled 'fadams.' *Banquet* would have been pronounced 'banket'. *Balcony* rhymed with *baloney* (Byron would soon rhyme it with *Giorgione*). *Barrage* was pronounced 'bair-idge' and apparently remained so pronounced up to the time of World War I. Words that we now pronounce with an interior *-ew* sound frequently lacked it then, so that *mute,* and *volume* would have been 'moot' and 'voloom'. Vowel sounds in general were much less settled and specific. Combinations that are now enunciated were then glossed over, so that many speakers said 'partickly' (or 'puhtickly') for *particularly*, 'actilly' for *actually*, 'poplar' for *popular* and so on.

Eighteenth-century users had a greater choice of contractions than now: as well as *can't, don't, isn't* and so on, there was *han't* (sometimes *hain't*) for 'have not' and *an't* for 'are not' and 'am not'. *An't*, first recorded in 1723 in print in America though probably older, evolved in two directions. Rhymed with 'taunt,' it took on the spelling *aren't* (the *r* being silent, as it still is in British English). Rhymed with 'taint,' it took on the spelling *ain't*. There was nothing intrinsically superior in one form or the other, but critics gradually developed a distaste for *ain't*. By the nineteenth century it was widely, if unreasonably, condemned as vulgar, a position from which it shows no sign of advancing.[24]

Contemporary writings, particularly by the indifferently educated, offer good clues as to pronunciation. Paul Revere wrote 'git' (for *get*), 'imeaditly' and 'prittie' and referred to blankets as being 'woren out'. Elsewhere we can find 'libity' for *liberty*, 'patchis' for *purchase*, 'ort' for *ought*,[25] 'weamin' for *women*, 'through' for *throw*, 'nater' for *nature*,[26] 'keer' for *care*, 'jest' for *just*; 'ole' for *old*, 'pizen' for *poison*, 'darter' (or even 'dafter') for *daughter*. 'Chaw' for *chew*, 'varmint' for *vermin*, 'stomp' for *stamp*, 'heist' for *hoist*, 'rile' for *roil*, 'hoss' for *horse*, and 'tetchy' for *touchy* were commonly, if not invariably, heard among educated speakers on both sides of the Atlantic. All of this suggests that if we wished to find a modern-day model for British and American speech of the late eighteenth century, we could probably do no better than Yosemite Sam.

To this day it remains a commonplace in England that American English is a corrupted form of British speech, that the inhabitants of the New World display a kind of helpless, chronic 'want of refinement' (in the words of Frances Trollope) every time they open their mouths and attempt to issue sounds. In fact, in several significant ways it is British speech that has become corrupted – or, to put it in less reactionary terms, has quietly evolved. The tendency to pronounce *fertile, mobile* and other such words as if spelled 'fertle' and 'moble', to give a *ŭ* sound to *hover, grovel* and *Coventry* rather than the rounded *o* of *hot*, to pronounce *schedule* with an initial *sk-* rather than a *sh-*, all reflect British speech patterns up to the close of the eighteenth century.* Even the feature that Americans most closely associate with modern British speech, the practice of saying 'bahth', 'cahn't' and 'banahna' for *bath, can't*

---

* It is, of course, no more than a tendency. Many Americans rhyme *grovel* with *novel*, and all of them say *mercantile, infantile* and *servile* in contradiction of the usual pattern.

and *banana,* appears to have been unknown among educated British speakers at the time of the American Revolution. Pronunciation guides until as late as 1809 give no hint of the existence of such a pronunciation in British speech, although there is some evidence to suggest that it was used by London's cockneys (which would make it one of the few instances in modern linguistics in which a manner of utterance travelled upward from the lower classes). Not only did English speakers of the day, Britons and Americans alike, say *bath* and *path* with a flat *a,* but even apparently such words as *jaunt, hardly, palm* and *father.* Two incidental relics of this old pattern of pronunciation are the general American pronunciation of *aunt* (i.e., 'ant') and *sassy,* which is simply how people once said *saucy.*

II

In the summer of 1776, when it occurred to the delegates assembled in Philadelphia that they needed a document to spell out the grounds of their dissatisfaction with Britain, the task was handed to Thomas Jefferson. To us, he seems the obvious choice. He was not.

In 1776 Thomas Jefferson was a fairly obscure figure, even in his own Virginia. Aged just thirty-three, he was the second youngest of the delegates and one of the least experienced. The second Continental Congress was in fact his first exposure to a wider world of affairs beyond those of his native colony. He had not been selected to attend the first Continental Congress and should not have been at the second. He was called only as a late replacement for Peyton Randolph, who had been summoned home to Virginia. Jefferson's reputation rested almost entirely on his *Summary View of the Rights of British America* written two years earlier. A rather aggressive and youthfully impudent essay advising the British on how they ought to conduct themselves in their principal overseas possession, it had gained him some attention as a writer. To his fellow Virginia delegates he was known as a dilettante (a word that did not yet have any pejorative overtones; taken from the Italian *dilettare,* it simply described one who found pleasure in the richness of human possibility) and admired for the breadth of his

49

reading in an age when that truly meant something. (He was adept at seven languages.)

By no means, however, did he have what we might call a national standing. Nor did he display any evidence of desiring one. He showed a distinct lack of keenness to get to Philadelphia, dawdling en route to shop for books and to buy a horse, and once there he said almost nothing. 'During the whole time I sat with him I never heard him utter three sentences together,' John Adams later marvelled. Moreover, he went home to Virginia in December 1775, in the midst of debates, and did not return for nearly five months. Had he been able, he would gladly have abandoned the Congress altogether, leaving the drafting of the Declaration of Independence to someone else in order to take part in drawing up a new constitution for Virginia, a matter much closer to his heart.[27]

None the less, because he showed a 'peculiar felicity for expression', in John Adams's words, he was one of five men chosen to draft the Declaration of Independence – John Adams, Benjamin Franklin, Roger Sherman and Robert R. Livingston were the others – and this Committee of Five in turn selected him to come up with a working draft. The purpose, as Jefferson saw it, was 'not to find out new principles, or new arguments, never before thought of, not merely to say things which had never been said before; but to place before mankind the common sense of the subject, in terms so plain and firm as to command their assent'.[28]

But of course the Declaration of Independence is much more than that. As Garry Wills has written, it stands as 'perhaps the only piece of practical politics that is also theoretical politics and also great literature'.[29] Consider the opening sentence:

> When in the Course of human events, it becomes necessary for one people to dissolve the political bands which have connected them with another, and to assume, among the powers of the earth, the separate and equal station to which the Laws of Nature and of Nature's God entitle them, a decent respect to the opinions of mankind requires that they should declare the causes which impel them to the separation.

In a single sentence, in clear, simple language that anyone can understand, Jefferson has not only encapsulated the philosophy of what is to follow, but set in motion a cadence that gradually becomes hypnotic. You can read the preamble to the Declaration of Independence for its rhythms alone. As Stephen E. Lucas notes, it captures in just 202 words 'what it took John Locke thousands of words to explain in his *Second Treatise of Government*. In its ability to compress complex ideas into a brief, clear statement, the preamble is a paradigm of eighteenth century prose style.'[30]

What is less well known is that the words are not entirely Jefferson's. George Mason's recently published draft of the *Virginia Declaration of Rights* provided what might most charitably be called liberal inspiration. Consider perhaps the most famous line in the Declaration:

> We hold these truths to be self-evident, that all men are created equal, that they are endowed by their Creator with certain unalienable Rights, that among these are Life, Liberty and the pursuit of happiness.'

Compare that with Mason's *Virginia Declaration*:

> All men are born equally free and independent, and have certain inherent natural rights, of which . . . they cannot, by any compact, deprive or divest their posterity; among which are the enjoyment of life and liberty, with the means of acquiring and possessing property, and pursuing and obtaining happiness and safety.

'Pursuit of happiness' may be argued to be a succinct improvement over 'pursuing and obtaining happiness and safety', but even that compelling phrase wasn't original with Jefferson. 'Pursuit of happiness' had been coined by John Locke almost a century before and had appeared frequently in political writings ever since.

Nor are the words in that famous, inspiring sentence the ones that Jefferson penned. His original version shows considerably less grace and rather more verbosity:

> We hold these truths to be sacred & undeniable; that all men are created equal and independant, that from that equal creation they derive rights inherent and inalienable, among which are the preservation of life, & liberty, & the pursuit of happiness.[31]

The sentence took on its final resonance only after it had been through the hands of the Committee of Five and then subjected to active debate in Congress itself. Congress did not hesitate to alter Jefferson's painstakingly crafted words. Altogether it ordered forty changes to the original text. It deleted 630 words, about a quarter of the total, and added 146. As with most writers who have been subjected to the editing process, Jefferson thought the final text depressingly inferior to his original, and, like most writers, he was wrong. Indeed, seldom has a writer been better served. Congress had the wisdom to leave untouched those sections that were unimprovable – notably the opening paragraph – and excised much that was irrelevant or otiose.

Though now one of the most famous passages in English political prose, the preamble attracted far less attention then than later. At the time the listing of grievances against the king, which takes up some 60 per cent of the entire text of the Declaration, was far more daring and arresting.

The twenty-seven charges against the king were mostly – sometimes recklessly – overstated. Charge four, for instance, accused him of compelling colonial assemblies to meet in locales that were 'unusual, uncomfortable and distant . . . for the sole purpose of fatiguing them into compliance with his measures'. In fact, in only three of the thirteen colonies were the assemblies ever compelled to move and in two of those it happened on only one occasion each. Only Massachusetts suffered it for an extended period and there the assembly was moved just four miles to Cambridge – hardly an odious imposition.

Or consider charge ten: 'He has erected a multitude of New Offices, and sent hither swarms of Officers to harass our people, and eat out their substance.' In fact, the swarms numbered no more than about fifty, and much of their activity, such as trying to stop smuggling (an activity which, incidentally, had helped to make John Hancock one of the richest men in New England), was legitimate by any standards.[32]

In Britain, the Declaration was received by many as arrant hogwash. The *Gentleman's Magazine* mocked the assertion that all men are created equal. 'In what are they created equal?' it asked. 'Is it in size, strength, understanding, figure, moral or civil accomplishments, or situation of life? Every plough-man knows that they are not created equal in any of these. All men, it is true, are equally created, but what is this to the purpose? It certainly is no reason why the Americans should turn rebels.'[33] Though the writer of that passage appears to have had perhaps one glass of Madeira too many at lunch, there was something in his argument. No one in America truly believed that all men were created equal. Samuel Johnson touched on the incontestable hypocrisy of the American position when he asked, 'How is it that we hear the loudest yelps for liberty among the drivers of Negroes?'[34]

Jefferson's draft of the Declaration contains several spellings and usages that strike us today – and indeed appear to have struck at least some of his contemporaries – as irregular. For one thing, Jefferson always wrote *it's* for the possessive form of *it*, a practice that looks decidedly illiterate today. In fact, there was some logic to it. As a possessive form, the argument went, *its* required an apostrophe in precisely the same way as did words like *children's* or *men's*. Others contended, however, that in certain common words like *ours* and *yours* it was customary to dispense with the apostrophe, and that *its* belonged in this camp. By about 1815, the non-apostrophists had their way almost everywhere, but in 1776 it was a fine point, and one to which Jefferson clearly did not subscribe.[35]

Jefferson also favoured some unusual spellings, notably *independant* (which Thomas Paine likewise preferred), *paiment* and *unacknoleged*, all of which were subsequently changed in the published version to their more conventional forms. He veered with apparent indecisiveness between the two forms for the singular third person present indicative of *have*, sometimes using the literary *hath* ('experience hath shown') and sometimes the more modern *has* ('He has kept among us . . .'). Two further orthographic uncertainties of the age are reflected in Jefferson's text – whether to write -*or* or -*our* in words like *honour* and whether to use -*ise* or -*ize* in words like *naturalize*. Jefferson was inconsistent on both counts.

Much is sometimes made of the irregularity of spelling among writers of English in the eighteenth century. Noting that Adam Smith's *Wealth of Nations* varied in its spellings between *public* and *publick*, *complete* and *compleat*, and *independent* and *independant*, David Simpson observes in *The Politics of American*

English: 'Except for Samuel Johnson, no one in 1776, on either side of the ocean, seems to show much concern for a standard spelling practice.'[36]

This is almost certainly overstating matters. Although Thomas Jefferson did have some spelling quirks – among many others, he persistently addressed his letters to 'Doctr. Franklyn' when he must surely have realized that the good doctor spelled his name otherwise[37] – to suggest that he or any other accomplished writer of his age was cavalier with his spelling does him an injustice. To begin with, such a statement contains the implied conceit that modern English is today somehow uniform in its spellings, which is far from true. In 1972 a scholar named Lee C. Deighton undertook the considerable task of comparing the spellings of every word in four leading American dictionaries and found that there are no fewer than 1,770 common words in modern English in which there is no general agreement on the preferred spelling. The *Random House Dictionary*, to take one example, gives *innuendos* as the preferred plural of *innuendo*, the American Heritage opts for *innuendoes*, *Webster's New World* prefers *innuendoes* but recognizes *innuendos*, and *Webster's Seventh* gives equal merit to both. The dictionaries are equally – we might fairly say hopelessly – split on whether to write *discussible* or *discussable*, *eyeopener*, *eye opener* or *eye-opener*, *dumfound* or *dumbfound*, *gladiolus* (for the plural), *gladioli* or *gladioluses*, *gobbledegook* or *gobbledygook*, *licenceable* or *licensable*, and many hundreds of others. (The champion of orthographic uncertainty appears to be *panatela*, which can also pass muster as *panatella*, *panetela* or *panetella*.) The principal difference between irregular spellings now and in Jefferson's day is that in Jefferson's day the number was very much larger – no less than you would expect in an age that was only just becoming acquainted with dictionaries. Just as we seldom note whether a particular writer uses *big-hearted* or *bighearted*, *omelette* or *omelet*, *OK* or *okay*, so I suspect Jefferson and Paine would think it singular that we had even noticed that they sometimes wrote *honour* and sometimes *honor*.

That is not to say that spelling or any other issue of usage in this period was considered inconsequential. In fact, the opposite is true. The second Continental Congress contained within it many men – Jefferson, Adams, John Jay, Benjamin Franklin, John Witherspoon (first president of Princeton University and the first authority on American English) – who constantly displayed a passionate interest in language and its consistent, careful application. They argued at length over whether the Declaration should use *independent* or *independant*, *inalienable* or *unalienable*, whether the principal nouns were to be capitalized as Franklin wished or presented lower case as Jefferson desired (and as was the rather racy new fashion among the younger set).* Anything to do with language exercised their interest greatly – we might almost say disproportionately. Just a month after the completion of the Declaration of Independence, at a time when the delegates might have been expected to occupy themselves with more pressing concerns – like how they were going to win the war and escape hanging – Congress quite extraordinarily found time to debate the business of a motto for the new nation. (Their choice, *E Pluribus Unum*, 'One From Many', was taken from, of all places, a recipe for salad in an early poem by Virgil.) Four years later, while the war still raged, John Adams was urging Congress to establish an American Academy along the lines of the Académie française with the express purpose of establishing national standards of usage. To suggest that these men showed 'not much concern' for matters of usage and spelling is to misread them utterly.

Where there was evident uncertainty was in what to call the new nation. The Declaration referred in a single sentence to 'the united States of America' and 'these United Colonies'. The first adopted form of the Declaration was given the title 'A Declaration by the Representatives of the United States of America, in General Congress Assembled', though this was improved in the final published version to the rather more robust and assertive 'The Unanimous Declaration of the Thirteen United States of America'. (It wasn't in fact unanimous at all. At least a quarter of the delegates were against it, but voting was done by delegation rather than by individuals, and each delegation carried a majority in favour.) It was the first time the country had been officially designated the United States of America, though in fact until 1778 the formal title was the United States of North America.[39] Even

---

* Among the words he lower-cased were *nature, creator* and even *God*. Most were later capitalized by the printer.[38]

after the Declaration, 'united' was often left lower case, as if to emphasize that it was merely descriptive, and the country was variously referred to throughout the war as 'the colonies', 'the united Colonies', the 'United Colonies of America' or 'the United Colonies of North America'. (The last two are the forms under which officers were commissioned into the army.)

That the signing of the Declaration of Independence is celebrated on 4 July is one of American history's more singular mistakes. America did not declare independence on 4 July 1776. That had happened two days earlier, when the proposal was adopted. The proceedings on 4 July were a mere formality endorsing the form of words that were to be used to announce this breach. Most people had no doubt that 2 July was the day that would ring through the ages. 'The second day of July, 1776 will be the most memorable Epocha in the History of America,' John Adams wrote to his wife Abigail on 3 July. Still less was the Declaration signed on 4 July, except by the president of the proceedings, John Hancock, and the secretary, Charles Thomson.* It was not signed on 4 July because it had first to be transcribed on to parchment. The official signing didn't begin until 2 August and wasn't concluded until 1781 when Thomas McKean of Delaware, the last of the fifty-six signatories, finally put his name to it. Such was the fear of reprisal that the names of the signers were not released until January 1777, six months after the Declaration's adoption.

Equally mistaken is the idea that the adoption of the Declaration of Independence was announced to a breathless Philadelphia on 4 July by the ringing of the Liberty Bell. For one thing, the Declaration was not read out in Philadelphia until 8 July, and there is no record of any bells being rung. Indeed, though the Liberty Bell was there, it was not so called until 1847 when the whole inspiring episode was recounted in a book titled *Washington and His Generals*, written by one George Lippard, whose previous literary efforts had been confined almost exclusively to producing mildly pornographic novels.[41] He made the whole thing up.

John Dunlap, a Philadelphia printer, hastily ran off an

---

* Though John Hancock became immediately famous for his cockily outsize signature on the Declaration, the expression 'Put your John Hancock here' for a signature didn't apparently occur to anyone until 1903.[40]

apparently unknown number of copies. (Until recently only twenty-four were thought to have survived – two in private hands and the rest lodged with institutions. But in 1992 a shopper at a flea market in Philadelphia found a copy folded into the back of a picture frame, apparently as padding. It was estimated to be worth up to $3 million.) Dunlap's version was dated 4 July and it was this, evidently, that persuaded the nation to make that the day of revelry. The next year, at any rate, the great event was being celebrated on the fourth, and so it has stayed ever since. It was celebrated 'with Pomp and Parade, with Shews, Games, Sports, Guns, Bells, Bonfires, and Illuminations from one End of this Continent to the other', in John Adams's words. The first anniversary saw the entrance of a new word into the language: *fireworks*. Fireworks themselves weren't new, but previously they had been called *rockets*.

America wasn't yet a nation, but more a loose confederation of thirteen independent sovereignties – what the Articles of Confederation would later call 'a firm league of friendship'. True nationhood would have to wait a further twelve perilous, unstable years for the adoption of the Constitution. Before we turn to that uneasy period, however, let us pause for a moment to consider the fate of poor Tom Paine, the man who set the whole process of revolution in motion.

Despite the huge success of *Common Sense*, the publication brought him no official position. By the end of 1776, he was a common foot soldier. After the war, Paine travelled to France, where he performed a similar catalytic role in the revolution there with his pamphlet *The Rights of Man* before falling foul of the erratic Robespierre, who had him clapped into prison for daring to suggest a merciful exile for King Louis XVI (on the grounds that Louis had supported the American rebels). Unappreciated in France and a pariah in his own country, he returned to America and sank almost at once into dereliction and obscurity.

Not long before he died, an old friend found Paine in a tavern in New Rochelle, New York, unconscious, dressed in tatters, and bearing 'the most disagreeable smell possible'. The friend hauled him to a tub of hot, soapy water and scrubbed him from head to foot three times before the odour was pacified. His nails had not been cut for years. Soon afterwards, this great man, who had once dined with the likes of Washington, Jay and Jefferson, who had been a central figure in the two great revolutions of the modern age, died broken and forgotten. William Cobbett, the essayist, stole his bones and took them back to England with him, but likewise died before he could find a suitable resting-place for them. And so the remains of one of the great polemicists of his or any other age were unceremoniously carted off by a rag-and-bone merchant and vanished for ever.

4

Making a Nation

It began with a dispute between oyster fishermen.

In 1632 Charles I placed the border between Virginia and Maryland not in the middle of the Potomac River, as was normal practice, but instead gave his chum Lord Baltimore the whole of the river up to the Virginia bank, to the dismay and frustration of Virginia fishermen who were thus deprived of their right to gather the river's delicious and lucrative bivalves. Over time, the dispute spread to Pennsylvania and Delaware, led to occasional skirmishes known collectively and somewhat grandly as the Oyster War, and eventually resulted in the calling of a gathering to try to sort out this and other matters involving trade and intrastate affairs.

Thus in May 1787 representatives from all over America began to assemble at the old State House in Philadelphia in what would come to be known as the Constitutional Convention. Though America had declared its independence eleven years earlier, it was not yet in any real sense a nation, but rather an uneasy alliance of states bound by a document known formally as the Articles of Confederation and Perpetual Union. Enacted in 1781, the Articles had established a central government of sorts, but had left it subordinate to the states and embarrassingly lacking in clout. In consequence, as the historian Charles L. Mee, jun., has put it, in 1787 the government of the United States 'could not reliably levy taxes, could not ensure that its laws would be obeyed, could not repay its debts, could not ensure that it would honour its treaty obligations. It was not clear, in fact, that it could be called a government at all.'[1]

Since the conclusion of the war with Britain four years before, the states had increasingly fallen to squabbling. Connecticut boldly claimed almost a third of the territory of Pennsylvania after many of its residents settled there. Pennsylvania bickered with Virginia over their common border and was so fearful of New York imposing tariffs on its manufactures that it insisted on having its own access to the Great Lakes. (If you have ever wondered why Pennsylvania's border takes an abrupt upward jag at its north-western end to give it an odd umbilicus to Lake Erie, that is why.) New York bickered over patches of land with little Rhode Island, and Vermont constantly threatened to leave the union. Clearly something needed to be done. The obvious solution would be a new agreement superseding the Articles of Confederation and creating a more powerful central government: in a word, a constitution. Without it, America could never hope to be a nation. As Page Smith has put it: 'The Revolution had created the possibility, not the reality, of a new nation. It is the Constitution that for all practical purposes is synonymous with our nationhood.'[2]

However, there were problems. To begin with, the delegates had no authority to form a constitution. Their assignment was to amend the Articles of Confederation, not replace them. (Which is why it wasn't called the Constitutional Convention until after-wards.)[3] Then, too, the scale of the American continent and the diversity of its parts seemed fated to thwart any hope of meaningful unification. With 1,500 miles of coastline and a vast inland wilderness, America was already one of the largest countries in the world – ten times larger than any previous federation in history – and the disparities in population, wealth and political outlook between the states presented seemingly insurmountable obstacles to finding a common purpose. If proportional representation were instituted, Virginia and Pennsylvania between them would possess one-third of the nation's political power, while Delaware would be entitled to a mere one-ninetieth. Little states thus feared big ones. Slave-owning states feared non-slave-owning states. Eastern states with fixed borders feared those to the west with an untapped continent on their doorsteps, suspecting that one day these western upstarts would overtake them in population and that they would find their destiny in the hands of rude frontiersmen in tassled buckskins – an unthinkable prospect. All the states, large and small, had proud, distinct histories, often going back nearly two centuries, and were reluctant to relinquish even the smallest measure of autonomy to an unproven central authority. The challenge of the Constitutional Convention was not to give powers to the states, but to take powers away from them, and to do it in a way that they would find palatable.

Some states refused even to entertain the notion. Rhode Island, which had declared independence from Britain two months before the rest of America had, now refused to send delegates to Philadelphia (and rather sulkily declined to join the union until 1790). Vermont likewise snubbed the convention and made it clear from the outset that it was disinclined to abide by its decisions. Others, like Maryland, could barely find people willing to go. The first five men selected as representatives all declined to attend, and at the opening of the convention the legislature was still trying to find willing delegates. New Hampshire was prepared to send two delegates, but refused to underwrite their expenses and as a result had no representatives at the convention for the first crucial weeks. Many delegates attended only fitfully, and six never came at all. Altogether only about thirty of the sixty-one elected delegates attended from start to finish.[4]

Fortunately, those who attended included some of the most steady, reflective and brilliant intellects any young nation has ever produced: Benjamin Franklin, Alexander Hamilton, James Madison, Roger Sherman, Gouverneur Morris, John Dickinson, Edmund Randolph, and of course the regal, rocklike George Washington whose benign presence as president of the convention lent the proceedings an authority and respectability they could not otherwise have expected. Of the leading political figures of the day only Thomas Jefferson and John Adams, both abroad on state business, were not there.

In many ways the most interesting of the delegates was Benjamin Franklin. Aged eighty-one, he was coming to the end of his long life – and in the view of many of his fellow delegates had long since passed the useful part of it. But what a life it had been. One of seventeen children of a Boston soap and candle maker, he had left home as a boy after receiving barely two years of schooling, and established himself as a printer in Philadelphia. By dint of hard work and steady application he had made himself into one of the most respected thinkers and wealthiest businessmen in the colonies. His experiments with electricity, unfairly diminished in the popular mind to inventing the lightning rod and nearly killing himself by foolishly flying a kite in a thunderstorm, were among the most exciting scientific achievements of the eighteenth century and made him one of the celebrated scientists of the day (though he was never called a scientist in his lifetime, the word not being coined until 1840; in the 1700s scientists were *natural philosophers*). The terms he created in the course of his experiments – *battery, armature, positive, negative* and *condenser*, among others[5] – show that he was a good deal more than a mildly quizzical fellow who just wanted to see what would happen if he nudged a kite into some storm clouds.

Franklin's life was one of relentless industry. He invented countless useful objects (which we shall discuss in a later chapter), helped to found America's first volunteer fire department, its first fire insurance company (the Hand-in-Hand), one of Philadelphia's first libraries, and the respected if somewhat overnamed American Philosophical Society for the Promotion of Useful Knowledge to be Held at Philadelphia.[6] He created an eternal literary character, the Richard of *Poor Richard's Almanack*, filled the world with maxims and *bons mots*, corresponded endlessly with the leading minds of Europe and America, wrote essays on everything from how to select a mistress (take an older woman) to how to avoid flatulence (drink perfume), and in 1737 drew up the first list of American slang terms for drunkenness. (He came up with 228.) He represented America overseas with intelligence and skill and, of course, was one of the shapers of both the Declaration of Independence and the Constitution. He dabbled in property speculation and ran a printing business with holdings as far afield as Jamaica and Antigua. He became the largest dealer in paper in the colonies and made *Poor Richard's Almanack* such an indispensable part of almost every American household that it was for twenty-five years the country's second best-selling publication (the Bible was first). Such was his commercial acumen that he was able to retire from active business in 1748 aged just forty-two and devote himself to gentlemanly pursuits like politics, science and writing.

And in between all this he somehow managed to find time – quite a lot of time – to pursue what was his greatest, if least celebrated, passion: namely, trying *to roger* just about any woman who passed before him. This curious expression, you may be surprised to learn, appears to be an Americanism. The earliest reference to it is from eighteenth-century Virginia, though we have no idea now which hyperactive Roger inspired the term or why it faded from use in the New World. We may as well have called it to *benjamin*, such was the portly Franklin's commitment to the pastime. From earliest adulthood, Franklin showed an unwavering inclination to engage in 'foolish Intrigues with low Women', as he himself sheepishly put it.[7] One such encounter resulted in an illegitimate son, William, born in 1730 or 1731 and raised in Franklin's house by his long-suffering common-law wife, Deborah. Throughout his long life Franklin's dynamic libido was a matter of wonder for his contemporaries. The artist Charles Willson Peale, calling on the great man in London, found him with a young woman on his knee[8] – or at least he was discreet enough to say it was his knee – and others commonly arrived for appointments to find him *in flagrante* with a parlourmaid or other yielding creature.

During his years in England he became close friends with Sir Francis Dashwood, who presided over a notorious den called the Order of St Francis, but more popularly known as the Hellfire Club, at his country house at West Wycombe in Buckinghamshire. Members took part in black masses and other wildly blasphemous ceremonies that invariably culminated in drunken orgies involving pliant women garbed as nuns. In his quieter moments, Dashwood was joint postmaster general of England and co-author with Franklin of a revised version of the *Book of Common Prayer*. There is no certain evidence that Franklin took part in these debauches, but it would have been a wrenching break with his character had he not. It is certainly known that he was a frequent, not to say eager, visitor to Dashwood's house and it would take a generous spirit indeed to suppose that he ventured there repeatedly just to discuss postal regulations and the semantic nuances of the *Book of Common Prayer*.

The eighteenth century, it must be remembered, was a decidedly earthy and free-spirited age. It was a period that teemed with indelicate locutions – *pisspot* for a doctor, *shit-sack* for a Nonconformist, *groper* for a blind person, *fartcatcher* for a footman (because he followed behind), to name just four. Words and metaphors that would bring blushes to a later age were used without hesitation or embarrassment. At the Constitutional Convention Elbridge Gerry would make a famous remark (curiously absent from modern high school textbooks) in which he compared a standing army to an erect penis – 'an excellent assurance of domestic tranquillity, but a dangerous temptation to foreign adventure'[9] – and no one thought it inapt or unseemly, at least in the company of men. Franklin himself peppered his almanacs with maxims that were, to modern ears, coarse to the point of witlessness: 'The greatest monarch on the proudest throne is obliged to sit upon his own arse'; 'He that lives upon hope, dies farting'; 'Relation without friendship, friendship without power, power without will . . . are not worth a farto.'

It is worth noting that few of his aphorisms, coarse or otherwise, were of his own devising. Though a few cannot be traced to earlier sources – for example, 'An empty bag cannot stand upright' and 'Experience keeps a dear school, yet fools will learn in no other' – most were plundered without hesitation or scruple from other similar publications of the day, such as James Howell's *Lexicon Tetraglotton*, Thomas Fuller's *Gnomologia* and other writings, George Herbert's *Outlandish Proverbs*, and, especially, Jonathan Swift's *Bickerstaff Papers*. It was from Swift that Franklin took the droll idea of predicting in the almanac's annual forecasts the imminent death of his leading competitor.[10] 'Why should I give my Readers bad lines of my own when good ones of other People's are so plenty?' he quipped.[11] (Nor did he hesitate to make up stories for his newspapers when the real news was thin and unarresting.)

He did, it must be said, often improve on others' maxims. He took the proverb 'God restoreth health and the physician hath the thanks', and made it into the pithier 'God heals and the doctor takes the fee.'[12] More often than not, however, he merely embellished them with a reference to flatulence, incontinence, sexual intercourse or some other frailty. His remark above about friendship without power being 'not worth a farto' originated with Thomas Fuller as the rather more prim 'A good friend is my nearest relation.' James Howell's 'A Fort which begins to parley is half gotten' he made into 'Neither a Fortress nor a Maidenhead will hold out long after they begin to parly.'[13]

No discussion of Franklin and language would be complete without a mention of his *Proposal for a Reformed Alphabet* of

1768. Though much is sometimes made of Franklin's tinkering with English spelling, and though he did offer occasional statements sympathetic to the cause of reform (namely, 'if Amendments are never attempted and things continue to grow worse and worse they must come to be in a wretched Condition at last'), it is not clear whether he regarded it as a serious attempt at orthographic reform or merely as an amusing way of writing mildly flirtatious letters to a pretty young correspondent.

Certainly there is no persuasive evidence that he worked very hard at the matter. The alphabet he came up with is a clumsy, illogical affair. It contained six additional letters, so it offered no improvements in terms of simplicity. Moreover, it was arbitrary, whimsical, hopelessly bewildering to the untutored, and routinely resulted in spellings that were far longer and more complex than those they were intended to replace. Under Franklin's reforms, for example, 'changes' became 'tseendsez' and 'Chinese' became 'Tsuiniiz.' His first letter in the new alphabet, dated July 20, 1768, is replete with spellings that suggest Franklin either had a peculiar sense of pronunciation or, more likely, carelessly applied his own pronunciation guide. According to his letter, *has* would be pronounced 'haze', *people* would be 'pee-peel', and *Richmond* would be 'Reechmund'.[14]

So used are we to regarding Franklin as a sage and mentor that it can come as a small shock to realize that he was not much venerated in his own day. John Adams, for one, detested him.[15] After Franklin's death in 1790, so little was his loss felt that the first edition of his collected writings did not appear until twenty-eight years later. His *Autobiography* aroused less interest still and did not appear in an American edition until 1868 – seventy-eight years after he died and long after it had been published elsewhere.[16] At the time of the Constitutional Convention Franklin was generally held to be at best of no real account, at worst little more than a doddering old fool. His infrequent proposals to the convention – that the President of the United States not be paid a salary, that each session be started with a prayer – were always roundly defeated. (His prayer motion failed to carry not because the delegates were ungodly but, as they patiently explained to him, because they had no funds to pay a chaplain.)

Franklin was merely a visible, wheezing reminder that the

business of America had passed in large part to a new generation. With the principal exception of the fifty-five-year-old General Washington (who in any case didn't take part in the debates), the delegates were strikingly youthful. Five were in their twenties, and most of the rest were in their thirties or forties. James Madison was thirty-five, Alexander Hamilton thirty-two. South Carolina's baby-faced Charles Pinckney was just twenty-nine, but to enhance his air of extreme youthfulness he vociferously insisted he was but twenty-four.[17] The oddest and least prepossessing figure of all was perhaps the most important: James Madison. Nothing about the young Virginian bespoke greatness. He was almost ridiculously short – no more than 'half a bar of soap' in the words of one contemporary – squeaky-voiced, pale, shy, and neurotically obsessed with his health. But he had a towering intellect and he tirelessly shunted between rival factions squeezing and cajoling compromise out of often obdurate delegates. No one else did more in that long, hot summer to make the Constitution a reality.

In not quite four months these thirty or so men created a framework for government that has lasted us to this day and was like nothing seen before. From 25 May to 17 September they worked in session five hours a day, six days a week, and often for long hours outside of that. It was, as Page Smith has put it with perhaps no more than a blush of hyperbole, 'the most remarkable example of sustained intellectual discourse in history'.[18] It is certainly no exaggeration to say that never before nor since has any gathering of Americans shown a more dazzling array of talent and of preparedness. Madison's background reading included the histories of Polybius, the orations of Demosthenes, Plutarch's *Lives*, Fortune Barthélemy de Felice's thirteen-volume *Code de l'Humanité* in the original French, and much, much else. Alexander Hamilton in a single speech bandied about references to the Amphictyonic Councils of ancient Greece and the Delian Confederacy. These were men who knew their stuff.

And they were great enough to put aside their differences. In the space of a single uncomfortable summer they created the foundations of American government: the legislature, the presidency, the courts, the system of checks and balances, the whole intricate framework of democracy – a legacy that is all the more arresting

66

when you consider that almost to a man they were against democracy in anything like the modern sense.

For a time they actually considered creating a monarchy, albeit one elected by the legislature. So real did this prospect seem that a rumour – quite without foundation – swept the colonies that the position was to be offered to the Duke of York, George III's second son. In fact, the idea of a monarch was quickly deemed incompatible with a republic. Alexander Hamilton suggested as an alternative a president and senate elected for life from men of property, with absolute power over the states.[19] Edmund Randolph preferred that the presidency be shared among three men, to give the executive office greater collective wisdom and less scope for despotism, sectionalism and corruption.[20] (The prospect of corruption worried them mightily.) Almost all envisioned an America ruled by a kind of informal aristocracy of propertied gentlemen – men much like themselves, in fact. So distant from their thinking was the idea of an open democracy that when James Wilson of Pennsylvania moved that the executive be chosen by popular vote, the delegates 'were entirely dumbfounded'. In the end they threw the matter of electing a President to the states, creating an electoral college and leaving each state to decide whether its collegial delegates would be chosen by the people or by the legislature.

In a spirit of compromise, they decreed that the House of Representatives would be chosen by the people, and the Senate by the states, an arrangement that remained in force until 1912 when senators at last were popularly elected. In the matter of the Vice-Presidency they decided – unwisely with the benefit of hindsight – that the job should fall to whoever came second in the Presidential poll. It seemed the fair thing to do, but it failed to take into account the distinct possibility that the Vice-President might represent a rival faction to that of the President. In 1804 the practice was abandoned and the custom of electing a two-man slate adopted.

When most of the rudiments were agreed, the delegates appointed a Committee of Detail to put their proposals on paper. One of the committee members, John Rutledge, was an admirer of the Iroquois, and recommended that the committee familiarize itself with the treaty of 1520 that had created the Iroquois

confederacy. It begins: 'We, the people, to form a union. . . .'[21]
These were of course essentially the very words they chose:

> We, the people of the United States, in Order to form a more
> perfect Union, establish Justice, insure domestic Tran-
> quility, provide for the common defence, promote the
> general Welfare, and secure the Blessings of Liberty to
> ourselves and our Posterity, do ordain and establish this
> Constitution for the United States of America.

After this simple statement of intent, there follow seven Articles, six
of which set out – sometimes sketchily, sometimes with fastidious
detail – the mechanisms of government, with a seventh announcing
that the document would take effect once it had been ratified by
nine states. (A number not chosen lightly; the delegates thought it
doubtful that more than nine states would ratify.)

At just twenty-five pages, the Constitution is a model of
concision. (The state constitution of Oklahoma, by contrast, is
158 pages long.)[22] On some matters it was explicit and forthright
– on the age and citizenship requirements for senators, representatives and the President, and most especially on the matter of
impeachment. The framers seemed cautious almost to the point of
paranoia about providing instructions for how to depose those
found to be disloyal or corrupt. However, on other matters it was
curiously vague. There was no mention of a cabinet, for instance.
It mandated the setting up of a Supreme Court, independent from
the other branches, but then rather airily decreed that the rest of
the judiciary should consist of 'such inferior courts as the
Congress may from time to time ordain and establish'. Sometimes
this vagueness was a consequence of oversight and sometimes of
an inability to arrive at a more specific compromise. Where it was
specific, it almost always left room for later change. After
decreeing that Congress should assemble at least once a year,
beginning on the first Monday in December, it thoughtfully added
'unless they shall by law appoint a different day'. The upshot is
that the Constitution is an extraordinarily adaptable set of ground
rules.

In terms of its composition, surprisingly few oddities of spelling
and syntax stand out. Three words are spelled in the British style,

behaviour, labour and *defence*, but not *tranquillity*, which even in 1787 was being given a single *l* in America. Only once is there an inconsistency of spelling – *empeachments* in one paragraph and *impeachment* in the next – and only two other words are spelled in an archaic way: *chuse* and *encreased*. The opening sentence contains a double superlative ('more perfect'), which might not survive the editing process today, though it was unexceptionable enough at the time. The occasional appearance of a discordant article and noun combination ('an uniform'), a rather more fastidious use of the subjunctive ('before it become a law', 'if he approve he shall sign it'), the occasional capitalization of nouns that would now be lower-cased ('our Posterity'), and the treating of 'the United States' as a plural (it would remain so treated until about the time of the Civil War),[23] more or less exhaust the list of distinctions.

The Constitution is more notable for what it does not include. The words *nation* and *national* appear nowhere in the document, and not by accident or oversight. The delegates carefully replaced the words wherever they appeared. They feared that *national* smacked of a system in which power was dangerously centralized. They instead used the more neutral and less emotive *federal*, derived from the Latin *fides*, 'faith', and in the eighteenth century still carrying the sense of a relationship resting on trust.[24]

The other part of the Constitution with which we are most familiar, the ten amendments known as the Bill of Rights, came later. They were not adopted until 1791 (and in the case of Massachusetts not until 150 years later, when it was discovered that their ratification had been accidentally overlooked). These guarantees of basic freedoms were as radical and novel as anything that preceded them – even now Britain has no bill of rights, but then it has no written constitution either – but it is worth bearing in mind that the framers often meant something quite different by them. Consider the wording of the First Amendment: 'Congress shall make no law respecting an establishment of religion, or prohibiting the free exercise thereof; or abridging the freedom of speech, or of the press, or of the right of the people peaceably to assemble . . .'* Note in particular those first five words: 'Congress shall make no law . . .' The founders were not trying to free

America from such restrictions, but merely endeavouring to ensure that matters of censorship and personal liberty were left to the states.[25] And at the risk of exciting correspondence from the National Rifle Association, the much vaunted right of the people to keep and bear arms was never intended as a carte blanche, semi- divine injunction to invest in a private arsenal for purposes of sport and personal defence, as the full sentence makes clear: 'A well regulated militia being necessary to the security of a free State, the right of the people to keep and bear Arms shall not be infringed.' The framers had in mind only the necessity of raising a defence force at short notice. If they did favour the idea of keeping guns for shooting animals and household intruders, they never said so.

Astonishingly, at the time of its adoption almost no one saw the Constitution as a great document. Most of the delegates left Philadelphia feeling that they had created an agreement so riddled with compromise as to be valueless – 'a weak and worthless fabric', as Alexander Hamilton dispiritedly described it. Samuel Adams, John Hancock and Patrick Henry were all opposed. Fifteen of the convention delegates refused to sign it, among them George Mason, Elbridge Gerry and even two of the five men who had written it, Edmund Randolph and Oliver Elsworth. (Randolph soon showed an even more breathtaking measure of hypocrisy by accepting the post as the nation's first attorney general, thus becoming the man most directly in charge of upholding the document he had lately disowned.) Even its heartiest proponents hoped for no more than that the Constitution might somehow hold the fragile nation together for a few years until something better could be devised.[26]

None the less, the document was duly ratified, Washington was selected as the first President, and 4 March 1789 was chosen as the day to begin the new government. Unfortunately, only eight senators and thirteen representatives troubled to show up on the first day. Another twenty-six days would have to pass before the

---

* 'Peaceably to assemble' is an interesting and early example of the ginger avoidance of a split infinitive. The curious conviction that infinitives should not be split had only recently come into fashion.

House of Representatives could muster a quorum and even longer before the Senate could find enough willing participants to begin productive work.[27]

One of the first orders of business was what to call the new Chief Executive. The Constitution had referred to 'the President of the United States', but such had been the pomp and costly splendour of Washington's inauguration and so stately the demeanour of the new office-holder as to encourage Congress to consider a title with a grander ring to it. Among the suggestions were *His Highness, His Mightiness, His Magistracy, His Supremacy*, and *His Highness the President of the United States and Protector of their Liberties*. This last was the title very nearly chosen before the Congressmen returned to their senses, and the original wording of the Constitution, and settled for the respectful but republican *President of the United States*. Even so, Martha was often referred to as 'Lady Washington'.

The Vice-Presidency seems to have caused no such difficulty, though some among the droller elements of Congress joked that the first incumbent, the portly John Adams, should be referred to as 'His Rotundity'.

Washington was a firm believer in the dignity of his office. Visitors were expected to remain standing in his presence and even his closest associates found him aloof and disquietingly kingly in his deportment (leading one to wonder if America had exchanged George III for George I). To be fair to Washington, he had to establish from the outset that a President should be treated with utmost respect. In the early days of his presidency people would actually wander in off the street, to wish him luck or ask how things were going. (Eventually, he hit on a system whereby twice a week he set aside time during which any 'respectably dressed person' could come and see him.) He was acutely aware that he was setting patterns of executive behaviour that would live beyond him. 'There is scarcely any part of my conduct which may not hereafter be drawn into precedent,' he wrote a trifle gloomily. After sitting through hours of inconclusive debates in the Senate, he fled, muttering that he 'would be damned' if he ever subjected himself to such unproductive tedium again, and since that time no American President has taken part in legislative debates, a striking departure from British practice, though there is nothing in the Constitution to forbid it.[28]

One of the more intractable myths of this period is that Congress (or the Constitutional Convention itself) considered adopting German as the national language. The story has been repeated so often, by so many respectable writers, that it has nearly attained the status of received wisdom.* So let me say this clearly: it is wholly without foundation. In 1789, 90 per cent of America's four million inhabitants were of English descent. The idea that they would in an act of petulance impose on themselves a foreign tongue is clearly risible. The only known occasion on which German was ever an issue was in 1795 when the House of Representatives briefly considered a proposal to publish federal laws in German as well as in English as a convenience to recent immigrants and the proposal was defeated.[29] Indeed, as early as 1778, the Continental Congress decreed that messages to foreign emissaries be issued 'in the language of the United States'.[30]

However, considerable thought *was* given in early Congresses to the possibility of renaming the country. From the start, many people recognized that *United States of America* was unsatisfactory. For one thing, it allowed of no convenient adjectival form. A citizen would have to be either a *United Statesian* or some other such clumsy locution, or an *American*, thereby arrogating to US citizens a title that belonged equally to the inhabitants of some three dozen other nations on two continents. Several alternative possibilities were considered – the *United States of Columbia, Appalachia, Alleghania,* and *Freedonia* or *Fredonia* (whose denizens would be called *Fredes*) – but none found sufficient support to displace the prevailing title.[31]

United States of Columbia was a somewhat unexpected choice, since for most of the previous 250 years Christopher Columbus had been virtually forgotten in America. His Spanish associations had made him suspect to the British, who preferred to see the glory

---

* Here, for instance, is Kingsley Amis: 'An early Congress of the United States debated what language the new nation was to speak. English symbolized the vanquished colonial oppressor, its sole virtue being that everyone used it. As so many of us know, it won the contest, narrowly beating German. There were also votes – not many – for Ancient Greek, as the language of the first democracy, and for a Red Indian language, perhaps Massachusetts or Cree, because it was American.' (*The Amis Collection*, p. 17.)

of North American discovery go to John Cabot. Not until after the Revolutionary War, when Americans began casting around for heroes unconnected with the British monarchy, was the name *Columbus* resurrected, generally in the more elegant Latinized form *Columbia*, and his memory generously imbued with a spirit of grit and independent fortitude that wasn't altogether merited.

The semi-deification of Columbus began with a few references in epic poems, but soon communities and institutions were falling over themselves to create new names in his honour. In 1784 King's College in New York became Columbia College and two years later South Carolina chose Columbia as the name for its capital. In 1791 an American captain on a ship named *Columbia* claimed a vast tract of the north-west for the young country and dubbed it Columbia. (It later became the states of Washington, Oregon and Idaho, though the original name lives on north of the border in British Columbia.) Journals, clubs and institutes (among them the Columbian Institute for the Promotion of the Arts and Sciences, better known today as the Smithsonian Institution*) were named for the great explorer. The song 'Hail Columbia' dates from 1798.[33]

After this encouraging start, Columbus's life was given a kick into the higher realms of myth by Washington Irving's ambitious, if resplendently inaccurate, *History of the Life and Voyages of Christopher Columbus*, which came out in 1828 and was a phenomenal best-seller in America, Europe and Latin America throughout the nineteenth century.

Irving later wrote a life of George Washington that was just as successful and no less indebted to his fictive powers. But it is Mason Locke Weems – or Parson Weems as history knows him – to whom we must turn for many of the most treasured misconceptions about the Father of the Country. His hugely successful *Life of Geòrge Washington: With Curious Anecdotes, Equally Honourable to Himself and Exemplary to His Young Countrymen*, first printed in

---

* It was renamed the Smithsonian in honour of a shadowy Englishman named James Smithson. The bastard son of a Duke of Northumberland, Smithson had never been to America and had no known American friends or connections, but he agreed to leave his considerable fortune of £100,000 to the government of the United States if it would name an institution of learning after him.[33]

book form in 1806, proved Weems to be not just a fictionalizer of rare gifts but a consummate liar.

Even for the time, the style of the book was more than a little saccharine. Consider the well-known story of Washington cutting down the cherry tree. We join the action at the point where George's father has asked him if by any chance he can explain how a productive fruit tree has come to be horizontal, and whether the hatchet in his hand might have something to do with it.

> 'I can't tell a lie, Pa; you know I can't tell a lie. I did cut it with my hatchet.'
>
> 'Run to my arms, you dearest boy,' cried his father in transports, 'run to my arms; glad am I, George, that you killed my tree; for you have paid me for it a thousand fold. Such an act of heroism in my son, is more worth than a thousand trees . . .'[34]

Weems of course made the whole thing up. Almost everything in the book beyond the hero's name and place of residence was made up or lavishly embellished. Even the title-page included a brazen falsehood. Weems advertised himself as the former 'Rector of Mount-Vernon Parish'. There was no such parish and never had been. None the less, the work went through some twenty editions and was the greatest seller of its age.

Washington was in fact more flawed and human than Weems or many subsequent chroniclers would have us believe. He was moody, remote and vain (he encouraged his fellow officers in the Revolutionary War to address him as 'Your Excellency'), he detested being touched by strangers and had an embarrassing proclivity to weep like a babe in public – for instance, when things weren't going well during the Revolution or when parting from his officers at the war's conclusion. He was not a gifted military commander. Far from being a hero of the French and Indian War, as Weems and others have suggested, he actually helped to provoke it. In 1754, while an inexperienced lieutenant-colonel with the Virginia Regiment, he led an unnecessary and essentially irrational attack on a party of Frenchman encamped in the Ohio valley, killing ten of them. This and other such incidents so outraged the French that they went to war with the British. To compound his haplessness, Washington shortly after was routed in battle and naïvely signed a document in which he apologized for the 'assassination' of the Frenchmen, thereby outraging his own masters.[35]

But there was about him an unquestionable greatness. He was brave, resolute and absolutely incorruptible. No one gave more time or endured greater risks or hardships to secure America's independence and democracy. For eight years he doggedly prosecuted a war in which neither the Continental Congress nor the people gave him anything like the support his valour deserved. During one long march across New Jersey, he watched in dismay as his army evaporated from 30,000 men to barely 3,400. To add to his problems, he often discovered he was being served by traitors. Benedict Arnold is the best-known example, but there were others, such as Major General Charles Lee, who while serving as one of Washington's aides-de-camp was simultaneously supplying the British with advice on how to beat the Americans.[36] It is no wonder that Washington sometimes wept.

He genuinely and nobly wanted only what was best for his country. Such was the hysteria that greeted his triumph over the British that he could have had any tribute he cared to ask for – a kingship, a lavish life pension, his own Blenheim Palace on the Potomac. He asked only to be allowed to return to a quiet life at Mount Vernon. When elected President he requested Congress not to pay him a salary, but only to meet his expenses – a position all the more honourable when you consider that he was chronically hard up. 'My estate for the last 11 years has not been able to make both ends meet,' he wrote in despair to his cousin shortly before becoming President, and when he made the trip from Mount Vernon to New York to be sworn in, he had to borrow £100 to pay his costs.[37] (Financial hardship was a common problem for Virginia planters. Jefferson was so chronically pressed for money that in 1815 he sold his beloved private library to Congress for a much needed $23,950, though he rather undid this achievement by almost immediately beginning to acquire another just as splendid. By the time of his death, he was over $100,000 in debt, and most of the contents of Monticello had to be auctioned off.)

Congress refused to heed Washington's request and insisted he take a salary of $25,000 a year. It also did him the honour of allowing him to choose the site of the nation's permanent capital –

not so much out of altruism but more because it couldn't decide on a location itself. At least forty sites had been considered and argued over, from Germantown, Pennsylvania, to Kingston, New York, before Washington was authorized to make his choice. He selected a ten-mile square alongside the Potomac River's head of navigation. (In 1846 Virginia reclaimed the portion on its side of the river, which explains why the modern Washington has ruler-straight boundaries on three sides but an irregular wriggle on the fourth.) In 1791 the city-to-be was named *Washington*; the 6,100-acre tract within which it was situated was called the *Territory of Columbia* (eventually of course changed to *District of Columbia*), thus neatly enshrining in one place the two great mythic names of the age.

Two years later, Washington laid the cornerstone for the Capitol, and in 1800 the city of Washington opened for business. America was on its way.

5

By the Dawn's Early Light: Forging a National Identity

Bombardments in the early nineteenth century provided a spectacle that must have been quite thrilling to anyone not on the receiving end. The art of the matter was to cut fuses to just the right length so that they would detonate at or near the moment of impact. In practice, they went off all over the place. Hence the 'bombs bursting in air' of the American national anthem. As most people know, the words to the anthem were inspired by the bombardment of Fort McHenry in Baltimore Harbour during the War of 1812. Francis Scott Key, a young lawyer, had been sent to try to negotiate the release of an American prisoner, and found himself detained aboard a British man-of-war.

Through the night Key watched as the British fleet ranged round the harbour threw a colourful fusillade of explosives at the embattled fort. When dawn broke and Key saw the American flag still flying, tattered but defiant, he was sufficiently moved to dash off a poem. The poem was frankly terrible, but it bore an emotional impact easily forgotten at this remove. Published under the title 'Defence of Fort M'Henry', and set to the decidedly funereal tune of an English song called 'To Anacreon in Heaven' (the beat has since been considerably enlivened), it became a sensation. Soon almost everyone had forgotten its original title and was calling it 'The Star-Spangled Banner', by which name it has been known ever since.

The flag that Key saw flying over Fort McHenry had fifteen stars and fifteen stripes. In the early years of independence, the custom was to add a star and a stripe to the flag each time a state joined the

Union. By 1818 Congress was flying a flag with no fewer than eighteen stripes and it was becoming evident that the practice would soon become unsustainable. Congress decided that enough was enough and officially decreed that henceforth flags should have thirteen stripes (one for each of the original colonies) and as many stars as there were states.

The War of 1812 also saw the rise of another American icon: Uncle Sam. He appears to have arisen in 1813 in Troy, New York, but little more than that is known.[1] Previously America had been personified by a character of obscure origins called Brother Jonathan, who usually appeared in apposition to the English John Bull. The inspiration for Uncle Sam is sometimes traced to one Samuel Wilson, an army inspector of Troy, but it seems more probable that the name was merely inspired by the initials *US*. The top-hatted, striped-trousered figure that we associate with the name came much later. It was popularized in the 1860s in the cartoons of Thomas Nast, and later reinforced by the famous I WANT *YOU* recruiting posters of the artist James Montgomery Flagg, in which Uncle Sam lost his genial sparkle and took on a severe, almost demonic look, which he has generally kept to this day.

Thus by the end of the second decade of the nineteenth century America had a national anthem (though it would not be officially recognized as such until 1931), a more or less fixed flag and a national symbol in the form of Uncle Sam. It was, in short, beginning to accumulate the rudiments of a national identity.

But in other ways America remained a collection of disparate parts, each following its own course. This was most arrestingly seen in the absence of uniform times. Until as late as 1883, there were no fixed times in America. When it was midnight in New York, it was 11.47 in Washington, and 11.55 in Philadelphia. In 1869, when Leland Stanford struck the golden spike that marked the completion of America's first transcontinental railway (in fact he couldn't manage to drive the spike in; the work had to be completed by someone more adept with a manual implement), the news was instantly telegraphed to a breathlessly waiting nation. In Promontory, Utah, the great event happened at 12.45, but in nearby Virginia City it was deemed to be 12.30. In San Francisco it was 11.46 or 11.44, depending on which authority you believed in, and in Pittsburgh the information was simultaneously received at six places and logged in at six different official times.

In an age when most information arrived by horseback, a few minutes here and there hardly mattered. But as the world became more technologically sophisticated, the problem of variable time-keeping did begin to matter. It was a particular headache for the railways and those who travelled on them. In an effort to arrive at some measure of conformity, most railway companies synchronized the clocks along their own lines, but often these bore no relationship to the times used either locally or by competing railways. Stations would often have a multiplicity of clocks – one showing the station time, another the local time and the rest showing the times on each of the lines serving that station. Passengers unfamiliar with local discrepancies would often arrive to catch a train only to find that it had recently departed. Making connections in a place like Chicago, where fifteen lines met, required the careful study of fat books of algorithms showing all the possible permutations.

Clearly something needed to be done. The first person to push for uniform time throughout the country was the rather unlikely figure of Charles F. Dowd, head of the Temple Grove Ladies' Seminary in Saratoga Springs, New York. In 1869, the year of Leland Stanford and the golden spike, Dowd began agitating for the adoption of four time zones very much along the lines of those used today. The idea met with surprisingly heated objections. Many thought it somehow ungodly to tinker with something as elemental as time, ignoring the consideration that clocks are not a divine concept. Some communities saw it as an impudence to expect them to change their clocks for the benefit of commercial interests like the railways and telegraph companies. Almost everyone found the entire notion strange and puzzling, particularly those who lived on or near the prospective time zone borders. People in a place like North Platte, Nebraska, couldn't for the life of them understand why their neighbours down the road in Ogallala should get to rise an hour later than they each day. The objections extended even to groups of the greatest eminence. The British Association for the Advancement of Science for one dismissed the idea as 'too utopian'.[2]

Finally in November 1883, after a meeting called the National

Railway Time Convention, it was agreed to introduce time zones and synchronize clocks. The date 18 November, dubbed 'the day of two noons,' was set for its inception. For two weeks, people everywhere fretted and fussed as if the country were about to be struck by an outsize meteor. Farmers worried that their hens would stop laying or that their cows would go dry. Workers in Chicago, suspecting they were to be compelled to work an extra nine minutes on the big day, threatened to strike. By the dawn of the appointed day, the nation was in a fever of uncertainty. Just before noon people everywhere began silently gathering by town halls and court-houses to watch the clocks change.

Although the time change had no legal authority – it was done solely at the behest of the railways – it was introduced almost everywhere, and almost everywhere the event proved to be disappointingly anticlimactic. Millions watched as the hands on their court-house clocks were summarily advanced or moved back a few notches, then pursed their lips and returned to business as it dawned on them that that was as exciting as it was going to get. Here and there local difficulties cropped up. In Washington, a disagreement between the US Attorney General and the head of the Naval Observatory meant that for several years government clocks in the city showed a different time to all others.[3] For the most part, however, America took to uniform timekeeping with barely a flutter and life grew easier because of it.

The fuss over introducing time zones was as nothing compared with the push, half a century later, for *summer time*, or *daylight-saving time* as it quickly came to be called. The driving force behind this idea was a businessman named William Willett, who wanted it primarily so that he would have more daylight to play golf in the evenings. Again the outcries were vociferous. The *New York Times* called it 'an act of madness' and others seriously suggested that they might equally change thermometers to make summers appear cooler and winters warmer. As one historian has put it, 'the idea of altering clocks to suit some human whim made daylight saving seem both unnatural and almost monstrous to its many opponents'.[4] Although America briefly instituted daylight saving as a way of conserving energy supplies during World War I, such was the antagonism to the idea in some quarters that it wasn't until 1966 that America got universal summer time.

Money, too, was a feature of American life that did not become standardized until relatively late in the day. Until the issuing of the first 'greenbacks' during the Civil War, the federal government in Washington produced no paper money, but only coins. Paper money was left to banks. As recently as the first half of the nineteenth century banks – and the word is used loosely to describe some of these institutions – were in the happy position of being able to print their own money. Types of bills proliferated wildly. In Zanesville, Ohio, to take one example, no fewer than thirty banks churned out money under such colourful appellations as the Virginia Saline Bank and the Owl Creek Bank. The bills were often of such dubious value that they were referred to as *shinplasters*.[5] Some banks' money was more respected than others'. The Citizens' Bank of New Orleans issued a particularly sought-after $10 bill. Because the French word for ten, *dix*, was inscribed on the back they became known as *Dixies*. As a descriptive term for the whole of the South, the word didn't really catch on until Daniel Decatur Emmett, a northerner, wrote the immensely successful song 'Dixie's Land' (which almost everyone thinks, wrongly, is called 'Dixie') in 1859.[6]

With so many types of money floating about, the situation would appear to have been hopelessly confused, but in fact it was a huge improvement on what had gone before. Throughout the long colonial period, the British had allowed very little British specie to circulate in the colonies. Though businesses kept their accounts in pounds, shillings and pence, they had to rely on whatever tender came to hand. A bewildering mixture of home-minted coins and foreign currency – Portuguese *johanneses* (familiarly known as *joes*), Spanish *doubloons* and *pistoles*, French *sous* and *picayunes*, Italian and Flemish *ducatoons*, American *fugios* (so called because the Latin *fugio*, 'I fly', was inscribed on one side) and other coins almost without number – circulated throughout the colonies, and business people had to know that 1s. 4d. was equal in value to one-sixth of a milled *peso* (the original 'piece of eight'), that a Spanish or Mexican *real* was worth twelve and a half cents, that a Portuguese *johannes* traded for $8.81, that 2s. 3d. was equivalent to half a Dutch *dollar*. Along the eastern seaboard, a *real* was generally called a shilling, but elsewhere it was more racily known as a *bit*.

First found in English in 1688, *bit* may be a translation of the Spanish *pieza*, 'piece' (which metamorphosed into *peso*), or it may be that the early coins were literally bits broken from larger silver coins. Because a bit was worth twelve and a half cents, a quarter dollar naturally became known as *two bits*, a half dollar as *four bits*, particularly west of the Mississippi. Ten cents was a *short bit*; a *long bit* was fifteen cents. Even after America began minting its own coins, foreign coins remained such an integral part of American commerce that they weren't withdrawn from circulation until 1857.

To add to the confusion, values varied from place to place. In Pennsylvania and Virginia, a half-*real* went by the alternative name *fipenny bit* or *fip* because it was equivalent in worth to an English five-penny piece. But in New York it was worth sixpence and in New England fourpence halfpenny. It is something of a wonder that any business got done at all – and even more wondrous when you consider that until after the Revolution there wasn't a single bank in America. Philadelphia got the first, in 1781; Boston and New York followed three years later.[7]

Not surprisingly, perhaps, many people dispensed with money and relied instead on barter, or *country pay* as it was often called. The goods used in barter were known as *truck* (from the Old French *troquer*, meaning *to peddle* or *trade*), a sense preserved in the expression *to have no truck with* and in *truck farm*, neither of which has anything to do with large wheeled vehicles. (In the vehicular sense, *truck* comes from the Latin *trochus*, 'wheel'.)

The decimalized monetary system based on dollars and cents was devised by Gouverneur Morris as assistant to the superintendent of finances, in consultation with Thomas Jefferson, and adopted in 1784 against the protests of bankers and businessmen, most of whom wanted to preserve English units and terms such as pounds and shillings. The names given to the earliest coins were something of an etymological rag-bag. In ascending order they were: *mill, cent, dime, dollar* and *eagle*. *Dollar* comes ultimately from *Joachimstaler*, a coin that was first made in the Bohemian town of Joachimstal in 1519 and then spread through Europe as *daler, thaler* and *taler*. In an American context *dollar* is first recorded in 1683.[8] *Dime*, or *disme* as it was spelled on the first coins, is a corruption of the French *dixième*, and was intended to be pronounced 'deem', though it appears that hardly anyone did. The word is not strictly an Americanism. *Dime* had been used occasionally in Britain as far back as 1377, though it had fallen out of use there long before, no doubt because in a non-decimal currency there was no use for a term meaning one-tenth. *Cent* of course comes from the Latin *centum*, 'one hundred', and was rather an odd choice of term because initially there were two hundred cents to a dollar.[9] The custom of referring to a single cent as a *penny* is a linguistic hold-over from the days of British control. No American coin has ever actually been called a penny. (The term appears to come from the Latin *pannus*, 'a piece of cloth', and dates from a time when cloth was sometimes used as a medium of exchange.)

A notable absentee from the list of early American coins is *nickel*. There was a coin worth five cents but it was called a *half dime* or *jitney*, from the French *jeton*, signifying a small coin or a token. When early in this century American cities began to fill with buses that charged a five-cent fare, *jitney* fell out of use for the coin and attached itself instead to the vehicles. *Nickel* didn't become synonymous with the five-cent piece until 1875; before that *nickel* signified either a one-cent or three-cent piece. The phrase 'don't take any wooden nickels' dates only from 1915 – and, no, there never was a time when wooden nickels circulated. Such a coin would have been immediately recognizable as counterfeit and in any case would have cost more to manufacture than it was worth.

One of the more durable controversies in the world of numismatics is where the dollar sign comes from. The first use of $ in an American context is in 1784 in a memorandum from Thomas Jefferson suggesting the dollar as the primary unit of currency, and some have deduced from this that he made it up there and then, either as a monogram based on his own initials (improbable; he was not that vain) or as a kind of doodle (equally improbable; he was not that unsystematic). A more widely held notion is that it originated as the letters *U* and *S* superimposed on each other and that the *U* eventually disintegrated into unconnected parallel lines. The problem with this theory is that $ as a symbol for *peso* far outdates its application to US dollars. (It is still widely used as a peso sign throughout Latin America.) The most likely explanation is that it is a modified form of the pillars of Hercules, wrapped around with a scroll, to be found on old Spanish pieces of eight.

Many slang terms and other like expressions associated with money date from the nineteenth century. Americans have been describing money as *beans* (as in 'I haven't got a bean') since 1810 and as *dough* since at least 1851, when it was first recorded in the *Yale Tomahawk*. *Small change* has been around since 1819, *not worth a cent* since the early 1820s, and *not worth a red cent* since 1839. *Upper crust* dates from 1832, *easy money* from 1836, *C-note* (short for *century note*) for a $100 bill from 1839, *flat broke* and *dead broke* from the 1840s. Americans have been referring to a dollar as a *buck* since 1856 (it comes from *buckskin*, an early unit of exchange). *Sound as a dollar, bet your bottom dollar, strike it rich, penny-ante* and *spondulicks* or *spondulix* (a term of wholly mysterious origin) all date from the 1850s. A $10 bill has been a *sawbuck* since the early 1860s. It was so called because the original bills had a roman numeral X on them, which brought to mind a saw-horse, or sawbuck. *Mazuma,* from a Yiddish slang term for money, dates from 1880, and *simoleon,* another word of uncertain provenance, meaning $1, dates from 1881.

But it wasn't just money terms that America developed in the nineteenth century. A flood, a positive torrent, of words and expressions of all types came out of the country in the period. The following is no more than a bare sampling: *to make the fur fly* (1804); *quick on the trigger* and *to whitewash* (1808); *having an ax to grind* (1811); *keep a stiff upper lip* (yes, it's an Americanism, 1815); *no two ways about it* (1818); *fly off the handle* (1825); *to move like greased lightning* (1826); *to have a knockdown and dragout fight* (1827); *to sit on the fence* and *to go the whole hog* (1828); *firecracker, hornswoggle, non-committal* and *to be in cahoots with* (1829); *ornery* and *talk turkey* (1830); *horse sense* and *nip and tuck* (often originally *rip and tuck*; no one knows why; 1832); *conniption fit, barking up the wrong tree* and *to keep one's eyes peeled* (1833); *close shave* and *rip-roaring* (1834); *hell-bent* (1835); *stool pigeon* (1836); *to have a chip on one's shoulder* and *to raise Cain* (1840); *to scoot* (1841); *to pull the wool over one's eyes* and *to get hitched*, in the sense of being married (1842); *hold your horses* (1844); *beeline* (1845); *to stub one's toe* (1846); *to be a goner* (1847); *to back down, to dicker, by the great horn spoon* and *highfalutin* (1848); *to face the music* (1850); *to paddle one's own canoe* and *to keep one's shirt on* (1854); *one-horse town* (1855); *to knock the spots off* and *stag party* (1856); *neither hide nor hair* (1857); *deadbeat* (1863); *to knuckle down* (1864); *to go haywire* (1865); *con man* and *to slather* (1866); *to go back on*, as with a promise (1868); *to get in on the ground floor* (1872); *to eat crow* (1877); *underdog* (1887); *cagey* in the sense of shrewd (1893); and *panhandler* and *to be out on a limb* (1897).

In addition, there were scores more that have since fallen out of use: *ground and lofty* (once a very common synonym for *fine and dandy*), *happify, to missionate, to consociate* (that is, to come together in an assembly), *dunderment* (bewilderment), *pucker-stoppled* (to be embarrassed), *from Dan to Beersheba*. This last, alluding to the northernmost and southernmost outposts of the Holy Land, was in daily use for at least two hundred years as a synonym for *wide-ranging, from A to Z*, but dropped from view in the nineteenth century and hasn't been seen much since.

Sometimes the meaning of nineteenth-century neologisms is self-evident, as with *to move like greased lightning* or *to have a close shave*. *To go haywire* evidently alludes to the lacerating effect of that material once a tightly wound bale is loosed, and *to talk turkey* may owe something to a once popular story about an Indian and frontiersman who often went hunting together. According to this tale, each time they came to divide the kill, the frontiersman would say, 'You may take the buzzard and I will take the turkey, or if you prefer I will take the turkey and you may take the buzzard.' After several such episodes, the Indian interrupts the frontiersman and says, 'But when do I get to talk turkey?' or words to that effect. The story is of course apocryphal, but it was widely told as a joke and thus perhaps is responsible for the popularity of the phrase.

More often, however, we are left with words and phrases that seem to have sprung from nowhere and that do not mean anything in particular – *even steven, fit as a fiddle, easy as a lead pipe cinch, to take a powder, to peter out, to paint the town red, to talk through one's hat, to josh, to root hog or die*. Explanations are frequently posited but all too often on unpersuasively flimsy evidence. The *Oxford English Dictionary* suggests that *josh* may be connected to the humorist Josh Billings, but in fact the term was current at least as early as 1845 and Josh Billings was unknown outside his neighbourhood until 1860. *To face the music,* first recorded in a publication called the *Worcester Spy,* may allude to a soldier being drummed out of service or possibly it may have some theatrical connection, perhaps to a nervous performer having to face the audience across the orchestra pit. No one knows. The mild expletives *doggone* and *doggone it* both date from the early nineteenth century, though no one has any idea what they meant. The mystery deepens when you realize that the first recorded citation has it as 'dog on't', reminiscent of the earlier 'a pox on't' and other like formations.

Phoney has been linked to any number of possibilities, from the Gaelic for *ring* (*fauney* or *fawney*; the explanation being that a street vendor known as a *fauney dropper* would show the gullible purchaser a ring of genuine quality, then slip him a cheap *fauney*) to an unscrupulous businessman named Forney. *Ballyhoo, blizzard, hunky dory, shanty, conniption fit* (at first also spelled *caniption* or *kniption*), *bogus, bamboozle* and many other durable Americanisms are of unknown, or at least decidedly uncertain, derivation. *To root hog or die,* first found in *A Narrative Life of David Crockett* in 1834, is similarly bewildering. The expression, meaning to fend for oneself or perish, evidently refers to the rooting practices of hogs, but precisely what Mr Crockett (or his ghost-writer) meant by it is uncertain. His contemporaries, it seems, were no wiser. They variously rendered the expression as 'root, hog, or die' (as if it were an admonition to a pig) or as 'root, hog or die' (as if presenting a list of three options). Clearly they hadn't the faintest idea what they wanted the poor hog to do, but the expression filled a gap in the American lexicon, and that is what mattered. As Gertrude Stein might have put it, an expression doesn't have to mean anything as long as it means something.

For a long time the most American of Americanisms, *OK*, fell resoundingly into this category. The explanations for its etymology have been as inspired as they have been various. Among the theories: that it is short for *only kissing,* that the semi-literate Andrew Jackson wrote it on papers as an abbreviation for *oll korrect* (in fact he was not that ignorant), that it came from *Orrin Kendall* crackers, that it was an abbreviation for the Greek *olla kalla* ('all good'), that it was from a prized brand of Haitian rum called *Aux Cayes*, that it was an early telegraphic abbreviation for *open key*, that it was from the Choctaw affirmative *okeh*, that it came from the Indian chief *Old Keokuk* or from the nickname for Martin Van Buren, *Old Kinderhook* (he was from Kinderhook, New York).

Learned papers were written in defence of various contentions. The matter was discussed at conferences. By 1941, when Allen Walker Read, a professor at Columbia University, began looking into the matter, *OK* was already the most widely understood Americanism in the world and the search for its origins was the etymological equivalent of the search for DNA. It took Read some twenty years of searching to nail the matter down, but thanks to his efforts we now know that OK first appeared in print in the *Boston Morning Post* on 23 March 1839, as a jocular abbreviation for 'Oll Korrect'. At the time there was a fashion for such concoctions – KY for 'Know Use', RTBS for 'Remains to Be Seen,' KG for 'Know Go,' WOOOFC for 'With One of Our First Citizens.' In 1840 Martin Van Buren ran for President, the Democratic OK Club was formed to promote his election, and *OK* raced into general usage, where it has remained ever since.[10]

As well as creating new words by the hundreds in the nineteenth century, Americans also gave new meanings to old ones. *Fix* and its offshoots accumulated so many uses that the *Dictionary of American English* needs nearly seven columns of text and some 5,000 words to discuss their specifically American applications. They added prepositions to common verbs to give them new or heightened significance: *to pass out, to check in, to show off, to beat up, to collide, to flare up, to start off, to stave off, to cave in, to fork over, to hold on, to hold out, to stay put, to brush off, to get away with*. They cut long words down – turning *penitentiary* into *pen*, *fanatic* into *fan*, *reformation* into *reform* – and simplified constructions, preferring *to graduate* over *to be graduated*. They created nouns from verbs – *dump* and *beat*, for example. Above all they turned nouns into verbs. The practice began as early as the late seventeenth century (*to scalp*, first noted in 1693, is one of the earliest) and continued throughout the eighteenth, but reached a kind of fever pitch in the nineteenth. The list of American verb formations is all but endless: *to interview, to bankroll, to highlight, to package, to panic, to audition, to curb, to bellyache, to demean, to progress, to corner, to endorse, to engineer, to predicate, to resurrect, to notice, to advocate, to splurge, to boost, to coast, to oppose, to demoralize, to placate, to donate, to peeve* (back-formed from *peevish*), *to locate, to evoke, to rattle, to deed, to boom, to park, to sidestep, to hustle, to bank, to lynch, to ready, to service, to enthuse* – all of these, and many more, are Americanisms without which the language would be much the poorer.[11]

The nineteenth century was in short the Americans' Elizabethan age, and the British hated them for it. Among the many neologisms that stirred their bile were *backwoodsman, balance* for remainder, *spell* in the context of time or weather, *round-up, once in a while, no great shakes, to make one's mind up, there's no two ways about it, influential, census, presidential, standpoint, outhouse, cross purposes, rambunctious, scrumptious, loan* for lend (not actually an Americanism at all), *portage, immigration, fork,* as in a road, *milage, gubernatorial, reliable,* and almost any new verb.

The first recorded attack on an American usage came in 1735 when an English visitor named Francis Moore referred to the young city of Savannah as standing upon a hill overlooking a river 'which they in barbarous English call a bluff' and thereby, in the words of H. L. Mencken, 'set the tone that English criticism has maintained ever since'.[12]

Samuel Johnson, who seldom passed up a chance to insult his colonial cousins (they were, in his much quoted phrase, 'a race of convicts, and ought to be grateful for anything we allow them short of hanging'), vilified an American book on geography for having the misguided audacity to use such terms as *creek, gap, branch* and *spur* when they had not been given a British benediction. Another critic attacked Noah Webster for including the Americanism *lengthy* in his dictionary. 'What are we coming to?' he despaired. 'If the word is permitted to stand, the next edition will authorize the word "strengthy".'[13] One Captain Basil Hall, a professional traveller, writer and, it would appear, halfwit, spoke for many when he remarked that America's penchant for neologisms was unnecessary because 'there are enough words already'.[14]

By the 1800s, the American continent fairly crawled with British observers who reported with patronizing glee on America's eccentric and irregular speech habits. Captain Frederick Marryat, best known for the novels *Mr Midshipman Easy* (1836) and

Masterman Ready (1841), recounted how one American had boasted to him that he had not just *trebled* an investment but 'fourbled and fivebled' it. It was Marryat who also reported the often recounted – and conveniently unverifiable – story of the family that clad its piano legs in little skirts so as not to excite any untoward sexual hankerings among the more impressionable of their visitors.

The classlessness of US English – the habit of calling every woman a *lady*, every man a *gentleman* – attracted particular vituperation. Charles Janson, a British writer, recorded how he made the mistake of referring to a young maid as a servant. 'I'd have you to know, man, that I am no sarvant,' she bristled. 'None but negers are sarvants.' She was, she informed him solemnly, her employer's *help*.[15] Though easy enough to mock, such semantic distinctions contributed mightily towards making America a less stratified society. Moreover, they underscored the essential openness of the American character. As Henry Steele Commager put it: 'The American was good natured, generous, hospitable and sociable, and he reversed the whole history of language to make the term "stranger" one of welcome.'[16]

Before long, it seemed, Americans could scarcely open their mouths without running the risk of ending up mocked between hard covers. Abuse was heaped upon the contemptible American habit of shortening or simplifying words – using *pants* for *trousers*, *thanks* in favour of *thank you*, *gents* instead of *gentlemen*. 'If I were naked and starving I would refuse to be clothed gratis in a "Gent's Furnishing Store",' sniffed one especially fastidious social commentator.[17] *Pants*, a shortening of *pantaloons*, is an Americanism first recorded in 1840 and attacked as a needless lexical affectation within the year. Incidentally, but not without interest, *panties* came into American English in 1845 and for a long time signified undershorts for males. They weren't regarded as a woman's article of clothing until 1908.

The British appeared unaware that their mockery had the capacity to make them look priggish and obtuse. Dickens, in his *American Notes*, professed to have been utterly baffled when a waiter asked him if he wanted his food served 'right away'. As Dillard points out, even if he had never heard the expression, he must have been a very dim traveller indeed to fail to grasp its meaning.[18]

Always there was a presumption that Americans should speak as Britons. In 1827 Frances Trollope, mother of the novelist Anthony Trollope, came to America at the rather advanced age of forty-seven to found a department store in Cincinnati. The enterprise failed and she lost everything, down to her household effects, but the experience gave her ample fodder for her enormously successful *Domestic Manners of the Americans*, published in 1832. Among her criticisms of American behaviour, she was struck again and again by how rarely during her time in the country she had heard a sentence 'correctly pronounced'. It appears never to have occurred to her that Americans had a perfect right, and sometimes possibly even a sound reason, to pronounce words in their own way.

All this would have been fractionally more bearable had the commentators not so often been given to blithe generalizations and careless reporting. Emerson noted with more than a hint of exasperation that most Americans didn't speak in anything like the manner that Dickens suggested. 'He has picked up and noted with eagerness each odd local phrase that he met with, and when he had a story to relate, has joined them together, so that the result is the broadest caricature.'[19] And all the while they were making capital out of America's foibles, the British observers were unwittingly picking up American habits. It was, ironically, Dickens's use of many Americanisms, notably *talented, lengthy, reliable* and *influential*, which he had absorbed on his travels and unthinkingly employed in *American Notes*, that at last brought them a measure of respectability in his homeland.[20]

For their part, Americans showed a streak of masochism as wide as the Mississippi. When *American Notes* was published it was such a sensation that people lined up fifty deep to acquire a copy. In Philadelphia it sold out in thirty-five minutes. Mrs Trollope's *Domestic Manners of the Americans* was even more successful, going through four editions in a year and so capturing America's attention that a British visitor was astonished to discover that her barbed observations on American social habits had almost entirely displaced a raging cholera epidemic as the principal topic of news in the papers and conversation in the taverns.

The attacks came from within as well as from without. In 1781 the eminent president of Princeton, John Witherspoon, a Scot by birth but one of the signers of the Declaration of Independence –

indeed a fierce proponent of American independence from Britain in all things but language – wrote a series of articles for the *Pennsylvania Journal and Weekly Advertiser* in which he attacked the lax linguistic habits that predominated in his adopted country even among educated speakers: using *notify* for *inform*, *mad* for *angry*, *clever* for *good*, and other such 'improprieties and vulgarisms which hardly any person in the same class in point of rank and literature would have fallen into in Great Britain'.[21] In the course of these writings he became the first to use *Americanism* in a linguistic sense, but by no means the last to use it pejoratively.

There was, it must be said, more than a dollop of toadying to be found among many Americans. When the Scottish philosopher David Hume criticized Franklin for employing *colonize* and other such New World novelties in his correspondence, Franklin contritely apologized and promised to abandon the practice at once. John Russell Bartlett compiled a *Dictionary of Americanisms*, but far from being a celebration of the inventive nature of American speech, the book dismissed Americanisms as 'perversions'. James Fenimore Cooper, in *The American Democrat*, opined: 'The common faults of American language are an ambition of effect, a want of simplicity and a turgid abuse of terms.'[22] Henry James, meanwhile, complained about the 'helpless slobber of disconnected vowel noises' that characterized American speech.

Many sincerely believed that America would cut itself off from its linguistic and cultural database (as it were) by forming an effectively separate dialect. Linguistic isolation was not a sensible or desirable goal for a small, young nation if it wished to be heard in the wider world of commerce, law and science. The *Knickerbocker Magazine* saw the 'greatest danger' in America's tendency towards linguistic innovation, and urged its readers to adhere to British precepts.

A few pointed out that the American continent required a more expansive vocabulary, like the anonymous essayist in the *North American Review* who plaintively noted: 'How tame will his language sound, who would describe Niagara in language fitted for the falls at London bridge, or attempt the majesty of the Mississippi in that which was made for the Thames?'[23] Or as Jefferson put it with somewhat greater simplicity: 'The new circumstances under which we are placed, call for new words, new phrases, and for the transfer of old words to new objects.'

Others saw Britain's linguistic hegemony as presumptuous and imperious. 'Our honour requires us to have a system of our own, in language as well as government,' argued Noah Webster in 1789. Echoing his sentiment, Rupert Hughes asked: 'Why should we permit the survival of the curious notion that our language is a mere loan from England, like a copper kettle that we must keep scoured and return without a dent?'[24]

Still others tried the defence – accurate if somewhat feeble – that many of the objectionable words were not Americanisms at all. Chaucer, it was pointed out, had used *gab*; Johnson had included *influential* in his dictionary; *afeared* had existed in English since Saxon times. *Son of a gun, bite the dust, beat it, I guess* and scores of other detestable 'Americanisms' all existed in England, it was explained, long before there were any American colonies. As the poet James Russell Lowell drily put it, Americans 'unhappily could bring over no English better than Shakespeare's'.[25] One dedicated scribbler named Alfred Elwyn compiled a *Glossary of Supposed Americanisms* in which he asserted passionately, but wrongly: 'The simple truth is, that almost without exception all those words or phrases that we have been ridiculed for using, are good old English; many of them are Anglo-Saxon in origin, and nearly all to be heard at this day in England.'

This tack struck many as more than a little pathetic. Lowell acidly observed: 'Surely we may sleep in peace now, and our English cousins will forgive us, since we have cleared ourselves from any suspicion of being original in the matter.'[26]

Lowell had a particular reason for feeling protective about the American dialect. His fame rested almost entirely on the creation of a fictional New England rustic, Hosea Biglow, whose comically quaint speech formed the basis of the hugely popular *Biglow Papers*. Unfortunately, Lowell's effectiveness as a defender of American speech was somewhat diminished by his growing antipathy for his own creation. When the reading public continually ignored his more earnest poetical compositions (and rightly; they were unceasingly mediocre) he went so far as to preface a volume of Biglow poems with a veiled insult to the reader: 'Margaritas, munde porcine, calcâsti: en, siliquas accipe', which translates as 'Oh, swinish world, you have trampled pearls; so take the husks.'[27]

None the less, he left behind an invaluable mass of material recording the habits of New England speech in the first half of the nineteenth century. As an extract shows, it was very different from that of today:

> Ez fer war, I call it murder, –
> There you hev it plain an' flat:
> I don't want to go no furder
> Than my Testyment fer that;
>
> God hez sed so plump an' fairly
> It's ez long ez it is broad,
> An' you've gut to git up airly
> Ef you want to take in God.

But this, it must be remembered, was the speech of an uneducated New Englander. Someone from a more refined background, like John Quincy Adams, say, would have sounded as different again. One of the paradoxes of the day was that as America was becoming more politically unified it was in danger of becoming linguistically fractured. Class differences and regional differences alike were acutely felt and remarked upon. The relative few who lived out along the frontier were not only cut off from changes in fashion but also changes in language. So when, for instance, Britons and eastern Americans began to change the diphthong in words like *boil* and *join* from *bile* and *jine*, or to insert a voiced *r* in some words while removing it from others, the frontier people were less likely to adopt the new trends. They continued for much longer (and in some cases continue yet) to say *bar* for *bear*, *consarn* for *concern*, *varmint* for *vermin*, *virtoo* for *virtue*, *fortin* for *fortune*, *enjine* for *engine*, *cattel* or *kittle* for *kettle*, *cuss* for *curse*, *thrash* for *thresh*, *tetchy* for *touchy*, *wrastle* for *wrestle*, *chaw* for *chew*, *gal* for *girl*, *riled* for *roiled*, *critter* for *creature* and so on. The further west one went the more pronounced the variations were, so that by mid-century when the English traveller Richard Francis Burton reached Salt Lake City he found the language scarcely recognizable as English.[28]

As the new breed of frontier people like Andrew Jackson, Davy Crockett and Abraham Lincoln brought their regional habits of speech to Washington, their distinctive turns of phrase and raw pronunciations increasingly grated on the sensibilities of their eastern colleagues and underlined the linguistic variability of the sprawling nation. Something of the flavour and pronunciation of frontier life is conveyed by a speech attributed to Davy Crockett (though in fact it was concocted in his behalf by a ghost-writer). 'We are called upon to show our grit like a chain lightning agin a pine log, to extarminate, mollify and calumniate the foe like a niggar put into a holler log . . . Cram his pesky carcass full of thunder and lightning like a stuffed sassidge and turtle him off with a red hot poker . . . Split his countenance with a live airthquake, and tarrify him with a rale Injun yell . . .' Though the words are not Crockett's there is no reason to suppose that the spellings are unfaithful to his pronunciations.[29]

Much the same country air applied to Lincoln, if at slightly less than gale force. However sophisticated his prose style, Lincoln's spoken English always had a whiff of the backwoods about it. His invariable greeting was 'Howdy' and his conversation was sprinkled with folksy colloquialisms like 'out yonder' and 'stay a spell', which must have caused at least some of Washington's more sophisticated politicos to cringe.[30] Though we cannot be sure in each case, he very probably pronounced more than a few of his words in the antiquated frontier style. Certainly we know that he enjoyed an earthy story and took delight in showing his associates a letter he received from a disgruntled citizen in 1860. It read: 'God damn your god damned old hellfired god damned soul to hell god damn you and goddam your god damned family's god damned hellfired god damned soul to hell and god damnation god damn them and god damn your god damn friends to hell.'[31] The letter came, it hardly needs saying, from the frontier.

The friction between the direct, colourful, independent language of the West and the more reserved and bookish diction of the East was a constant leitmotif of American speech throughout the nineteenth century. And nowhere was it made more arrestingly manifest than at the commemoration of a cemetery for Civil War soldiers in the little Pennsylvania town of Gettysburg on 19 November 1863.

The main speaker of the day was not Lincoln, but the orator Edward Everett – an easterner, naturally. Everett droned on for two hours. As was the custom of the day, his speech was full of literary allusions, Ciceronian pomp and obscure historical references that bore only the scantest significance to the occasion. The syntax was high-flown and decked out with phalanxes of subordinate clauses, convoluted constructions, and parenthetical excursions. Almost every sentence had an acre of flowery verbiage between the subject and predicate. A single sentence gives some hint of its denseness:

> Lord Bacon, in 'the true marshalling of the sovereign degrees of honour,' assigns the first place to 'the Condirotores Imperiorum, founders of States and Commonwealths;' and truly, to build up from the discordant elements of our nature, the passions, the interests and the opinions of the individual man, the rivalries of family, clan and tribe, the influences of climate and geographical position, the accidents of peace and war accumulated for ages – to build up from those often-times warring elements a well-compacted, prosperous and powerful State, if it were to be accomplished by one effort or in one generation would require a more than mortal skill.

And this was just one of some 1,500 equally windy sentences. At 2 p.m., two long, cold hours after starting, Everett concluded his speech to thunderous applause – motivated, one is bound to suspect, more by the joy of realizing it was over than by any message derived from the content – and turned the dais over to President Lincoln. The audience of perhaps 15,000 people had been standing for four hours, and was tired, cold and hungry. Lincoln rose awkwardly, 'like a telescope drawing out', as one contemporary put it, adjusted his glasses, held the paper directly in front of his face and in a high, reedy voice delivered his address. 'He barely took his eyes off the manuscript,' according to one witness, as he intoned those famous words:

> Four score and seven years ago our fathers brought forth on this continent a new nation, conceived in liberty and dedicated to the proposition that all men are created equal.
> Now we are engaged in a great civil war, testing whether that nation or any nation so conceived and so dedicated can long endure. We are met on a great battlefield of that war. We have come to dedicate a portion of that field as a final resting place for those who here gave their lives that that nation might live. It is altogether fitting and proper that we should do this
> But, in a larger sense, we cannot dedicate – we cannot

consecrate – we cannot hallow – this ground. The brave men, living and dead, who struggled here have consecrated it far above our poor power to add or detract. The world will little note nor long remember what we say here, but it can never forget what they did here. It is for us, the living, rather, to be dedicated here to the unfinished work which they who fought here have thus far so nobly advanced.

It is rather for us to be here dedicated to the great task remaining before us that from these honoured dead we take increased devotion to that cause for which they gave the last full measure of devotion; that we here highly resolve that these dead shall not have died in vain; that this nation, under God, shall have a new birth of freedom; and that government of the people, by the people, for the people shall not perish from the earth.

Though Lincoln was never intended to provide anything other than some concluding remarks, this was breathtakingly brief. The Gettysburg address contained just 268 words, two-thirds of them of only one syllable, in ten mostly short, direct and memorably crystalline sentences. It took only a fraction over two minutes to deliver – so little, according to several contemporary accounts, that the official photographer was still making preliminary adjustments to his camera when the President sat down.

Far from taking the listener on a discursive trip through the majesties of imperial Rome or the glory that was Greece, the address contained no proper nouns at all. As Wills notes, it doesn't mention Gettysburg or slavery or even the Union.[32] Lincoln thought it a failure. 'I failed: I failed: and that is about all that can be said about it,' he remarked forlornly to Everett. Many agreed with him. The *Chicago Times* wrote: 'The cheek of every American must tingle with shame as he reads the silly, flat and dishwatery utterances of the man who has to be pointed out to intelligent foreigners as the President of the United States.' Even those newspapers sympathetic to Lincoln scarcely noted his address. Not until considerably later was it perceived as perhaps the greatest of American speeches.

The Gettysburg address also marked a small but telling lexical transition. Before the Civil War people generally spoke of *the Union*, with its implied emphasis on the voluntariness of the American confederation. In his first inaugural address Lincoln used

Union twenty times, and *nation* not at all. By the time of the Gettysburg address, the position was reversed. The address contains five mentions of *nation* and not one of *union*.

We have come to take for granted the directness and accessibility of Lincoln's prose, but we should remember that this was an age of ludicrously inflated diction, not only among politicians, orators and literary aesthetes, but even in newspapers. As Cmiel notes, no nineteenth-century journalist with any self-respect would write that a house had burned down, but must instead say that 'a great conflagration consumed the edifice'. Nor would he be content with a sentiment as unexpressive as 'a crowd came to see' but instead would write 'a vast concourse was assembled to witness'.[33]

In an era when no speaker would use two words when eight would do, or dream of using the same word twice in the same week, Lincoln revelled in simplicity and repetition. William Seward, his Secretary of State, drafted Lincoln's first inaugural address. It was a masterpiece of the times. Lincoln pruned it and made it timeless. Where Seward wrote: 'We are not, we must not be, aliens or enemies, but fellow-countrymen and brethren,' Lincoln changed it to 'We are not enemies, but friends. We must not be enemies.'[34] Such succinctness and repetition were not just novel, but daring.

His speeches were constantly marked by a distinctive rhythm – what Garry Wills calls 'preliminary eddyings that yield to lapidary monosyllables', as in 'The world will little note, nor long remember, what we say here' and 'We shall nobly save, or meanly lose, the last best hope of earth.'[35] Always there was a directness about his words that stood in marked contrast to the lofty circumlocutions of the East and marked him as a product of the frontier. 'With malice towards none; with charity for all; with firmness in the right . . . let us strive . . . to do all which may achieve and cherish a just, and a lasting peace, among ourselves, and with all nations' from Lincoln's second inaugural address may not seem on the face of it to have a great deal in common with Davy Crockett's 'like a chain lightning agin a pine log', but in fact it has precisely the same directness and simplicity of purpose, if phrased with somewhat more thoughtful elegance.

American English had at last found a voice to go with its flag and anthem and national symbol in the shape of Uncle Sam. At the same time it had found something else even more gratifying and more certain to guarantee its prospects in the world. It had found wealth – wealth beyond the dreams of other nations. And for that story we must embark on another chapter.

Dame Railway and Her Choo-Choo Court, Cincinnati
Ironmongery Fair, 1852

6

We're in the Money: The Age of Invention

On the morning of 2 July 1881 President James Garfield, accompanied by his Secretary of State, James G. Blaine, was passing through the central railway station in Washington, DC, to spend the Fourth of July holiday on the New Jersey shore with his family. His wife had only recently recovered from a nearly fatal bout of malaria and he was naturally anxious to be with her. In those days there was no Secret Service protection for the President. On occasions such as this the President was quite literally a public figure. Anyone could approach him, and one man did – a quietly deranged lawyer named Charles Guiteau, who walked up to the President and calmly shot him twice with a .44-calibre revolver, then stepped aside and awaited arrest. Despite a notable absence of qualifications Guiteau had long pestered the President to make him chief consul in Paris.

The nation waited breathlessly for news of the President's recovery. Newspapers all over the country posted frequent, not to say strikingly candid, bulletins outside their main offices. 'The President was somewhat restless and vomited several times during the early part of the night. Nutritious enemata were successfully employed to sustain him,' read a typical one on the façade of the *New York Herald* office.[1]

As the President slipped in and out of consciousness, the greatest minds in the country were brought to his bedside in the hope that someone could offer something more positively beneficial than rectal sustenance. Alexander Graham Bell, at the peak of his fame, devised a makeshift metal-detector, which he called an 'induction balance' and which employed his recently invented telephone as a listening aid. The intention was to locate the bullets lodged in the President's frame, but to Bell's considerable consternation, it appeared to show bullets practically everywhere in the President's body. Not until much later was it realized that the device had been reading the bed springs.

The summer of 1881 was one of the sultriest for years in the nation's capital. To provide some relief for the stricken President, a corps of naval engineers who specialized in ventilating mine shafts was summoned to the White House and instructed to build a cooling device. They rigged up a large iron box filled with ice, salt and water, and a series of terry-cloth filters which were saturated by the melting ice. A fan drew in warm air from outside, which was cooled as it passed over the damp terry-cloth and cleansed by charcoal filters, and was propelled onwards into the President's bedroom. The device was not terribly efficient – in fifty-eight days it consumed a quarter of a million tons of ice – but it worked up to a point. It cooled the President's room to a more or less tolerable 81°F, and stands in history as the world's first air-conditioner.[2]

Nothing, alas, could revive the sinking President, and on the evening of 19 September, two and a half months after he had been shot, he quietly passed away.

The shooting of President Garfield was significant in two ways. First, it proved once and for all the folly of the spoils system, a term inspired by the famous utterance of New York politician William E. Marcy sixty years earlier: 'To the victor belong the spoils.'[3] Under the spoils system it fell to a newly elected President to appoint hundreds of officials, from rural postmasters and lighthouse keepers to ambassadors. It was a handy way to reward political loyalty, but it was a tediously time-consuming process for a new President and – as Charles Guiteau conclusively demonstrated – it bred dissatisfaction among disappointed aspirants. Two years later Congress abolished the practice. But the shooting of the President – or more precisely the response to the shooting – was significant in another way. It underlined the distinctively American belief that almost any problem, whether it be finding a bullet buried in soft tissue or cooling the bedroom of a dying Chief Executive, could be solved with the judicious application of a little know-how.

Know-how, dating from 1857, is a quintessentially American term and something of a leitmotif for the nineteenth century. Thanks to it, and some other not insignificant factors like an abundance of natural resources and a steady supply of cheap immigrant labour, America was by 1881 well on its way to completing a remarkable transformation from an agrarian society on the periphery of world events to an economic colossus. In the thirty years that lay either side of Garfield's death America enjoyed a period of growth unlike that seen anywhere in history. In almost every area of economic activity, America rose like a giant, producing quantities of raw materials and finished products that dwarfed the output of other countries – sometimes dwarfed the output of all other countries put together. Between 1850 and 1900, American coal production rose from 14 million tons to over 100 million, steel output went from barely 1 million tons to over 25 million, paper production increased ninefold, pig-iron production sevenfold, cotton-seed oil by a factor of fourteen, copper wire by a factor of almost twenty. In 1850 America's 23 million people had a cumulative wealth of $7.1 billion. Fifty years later, the population had tripled to 76 million, but the wealth had increased thirteenfold to $94.3 billion.[4] In 1894 America displaced Britain as the world's leading manufacturer. By 1914 it was the world's leading producer of coal, natural gas, oil, copper, iron ore and silver, and its factories were producing more goods than those of Britain, Germany and France together. Within thirty years of Garfield's death, one-fourth of all the world's wealth was in American hands.

For the average American, progress was not, in the words of Henry Steele Commager, 'a philosophical idea but a commonplace of experience . . . Nothing in all history had ever succeeded like America, and every American knew it.'[5] In no other country could the common person enjoy such an intoxicating possibility of accumulating wealth. An obsession with money – and more specifically with the making of money – had long been evident in the national speech. As early as the eighteenth century, Benjamin Franklin was reminding his readers that 'time is money' and foreign visitors were remarking on the distinctly American expression 'to net a cool thousand',[6] and on the custom of defining a person as being 'worth so-and-so many dollars'. Long before Henry Clay thought up the term in 1832, America was the land of the 'self-made man'.[7] At about the same time people began referring to the shapers of the American economy as 'businessmen'. The word had existed in English since at least 1670, but previously it had suggested only someone engaged in public affairs.[8] In the sense of a person concerned with the serious matter of creating wealth it is an Americanism dating from 1830. As the century progressed people could be *well-fixed* (1822), *well-to-do* (1825), *in the dimes* (1843), *in clover* (1847), *heeled* (1867; *well-heeled* didn't come until the twentieth century), a *high roller* (1881), or a *money-bag* (1896, and made into the plural *money-bags* early in this century). As early as the 1850s they could hope *to strike it rich* and by the 1880s they could dream of *living the life of Riley* (from a popular song of the period, 'Is That Mr Reilly?', in which the hero speculates on what he would do with a fortune).[9]

Not everyone liked this new thrusting America. In 1844 Philip Hone, a mayor of New York and a noted social critic, wrote 'Oh, for the good old days', the first use of the phrase.[10] But most people, then as now, wanted nothing more than to get their hands on 'the almighty dollar', an expression coined by Washington Irving in 1836 in an article in the *Knickerbocker Magazine*.[11]

A great many of them did. As early as the mid-1820s, Americans were talking admiringly of *millionaires*, a term borrowed from the British who had in turn taken it from the French, and by 1850 were supplementing the word with a more aggressive version of their own devising: *multimillionaires*.[12] An American lucky enough to *get in on the ground floor* (1872) with an arresting invention or a timely investment might reasonably hope to become a millionaire himself. In 1840 the country had no more than twenty millionaires. By 1915 there were 40,000.[13]

The new class of *tycoons* (from the Japanese *taikun*, 'military commander', and first applied to business leaders in the 1870s) enjoyed a concentration of money and power that is almost unimaginable now. In 1891 John D. Rockefeller and Standard Oil controlled 70 per cent of the world market for oil. J. P. Morgan's House of Morgan and its associate companies in 1912 were worth more 'than the assessed value of all the property in the 22 states and territories west of the Mississippi'.[14] With great wealth came the luxury of eccentricity. James Hill of the Great Northern Railroad reportedly fired an employee because the man's name was Spittles. The servants at J. P. Morgan's London residence nightly prepared dinner, turned down the bed and laid out nightclothes for their master even when he was known beyond doubt to be three thousand miles away in New York. The industrialist John M. Longyear, disturbed by the opening of a railroad line past his Michigan residence, had the entire estate packed up – sixty-room house, hedges, trees, shrubs, fountains, the works – and re-erected in Brookline, Massachusetts.[15] James Gordon Bennett, a newspaper baron, liked to announce his arrival in a restaurant by yanking the tablecloths from all the tables he passed. He would then hand the manager a wad of cash with which to compensate his victims for their lost meals and spattered attire. Though long forgotten in his native land, Bennett and his exploits – invariably involving prodigious drinking before and lavish restitution after – were once world famous, and indeed his name lives on in England in the cry 'Gordon Bennett!', usually uttered by someone who has just been drenched by a clumsy waiter or otherwise exposed to some exasperating indignity.

The indulgences of the rich become all the more insufferable when contrasted with the miserable condition of those whose labours sustained their wealth. Through the 1860s, workers in factories – or *manufactories* as they were still often called – routinely worked sixteen-hour days six days a week for less than twenty cents a day. Often they were paid in scrip, which they could spend only at the factory store. Workplaces were often ill-lit, ill-heated and filled with dangerous machinery and perilous substances. A physician in the mill town of Lawrence, Massachusetts, noted just after the turn of the century that 36 per cent of factory workers there didn't live to see their twenty-fifth birthdays.[16]

As America prospered, less attractive words entered the language, like *slum* (a word of uncertain origin, but probably based on a British dialectal variant of slime) and *sweatshop* (commonly shortened to *sweater* and first recorded in 1867), and *tenderloin* for the less salubrious areas of cities. This last named has been traced to a New York policeman who announced upon being assigned to the district around Forty-second Street that the opportunities for graft would enable him to stop eating ground beef and switch to tenderloin. The obvious pun on a prostitute's salient anatomical feature no doubt helped to reinforce the term.[17] Older words, too, sometimes took on new, more sinister meanings. *Tenement* originally described any tenanted dwelling. In America, where only the poor lived in shared housing, it had by the 1840s taken on the sense of a crowded, fetid building inhabited by the lowest orders.

Out in the sunshine of prosperity, however, it was a dazzling age. A brief list of just some American inventions of the period may give an idea of the dynamism that seized the country: the passenger elevator, escalator, telephone, phonograph, air-brake, cash register, electric light, fountain-pen, linotype, box camera, pneumatic tire, adding machine, revolving door, safety pin, and typewriter. All were invented in America, mostly in the frantic last quarter of the nineteenth century, and all were designed to relieve people of some everyday inconvenience. Where other countries tied their fortunes to revolutionary industrial processes – Bessemer steel, Jacquard looms, steam presses – Americans churned out appliances that made life easier. They took to heart Ralph Waldo Emerson's famous apophthegm: 'Build a better mousetrap and the world will beat a path to your door.' Or they would have, had Emerson ever said any such thing. In fact, what Emerson said didn't mention mousetraps and was a good deal more prolix: 'If a man has good corn, or wood, or boards, or pigs, to sell, or can make better chairs or knives, crucibles or church organs, than anybody else, you will find a broad hard-beaten road to his house, though it be in the woods.'[18] (Nor, by the way, did he say, 'Consistency is the hobgoblin of little minds.' He said, 'A foolish consistency is the hobgoblin of little minds' – quite another matter.)[19] But they took the sentiment to heart anyway.

America had a long tradition of productive tinkering. Jefferson invented a plough, which secured him a *prix d'honneur* from a French agricultural academy (though in fact it didn't actually work very well), and filled Monticello, his classical Virginia mansion, with self-invented contrivances designed to thwart small everyday irritants. Franklin, as everyone knows, was a manic inventor. He gave the world bifocals, the lightning rod, extendable grippers for taking items off high shelves, possibly the rocking-chair and certainly the Franklin stove (though for its first forty years it was more generally known as the *Pennsylvania fireplace*) – and always, always with a practical bent. 'What signifies philosophy that does not apply to some use?' he asked. Like Jefferson, he never profited from any of them.

It was at Jefferson's insistence that the US Patent Office was set up in 1790. At first, the patent board consisted of the Attorney General, the Secretary of State and the Secretary of War, who were given the job of vetting inventions as an extra little something to keep them occupied between more pressing assignments. They don't appear to have been run off their feet. In the first year just three patents were issued. (For the record, the first American patent went to a Samuel Hopkins for a new way of making potash.) By 1802, however, patents were pouring in so fast that a proper patent board had to be organized. Suddenly the country teemed with tinkerer-inventors. In other nations, inventions emerged from laboratories. In America they came out of kitchens and tool-sheds. Everyone, it seemed, got in on the act. Even Abraham Lincoln found time to take out a patent (No. 6469: A Device for Buoying Vessels over Shoals).[20]

Typical of the age was Charles Goodyear, the man who gave the world vulcanised rubber. Goodyear personified most of the qualities of the classic American inventor – total belief in the product, years of sacrifice, blind devotion to an idea – but with one engaging difference. He didn't have the faintest idea what he was doing. Described by one biographer as a 'gentle lunatic', Goodyear in 1834 became fascinated with rubber. It was a wonderfully promising material – pliant, waterproof, rugged and durable – but it had many intractable shortcomings. For one thing, it had a low melting-point. Boots made of rubber were fine in winter, but at the first sign of warm weather they would gooily decompose and quickly begin to stink.

Goodyear decided to make it his life's work to solve these problems. To say that he became obsessed only begins to hint at the degree of his commitment. Over the next nine years, he sold or pawned everything he owned, raced through his friends' and family's money, occasionally resorted to begging, and generally inflicted loving but untold hardship on his long-suffering wife and numerous children. He turned the family kitchen into a laboratory and, with only the most basic understanding of the chemistry involved, frequently filled the house with noxious gases and at least once nearly asphyxiated himself. Nothing he tried worked. To demonstrate the material's versatility, he took to wearing a suit made entirely of rubber, but this merely underlined its acute malodorousness and its owner's faltering grip on reality. Amazingly, everyone stood by him. His wife did whatever he asked of her and relatives gladly handed him their fortunes. One brother-in-law parted with $46,000 and never whimpered when all it resulted in was tubs of noisome slop. With implacable resolve Goodyear churned out one product after another – rubber mailbags, life-preservers, boots, rainwear – that proved disastrously ineffective. Even with the lavish support of friends and relatives, Goodyear several times ended up in debtors' prisons. In 1840, when his two-year-old son died, the family couldn't even afford a coffin.

Finally in 1843, entirely by accident, he had his breakthrough. He spilled some India rubber and sulphur on the top of his stove and in so doing discovered the secret of producing a rubber that was waterproof, pliant, resistant to extremes of heat and cold, made an ideal insulator, didn't break when dropped or struck, and, above all, was practically odourless. Goodyear hastily secured a patent and formed the Naugatuck India-Rubber Company. At long last he and his family were poised for the fame and fortune that their years of sacrifice so clearly warranted.

It was not to be. Goodyear's process was so easily duplicated that other manufacturers simply stole it. Even the name by which the process became known, *vulcanization*, was coined by an English pirate. Goodyear had endless problems protecting his patents. The French gave him a patent but then withdrew it on a technicality, and when he travelled to France to protest the matter, he found himself tossed yet again into a debtors' prison. He made more money from his autobiography – a book with the slightly less than compelling title *Gum-Elastic* – than he ever did from his invention. When he died in 1860, he left his family saddled with debts.[21] The company that proudly bears his name, the Goodyear Tire & Rubber Company, had nothing to do with him or his descendants. It was named Goodyear by two brothers in Akron, Ohio, Frank and Charles Seiberling, who simply admired him.[22]

Many of the most prolific and important inventors of the age are now almost wholly forgotten. One such was Walter Hunt, who took out patents by the score on fountain-pens, a process for manufacturing paper collars, a machine to make nails and rivets, and the prototype of the breech-loading Winchester rifle. Perhaps his most lasting invention was the safety pin, which he devised in 1849 after a couple of hours of fiddling with a piece of wire. Never much of a businessman, he immediately sold the rights to the device for $400. Slightly earlier, but in much the same mould, was Eli Whitney. While still a youth, he had devised novel processes for manufacturing nails, pins and men's walking-sticks, and later in life would be instrumental in developing the idea of interchangeable mass-produced parts, an approach that came to be known as the uniformity, or Whitney, system. But what he is chiefly remembered for is the cotton gin, and rightly so. It was one of the great inventions of the age. If you have ever wondered how an intoxicating drink became associated with a device for combing cotton the answer is it didn't. *Gin* is merely a shortening of *engine*.

Whitney hit upon the invention while visiting a cotton plantation in Georgia. As a New Englander unacquainted with the region, Whitney took a keen interest in how the plantation worked, and was immediately struck by how slow and labour-intensive was the process of deseeding cotton by hand. He knocked together a contraption that consisted essentially of two contra-rotating drums with teeth that effectively parted the cotton from the seeds. It was ingeniously simple, but it transformed the plantation economy of the South. Indeed, perhaps no other simple invention in history other than the wheel has had a more sensational and immediate payback in terms of increased efficiency. A single gin could do the work of a thousand slaves. In ten years, exports of cotton from the South increased from 189,500 pounds to 41 million pounds. Slavery across large parts of the South was suddenly not just morally indefensible but economically unnecessary. But what is notable here is that Whitney wasn't thinking of a revolutionary device that would alter history or secure his fortune – at least not at first – but of a simple machine that would make a friend's life simpler and more efficient.

When it did occur to Whitney that the gin was revolutionary and that there ought to be money in it, he hastily secured a patent. As so often with nineteenth-century inventors, he found himself cheated at every step and spent much of his life fighting costly court battles that gained him little but lawyers' bills. At least he had the satisfaction of being famed for his achievement, which is more than many got.

Consider the fate of poor Elias Howe, a young Boston native who in 1846 produced the first workable sewing-machine. The trouble was that no one wanted it. Depressed by his failure, Howe suffered a nervous breakdown and fled to England, where he hoped his ingenious invention might be given a more congenial reception. It was not. After two years of tramping the streets, he was so destitute that he had to work his passage home on a merchant ship. Arriving penniless in Boston he discovered that in his absence one Isaac Singer had stolen his patent, set up a sewing-machine factory and was making money hand over fist. Howe took Singer to court, where it became apparent that Singer had not a leg to stand on but was making so much money from Howe's invention that he could afford to hire the sharpest lawyers. After a protracted fight, Singer was compelled to pay Howe a decent royalty on every machine built. (Having secured his fortune, Howe promptly enlisted in the Union Army as a common foot-soldier; it was an age of eccentrics as well as inventors.) None the less, it is Singer's name, not Howe's, that is indelibly associated in the popular mind with the sewing-machine.[23]

Equally unlucky was J. Murray Spangler, who invented the vacuum cleaner – or *electric suction sweeper* as he called it – at the turn of the century in New Berlin, Ohio. Unable to make a success of it, he turned for advice to W. H. Hoover, a local leather-goods maker who knew nothing about electrical appliances but did recognize a business opportunity when it fell in his lap. Before long there were Hoover factories all over the world, Hoover was credited with a great invention he had nothing to do with, the British were turning his name into a verb, and J. Murray Spangler was forgotten.

But perhaps the greatest historical snub was that meted out to Professor Joseph Henry of Princeton, who in 1831 invented the telegraph. The word itself had been coined thirty-seven years earlier by a Frenchman named Claude Chappe, for a kind of semaphore system employed during the French Revolution, and by 1802 was being employed to describe long-distance messages of all types. Henry not only had the idea of transmitting messages as coded electrical impulses via wires, but worked out all the essentials that would be necessary to make such a system feasible, but for some reason he never bothered to perfect, or more crucially patent, the process.

That fell to a talented, well-connected, but generally unattractive fellow from Charlestown, Massachusetts, named Samuel Finley Breese Morse. Morse — Finley to family and friends — would have been a man of distinction even if he had never perfected the telegraph. The scion of a leading New England clan (his grandfather had been president of Princeton), he was an accomplished artist, a member of Britain's Royal Academy, a professor of fine arts at New York University, a dedicated dabbler in the creative sciences, and a would-be politician of distinctly reactionary bent (he ran twice for mayor of New York on a virulently anti-Catholic ticket and believed, among other things, that slavery was not just a good thing but divinely inspired). His consuming passion, however, was the idea of transmitting messages along wires, to the extent that he abandoned his career and spent five desperately impoverished years perfecting the telegraph and lobbying Congress for funding. Finally, in 1842, Congress — proving that it is seldom more than half smart — appropriated $30,000 for Morse's experiments and $30,000 to be spent on the equally exciting new science of mesmerism.

With his share of the funds, Morse strung a wire between Washington and Baltimore and on 11 May 1844 sent the first telegraphic message (it would not be called a telegram for another twelve years). Every schoolchild knows that this first message was 'What hath God wrought?' In fact, it was not. The first message was 'Everything worked well.' The more famous and ringing words, chosen not by Morse but by the daughter of the Commissioner of Patents, came at a later public demonstration. Morse's only real invention was the simple code that bears his name.* Much of the rest was utterly beyond him. To build a working telegraph, Morse not only stole lavishly from Henry's original papers, but when stuck would call on the eminent scientist for guidance. For years, Henry encouraged and assisted his efforts. Yet later, when Morse had grown immensely famous and rich, he refused to acknowledge even the slightest degree of debt to his mentor.

---

* It is a myth, incidentally, that *SOS* stands for *save our ship* or *save our souls*. It stands for nothing. It was chosen as a distress signal at an international conference in 1906 not because it had any meaning but because its nine keystrokes (three dots, three dashes, three dots) were simple to transmit.[24]

Throughout his career Morse was the lucky beneficiary of men more generous and gifted than he. In Paris he persuaded Louis Daguerre to show him how his newly invented photographic process worked. He then took it home with him to America and handsomely supplemented his fortune by making pictures and selling them (becoming in the process the first to photograph a living person). On the same trip, he actually stole a magnet crucial to long-distance telegraphy invented by Louis Breguet, and took it home with him to study at leisure.

It is almost impossible to conceive at this remove how the telegraph astonished and captivated the world. That news from remote places could be conveyed instantaneously to locations hundreds of miles away was as miraculous to Americans as it would be today if someone announced a way to teleport humans between continents. It was too miraculous for words. Within just four years of Morse's first public demonstration, America had five thousand miles of telegraph wire and Morse was widely regarded as the greatest man of his age.[25]

Morse was knocked from the pantheon by an invention more useful and lasting, and far more ingenious, than the telegraph. I refer to the telephone, invented by Alexander Graham Bell in 1876 (and not strictly an American invention since Bell, a native of Edinburgh, Scotland, didn't become a US citizen until six years later). Bell did not coin the term *telephone*. The word had been around since the 1830s, and had been applied to a number of devices designed to produce noise, from a kind of musical instrument to a particularly loud foghorn. Bell described his appliance on the patent application as a new kind of 'telegraphy' and soon afterwards began referring to it an 'electrical speaking telephone'. Others commonly referred to it in its early days as a 'speaking telegraph'.

Bell had become interested in the possibility of long-distance speech through his work with the deaf (a misfortune that extended to both his wife and mother). He was just twenty-eight and his assistant, Thomas A. Watson, just twenty-one, when they made their breakthrough on 10 March 1876. Despite their long and close association, there was a formality in their relationship that was somehow touching. It is notable that Bell's first telephonic communication was not 'Tom, come here, I want you,' but 'Mr Watson, come here, I want you.'

Flushed with excitement, Bell and Watson demonstrated their new device to Western Union, but the company's executives – why does this seem so inevitable? – failed to see its potential. 'Mr Bell,' they wrote to him, 'after careful consideration of your invention, while it is a very interesting novelty, we have come to the conclusion that it has no commercial possibilities,' adding that they saw no future for 'an electrical toy'.[26] Fortunately for Bell, others were not so short-sighted. Within just four years of its invention, America had 60,000 telephones. In the next twenty years that figure would increase to over six million, and Bell's telephone company, renamed American Telephone and Telegraph, would become the largest corporation in America, with stock worth $1,000 a share. The Bell patent (No. 174,465) became the single most valuable patent in history.[27] The speed with which the telephone insinuated itself into American life is indicated by the fact that by the early 1880s when a person said 'I'll call you' it was taken to mean by telephone – or phone, as it was it was already familiarly known.

Bell sold his interests in the telephone in 1881 and devoted himself to other scientific pursuits. He invented ailerons for airplanes, and made significant contributions to the phonograph, the iron lung, the photoelectric cell and water desalination.[28] When President Garfield lay dying from bullet wounds, Bell was the natural candidate to try to save him.

The telephone not only brought instant communication to millions, but enriched American English in a way the telegraph never had. Scores of new words entered the language or were given new meaning. *Operator* was current by the late 1870s, as was 'Hello, central', the phrase universally used before the introduction of dial phones. 'Number, please?' dates from 1895, as does *telephone booth. Yellow pages* and *information* first appeared in 1906, *telephone directory* in 1907 (the first, listing fifty subscribers, appeared in New Haven, Connecticut), and *telephone book* in 1915.[29] That year also saw the introduction of *coast-to-coast service*. It took almost half an hour to make all the connections and the minimum charge was $20.70.

At first people were not sure what to say in response to a ringing phone. Edison thought callers should answer with a jaunty 'Ahoy!' and that was the word habitually used by the first telephone operator, one George Coy of New Haven. (Only male operators were employed at first. As so often happens with new technologies, women weren't allowed anywhere near it until the novelty had worn off.) Others said, 'Yes!' or 'What?' and many merely picked up the receiver and listened hopefully. The problem was such that magazines ran long articles explaining the etiquette of phone use.

Today, America is the most phone-dependent nation on earth. Ninety-three per cent of American homes have a phone and almost 70 per cent have two phones, a level of penetration no other nation but Canada comes anywhere near equalling, and each household makes or receives on average 3,516 calls per year,[30] a figure astonishing to almost all other people in the world.

Such was the outpouring of inventions in the late nineteenth century that in 1899 Charles Duell resigned as head of the US Patent Office declaring that 'everything that can be invented has been invented'.[31] As patent applications proliferated and grew ever more arcane, the definition of what constitutes a patentable invention had to be revised. In the early years a product or device had not only to be new but also demonstrably useful. From 1880 to 1952 the law was refined to require that an invention constitute a genuine breakthrough rather than a mere modification. By 1952 that definition was held to be too ambiguous and a new standard was adopted. Since then, an invention must merely be 'nonobvious'.[32]

From the linguistic point of view, it is interesting to note how seldom inventions were patented under the names by which we now know them. Bell, as we have seen, described his most famous invention as 'telegraphy'. Hiram Maxim didn't use the word machine-gun – and quite rightly since all guns were machines – but the more precise 'automatic gun'. Edison called his light-bulb an 'electric lamp'. Joseph Glidden showed a small stroke of genius in inventing barbed wire, a material that transformed the West, but rather less in naming it; he described it on the patent application as 'wire-fences'. The cash register began life as the 'Incorruptible Cashier' – so called because every dip into the till was announced with a noisy bell, thus making it harder for cashiers to engage in illicit delvings among the takings. (For much the same reason, early owners discovered that if they charged odd amounts like forty-nine cents or ninety-nine cents the cashier would very probably have to open the drawer to extract a penny change, thus obviating the possibility of the dreaded unrecorded transaction. It was only later that it dawned on merchants that a sum like $1.99 had the odd subliminal quality of seeming markedly cheaper than $2.) The escalator began life as the 'Reno Inclined Elevator', named for its inventor, Jesse Reno, who installed the first one at the Old Iron Pier on Coney Island in 1896. *Escalator* was the trade name used by the Otis Elevator Company when it joined the market with a version of its own in 1900, but for years afterwards most people called it a *movable stairway*. (The modern word *escalate*, incidentally, is a back-formation from escalator.)[33]

Among such company, the typewriter, patented in 1868 by Christopher Latham Sholes of Milwaukee as the *Type-Writer*, was unusual for preserving its original designation, though earlier models went by a variety of names, from *pterotype* to *mechanical chirographer,* and Sholes himself considered calling it a *writing machine* or *printing machine*. Sholes's earliest models had some notable drawbacks. They printed only capital letters and the keys tended to jam. At first, the letters were arrayed in alphabetical order, an arrangement hinted at on modern keyboards by the sequences *F–G–H, J–K–L* and *O–P*, but the fact that no two other letters are alphabetical, that the most popular letters are not only banished to the periphery but given mostly to the left hand while the right is left with a sprinkling of secondary letters, punctuation marks and little-used symbols, are vivid reminders of the extent to which Sholes had to abandon common sense and order just to make the damn thing work. There is a certain piquant irony in the thought that every time you stab ineptly at the letter *a* with the little finger of your left hand, you are commemorating the engineering inadequacies of a nineteenth-century inventor.

To test the machines, a mechanic at Sholes's Milwaukee factory reportedly took to typing 'Now is the time for all good men to come to the aid of the party' – no one knows why – which is apparently how this rousing sentiment became indelibly associated with testing a keyboard or limbering up the fingers.[34] Mark Twain, incidentally, was the first person to write a book on a typewriter, or *typemachine* as he insisted on calling it. He claimed in an autobiographical note that it was *The Adventures of Tom Sawyer*, but his memory was faulty. It was in fact *Life on the Mississippi*.[35]

As the twentieth century dawned, still more terms designating wealth entered the language: *to be on easy street* (1901), *high flier* (1904), *sitting pretty* (1910). And inventors continued giving names to their processes that the world ignored. When a twenty-year-old recent graduate of Cornell named Willis Carrier developed the first modern air-conditioner in 1902, he didn't call it that, but an 'Apparatus for Treating Air'. The first electric stove was called a 'fireless cooker'. The first ball-point pen was patented as a 'non-leaking, high altitude writing stick'. Radio and television, as we shall see elsewhere, went by any number of names before settling into their present, seemingly inevitable forms. Chester Carlson invented xerography in 1942, but called it 'electro-photography'. And the transistor, invented by three researchers at AT&T Bell Laboratories in 1950, was described on the patent application as a 'three-electrode circuit element utilizing semi-conductive materials'.[36]

Although America was unsurpassed at devising new conveniences, its constant bent towards practicality – or *pragmatism*, a term coined by William James in 1863 – meant that it wasn't always so good at dealing with more complicated systems. Many of the great technological breakthroughs of the nineteenth century didn't occur in America but in Europe. The car was invented in Germany and the radio in Italy, just as radar, the computer and the jet engine would later be invented in Britain. But where America couldn't be touched was in its capacity to exploit new technologies, and no one was better at this than Thomas Alva Edison.

Edison was the archetypal American pragmatist. Latin, philosophy and other such esoteric pursuits he dismissed as 'ninny stuff'.[37] What he wanted were useful inventions that would make life more agreeable for the user and bring untold wealth to him. With 1,093 patents to his name (though many of these were in fact invented by his employees) Edison has almost twice as many patents as his nearest rival, Edwin Land (inventor of the Polaroid camera), and no one gave the world a greater range of products that have become central to modern life.

Edison's character was not, to put it charitably, altogether unflawed. He connived against competitors, took personal credit for inventions that were not his, drove his assistants to breaking point (they were known as the *Insomnia Squad*)[38] and when all else failed did not hesitate to resort to bribery, slipping New Jersey legislators $1,000 each to produce laws favourable to his interests.[39] If not an outright liar, he was certainly often economical with the truth. The popular story, which he did nothing to dispel, was that a width of 35 mm was chosen for movie film because when one of his minions asked how wide the film should be he crooked a finger and thumb and said, 'Oh, about this wide.' In fact, as Douglas Collins points out, it is far more probable that rather than devise his own film, he used Kodak film, which was not only 70 mm wide but 50 feet long. When cut down the middle it would conveniently yield 100 feet of 35 mm film – curiously, the precise dimensions of Edison's first reels.[40]

When George Westinghouse's novel and, in retrospect, superior alternating current electrical system began to challenge the direct current system in which Edison had invested much effort and money, Edison produced an eighty-three-page booklet entitled *A Warning! From The Edison Electric Light Co.* filled with alarming (and possibly fictitious) tales of innocent people who had been killed by coming in contact with Westinghouse's dangerously unreliable AC cables.* To drive home his point, he paid neighbourhood children twenty-five cents each to bring him stray dogs, then staged elaborate demonstrations for the press at which the animals were dampened to improve their conductivity, strapped to tin sheets and slowly dispatched with increasing doses of alternating current.[41]

But his boldest – and certainly tackiest – public relations exercise was to engineer the world's first electrical execution using his rival's alternating current in the hope of proving once and for all its inherent dangers. The victim selected for the exercise was one William Kemmler, an inmate at Auburn State Prison in New York, who had got himself into this unfortunate fix by bludgeoning to death his girlfriend. The experiment was not a success. Strapped into an electric chair with his hands immersed in buckets of salt water, Kemmler was subjected to 1,600 volts of alternating current

---

* Though Westinghouse is associated in the popular mind with electricity, his initial fame came from the invention of air-brakes for trains. Before this useful development trains could only stop in one of two ways: by having brakemen manually turn a hand-wheel on each car, a laborious process, or by crashing into something solid, like another train.

for fifty seconds. He gasped a great deal, lost consciousness and even began to smoulder a little, but conspicuously he failed to die. Not until a second, more forceful charge was applied did he finally expire. It was a messy, ugly death and wholly undermined Edison's intentions. Alternating current was soon the norm.

Of linguistic interest is the small, forgotten argument over what to call the business of depriving a person of his life by means of a severe electrical discharge. Edison, always an enthusiast for novel nomenclature, variously suggested *electromort, dynamort* and *ampermort* before seizing with telling enthusiasm on *to westinghouse,* but none of these caught on. Many newspapers at first wrote that Kemmler was to be *electrized*, but soon changed that to *electrocuted* and before long *electrocution* was a word familiar to everyone, not least those on death row.

Edison was to be sure a brilliant inventor, with a rare gift for coaxing genius from his employees, but where he truly excelled was as an organizer of systems. The invention of the light-bulb* was a wondrous thing, but of not much practical use when no one had a socket to plug it into. Edison and his tireless workers had to design and build the entire system from scratch, from power stations to cheap and reliable wiring, to lamp-stands and switches. In this he left Westinghouse and all other competitors standing.

The first experimental power plant was built in two semi-derelict buildings on Pearl Street, lower Manhattan, and on 4 September 1882 Edison threw a switch that illuminated, if but faintly, 800 flickering bulbs all over southern Manhattan. With incredible speed electric lighting became the wonder of the age.[42] Within months Edison had set up no fewer than 334 small electrical plants all over the world. Cannily he put them in places where they would be sure to achieve maximum impact: on the New York Stock

---

* Curiously, although everyone refers to the object as a *light bulb*, few dictionaries do. The *American Heritage* (first edition) has *lighthouse, light-headed, light meter* and many others in similar vein, but no *light bulb*. If you wish to know what that object is, you must look under *incandescent light, electric light* or *electric lamp*. *Funk & Wagnalls Revised Standard Dictionary* devotes 6,500 words to *light* and its derivatives, but again makes no mention of *light bulb*. *Webster's Second New International* similarly makes no mention of *light bulb*. The third edition does – although it has just this to say: 'light bulb n: incandescent lamp'. For full details you still have to turn to *incandescent lamp*. In my experience, most dictionaries are the same. I can't explain it.

Exchange, in the Palmer House Hotel in Chicago, La Scala opera house in Milan, the dining-room of the House of Commons in London. All this made Edison, and America, immensely rich. By 1920 it was estimated that the industries spawned by his inventions and business pursuits – from electric lighting to motion pictures – were worth an aggregate $21.6 billion. No other person did more to make America an economic power.[43]

Edison's other great innovation was the setting up of a laboratory with the express purpose of making technological breakthroughs with commercial potential. Before long many leading corporations, notably AT&T, General Electric and DuPont, were doing the same. Practical science, elsewhere the preserve of academics, had become in America the work of capitalists.

As the nineteenth century progressed and small companies grew into mighty corporations, the new breed of magnates required increasingly grand and imposing headquarters. Fortunately, their need for office space coincided with the development of a radical type of building: the skyscraper. Before the 1880s, buildings of more than eight or nine storeys were impracticable. Such a structure, made of brick, would require so much support as to preclude openings for windows and doors on the lower floors. However, a number of small innovations and one large one suddenly made skyscrapers a practical proposition. The large innovation was curtain walling, a cladding of non-weight-bearing materials hung on a steel skeleton, which made tall buildings much easier to build.

Skyscraper had existed in English since 1794, but had been applied to any number of other things: a top hat, a high pop-up in early baseball, the loftiest sail on a merchant ship. It was first applied to a building in 1888 (though *skyscraping building* was used four years earlier), and not in New York, as one might expect, but in Chicago. Throughout the last quarter of the nineteenth century Chicago led the world in the engineering of large structures, and for one very good reason: it had burned down in 1871. The first skyscraper was the Home Insurance Building in Chicago, built in 1883–5, and soon followed by the Leiter Building (1889), the Reliance Building (1894), and the Carson, Pirie, Scott Building (1899). Soon skyscrapers were transforming *cityscapes* (an

Americanism of 1850) all across the nation and so altering people's way of looking at cities as to give new meaning to the word *skyline*, which originally was a synonym for horizon but took on its modern sense in 1896.

If Chicago was the birthplace of the skyscraper, New York soon became its spiritual home. The city's first skyscraper, the twenty-two-storey New York World Building, opened in 1890 and soon Manhattan was gleaming with tall towers – the Pulitzer Building of 1892 (309 feet), the Flatiron Building (1903; 285 feet), Times Tower (1904; 362 feet), Singer Building (1908; 600 feet), Metropolitan Life Tower (1909; 700 feet), and finally the Woolworth Building, built in 1913 and soaring to 792 feet.[44]

With 58 floors and space for 14,000 workers, the Woolworth Building seemed unsurpassable – and for seventeen years it remained the world's tallest building. Not until 1930 was the Woolworth Building displaced by the Chrysler Building, which with 77 storeys and a height of 1,048 feet was nearly half as big again. The Chrysler Building was only planned to be 925 feet tall, but at the same time a rival developer began work on a building at 40 Wall Street that was planned to be two feet higher. In order not to be beaten, the Chrysler Building's architect, William Van Alen, hastily and secretly designed the 123-foot-high art deco spire that remains to this day the building's glory. The spire was assembled inside the building and hoisted triumphantly into place just as 40 Wall Street was being completed.[45] The Chrysler Building's undisputed eminence was painfully short-lived. Before it was even completed work had begun on a more ambitious project on Fifth Avenue, on the site of the original Waldorf-Astoria Hotel. There the Empire State Building began to rise. When completed the following year it soared 1,250 feet and 102 storeys, a record that would stand for forty-three years until the erection of the 110-storey, 1,454-foot-high and heart-stoppingly ugly Sears Tower in Chicago in 1974.

Steel-frame construction and curtain walling made tall buildings possible, but they didn't make them necessarily usable. For that, countless secondary innovations were needed, among them the revolving door, without which draughts would be all but uncontrollable, heightening fire risks and making effective heating and cooling an impossibility, and, above all, swift, safe passenger lifts.

The lift was not, as is commonly supposed and even sometimes stated, the invention of Elisha Graves Otis. Hoists and lifts had been around for years when Otis sprang to fame in the late 1850s. Otis never pretended to have invented the lift. His contribution was merely to come up with a simple, reliable device – a spring mechanism with gripper cogs – that made vertical passenger travel safe. A born showman, Otis travelled the world giving demonstrations of the safety of his lifts. Standing in a heavily weighted lift, he would have himself hoisted thirty feet or so above the ground, and would then call to an assistant to cut the rope. The audience would gasp, but instead of crashing to the floor, the lift would merely drop an inch or so and stay there. He sold the devices by the hundreds. (Even so, early lifts were by no means foolproof. In 1911 the *New York Tribune* reported that in the previous two years at least 2,600 people had been injured or killed in lift accidents.)

Skyscrapers may have transformed the appearance of the American city, but they have done surprisingly little for it linguistically. According to several sources, the Flatiron Building in New York was responsible for the expression *twenty-three skiddoo*, the idea being that the curious angular geometry of the building created unusual draughts that lifted the skirts of women passing on Twenty-third Street, to such an extent that men began hanging out there in the hopes of catching a glimpse of stockinged leg. And the police, in response, took to moving them on with the growled entreaty 'Hey, you – twenty-three skiddoo!' Unfortunately, there is not a shred of evidence to support the story. *Skiddoo*, meaning 'scram' or 'scat', is known to have been the invention of the linguistically prolific cartoonist T. A. 'Tad' Dorgan in the early years of this century, but how or why *twenty-three* became immutably associated with it is, like so much else, anybody's guess.

7

Names

I

Soon after the Milwaukee Railroad began laying track across Washington state in the 1870s, a vice-president of the company was given the task of naming thirty-two new communities that were to be built along the line. Evidently not a man with poetry in his soul, he appears to have selected the names by wandering through his house and choosing whatever objects his eye happened to light on. He named the towns after everything from poets (*Whittier*) and plays (*Othello*) to common household foods (*Ralston* and *Purina*). One town he named *Laconia* 'after what I thought was Laconia in Switzerland located high up among the Alps, but in looking over the Swiss map this morning I am unable to find a place of that name there'.[1] Never mind. Laconia at least had a kind of ring to it.

This is by way of making the point that no people in modern history have been confronted with a larger patch of emptiness to fill with names than those who settled America, or have gone about it in more strikingly diverse ways. According to George R. Stewart, the greatest of American toponymists (that is, one who studies place-names), as of 1970 America had probably 3.5 million named places, plus another million or so named places that no longer existed (among them, Purina and Laconia, Washington). There is almost nothing, it would appear, that hasn't inspired an American place name at some time or other. In addition to breakfast foods and Shakespearean plays, Americans have had towns named for radio programmes (Truth or Consequences, New Mexico), towns named for cowboy stars (Gene Autrey, Oklahoma), towns named for forgotten heroes (Hamtramck, Michigan, named for a Major John Hamtramck), towns that you may give thanks you don't come from (Toad Suck, Arkansas, and Idiotville, Oregon, spring to mind), at least one town named for a person too modest to leave his name (Modesto, California) and thousands upon thousands of others with more prosaic or boring etymologies (not forgetting Boring, Maryland).

The first colonists, as we noted earlier, were spared the immediate task of giving names to the land since much of the eastern seaboard was named already. But as they spread out and formed new settlements they had to arrive at some system for labelling unfamiliar landmarks and new communities. The most convenient device was to transfer names from England. Thus the older states abound in names that have counterparts across the sea: Boston, Dedham, Braintree, Greenwich, Ipswich, Sudbury, Cambridge and scores of others. An equally simple expedient was to honour members of the royal family, as with Charlestown, Jamestown, Maryland and Carolina. Many of these names, it is worth noting, were pronounced quite differently in the seventeenth century. Charlestown, Massachusetts, was 'Charlton'. Jamestown was 'Jimston' or even 'Jimson' – a pronunciation preserved in *jimson weed*, a poisonous plant found growing there in alarming quantities.[2] Greenwich was pronounced 'grennitch', but over time came to be pronounced as spelled. Only since about 1925, according to Krapp, has it reverted to the original.[3]

But the colonists employed a third, rather less obvious, method for place-naming. They borrowed from the Indians. As we know, the native languages of the eastern seaboard were forbiddingly complex and nowhere more so than with their names, yet the colonists showed an extraordinary willingness not only to use Indian names but to record them with some fidelity. Even now the eastern states are scattered with Indian names of arresting density: Anasagunticook, Mattawamkeag, Nesowadnehunk, Nollidewanticook, Nukacongamoc, and Pongowayhaymock, Maine; Youghiogheny and Kishecoquillas, Pennsylvania; Quacumquasit and Cochichewick, Massachusetts; Wappaquasset, Connecticut; Nissequogue, New York.

Once there were many more. Until 1916, New Hampshire had a

stream called the Quohquinapassakessamanagnog, but then the cheerless bureaucrats at the Board on Geographic Names in Washington arbitrarily changed it to Beaver Creek. In like fashion the much loved Conamabsqunooncant River was transformed into the succinctly unmemorable Duck.[4] The people of Webster, Massachusetts (especially those who sell postcards), continue to take pride in the local body of water named on a signboard as 'Lake Chargoggagoggmanchauggauggagoggchaubunagungamaugg,' which is said to be Nipmuck for 'You fish on that side, I'll fish on this side, and no one will fish in the middle.' Such is the hypnotic formidableness of its many syllables that the sign painter added an extra one; the *gaugg* roughly midway along shouldn't be there. In any case, the name is no longer official.

Often, as you might expect, Indian names went through many mutations before settling into their modern forms. *Connecticut* was variously recorded as *Quonectacut*, *Quonaughticut*, *Qunnihticut*, *Conecticot* and many others before arriving at a permanent arrangement of letters. *Cuyahoga* was at first often spelled *Cajahoga*. John Smith recorded *Susquehanna* as *Sasquesahanock* and *Potomac* as *Patowomek*.[5] *Kentucky*, from the Iroquoian *kenta-ke*, appeared in a variety of guises – *Kaintuck*, *Caintuck*, *Kentuck* and *Kentucke* – and was generally pronounced with just two syllables until the nineteenth century. More than 132 spellings have been recorded for *Winnipesaukee*, perhaps not surprisingly. *Minnesota* has been everything from *Menesotor* to *Menisothé* to *Minnay Sotor*.[6] *Oregon* has appeared as *Ouaricon*, *Ouragon*, *Ourgan* and *Ourigan*. Even *Kansas* has had 140 spellings. *Milwaukee*, first recorded in 1679 as *Melleoki*, roamed freely through the alphabet as *Meleke*, *Millioki*, *Milwarik*, *Milwacky*, *Muilwahkie* and many others before settling into its permanent form as recently as 1844. Probably the liveliest diversity of spellings belongs to Chicago, which in its early days was rendered as *Schuerkaigo*, *Psceschaggo*, *Shikkago*, *Tsckakko*, *Ztschaggo*, *Shecago*, *Shakakko*, *Stkachango* and almost any other remotely similar combination you could think of.

Indian names frequently evolved into forms that disguised their native origins. *Kepaneddik* became *Cape Neddick*. *Norwauk* transmuted into *Norwalk*. The arresting *Waycake Creek*, New Jersey, grew out of *Waakaack*, while Long Island's *Rockaways* had their origins in *Rackawackes*. *Moskitu-auke* became, almost inevitably, *Mosquito Hawk*. *Oxopaugsgaug* became the jauntily accessible *Oxyboxy*. *No Man's Land* island in Massachusetts commemorates not some forgotten incident, but is taken from an Indian chief named Teque*noman*. The list goes on and on. *Ticklenaked*, *Smackover*, *Pohamoonshine*, *Poo Run*, *Zilly Boy* and countless other resonant place-names are the result of the confusion or comic adaptability of early colonial settlers.

Non-Indian names likewise sometimes underwent a kind of folk evolution. *Burlington*, Delaware, was originally called *Bridlington*, after the town in Yorkshire.[7] *Newark* is a shortening of *New Ark of the Covenant*. *Teaneck* was a folk adaptation of the Dutch family name *Teneyck*. *Newport News* has nothing to do with news; it was originally *New Port Newce* and named for the Newce family that settled there.[8]

Although Indian names occasionally were lost in this process – as when *Cappawack* became *Martha's Vineyard* or *Mattapan* was turned into *Dorchester* – for the most part Native American names have proved remarkably durable. You have only to cast an eye over a map of the United States to see how extraordinarily rich its heritage of Indian names is. In his classic study *Names on the Land*, George R. Stewart notes that '26 states [now 27; Alaska has been added since he wrote], 18 of the greatest cities, and most of the larger lakes and longer rivers' all owe their names to the Indians.[9] The sentiment is true enough, but the specifics demand some qualifying. For one thing, many 'Indian' names were never uttered by any Indian – *Indiana* being the most obvious example. *Oklahoma* was a word coined in Congress. It employed Choctaw elements but not in any way ever used by the Choctaws themselves. *Wyoming* was taken from a sentimental poem of the early 1800s called 'Gertrude of Wyoming', commemorating a massacre. The poem was so popular that communities all over the country were given the name before it was applied in 1868 to a Western territory in which it had no linguistic relevance. *Idaho*, even more absurdly, had no meaning whatever. It simply sounded to nineteenth-century Congressmen like a good Indian word.

Indian town names, too, often arose not out of any historical connection, but under the impulse of the romanticism that swept the country in the nineteenth century. All the many *Hiawathas* owe their existence not to the Mohawk chief but to the poem by Longfellow. The great Seminole chief Osceola never went anywhere near Iowa, but there is a town there named for him. Even when an Indian place-name has some historical veracity, it was often applied relatively late. Agawam, Connecticut, for instance, took its place on the map two hundred years after the nearby town of Ipswich did.

As America moved west, the need for names grew apace. For a time, the fashion was to give classical names to new communities – hence the proliferation, particularly among those states that received the first westward migrations, of classical names: *Cincinnati, Troy, Utica, Athens, Corinth, Memphis, Sparta, Cicero, Carthage, Cairo, Hannibal,* even *Romeo* and *Juliet.* The residents of one town in New York evidently grew so wearied by the various spellings that attached themselves to their town –*Sinneken, Sinnegar, Sennicky* – that they seized the opportunity to give the place both consistency and classical credibility by making it *Seneca.*

Another approach, and one that grew increasingly common as Americans plunged still further west, was to name places and landmarks after people, usually their founders but often someone deemed to have admirable qualities. In the Midwest especially, every state is dotted with communities bearing the name of some forgotten pioneer or hero of the nineteenth century. In Iowa you can find *Webster City, Mason City, Ames, Audubon, Charles City, Grinnell* (named by and for the man who took Horace Greeley's advice to 'go west, young man') and perhaps two hundred others in a similar vein. A notable (if seldom noted) feature of American place-names is how many of the larger cities honour people hardly anyone has ever heard of. There are no great cities named Franklin or Jefferson, but there is a Dallas. It was named for George Mifflin Dallas, who rose to the certain obscurity of the Vice-Presidency under James K. Polk and then sank from history like a stone dropped in deep water. Cleveland (originally spelled *Cleaveland*) is named for a forgotten Connecticut lawyer, Moses Cleaveland, who owned the land on which it stood but never bothered to visit the community that bears his name. Denver commemorates a governor of the Kansas Territory. It is not that these people were deemed especially worthy of having great cities named after them, but that the communities grew to greatness later.

Timing was all in these matters. Lewis Cass's nearest brush with immortality was to be defeated by Zachary Taylor in the 1848 presidential election, but counties in nine states are named for him none the less. Taylor had to be content with just seven county names – though that is perhaps seven more than a longer view of history would grant him. Henry Clay, the Kentucky senator and twice failed presidential candidate, did better than both put together. He is honoured with county names in no fewer than eighteen states. You can search the West for notable commemorations of Lewis and Clark and find almost nothing, but Zebulon Pike is grandly honoured with a mountain peak he never climbed or even got very close to (he merely sighted it from afar). Even Warren G. Harding, a President whose greatest contribution to American history was to die in office, has a county named in his honour in New Mexico. Only George Washington got anything approaching his just reward, receiving the approbation of a state, the nation's capital, 31 counties and at least 120 communities.[10] Once there were even more. Cincinnati, for example, began life as Fort Washington.

Often Americans arrived in a place to find it already named. The process began with the names the Dutch left behind when they gave up their hold on Nieuw Amsterdam. The British hastily changed that to New York – in honour of the Duke of York, and not the historic English city – but others required a little linguistic surgery. *Haarlem* was shorn of a vowel, *Vlissingen* was transformed into *Flushing*, and *Breukelyn* became *Brooklyn* (and at one point looked like evolving further into Brookland).[11] *Deutel Bogt* begat *Turtle Bay*, *Vlachte Bosch* became *Flatbush*, *Thynevly* became *Tenafly*, *Bompties Hoek* became *Bombay Hook*, and *Antonies Neus* became *Anthony's Nose*. As with the English and French, the Dutch often took Indian names and rendered them into something more palatable to their tongues. Thus *Hopoakan,* a village across the river from Manhattan, became *Hoboken*.

Further west, the French left many hundreds of names. In a single summer in 1673, the explorers Marquette and Jolliet set down eleven important names that live on yet in the names of rivers or cities (often both): Chicago, Des Moines, Wisconsin, Peoria, Missouri, Osage, Omaha, Kansas, Iowa, Wabash and Arkansas, though those weren't quite the spellings they used. To Marquette and Jolliet, the river was the *Mesconsing*. For reasons unknown, this was gradually altered to *Ouisconsing* before eventually settling into English as *Wisconsin*. Similarly *Wabash* evolved from *Ouabasche* and *Peoria* from *Peouarea*. *Iowa* began life as the somewhat formidable *Ouaouiatonon*. The French quickly shortened this to the still challenging *Ouaouia* before English-speaking settlers finished the job for them.

In Marquette and Jolliet's wake came French trappers, traders and explorers. For a century and a half much of America west of the Appalachians was under French control and the names on the landscape record the fact: Michigan, Illinois, Louisiana, Detroit, Baton Rouge, St Louis, Chicago and countless others. Many of these names are of uncertain significance. Chicago appears to be from an Indian word meaning 'place that stinks of onions', and Baton Rouge was evidently so called because in 1700 a party of explorers came upon a red stake – a *baton rouge* – marking the boundary between two Indian hunting-grounds and built a trading post there, but Coeur d'Alene, the city in Idaho, is utterly baffling. It translates as 'heart of awl', and quite what the founders had in mind by that is anybody's guess.[12]

No less of a mark was made by the Spanish. Though we tend to associate the Spanish with the south-west, Spain's American dominions stretched at one time across most of the continent, from the Florida Keys as far north as Alaska. Memphis was once known as San Fernando and Vicksburg as Nogales.[13] But, preoccupied with their holdings in Central and South America and convinced that North America was mostly worthless desert, the Spanish never made much of the lands to the north. By 1821, when Spain withdrew from North America, its estate north of the border consisted of only a few scattered garrisons and just three towns worthy of the name – Santa Fe, San Antonio and St Augustine, though even they couldn't muster 10,000 citizens between them. (Mexico City by contrast had a population comfortably above 150,000.) Even so, as I need hardly tell you, the Spanish left hundreds of names on the American landscape, including the oldest non-Amerindian place-name in the United States – Florida, or 'place of flowers', so dubbed by Juan Ponce de León when he became the first known European to set foot on what would eventually become US soil, on 2 April 1513. Missions and other small settlements soon followed, among them Tortugas (the second oldest European place-name in North America), St Augustine and Apalchen. This last named was never anything more than a hamlet, but the name somehow came to be applied to the vaguely defined mountainous interior. Eventually it attached itself to the mountain themselves – hence, *Appalachians*.

If the Spanish were modest in peopling their North American settlements, they were often lavish, not to say excessive, when it came to bestowing names upon them. To them Santa Fe was not just Santa Fe but La Villa Real de la Santa Fe de San Francisco (The Royal City of the Holy Faith of Saint Francis), while the California community that we know as Los Angeles went by the dauntingly ambitious name of El Pueblo de Nuestra Señora la Reina de los Angeles del Río Porciúncula (The Town of Our Lady the Queen of the Angels by the Little-Portion River), giving it nearly as many syllables as residents.

Often, as with Los Angeles and Santa Fe, these names left behind by the French and Spanish had to be shortened, re-spelled, or otherwise modified to make them sit more comfortably on English-speaking tongues. Thus L'Eau Froid ('cold water'), a lake in Arkansas, was turned into Low Freight. Mont Beau, North Carolina, evolved into Monbo. Les Mont Verts became Lemon Fair. Similarly the Siskiyou Mountains may be an adaptation of the French *six cailloux*, 'six stones'. Waco, Texas, began as the Spanish *Hueco*, while Key West was corrupted from *Cayo Hueso*. Bob Ruly, Michigan, started life as *Bois Brulé*.[14] More often the English-speaking settlers kept the spelling but adapted its pronunciation. Des Moines, Detroit, St Louis and Illinois are obvious examples of French words with non-French pronunciations, but there are countless lesser-known ones, like Bois D'Arc, Missouri, pronounced 'bodark', and De Blieux, Fortier, and Breazale, Louisiana, pronounced respectively 'double-you', 'foshee' and 'brazil'.[15]

Odd pronunciations are by no means exclusive to communities with a foreign pedigree. Often founders of towns selected an exotic name and then either didn't know how to pronounce it or decided they had a better way. Thus we find Pompeii, Michigan, pronounced 'pom-pay-eye', Russiaville and Peru, Indiana, as 'roosha-ville' and 'pee-roo', Versailles, Kentucky as 'vur-sales', Pierre,

South Dakota, as 'peer', Bonne Terre, Missouri, as 'bonny tar', Beatrice, Nebraska, as 'be-*at*-riss', Dante and Fries, Virginia, as 'dant' and 'freeze'. (The joke in Fries is that it is 'fries' in summer and 'freeze' in winter.)

If America had a golden age of place-naming it would be the middle portion of the nineteenth century when in quick order Oregon fever, the California gold rush and the opening of a transcontinental railway saw hundreds of new communities spring up practically overnight. Often, as we saw at the start of the chapter, the naming of towns was left to the railways, which not only arbitrarily bestowed titles on new communities but sometimes took the opportunity to rename existing ones. Marthasville, Georgia, had its new name – Atlanta – forced on it entirely against its wishes by a railway official in 1845. Occasionally, as Mencken notes, the first passengers on a new line were given the privilege of naming the towns along the way.[16] Post Office officials also enjoyed free rein. One official, Stewart relates, was said to have named post offices all over the West 'for practically all the kids and babies in his immediate neighbourhood'.[17]

When the naming was left to unofficial sources, as with the towns that sprang up around the mining camps in California, the results were generally livelier. California briefly revelled in such arresting geographic designations as Murderer's Gulch, Guano Hill, Chucklehead Diggings, Delirium Tremens, Whiskey Diggings, You Bet, Chicken Thief Flat, Poker Flat, Git-Up-And-Git, Dead Mule, One Eye, Hell-out-for-Noon City, Puke and Shitbritches Creek.[18] The practice was by no means confined to California. The whole of the West was soon dotted with colourful nomenclature – Tombstone, Arizona; Cripple Creek, Colorado; Whiskey Dick Mountain, Washington; Dead Bastard Peak, Wyoming; and others beyond counting. Often the more colourful of these names were later quietly changed for reasons that don't always require elucidation, as with Two Tits, California, and Shit-House Mountain, Arizona. Once, doubtless in consequence of the loneliness of western life, the West had more Nipple Mountains, Tit Buttes and the like than you could shake a stick at. Today we must make do with the Teton Mountains, whose mammary implications are evident only to those who are proficient in French.

*

Colourful appellations are not a uniquely western phenomenon, however. Lunenberg County, Virginia, once boasted a Fucking Creek and a Tickle Cunt Branch,[19] North Carolina had a Coldass Creek, and Kentucky still proudly boasts a Sugar Tit. Indeed, oddball names know no geographical bounds, as a brief sampling shows:

Who'd A Thought It, Alabama
Eek, Alaska
Greasy Corner, Toad Suck and Turkey Scratch, Arkansas
Zyzx Springs, California
Two Egg, Florida
Zook Spur and What Cheer, Iowa
Rabbit Hash, Bug, and OK, Kentucky
Bald Friar and Number Nine, Maryland.
Teaticket, Massachusetts
Sleepy Eye and Dinkytown, Minnesota
Tightwad, Peculiar, and Jerk Tail, Missouri
Hot Coffee and Goodfood, Mississippi
Wynot, Nebraska
Brainy Boro and Cheesequake, New Jersey
Rabbit Shuffle, Stifflknee Knob and Shoofly, North
   Carolina
Knockemstiff, Pee Pee, Lickskillet, and Mudsock, Ohio
Bowlegs, Oklahoma
East Due West, South Carolina
Yell, Bugscuffle, Gizzards Cove and Zu Zu,Tennessee
Lick Skillet, Bugtussle, Chocolate Bayou, Ding Dong,
   Looneyville, Jot 'Em Down, and Cut and Shoot, Texas
Lick Fork, Unthanks and Tizzle Flats, Virginia
Humptulips and Shittim Gulch, Washington
Superior Bottom, West Virginia
Embarrass, Wisconsin

Often a prosaic explanation lies buried in an arresting name. Goodnight, Texas, has nothing to do with a memorable evening or bedtime salutation. It simply recalls a Mr Goodnight. So, too, Humble and Oatmeal (named for a Mr Othneil), Texas, and Riddle, Idaho. Chagrin Falls, Ohio, does not, as the name would seem to suggest, have any connection with some early exploratory setback, but is simply a misrendering of the surname of François Séguin, an early French trader who settled along the river from which the town takes its name.[20] The town and river were both commonly spelled *Shaguin* until well into the nineteenth century.

In the eastern states, colourful names often have their roots in the name of a tavern or inn. Such, a bit disappointingly, is the case with King of Prussia, Blue Ball, Bird-in-Hand, Rising Sun, Bishop's Head, Cross Keys and many other curiously named towns lying mostly in or between Pennsylvania and Virginia.

The twentieth century has seen an odd, and mercifully intermittent, fashion for giving towns names that it was hoped would somehow put them on the map. Breakthroughs in science often prompting towns to name (or more often rename) themselves *Xray, Radio, Gasoline, Electron* and *Radium*. Bee Pee, Kansas, after putting up for years with jokes concerning the urinary habits of honey-making insects, decided to change its name to something less risible – and opted for *Chevrolet*.

Changing their names is something that towns do more often than you might expect. Few communities have not changed their names at least once. Scranton, Pennsylvania, has gone through no fewer than eight names, the most notable of which perhaps was its first: Skunk's Misery. Sometimes names are changed for reasons of delicacy – as when Screamerville became Chancellor or when Swastika, Arizona, transmuted into Brilliant – but just as often it was a desire by some real-estate developer to make the place sound more desirable. Thus Willmore City, California, became Long Beach, Roscoe became Sun Valley, Girard became Woodland Hills, and parts of Van Nuys and North Hollywood declared independence as, respectively, Chandler Estates and Valley Village. Merely changing the name can reportedly give property values an instant boost of up to 15 per cent.[21] Mellifluousness is generally given priority over etymological considerations, as with Glendale, California, a name that combines the Scottish-Gaelic *glen* with the northern English *dale* to form a name that means 'valley-valley'. Practically every city in America can boast subdivisions whose names owe nothing to anything other than their developers' vision of what sounds appealing: Wellington Heights, Canterbury Hills, Vista View Estates and the like. Somewhere, I suspect, there may even be a Laconia Heights.

By the late nineteenth century, America had accumulated so many names for towns, lakes, mountains and other topographical entities that the situation had grown confusing. Many states had as many as five towns with the same name, causing constant headaches for the postal service. Hundreds of other features on the landscape went by two or more names, like the mountain near San Diego sometimes called Cloud Peak and sometimes called Cuyamaca. Then, too, there were hundreds of places with variant spellings – like Alleghany, Virginia; Allegany, New York; and Allegheny, Pennsylvania.

In 1890, to sort out the mess, President Benjamin Harrison founded the ten-man Board on Geographic Names. The board was chronically underfunded – it didn't get its first paid secretary until 1929 – and had no great authority. It could order government offices to use its spellings, but no one else had to, and at first many people didn't. Gradually, however, most communities gave in to its decisions whether they liked them or not, rather in the way that most people have quietly acceded to the Postal Service's insistence on two-letter abbreviations for state names.

Early on the board established thirteen guiding principles. The first of these was the sensible conclusion that in general it would be best to follow local custom. Unfortunately, this was not consistent with the other twelve, all of which called for some deviation or other from historic practice. One ruling was that places should be shorn of unnecessary punctuation, so that Coeur d'Alêne lost its stately circumflex (though not its apostrophe) and San José was deprived of a sliver of its Spanish heritage.[22] At the same time, all towns terminating in *-burgh* were instructed to change to *-burg*, while all those ending in *-borough* were henceforth to read *-boro*. Deviant spellings like *Centre* were ordered Americanized. *City* and *Town*, the board decreed, should be removed from place-names, and names involving multiple words should be made one word, so that all the *New Castles* and *La Fayettes* became *Newcastles* and *Lafayettes*. Many hundreds of names were changed or shortened so that a place as formidably unpronounceable as Popocatepetl Mount in Oregon or Nunathloogagamiutbingoi Dunes, Alaska (at twenty-three letters, the longest name on the American landscape today), is now a rarity.

All of this would have been fractionally more tolerable had it been applied with some degree of consistency, of which the board seemed wholly incapable. It couldn't even settle on a name for itself. After starting as the Board on Geographic Names, it became the Geographic Board, then the Board on Geographical Names and now is once again the Board on Geographic Names.

In consequence of its decisions, American toponymic spelling lost much of its distinctiveness and charm, and a good deal of its clarity (an outsider could make a better stab at pronouncing Wilks-Barré than Wilks-Barre), without gaining anything much in the way of uniformity. Its decisions had an air of whimsicality. It took the apostrophe out of Pikes Peak, but left it in Martha's Vineyard. It ordered hundreds of communities to amalgamate their names – making all the El Dorados into Eldorados, for instance – but quickly realized that no one would accept Newyork or Losangeles or Elpaso. It threw out hundreds of Indian names, but kept hundreds of others. Almost its only act of incontestable virtue was to try to ameliorate racist names – changing Chinaman's Springs to Chinese Springs, Nigger Creek to Negro Creek and so on – but even here it didn't generally begin to act until the 1960s, long after they had become an embarrassment.[23]

On the matter of *-burg* and *-boro* terminations, however, the board was nothing short of relentless, and even now you can search a gazetteer long and hard before you find an exception to these two terminations. The main and most obvious one is Pittsburgh, which, curiously, often styled itself Pittsburg before the board came along and got the city's collective dander up. (Pittsburgh was named, incidentally, for the British statesman William Pitt by a Scottish immigrant who almost certainly intended it to be pronounced 'pittsburra'.) In 1891, in one of its earliest decisions, the board ordered the city to call itself Pittsburg. The Post Office diligently followed its instructions, but almost everyone else became resentful, and most of the city's leading institutions – the University of Pittsburgh, the Pittsburgh Stock Exchange, the *Pittsburgh Gazette* newspaper – refused to buckle under. After twenty years of squabbling, the board finally reversed its decision and on 19 July 1911 the city officially became Pittsburgh.[24]

Just as hundreds of towns have changed their names, so too have states. Maine was once New Somerset. New Jersey was briefly called Albania and later bore the alternative name of New Cesarea. Vermont was called generally New Connecticut until the inhabitants came up with the contrived, and inescapably non-sensical, name Vermont. If, as is apparent, their intention was to name it for the Green Mountains, they should have called it Les Monts Verts. As it is, in so far as it means anything at all, it means 'worm-mountain'.[25]

But then quite a number of state names are, when you pause to consider them, at least faintly nonsensical. Mississippi is a curious name for a state that possesses neither the source nor the mouth of the river for which it is named and indeed owns only part of one bank. Missouri has more of the Mississippi River than Mississippi has – but then Missouri also has more of the Mississippi River than it has of the Missouri River, and yet we call it Missouri. Rhode Island is not only not an island, but is not named for anyone or anything called Rhode. Nevada is named for a chain of mountains that lies almost entirely in California. Wyoming is named for a forgotten poem, California for a mythical queen. Maine has no particular reason for being called that. Montana and Idaho are named for nothing at all.

The explanations behind all these are various. Rhode Island originally referred only to the island in Narragansett Bay on which Newport now stands. An early Dutch explorer called it Roodt Eylandt (or Red Island, after the colour of its soil) and the name eventually evolved into a form more palatable to English sensibilities after Roger Williams founded Providence Plantation there in 1636. The state's full official name is Rhode Island and Providence Plantations. Maine comes from an archaic sense of *main* meaning *great* or *principal*. The Atlantic was sometimes referred to as the Main Sea – hence 'to sail the Spanish main'. The use is retained in the term *mainland* – and, less explicitly, in the name of the twenty-third state. Missouri is named not directly for the river, but for the Missouri Territory of which it was the most important part, and Mississippi came about more or less because no one else had taken the name. It was almost called Washington.

Many states also almost went by other names. West Virginia was nearly called Kanawha. Washington state nearly became Columbia. Idaho might have been Esmerelda, Oro Plata, Sierra Plata or Humboldt. Nevada might have been Bullion or Washoe, the name by which the region was generally known before Congress decided to name it Nevada after the mountains that feature only incidentally in its geography. From the outset, the question of what names to bestow on new states was one that generated hot debate and exercised the minds of men whose talents might better have been applied to more consequential matters. In 1784, in one of his few truly misguided efforts, Thomas Jefferson drew up a list of fashionably neoclassical but inescapably inane names that he suggested be bestowed on the territories of the West. Among his choices: *Polypotamia, Assenisipia, Pelisipia, Chersonesus, Macropotamia* and *Metropotamia*.[26]

Jefferson never got his way with his fancy names, but he did have somewhat greater success with a second proposal, namely that western states be divided in a neat chequer-board pattern. Every state west of the Mississippi has at least two straight (or nearly straight) borders except for Oregon, Minnesota and Texas, though only two, Colorado and Wyoming, are rectangular. In terms of their interior organization, the western states had an almost brutal orderliness imposed upon them, and one that made little allowance for topographical features like rivers and mountains. Land was divided into one-mile squares, or 640-acre sections. Six sections formed a township. Sections were divided into sixteen 40-acre squares, which accounts for those familiar farm expressions like 'north 40'. One problem with such a set-up is that a spherical planet doesn't lend itself to square corners. As you move nearer the poles, the closer the lines of longitude grow – which is why, if you look at a map, Wyoming is perceptibly narrower at the top than at the bottom. To get around this problem, longitudinal lines were adjusted every twenty-four miles. That explains why north–south roads in places like Nebraska and Kansas so often take a mysterious jag where they intersect with state highways.

Debates over state names often dragged on for days and never failed to inflame passions. Among the names suggested for Colorado were Colona (a rather odd feminization of the Spanish for Columbus, Colón), Jefferson, Franklin, Jackson, Lafayette, Yampa, San Juan, Lula, Arapahoe, Tahosa and Idaho. Idaho had a strange and almost mystical popularity among some Congressmen. Despite having no meaning whatever, it was suggested over and over again for thirty-one years until it was finally adopted for the forty-third state in 1890. Once it was out of the way, other names took its place in the line-up of hopefuls. Among those considered for Arizona were Gadsonia – after James Gadsden of Gadsden Purchase fame – and Pimeria. For New Mexico the suggestions included Hamilton, Lincoln, Montezuma and Acoma (a concocted name designed for no purpose other than that it would put the state first in the nation alphabetically).

Even more improbable in their way are state nicknames. Considering how widely used these nicknames are, it is surprising that their origins are often nowadays a mystery. No one knows for sure why Iowans are called Hawkeyes, why North Carolinians are Tarheels, why Kansans are Jayhawkers (there is no such bird) or why Indianans are Hoosiers. We know that Delaware has been called the Blue Hen State since at least 1840, but we don't know why. Various, sometimes ingenious explanations have been adduced – someone, for instance, traced *hoosier* to a Cumberland dialect word, *hooser* – but the evidence in each case is at best inconclusive and often merely fanciful.[27]

Most states have a discarded nickname somewhere in their past. Arkansas has been called the Hot Water State and the Toothpick State, Georgia the Buzzard State, Goober State and Cracker State. (The cracker in *Georgia cracker* has nothing to do with crisp baked wafers. It comes from the practice of cracking corn to make cornmeal.) Missouri was once widely known as the Puke State, Illinois as the Sucker State and Montana as the Stub-Toe State – though again in each case no one seems to know why. We do know, however, the derivation of Missouri's current slogan, the Show Me State. The expression was coined as an insult by outsiders and was meant to suggest that Missourians were so stupid that they had to be shown how to do everything. The state's inhabitants, however, contrarily took it as a compliment, persuading themselves that it implied a certain shrewd caution on their part.

As you might expect, state legislatures from time to time come up with more flattering nicknames for themselves, even at the risk of seeming a shade overambitious. New Jersey for a time called itself the Switzerland of America while Arkansas opted for the Wonder State. New Mexico appears to have suffered from the most severe outbreak of narcissism, calling itself at various times the Land of Heart's Desire, the Land of Opportunity, the Land of the Delight Makers and the Land of Enchantment.

For the honour of nickname least likely to make you pack up

your bags and head on out, there has been no shortage of contenders. Among the perennial front runners in this category we find the Tree Planters State (Indiana), the Wheat State (Kansas), the Blizzard State (South Dakota), the Hog and Hominy State (Tennessee), the Iodine State (South Carolina), the Mosquito State (New Jersey) and the apt if resplendently self-evident Land of the Dakotas (North Dakota).

II

And so, more briefly, to personal names. One of the more striking features of life in the early colonial period is how casual people were with the spellings of their names. Shakespeare, as is commonly noted, never spelled his name the same way twice in any of his surviving six signatures, even employing two spellings on a single document. His contemporaries were even more approximate in their renderings, leaving us with eighty-three different spellings of his name. Curiously, the one spelling Shakespeare himself didn't appear to use was *Shakespeare*. Sir Walter Raleigh likewise changed the spelling of his surname as one might change a shirt, sometimes styling himself *Rawleyghe*, sometimes *Rawley*, sometimes *Ralegh*.* His friends and associates were even less specific, addressing him as *Ralo, Ralle, Raulie, Rawlegh, Rawlighe, Rawlye* and some sixty-five other seemingly whimsical variants. Again, the one spelling he never apparently used is the one most commonly applied to him today: *Raleigh*.[28]

Abraham Lincoln's ancestors are recorded in early church and property rolls in such forms as *Lyncoln, Linccolne* and *Linkhorn*, Jefferson's as *Giffersonne* and *Jeffreson*, and Andrew Jackson's as *Jaxon, Jackeson, Jakeson* and *Jakson*. John Winthrop, first governor of Massachusetts (or *Masathusets* as it appeared on the first colonial-minted coins, place-names being equally subject to orthographic variability), sometimes styled himself *Wyntropp*, which is in fact how he pronounced the name,[29] and the records of

---

* Nearly all the spellings suggest, incidentally, that the modern American pronunciation of his name, 'rawly', is more faithful to the original than the modern British pronunciation, 'rally'.

early colonial towns are so full of multiple spellings for the same name – *Mayo/Mayhew, Smith/Smythe, Moore/Muir* and so on – as to suggest that few in that busy age saw any special merit or purpose in consistency of spelling or even pronunciation.

As early colonists employed odd spellings, so too they often brought unexpected pronunciations with them. This was particularly the case in Virginia where the leading families had a special fondness for pronouncing their family names in improbable ways, so that *Sclater* became 'Slaughter', *Munford* became 'Mumfud', *Randolph* was 'Randall', *Wyatt* was 'Wait', *Devereaux* was 'Deverecks', *Callowhill* was 'Carroll', *Higginson* was 'Hickerson', *Norsworthy* was 'Nazary', and *Taliaferro* became a somewhat less than self-evident 'Tolliver'. Still more unlikely were the Crenshaws, who were said to pronounce the name 'Granger', and a branch of the Enroughty clan, which altered the pronunciation to 'Darby', evidently as a way of distinguishing themselves from those members who said 'Enruffty'. Almost always these aberrant pronunciations arose not in the New World but were brought from England, and presumably treasured as rather eccentric heirlooms. In contrast to Britain, where bewildering pronunciations are affectionately preserved, in most cases in America the pronunciations gradually fell into line with their spellings, as when the forebears of John Wilkes Booth, Lincoln's assassin, stopped rhyming the name with 'south' and instead made it rhyme with 'truth'.

The practice was less common in the north but not unknown. Franklin Pierce of New Hampshire, the fourteenth President, pronounced his name 'Purse' throughout his life, but even such modest phonetic unorthodoxy was rare. New Englanders saved their creative impulses for their forenames, finding a certain comfort in endowing their children with names that denoted virtuous qualities. Among the *Mayflower* passengers we find Love and Wrastle Brewster, Resolved White, Humility Cooper, Desire Minter and Remember Allerton. Such names, as far as we can tell, appear only among the *Mayflower* children, suggesting that in 1620 the practice was quite new. We can not be entirely sure because the records are patchy. William Bradford compiled a 'compleat' list of *Mayflower* passengers in which he recorded the names of all of the men and most of the children and menservants, but only a few of the women, as if they were somewhat incidental to the enterprise. We therefore know, for instance, the name of Christopher Martin's two menservants, but have no idea what his wife was called. As wives gave up their surnames upon marriage, so it would appear that they relinquished their forenames except among their familiars, being known in the wider world – or at least to William Bradford – simply as 'Mistress Martin' or 'Mistress Jones'.

At first descriptive names were confined to a single virtue: Faith, Hope, Love, Charity, Increase, Continent and the like, but within a generation Puritan parents were giving their children names that positively rang with righteousness: Flie-Fornication, Misericordia-Adulterina, Job-Raked-Out-of-the-Ashes, Small-Hope, Praise-God, Fear-Not, The-Lord-Is-Near. Names began to sound rather like cheerleaders' chants, so that among the early Pilgrims we find Fight-the-Good-Fight-of-Faith Wilson, Be-Courteous Cole, Kill-Sin Pemble, and the memorably euphonious Safely-on-High Snat. Occasionally the desire for biblical fidelity resulted in names of daunting sonorosity: Mahershalalhasbaz, Zaphenathpaneah, Zerubbabel and Mene Mene Tekel Upharsin. And sometimes parents simply closed their eyes and stabbed blindly at the Bible, placing their faith in Providence to direct them to an apposite word, which accounts for the occasional occurrence of such relative inanities as Maybe Barnes and Notwithstanding Griswold.[30]

Although these memorable appellations naturally attract our attention, they were not in fact all that numerous. Careful tabulation has shown that no more than 4 per cent of Puritan children were given unconventional names. Most infants were in fact endowed with names that were unimaginative to the point of timidity. Just three names – Sarah, Elizabeth and Mary – accounted for more than half of all the females christened in the Massachusetts Bay Colony in the 1600s.[31] Where parents applied more adventurous names, generally it was not to venerate the Bible, but to honour some progenitor – as with the celebrated clergyman and author Cotton Mather, who was named not for that useful fibre, but for his mother Maria Cotton (who was, entirely incidentally, the stepsister of her husband, Increase Mather, and thus was not only Cotton's mother but simultaneously his aunt).[32]

By the turn of the eighteenth century, striking forenames had

fallen out of use almost entirely. At the same time, there arose a
tendency to encourage a measure of uniformity with surnames. In
Britain family names often came, indeed still come, with a variety
of acceptable spellings: *Lea/Leigh/Lee, More/Mohr/Moore, Coke/
Cook, Cooper/Cowper, Smith/Smythe* (and even in my acquaintance *Shmith*). Early on in America names tended to standardize
around a single simplified spelling, so that *Browne* generally
became *Brown, Hull* became *Hall, Newsholme* became *Newsom*
and so on.[33]

From the earliest days, immigrants from non-English-speaking
countries likewise adapted their names to ease their way into
American society. Paul Revere's father, a French Huguenot
refugee, arrived in America as Apollos Rivoire.[34] James Bowdoin,
the Massachusetts revolutionary leader and founder of Bowdoin
College, was the son of a Pierre Baudoin. George Custer, of Last
Stand fame, emerged from a long line of Kösters. The Rockefellers
began as Roggenfelders, the Westinghouses as Wistinghausens.
Billy Sunday, the baseball player and evangelist, came from a
family of Sonntags. Buffalo Bill Cody's family name was adapted
from Kóthe. President Hoover's forebears were Hubers.[35] Wendell
Willkie's father was named Willcke.

Often the transition was relatively straightforward. Langestraet
easily became Longstreet, as Wannemacher turned naturally into
Wanamaker, Schumacher into Shoemaker, Jung into Young,
Schmidt and Müller into Smith and Miller, Blumental into
Bloomingdale, Braun into Brown, Grün into Green, Blum into
Bloom, Fjeld into Field, Oehms into Ames, Koch into Cook,
Nieuwhuis into Newhouse, Pfoersching into Pershing, Jansson,
Jonsson and Johansson into Johnson, Olesen and Olsson into
Olsen. Occasionally slightly more ingenuity was required, as when
Bon Coeur was turned into Bunker and Wittenachts became
Whitenecks. When folk etymology wouldn't do, direct translation
was often the most convenient solution, which is how the French
Feuillevert evolved into the *Greenleaf* in John Greenleaf Whittier.
The result is that American surnames often have an Anglo-Saxon
homogeneity that belies their origins. Miller and Johnson, for
instance, are far more common family names in America than in
Britain, and almost entirely because of adoption by Germans and
Scandinavians with similar, but other, names.

As America moved into the second half of the nineteenth century, immigration increasingly moved away from the comfortably adaptable Germanic heartland of Europe and to the southern and eastern fringes. People began arriving on American shores bearing names far less accommodating to English sensibilities and phonetics. Polish names like Krzyanowski, Szybczyński, Mikolajezyk and Gwzcarczyszyn[36] clearly represented a greater linguistic challenge than Braun or Olesen. Even the shortest of eastern European names – notably such Czech manifestations as Krč, Chrt, Hnát and Srch – often seemed to defy easy assimilation. There was the problem, too, that some groups like the Hungarians put their last names first and others, notably Armenians, didn't normally go in for last names at all. Sometimes a foreign name could be translated into an English equivalent, so that many Poles named Kowalczyk and Czechs named Kovář became Smiths. Sometimes a more manageable middle name was pressed into service, as when Josef Konrad Korzienowski became the writer Joseph Conrad. Long names were generally truncated, so that Greeks with names like Pappadimitracoupoulos became, almost inevitably, Pappas, and Poles named Mikolajezyk became Mikos (and often further refined to some less visibly ethnic form like Michaels).

Sometimes the old name was abandoned altogether to be replaced with a shiny new name with a good American ring to it, as when the Italian boxer Andrea Chiariglione became the American boxer Jim Flynn. Not infrequently, some members of a family would adapt the family name while others would stay faithful to their cultural heritage. Thus the novelist Theodore Dreiser and the song writer Paul Dresser ('On the Banks of the Wabash') were brothers.[37]

For Jewish immigrants the question of an American identity had an additional dimension. For those who wished to function in the wider world – for instance in show business – a visibly Jewish name could be a handicap, so Israel Baline became Irving Berlin, Mendel Berlinger turned into Milton Berle and Nathan Birnbaum took to the stage as George Burns. This was hardly a new problem for Jews. Mencken quotes a tale from Samuel Pepys's diary about a Dr Levy who had petitioned a court to let him change his name to Sullivan and then a month later sought permission to change it again to

Kilpatrick. 'On request for ye reason, he telleth ye court that ye patients continually ask of him, "What was your name *before*?" If granted ye change, he shall then tell them "Sullivan".'[38] Often, Jews had no particular attachment to their surnames. Those from Austria and parts of Germany had been compelled to adopt German surnames only sixty or seventy years before. Often the names imposed on them had been unattractive to begin with, as with Geldwässer ('gold water'), a venerable euphemism for urine, Wanzenknicker ('louse picker') and Eselkopf ('ass's head'), and they were only too glad to shed them.

Pronunciations were adapted too to conform to American patterns, especially among Italians with names like Capone and Stallone, where the final vowel, always voiced in Italy, often became silent in America. This happened with English names as well, so that *Cecil, Purcell, Maurice* and *Barnett* became in America 'seesil', 'pur-*sell*', 'mo-*reece*' and 'bar-*nett*'.

Despite the manifold pressures to conform, and the incontestable convenience that came with adopting a simple American name, millions stuck loyally to whatever monicker fate and geography had brought them. A glance through the index of a book on the history of American football, which I happen to have before me, throws up such uncompromisingly un-American names as Dick Modjelewski, Ed Abbatticchio, Knute Rockne, Bronsilaw 'Bronko' Nagurski, Fred Benirschke, Harry Stuhldreder, Zeke Bratkowski, W. W. Heffelfinger, Jim Kiick, Dan Pasquariello and Alex Wojchiechowicz, and virtually any other list of Americans (except for Presidents and film stars) would show equal ethnic diversity. Indeed, there is a growing tendency to resurrect old family names, as with the actor Emilio Estevez, the son of the actor Martin Sheen (né Ramon Estevez) and the writer David Wallechinsky, son of Irving Wallace.

Finally, there remains a group of immigrants that tends to get left out of discussions of this type: American blacks. Conventional wisdom has it that blacks, long denied the dignity of a surname under slavery, conveniently took the names of their former owners upon being freed. However, the evidence – not to mention common sense – suggests that blacks showed no special affection for the names of their masters. Those names that feature most prominently among southern slave-holders – Pinckney, Randolph and

Rutledge, for instance – appear only incidentally among any list of black names. It appears that most freed slaves either adopted an innocuous American name – Johnson, Jones, Smith, Robinson and the like – or named themselves for a hero. Hence the relatively large number of Afro-Americans named Washington, Jefferson, Brown (from the abolitionist John Brown) and Howard (after General O. O. Howard, head of the Freedmen's Bureau in the years just after the Civil War) – but not, oddly and inexplicably, Lincoln.

8

'Manifest Destiny': Taming the West

In 1803, Thomas Jefferson made one of history's better buys. For about three cents an acre, he purchased from the French all or most of what would become twelve states – Arkansas, Iowa, Kansas, Louisiana, Minnesota, Missouri, Montana, Nebraska, Oklahoma, Wyoming and the two Dakotas – at a stroke more than doubling the size of the United States. It was known as the Louisiana Purchase.

The natural thing was to commission someone to explore and chart the new territory. In fact Jefferson already had. Months before the Louisiana Purchase had been considered even a possibility, he had authorized Meriwether Lewis to lead an illegal exploratory party across the western territories. By the time word reached Lewis that most of the country to the west was now in American hands, he was already halfway to St Louis.

Lewis had grown up near Monticello as Jefferson's protégé, 'almost a son' to him, in the words of one biographer,[1] and was something of an odd choice to lead the expedition. Though he had military experience, he was not particularly acquainted with wilderness travel and for the past two years had led a decidedly soft life as Jefferson's private secretary in the White House. His schooling was minimal. He had no training as a botanist or cartographer and spoke no Indian languages. More ominously, he was given to disturbing mood swings euphemistically called 'hypochondriac affections'. For co-leader he turned to his friend William Clark. Despite coming from a distinguished family (his

brother was the Revolutionary War general George Rogers Clark),
Clark had even less schooling than Lewis and had about him the
perennial air of a frontiersman, but he was steady, resourceful and
brave. They made, almost miraculously, a perfect pair of leaders.

On 14 May 1804 they set off up the Missouri at the head of a
ragtag party consisting of thirty-two soldiers, ten civilians, one
slave (Lieutenant Clark's servant, York), a teenaged Indian guide
and interpreter named Sacagawea and her new-born baby, two
other interpreters and Lewis's dog Scannon. They would be gone
almost two and a half years and would travel some eight thousand
miles through unknown and often hostile territory, yet just one
member of the party would die, from a ruptured appendix.

They were by no means the first whites to venture into the vast
North American interior. As early as 1680, some eight hundred
French fur trappers were at work in the West,[2] and by 1804 both
French and English traders and trappers were a common sight all
along the sprawling watershed of the Missouri River. In 1792-3 a
Briton named Alexander Mackenzie had travelled over the
Canadian Rockies to British Columbia, and in doing so had
become the first person of European descent to reach the Pacific
overland. Many more had reached the west coast by sea, as Lewis
and Clark discovered when Pacific North-west Indians greeted
their arrival with a hearty 'son-of-a-pitch' in the evident belief that
this was an English call of friendship.[3] They also encountered an
Indian woman with the name 'Jonathan Bowman' crudely tattooed
on her leg.[4] In 1801 the explorer Mackenzie published an
influential book, *Voyages from Montreal . . . through the Continent
of North America, to the Frozen and Pacific Oceans,* in which he
suggested that the British pre-empt the United States in the western
territories while the chance was there. It was this alarming prospect
that had led Jefferson to initiate the Lewis and Clark expedition.

Though Lewis and Clark were not the first to venture into the
western territories they were the first to approach the matter
scientifically. With unflagging diligence they labelled, mapped and
inspected everything that passed before them, recording their
findings in their famous journals, which still make marvellous
reading today. It is impossible to read Clark's notes in particular
without developing a swift affection for his rough spelling and
erratic grammar, which at times, in the words of George R.

Stewart, 'approached the inspired'. From his first entry upon setting off – 'We proceeded on under a jentle brease up the Missourie'[5] – his directness of description and eccentricity of composition make the whole hazardous undertaking come alive:

> Sunday 25th a fair morning river rose 14 Inch last night, the men find numbers of Bee Trees, & take great quantities of honey, at 11 oClock 24 Sauckees Came pass from St Louis, and asked for Provisions.... Guterge [his spelling of Goodrich] returned with Eggs & [illegible], Willard brought in 10 pr. Hinges George Shannon Caught 3 large Cat fish – The musquetors are verry bad this evening.[6]

Under his uncertain hand, *circumference* became *secumpherance*, *rheumatism* became *rhumertism*, and *Missouri* became almost anything – *Missouris, Missouries, Missourie* – often taking on two spellings in the same line. *Sacagawea*, the heroic Indian girl who guided the party across the wilderness, he wisely steered clear of, referring to her as 'the squar'. Lewis, though himself an erratic speller, brought a more assured style to the journals. Between them they coined almost a thousand terms for animals, plants and features previously unrecorded on the landscape. They discovered 178 plants and 122 animals, among them the grizzly bear and great-tailed fox, and several species of pike, catfish and squirrels. No other explorers or naturalists in American history have named more objects.

Among the words not previously recorded in English are *great plains, prairie dog* (though Clark preferred *ground rat*) and *cache* for a secret hole in the ground (taken evidently from French trappers and spelled, almost inevitably, 'carsh' by Clark). Some of their words didn't catch on. Their term *small wolves* was eventually displaced by the Mexican-Spanish *coyote* (from the Nahuatl *coyotl*). They also named every feature of the landscape that didn't have a known name already, though quite a number did. *Yellowstone*, for instance, is no more than Lewis's literal translation of the French trappers' *Roche Jaune*. Yet relatively few of their geographic names survived. They gave the noble name Philanthropy River to a tributary of the Missouri, but it didn't stick. Later passers-by renamed it Stinking Water. The Lewis River later became the Shoshone. Philosophy River became Willow Creek.

Despite having three interpreters to call on, Lewis and Clark often encountered extraordinary language difficulties with the native Americans. At one meeting, in a kind of pass-the-parcel round of translating, Lewis's English was translated into French by one listener, from French into Minitari by another, from Minitari into Shoshone by the next person in line and finally from Shoshone into Nez Percé. The Indians themselves obviated such difficulties with a universal sign language of about a hundred gestures, which could communicate, if baldly, most needs. The party also experienced remarkable good fortune, most notably during a potentially tense encounter with Indians when Sacagawea realized that one of the opposing braves was her brother.

After the expedition Jefferson appointed Lewis governor of the Louisiana Territory. In October 1809, three years after the expedition's completion and while aged just thirty-four, the great explorer died in exceedingly odd circumstances in a back-country inn called Grinder's Tavern along the Natchez Trace in Tennessee. Clearly suffering a severe outbreak of his 'hypochondriac affections', he began behaving in an odd and paranoid manner – to the extent that the proprietor of the lodgings moved out of the house and into an outbuilding. For hours Lewis could be heard talking and shouting to himself. Then at some time late in the night gunshots were heard and all went quiet. In the morning Lewis was found with terrible wounds – half his skull was blown away and he had other self-inflicted injuries all over – but still conscious. He begged the proprietor to put him out of his misery, but the proprietor refused. Lewis died later that day. His friend and colleague William Clark fared rather better. He became governor of the Missouri Territory and commanded it with distinction, though he never did learn to spell.

For the better part of a century Lewis and Clark's scientific and linguistic achievements went almost wholly unremarked. Not until 1893, when a researcher and naturalist named Elliott Coues rediscovered their all but forgotten manuscripts mouldering in a cupboard at the American Philosophical Society in Philadelphia and produced an annotated edition of their journals, were they at last accorded recognition as naturalists, cartographers and ethnologists.[7]

Jefferson thought it would take a thousand years for Americans to populate the vast emptiness of the West,[8] but he hadn't reckoned on the great waves of immigration of the nineteenth century and the odd 'restlessness of character' that so fascinated Tocqueville.[9] From the start, Americans seldom stayed anywhere long. Jamestown was a ghost town less than a century after it was founded. Few states haven't seen their state capitals move at least once and often more. Just between the Revolution and War of 1812, a period of roughly thirty-five years, eight of the original thirteen colonies moved their seats of government. Further west, capitals changed even more often. Indiana moved its from Vincennes to Corydon and finally to Indianapolis. Illinois went from Kaskaskia to Vandalia and on to Springfield.[10] *Frontier,* which meant (and still means) a national border in British English, took on in America the new sense of the ever-moving dividing line between wilderness and civilization.

Towns were established with high hopes and, if things didn't work out, abandoned without hesitation. In 1831 Abraham Lincoln moved to New Salem, Illinois. Six years later, trade on the nearby Sangamon River proving disappointing, he and everyone else abandoned the community and scattered to more promising parts. All over the West towns came and went. For every Chicago and Milwaukee that thrived thousands of others passed quietly away. Iowa alone had 2,205 communities fade into ghost towns in its first century.[11]

Before the 1800s *city* was a term usually reserved for substantial communities, but in nineteenth-century America it began to be applied to almost any cluster of houses, however modest. To this day America is dotted with 'cities' for which the term is patently overambitious – places like Republican City, Nebraska (pop. 231), Barnes City, Iowa (pop. 266), Rock City, Illinois (pop. 286). But what we tend to forget is that in America dusty hamlets *could* become cities, and almost overnight.

The boom town *par excellence* was a little community on the shores of Lake Michigan called Fort Dearborn. In 1832 it had fewer than a hundred inhabitants. Sixty years later, renamed Chicago, it boasted a million inhabitants and was the largest grain market in the world.[12] No community in history has risen to greatness so swiftly. As Daniel Boorstin has noted: 'Mankind had required at least a million years to produce its first urban community of a million people. Chicagoans accomplished this feat in less than a century.'[13] What made it possible to house such a mass of people in so short a period was a Chicago invention that went by the odd name of *balloon frame construction*. This revolutionary method of building, in which light but sturdy timber frames are hammered together, then hoisted into place, was invented by Augustine Taylor in Chicago in 1833, and was so ingeniously unimprovable that it is still almost universally used in the building of American homes. *Balloon frame* was not Taylor's term. It was coined by sceptical carpenters to denigrate the method because of its extraordinary lightness and presumed frailty.[14] When Taylor used the method to construct Chicago's first Catholic church, nearly everyone thought that the building would be carried off like a tent by the first strong winds. Needless to say it was not, and soon the method was being copied everywhere.

To Americans 'the West' was an ever-changing concept. At the time of the first federal census in 1790, 95 per cent of America's four million people lived hard by the eastern seaboard and 'the West' was virtually everything else. By the 1820s, it extended not much beyond the Appalachians. Kentucky's leading paper of the day was called the *Argus of Western America*. Even as late as mid- century a chronicler like Charles Dickens could venture only as far as St Louis, still the better part of a thousand miles short of the Rockies, and plausibly claim to have seen the West.

The move to the West as we now know it began in earnest in the mid-1840s when the expression *Oregon fever* erupted. Encouraged by the government to settle the north-western territory claimed also by Britain, homesteaders set off in their thousands for a new life at the end of the Oregon Trail, following a route blazed by trappers twenty years before. The phrase that summed up America's new assertive attitude to western development was coined by the editor of the *Democratic Review*, John O'Sullivan, in 1845 when he wrote that it was 'our manifest destiny to overspread the continent allotted by Providence for the free development of our yearly multiplying millions'.[15] The peopling of the West became not just an opportunity to be seized, but a kind of mission.

Oregon Trail is a somewhat misleading term. For one thing, it wasn't a trail in the sense of a well-defined track. It was almost entirely a notional corridor, highly variable in width, across the grassy plains. Moreover, after the first few years relatively few of those who travelled the trail were heading for Oregon. Once past the Rockies, they instead broke off and made for the gold fields of California.

One of the great myths of the westward migration, compounded by a thousand movies, was that the immigrants lumbered over the prairies in Conestoga wagons. These sturdy vehicles were, in the words of the historian George R. Stewart, 'uselessly heavy for the long pull to Oregon or California'.[16] They did haul some freight west, but almost never did they transport families. Instead westward immigrants used lighter, smaller and much nimbler wagons universally known as *prairie schooners*. These were hauled not by horses, but by mules or oxen, which could withstand the hardships of prairie crossings far better than any horse could. A final myth engendered by Hollywood was that wagons gathered in a circle whenever under attack by Indians. They didn't, and for the simple reason that the process would have been so laborious to organize that the party would very probably have been slaughtered before the job was even a quarter accomplished.

Wagons were covered with canvas, as in the movies, though that word was seldom used; the material was more generally known in the nineteenth century as *twill*. Though *wagon train* was also used (it is first recorded in 1849), the term wasn't particularly apt. For much of the journey the wagons fanned out into an advancing line up to ten miles wide to avoid each other's dust and the ruts of earlier travellers – and providing yet another obstacle to their forming into circles.

Many of the early homesteaders had only the faintest idea of what they were letting themselves in for, and often through no fault of their own. Until well into the third decade of the nineteenth century ignorance of the West remained so profound that maps were frequently sprinkled with fanciful rivers – the Multnomah, the Los Mongos, the Buenaventura – and with a great inland sea called the Timpanogos. Those who went west, incidentally, didn't think of themselves as still being in America. Until about the time of the Civil War, *America* was generally taken to signify the eastern states, so that accounts of the time commonly contain statements like 'Some people here [in Oregon] are talking about going back to

America' or 'We'll go back to America. Dressed up slick and fine' (from, respectively, the *New York Tribune* in 1857 and the *Rocky Mountain News* in 1860).

The landscape they found was so strikingly different that it required new words. Although *great plains* had been used as early as 1806, the grassy flatlands west of the Missouri were usually called *the barrens*, or sometimes *the great dismal*, until the French *prairie* began to supersede it. *Prairie*, from an old French word for meadow, had been in use in America since colonial times, originally signifying a piece of wild open ground enclosed by forest. *Desert*, too, was modified to suit the peculiar landscape of the West. Originally it had signified any uninhabited place (a sense preserved in *deserted*). Thus *Great American Desert*, first noted in 1834, described not just the scrubby arid lands of the south-west, but also the rich grasslands to the north. Much of the landscape that we now think of as desolate and forbidding was nothing like as barren then as it is today. When the western migrants arrived, much of the south-west was covered in waving grass. They simply grazed it away.[17] Even so, there was no shortage of places that proved treacherous beyond endurance. One party that tried taking a short cut to California in 1849 discovered to its cost a killing expanse that they named Death Valley.

The traditional western stagecoach, notwithstanding its perennial role in movies and TV programmes, saw active service for only a little over a decade. The first service was inaugurated in 1858 when the Overland Mail Company began twice-weekly trips from St Louis to San Francisco. Its Concord coaches (named for Concord, New Hampshire, where they were developed) were intended principally to carry mail and freight but also carried up to nine passengers at $200 each for the westward trip and $150 for the eastward. (Eastward was cheaper because the traffic was largely one way.) All being well, the trip took a little over three weeks. In 1866 the Overland Mail Company was sold to Wells, Fargo and Co., but it was put out of business by the opening of the first transcontinental railway three years later.

Even more short-lived was the Pony Express. Inaugurated on 3 April 1860, it was designed to carry mail as quickly as possible from St Joseph, Missouri, to Sacramento, California. Riders rode in relays, each averaging fifty to eighty miles a day (though some occasionally went as far as three hundred miles without a rest), carrying a mail pouch or *mochila*, as it was more normally called. On an average run, seventy-five riders would cover the two thousand miles between Missouri and California in ten and a half days. It was a fabulous achievement, but economic folly. Setting up and maintaining riders, horses and way stations was an exceedingly costly business. The express's investors sank $700,000 into the service and, despite charging a whopping $5 an ounce for letters, never made back more than a fraction of their costs. By late 1861, barely nineteen months after starting, the Pony Express was out of business, a victim of the newly installed telegraph and its own inescapable costs.

For those who wished not to face the perils and discomforts of travelling overland, the alternative was to go by sea. One option was to take a ship to Panama through the Gulf of Mexico, cross the fifty-mile-wide Isthmus of Panama (or Isthmus of Darien as it was then commonly called) on horseback and catch another ship up the Pacific coast. But connections were uncertain and it was not uncommon to be stranded there for weeks at the mercy of steamy heat and yellow fever. The other option was to go by ship around Cape Horn, a 15,000-mile journey that seldom took less than six months and sometimes twice that in conditions that rarely rose above the squalid. Altogether, getting to California was a dangerous and uncomfortable affair.

But that didn't stop anyone – not at least after gold was found there in 1849. In the first four years of the gold rush, the population of California went from 20,000 to just under 225,000. In those same four years, $220 million in gold was pulled from the ground or sluiced from its glittering creeks. The gold rush not only enriched a fortunate few, but enlivened the language. Many of the terms that arose from it soon made their way into more general usage, among them *pay dirt, pan out, to stake a claim* and *to strike it rich*,[18] all of which were soon being used in senses far removed from the idea of scrabbling in the earth for nuggets of gold.

One of the many side-effects of the gold rush was the invention of hard-wearing canvas trousers and bib overalls in San Francisco in the 1850s. The inventor was of course Levi Strauss, who had travelled west with a load of canvas (or twill) intending to make tents, but found a much greater demand for trousers that would stand up to the wear and tear of life in the mining camps. He didn't call them *jeans*. In the 1850s the word signified not an item of apparel but a type of cloth. It is a corruption of *Genoa*, the Italian city where it was first woven. Not until this century did denim (itself a corruption of *serge de Nîmes,* from the French city) trousers become generally known as jeans and not until the 1940s were people calling them *Levis*.

The traffic to California wasn't all from east to west. Many thousands came from China. At the beginning of the gold rush, just 325 Chinese lived in California; two years later the number had jumped to 25,000. In the next three decades it increased twelvefold, to over 300,000, or nearly one-tenth of the population. Because of political turmoil in China, almost all of them came from just six small districts in Guangdong province.

The Chinese, who for entirely mysterious reasons were commonly known in the West as 'Johnnies', were treated exceptionally badly. Because they were prepared to work hard for little pay, and because their appearance precluded easy assimilation, they were often pointlessly attacked and occasionally even massacred. Even banding together didn't provide much protection. In 1885, in Rock Springs, Wyoming, a mob swooped on a community of five hundred Chinese for no reason other than that they didn't like them, and left twenty-eight dead. Such was the prejudice against the Chinese that in some western courts they were not even permitted to plead self-defence. Thus there arose the telling western expression 'He doesn't have a Chinaman's chance.'

Many of the terms that we most closely associate with the West were not coined there at all. Abigail Adams used *desperadoes* to describe the participants in Shays' Rebellion long before the word attached itself to western bandits.[20] Though the chuck wagon (from a slang term for food, which survives incidentally in the expression *upchuck*) became widely used in the West – one of the most popular models was built by the Studebaker Company of Detroit – the term was widely used in Kentucky long before the Oregon Trail was even thought of. *Son of a gun* and *to bite the dust* were both Anglicisms brought to America by early colonists. *Posse* has been in English since the Middle Ages. Much of the inflated speech that seems such a natural accompaniment to the high-spirited lifestyle of the West – formations like *absquatulate* and *rambunctious* – had originated long before in New England.[21] Likewise, the *Stetson* hat, also often called a *John B.*, was an eastern innovation. Its originator, John Batterson Stetson, was a Philadelphian who never intended the hat to be exclusively associated with guys on horses.

Even *cowboy* was an old term. It was first used during the Revolutionary War as a disparaging epithet for loyalists. In its modern sense it dates from 1867 when an entrepreneur named Joseph McCoy (another oft-named candidate for the source of the expression *the real McCoy*) began employing cowboys to run longhorn cattle up the Chisholm Trail from Texas to his railhead at Abilene, Kansas. He became immensely successful and by the early 1870s was shipping out up to 500,000 head of cattle a year from the dusty town. (*Cow town* didn't enter the language until 1885.)

To distinguish one herd of cattle from another, ranchers began using brands, and these developed a complicated argot of their own. A letter tipped on its side was called 'lazy'. A line underneath a letter was a 'bar'. A letter written with curving lines rather than straight ones was called 'running'. And from these came the names of many ranches: the Lazy X Bar, the Running W and so on.[22] There were literally thousands of brands – 5,000 in Wyoming and nearly 12,000 in Montana by the early 1890s – and publishers made a good income from producing annual brand books. Unmarked cattle were called *mavericks*. The name comes from a Texas rancher named Samuel A. Maverick who refused to brand his cattle – though whether because he was eccentric or lazy or simply hoped to claim all unmarked cattle as his own is a matter of long dispute among western historians.[23]

Hollywood has left us with the impression that the West was peopled by little but cowboys. In fact, farmers outnumbered them by about a thousand to one. Even at their peak there were fewer than 10,000 working cowboys, at least a quarter of them black or Mexican (and the remainder not a great deal higher up the nineteenth-century social scale).[24]

The cowboy of popular imagination was largely the invention of two highly unlikely easterners. The first was the artist Frederic Remington, whose action-filled, hyper-realist paintings were in fact largely studio creations based on a lively imagination. He never saw any real cowboys in action. For one thing he was immensely fat

– much too fat to get on a horse, let alone ride it into the midst of Indian battles. Even more crucially, by the time he made his first trip to the West the cowboy age was all but over.

No less disconnected from life around the camp-fire was his close friend Owen Wister, who mythologized cowboys on paper in much the same way that Remington mythologized them on canvas. Cowboys had begun to appear as heroes in dime novels as early as the 1880s (the genre appears to have been the invention of one Prentiss Ingraham), but it wasn't until Wister published *The Virginian* in 1902 that the cowboy (or *cow-boy* as Wister insisted on spelling it) truly became a national figure. Wister was the quintessential *dude* (a word of unknown origin dating in a western context only from 1883, though it was used earlier in the East). Scion of a wealthy Philadelphia family and grandson of the celebrated actress Fanny Kemble, he was a Phi Beta Kappa at Harvard, a close friend of Teddy Roosevelt, and of a decidedly delicate disposition. Unlike Remington, he actually travelled in the West, though he hardly hit the dusty trail. He was sent west by his parents to recover from a nervous breakdown and was chaperoned throughout by two spinsters.

Although Wister introduced many of the conventions of cowboy fiction – the use of a hero without a name, the introduction of a climactic shoot-out between the hero and villain, the immortal line 'When you call me that, *smile!*' – his main achievement was to make the cowboy a respectable figure for fictionalization. He began the process with a now forgotten novel called *Lin McLean,* but brought it to full fruition with *The Virginian.* The story of an easterner (unnamed of course) who goes west, it struck a chord with millions of Americans, but particularly among the better educated at whom it was aimed. The book sold 50,000 copies in its first four months and three million copies overall, went through fifteen printings in its first seven years, and was made into a Broadway play that ran for ten years, and subsequently into a seminal film.

The mythologizing of the West was consolidated in the immensely popular novels of writers like C. J. Mulford, creator of the absurdly uncowboylike Hopalong Cassidy, and Zane Grey, a New York dentist who knew almost nothing of the West but refused to let that get in the way of a good tale.[25] The first movie western, *The*

Great Train Robbery, came in 1903. By the 1920s, westerns accounted for nearly a third of all Hollywood features. But their real peak came in the 1950s on television. During their zenith year, 1959, the American television viewer could choose among twenty-eight western series running on network television – an average of four a night.[26]

It is decidedly odd that these figures of the West, whose lives consisted mostly of herding cows across lonely plains and whose idea of ultimate excitement was a bath and a shave and a night on the town in a place like Abilene, should have exerted such a grip on the popular imagination. As the historian William W. Savage has put it: 'The cattle business and cowboy life were hardly the stuff of which legends are made ... The cowboy is a symbol for many things – courage, honour, chivalry, individualism – few of which have much foundation in fact.'[27]

Cowboys certainly didn't spend a lot of time shooting each other. In the ten years that Dodge City was the biggest, rowdiest cow town in the world, only thirty-four people were buried in the infamous Boot Hill Cemetery, and almost all of them had died of natural causes. Incidents like the shoot-out at the OK Corral or the murder of Wild Bill Hickock became famous by dint of their being so unusual. Those who *were* shot seldom got up again. Scarcely a western movie has been made in which at least one character hasn't taken a bullet in the thigh or shoulder but shrugged it off with a manly wince and continued firing. As one observer has put it: 'One would think that the human shoulder was made of some self-healing material, rather like a puncture-proof tire.'[28] In fact, nineteenth-century bullets were so slow, relatively speaking, and so soft that they almost never moved cleanly through the victim's body. Instead, they bounced around like a pinball and exited through a hole like that created by a fist punched through paper. Even if a bullet miraculously missed the victim's vital organs, he would almost invariably suffer deep and incapacitating shock and bleed to death within minutes.

For the most part, trust and goodwill were no more lacking in the lawless environment of the West than elsewhere. As Boorstin notes, it is no accident that the term *pardner* – originally conveying a sense much deeper and more trusting than that of a casual friendship – entered the language in the gold fields of California around 1850.[29]

Justice was often peremptory and swift – thieves and cheats on riverboats were generally put down on the nearest sand-bar and left to make their way back to civilization, if they could – but at least justice there was. Land-based miscreants were often dealt with by *kangaroo courts* – impromptu convocations that seldom bothered with the niceties of due process. This rather odd and interesting term has been traced to Texas, a place notably deficient in antipodean marsupials, and was first recorded in 1849. It appears to have no connection to Australia – the expression was unknown there until introduced from America – and may derive from the idea of a criminal being bounced like a kangaroo to the gallows, but that is no more than conjecture.

Among other terms that appear to have arisen in the West are *bogus, rip-roaring, joint* in the sense of a gathering spot, *piker* for an untrustworthy character (it is sometimes said to be a reference to the inhabitants of Pike County, Missouri, but more probably comes from *turnpike*), *to be caught between a rock and a hard place, six-shooter* for a Colt revolver, *gunplay, holdup,* and *crook,* plus scores of others that didn't survive into the twentieth century, such as *dying with throat trouble* and *the big jump* for being hanged. *Bogus* is wholly mysterious and *crook* only slightly less so. *Crook* may have something to do with the fact that a shepherd's crook is not straight but bent (*bent* was in the nineteenth century a common adjective for a criminal, and still is in Britain) but written evidence is lacking.

Many of the terms we most closely associate with cowboys and life amid the purple sage didn't appear in the West until much later, if at all. *Dogy,* a motherless calf, memorialized in the song lyrics 'git along, little dogy, git along', has not been found earlier than 1903.[30] *Hoosegow,* for a jail, didn't enter the language until 1920. Bandits were seldom called that; *banditti* was the more common term. *Bounty hunter, gunslinger* and *to have an itchy trigger finger* were all the inventions of Hollywood scriptwriters.[31]

The lexical creations of cowboys, miners and other western Americans become incidental when compared with the legacy of Spanish terms from the West. These at one time numbered well over a hundred. Among the more notable survivors we find *lasso* (1819), *sombrero* (1823), *patio* (1827), *corral* (1829), *lariat* (from *la reata*, 'the rope', 1831), *canyon* (1834), *plaza* (1836), *burro, stampede* and *rodeo* (1844), *bonanza* (1844), *bronco* and *pronto* (1850), *alfalfa* (1855), *cinch* (from *cincha*, a saddle girth; 1859), *pinto* (1860) and *vigilante* (1865).[32]

Often these words had to be wrestled into shape. *Wrangler* comes from *caballerangero*. *Vamos* became *vamoose* and then *mosey*. *Vaquero*, literally 'cow handler', went through any number of variations – *buckhara*, *bakkarer*, *backayro*, *buccahro* – before finally settling into English as *buckaroo*. The *ten-gallon hat* is named not for its capacity to hold liquids (it would have to be the size of a bath-tub for that) but for the braid with which it was decorated; the Spanish for braid is *galón*.

Sometimes the English spellings of Spanish words took some time to become established. As late as the 1920s, *bronco* appeared in a famous ad for Jordan cars in this manner: 'Somewhere west of Laramie, there's a broncho-busting, steer-roping girl who knows what I'm talking about.' In the same way, G. M. Anderson, the first cowboy movie star, was sometimes represented to his fans as *Broncho Billy*, and the evidence suggests that it was pronounced by some as spelled. Meanwhile, *rancher*, from the Mexican-Spanish *rancho*, or 'mess-room', was often originally pronounced 'ranker'.

The first English-speaking immigrants to the south-west also encountered Spanish-Mexican cuisine for the first time: tacos, enchiladas, tortillas and the like. Nachos are said to be named for a certain Ignacio who made them particularly well, but the story, if true, is unsubstantiated. Unquestionably apocryphal is the old tale that Mexicans began calling Americans *gringos* because a popular marching song during the Mexican war contained the words 'Green grow the rushes'. In fact, *gringo* is not a New World term at all. It was in common use in Spain in the eighteenth century. It is a corruption of *Griego*, 'Greek', signifying unintelligible foreign babble, in much the same way as we say 'It's Greek to me.'[33]

Many other terms that are sometimes lumped in with Spanish expressions brought into English by cowboys and ranchers actually entered English much earlier, among them *adobe* and *mesa* as early as 1759, *calaboose* (from *calabozo*, 'dungeon') by 1792, and *mustang* (from *mesteño* or *mestengo*, signifying stray animals) in 1808. One of the more breathtakingly complex of these early adaptations was *maroon*. In the sense of being stranded, it began life as the Spanish *cimarrón* (literally 'one who lives on the mountain tops'), and originally signified a fugitive slave in the West Indies. Then it came to mean the offspring of such a slave. Finally it arrived at its modern sense of suffering abandonment. But the Spanish also applied the word to a tribe of Muskhogean Indians (the ones we know as *Seminoles*). In the mean time, the French had picked up the word, changed it to *marron* (their word for chestnut), and it was from there that the English naturalized it into *maroon*. Ironically, when the Seminoles were eventually driven from Florida, they were resettled in Oklahoma near the Cimmaron River. Rather less challenging was *el lagarto*, 'the lizard', which became naturalized in English as *alligator*.

Further north, French-speaking trappers provided many useful words to the settlers, notably *gopher, rendezvous, peak* for a mountain top (from the French *pic*), *badlands* (translated literally from the French *mauvaises terres*), and *park* in the sense of a mountain valley. This last named didn't survive in a general sense but lives on in some place-names, such as Estes Park, Colorado. As with Spanish, many French words came into English well ahead of the western migrations, among them *chute* (1804), *butte* and *picayune* (1805), *coulee* (1807), *depot* (1832) and *to sashay* (1836). Often they, too, went through convoluted transformations. *Lagniappe*, usually attributed to the French of New Orleans, in fact originated among the Kechuan Indians of Peru as *yapa*. The Spanish adopted it as *ñapa*. The French then took it from the Spanish and we from the French.

If the English-speaking settlers of the West didn't shoot each other much, they did shoot a lot of buffalo and a lot of Indians. The two were not unconnected. Between 1830 and 1895, the 70 million buffalo that roamed the great plains were reduced in number to just 800, most of those in zoos or touring shows. The virtual extermination of the buffalo was not simply a matter of sloppy overkill, as we are often led to believe, but the result of 'a conscious policy connived at by the railways, the army and the cattle ranchers as a means of subduing the Indians and keeping them on their reservations'.[34] During roughly the same period, the number of Indians fell from 2 million to 90,000 as war, disease, and poverty born of the loss of their lands and livelihood took their brutal toll.

To say that the Indians were often treated abysmally barely conveys at the scale of the indignity heaped upon them. Again and again, they were uprooted and moved on until they were crowded on to the meanest, most unproductive land. Though America's wars with the Indians ended in 1886 with the surrender of the great Apache chief Geronimo, their mistreatment did not end there. Between 1887 and 1934, they were deprived of a further 86 million acres. Altogether, as Howard Zinn notes, the United States made 400 treaties with the Indians and broke every one of them. They weren't even made citizens until 1924.[35]

Today no one knows how many Indians there are. All we know is how many people think they are Indians, which is of course not the same thing. Some two million Americans claimed on the 1990 census to be Indian, but that was a rise of almost 40 per cent from the 1980 census – clearly not in line with population growth.[36]

Some 300 tribes remain in America today, but much of the linguistic diversity that once existed is gone for ever. According to Dr Duane King of the National Museum of the American Indian, 'fewer than 200 [Native American] languages are spoken today, and 80 to 100 of those will probably disappear within a generation'.[37] Among those most perilously on the brink of extinction are Mandan (with only six known speakers left in 1991), and Osage (spoken by only five). Lakota, the language used in the movie *Dances with Wolves*, appears to be dead. No native speaker could be found to act as adviser to the film crew. In only half a century or so America conquered the West, but at a terrible price to its own native cultures.

The Melting-Pot: Immigration in America

I

By the early 1830s America's cotton trade with Britain had become so vast that up to a thousand ships at a time, a significant portion of the Atlantic fleet, were engaged in carrying cotton to Liverpool. The problem was that most made the return journey largely empty. Seeking out a convenient cargo for the return trip, the shipowners hit on an unusual one: people.

Never mind that their ships were never intended for passengers, that a crossing could take up to three months with the human freight crowded into fetid holds that were breeding grounds for diseases like trachoma and malignant typhus, which in the nineteenth century was so closely associated with Atlantic crossings that it was called *ship fever*. People were willing to endure almost any hardship to get to America if the price was right, and by packing the passengers in and giving them almost nothing in the way of civilizing comforts, the fares could be made not just low but effectively irresistible. By mid-century a one-way ticket in steerage (so called because it was near the ship's steering mechanism and thus noisy) could be had for as little as $12 from Liverpool to New York, and for less than $10 from Dublin. All but the most miserably destitute could scrape together that.[1]

Millions did. From 150,000 in the 1820s, the number of immigrants to America climbed steadily with each successive decade: to 600,000 in the 1830s, 1.7 million in the 1840s, 2.3 million in the 1850s. All this was happening in a much more thinly populated America, of course. The 3 million immigrants who came to the United States in the decade 1845–55 arrived in a country that had a population of only 20 million to begin with. In just twenty years, 1830–50, the proportion of foreign-born immigrants in America rose from one in a hundred to one in ten.

Never before had there been such a global exodus – and not just to America, but to Australia, Argentina, New Zealand, anywhere that showed promise, though America had by far the largest share. Between 1815 and 1915 it took in 35 million people, equivalent to the modern populations of Norway, Sweden, Austria, Ireland, Denmark and Switzerland. Seven million came from Germany, roughly 5 million each from Italy and Ireland (1.5 million more than live in Ireland today), 3.3 million from Russia, 2.5 million from Scandinavia, and in the hundreds of thousands from almost everywhere else – from Greece, Portugal, Turkey, the Netherlands, Mexico, the Caribbean, China, Japan. Even Canada provided a quarter of a million immigrants between 1815 and 1860, and nearly a million more in the 1920s.[2] For smaller countries like Sweden, Norway and Ireland, and for regions within countries, like Sicily and the Mezzogiorno in Italy, the numbers represented a significant drain on human resources. This was especially true of Ireland. In 1807 it was the most densely populated country in Europe; by the 1860s it was one of the least.[3]

Once across the ocean the immigrants tended naturally to congregate in enclaves. Almost all the migrants from Norway between 1815 and 1860 settled in just four states, Wisconsin, Minnesota, Iowa and Illinois. In much the same way, two-thirds of the Dutch were to be found in Michigan, New York, Wisconsin and Iowa. Sometimes they were given active encouragement to congregate. In the first half of the nineteenth century several German societies were formed with the express intention of so concentrating immigration in a particular area that they could in effect take it over. One German spoke for many when he dreamed of Pennsylvania becoming 'an entirely German state where . . . the beautiful German language would be used in the legislative halls and the courts of justice'. Not just in Pennsylvania, but in Texas, Missouri and Wisconsin, there were earnest hopes of colonizing all or at least a significant part of those states.[4]

In factory towns, too, immigrant groups were often concentrated to an extraordinary degree. In 1910 Hungry Hollow,

Illinois, a steel town, was home to 15,000 Bulgarians. At the same time, of the 14,300 people employed in Carnegie steel mills, almost 12,000 were from eastern Europe.[5]

Those who had neither the inclination to work in heavy industry nor the wherewithal to take up farming generally clustered in cities – even if, as was almost always the case, their backgrounds were agricultural. So effortlessly did Irish, Poles and Italians settle into urban life that we easily forget that most came from rural stock and had perhaps never seen a five-storey building or a crowd of a thousand people before leaving home. Often they arrived in such numbers as to overturn the prevailing demographics. In a single year, 1851, a quarter of a million Irish came to America, and almost all of them settled in New York or Boston. By 1855 one-third of New York's population was Irish born.[6] As immigration from northern Europe eased in the third quarter of the century, the slack was taken up by eastern European Jews. Between 1880 and 1900 an estimated one-third of the Jewish population of Europe came to America, and again settled almost exclusively in New York.[7]

By the turn of the century, New York had become easily the most cosmopolitan city the world had ever seen. Eighty per cent of its five million inhabitants were either foreign born or the children of immigrants.[8] It had more Italians than the combined populations of Florence, Genoa and Venice, more Irish than anywhere but Dublin, more Russians than Kiev. As Herman Melville put it: 'We are not so much a nation as a world.' In 1908 a British Zionist named Israel Zangwill wrote a play about the immigration experience that gave Americans a term for the phenomenon. He called it *The Melting-Pot*.

The popular image, recreated in countless movies and books from *The Godfather* to *Kane and Abel*, is of an immigrant arriving wide-eyed and bewildered at Ellis Island, being herded into a gloomy hall, subjected to an intimidating battery of medical tests and interviews, being issued a mysterious new name by a gruff and distracted immigration official, and finally stepping into the sunshine to realize that he has made it to the New World. Except possibly for the last part, it wasn't quite like that.

For one thing, until 1897 immigrants didn't pass through Ellis

Island, but through Castle Garden, a former opera house on the Battery. Even after immigration facilities were transferred to Ellis Island only steerage passengers were taken there. First- and second-class passengers were dealt with aboard their ships. Nor was Ellis Island (named, incidentally, for an eighteenth-century owner, Samuel Ellis) the drab, cheerless institution we might imagine. It was a beautiful, richly decorated complex with first-class health facilities, a roof garden with inspiring views of lower Manhattan and the Statue of Liberty, and good food for the relative few who were subjected to detention. Its Registration Hall, with its brass chandeliers and vaulted ceiling containing 29,000 tiles, each one set by hand by Italian craftsmen, was possibly 'the grandest single space in New York', according to one account.[9] Although the immigration officials were unquestionably hard-worked – they processed up to 5,000 arrivals a day and just over 1 million, four times Ellis Island's supposed capacity, in a single peak year, 1907[10] – they performed their duties with efficiency, dispatch and not a little compassion. (Many were themselves immigrants.)

Though the list of those who could be denied admission was formidable – it included prostitutes, lunatics, polygamists, anarchists, those with 'loathsome or contagious diseases', those deemed likely to become public charges, and some ninety other categories of undesirables – only about 2 per cent of applicants were denied entrance, and so few were given names they didn't willingly accede to as to make the notion effectively mythical. Far from being a cold and insensitive introduction to the New World, it was a dazzling display of America's wealth, efficiency and respect for the common person – and one that made many truly believe that they had passed into an earthly paradise.

Once landed on Manhattan the new immigrants would immediately find further manifestations of the wondrousness of America. At the landing point they would often be approached by fellow countrymen who spoke their language, but who were friendlier, easier in their manner and far more nattily dressed than any they had seen at home. With astounding magnanimity, these instant friends would offer to help the newly arrived immigrant find a job or lodgings, and even insist on carrying the grip into which he had packed his few valuables – one couldn't be too careful in New York, the immigrant would be solemnly cautioned. And then at some point the immigrant would turn to discover that his new friend had vanished with his belongings, and that he had just learned his first important lesson about life in a new land. Few newly arrived immigrants were not fleeced in some way within their first days.

Most of the millions of lower-class immigrants settled in the four square miles that were the Lower East Side, often in conditions of appalling squalor, with as many as twenty-five people sharing a single windowless room. As early as the 1860s, three-quarters of New York City's population – more than 1.2 million people – were packed into just 37,000 tenements. By the end of the century the population density of the Lower East Side was greater than in the slums of Bombay.[11] In an effort to improve conditions, a law was passed in 1869 requiring that every bedroom have a window. The result was the air-shaft. Though a commendable notion in principle, air-shafts turned out to be a natural receptacle for garbage and household slop, and thus became conduits of even greater filth and pestilence.

Crime, prostitution, begging, disease and almost every other indicator of social deprivation existed at levels that are all but inconceivable now. (Murder, however, was the exception to this rule; the rate is ten times higher today.) A study of Irish immigrants to Boston around mid-century found that on average they survived for just fourteen years in America. In 1888 the infant death rate in the Italian quarter was 325 per 1,000. That is, one-third of all babies did not survive their first year.[12]

Gangs with names like the Plug Uglies, Dead Rabbits and Bowery B'hoys roamed the streets, robbing and mugging (an Americanism dating from 1863; also sometimes called *yoking*) with something approaching impunity. Although New York had had a police force since 1845, by the second half of the nineteenth century it was thoroughly corrupt and ineffectual. Typical of the breed was Chief Inspector Alexander 'Clubber' Williams, who was brought up on charges no fewer than 358 times, but was never dismissed or even apparently disciplined. Such was his gift for corruption that by the time of his retirement he had accumulated a yacht, a house in Connecticut and savings of $300,000.[13]

Against such a background, it is hardly surprising that many immigrants fled back to Europe. At one point, for every 100

Italians who arrived in New York each year, 73 left. Perhaps as many as one third of all immigrants eventually returned to their native soil.[14]

None the less, the trend was relentlessly upward. The pattern was for one immigrant group to settle in an enclave and then disperse after a generation or so, with a new concentration of immigrants taking its place. Thus when the Irish abandoned their traditional stronghold of the Five Points area, their place was taken immediately by Italians. The old German neighbourhoods were taken over by Russian and Polish Jews. But there were finer gradations than this, particularly among the Italians. Natives of Genoa tended to accumulate along Baxter Street, while Elizabeth Street housed a large community of Sicilians. Calabrians congregated in the neighbourhood known as Mulberry Bend. Alpine Italians – those from areas like Ticino in Switzerland and the Tyrol near Austria – were almost invariably to be found on Sixty-ninth Street.

Immigrant groups had their own theatres, newspapers, libraries, schools, clubs, stores, taverns and places of worship. Germans alone could choose between 133 German-language newspapers by 1850, some of them, like the *New York Staats-Zeitung* and the *Cincinnati Volksblatt*, nearly as large and influential as their English-language counterparts.[15] Yiddish-speaking New Yorkers could in 1935 choose from a dozen daily newspapers, one of which, the *Jewish Daily Forward*, had a circulation of 125,000. Even Norwegians had forty papers in their own tongue to choose from across the nation as a whole. It was possible – indeed, in some cases normal – to live an entire life in the United States and never speak English.

Dutch, for instance, remained widely spoken in rural New York well into the nineteenth century, some two hundred years after the Netherlands had retreated from the continent. The celebrated feminist and public speaker Sojourner Truth, for instance, was raised in a Dutch household in Albany and spoke only Dutch until she reached adulthood.[16] According to Raven I. McDavid, jun., 'a few native speakers [of Dutch] survived in the remoter parts of the Hudson Valley as late as 1941'.[17]

Though the Dutch were only a passing political presence in America, their linguistic legacy is immense. From their earliest days of contact, Americans freely appropriated Dutch terms –

blunderbuss (literally 'thunder gun') as early as 1654, *scow* in 1660, *sleigh* in 1703. By the mid-eighteenth century Dutch words flooded into American English: *stoop, span, coleslaw, boss, pit* in the sense of the stone of a fruit, *bedpan, bedspread* (previously known as a *counterpane*), *cookie, waffle, nitwit* (the Dutch for 'I don't know' is 'Ik niet wiet'), the distinctive American interrogative *how come?* (a literal translation of the Dutch *hoekom*), *poppycock* (from *pappekak*, 'soft dung'), *dunderhead*, and probably the *caboodle* in *kit and caboodle*. (*Boedel* in Dutch is a word for household effects, though Dillard, it is worth noting, mentions its resemblance to the Krio *kabudu* of West Africa.)[18]

Two particularly durable Americanisms that emanate from Dutch are *Santa Claus* (out of *Sinter Klaas*, a familiar form of *St Nicholas*), first recorded in American English in 1773, and *Yankee* (probably from either *Janke*, a diminutive equivalent to the English *Johnny*, or *Jan Kees*, 'John Cheese', intended originally as a mild insult). Often Dutch words were given entirely new senses. *Snoepen*, meaning to slip candy into one's mouth when no one is watching, was transformed into the English *snoop*, meaning to spy or otherwise manifest nosiness.[19] *Docke*, 'doll', became *doxy*, a woman of easy virtue. *Hokester*, an innocuous tradesman, became *huckster*, someone not to be entirely trusted. *Doop* to the Dutch signified a type of sauce. In America, transliterated as *dope*, it began with that sense in 1807, but gradually took on many others, from a person of limited mental acuity (1851), to a kind of lubricant (1870s), to a form of opium (1889), to any kind of narcotic drug (1890s), to a preparation designed to affect a horse's performance (1900), to inside information (1910). Along the way it spawned several compounds, notably *dope fiend* (1896) and *dope addict* (1933).

Still other Dutch terms came to English by way of nautical contacts, reflecting the Netherlands' days of eminence on the seas, among them *hoist, bumpkin* (originally a short projecting spar; how it became transferred to a rustic character is unclear), *bulwark, caboose* (originally a ship's galley), *freebooter, hold, boom* and *sloop*.

As Dutch demonstrates, a group's linguistic influence bears scant relation to the numbers of people who spoke it. The Irish came in their millions, but supplied only a handful of words, notably *smithereens, lallapalooza, speakeasy, hooligan* (from Gaelic *uallachán*, a braggart[20]) and *slew* (Gaelic *sluagh*), plus one or two semantic nuances, notably a more casual approach to the distinctions between *shall* and *will*, and the habit of attaching definite articles to conditions that previously lacked them, so that whereas a Briton might go into hospital with flu or measles, Americans go to *the* hospital and suffer from *the* flu and *the* measles.

The Scandinavians imparted even less. With the exception of a very few food words like *gravlaks* and *smorgasbord*, and a few regional terms like *lutfisk* (a fish dish) and *lefse* (a pancake) that are generally unknown outside the upper Midwest and the books of Garrison Keillor, their linguistic presence in America left no trace.

Italian was slightly more productive, though again only with food words – *spaghetti, pasta, macaroni, ravioli, pizza* and the like. The few non-food Italian terms that have found a home in English, like *ciao* and *paparazzo*, came much later and not through the medium of immigration.

German by contrast prospered on American soil. Germans had been present in America from early colonial times – by 1683 they had formed their own community, Germantown, near Philadelphia – but the bulk of their immigration came in two relatively short, subsequent bursts. The first, numbering some 90,000, happened mostly in the five years from 1749 to 1754 and was largely completed by the time of the American Revolution.[21] From 1830–50 there was a second, larger influx focused mostly on urban areas like St Louis, Cincinnati, Chicago, Milwaukee, Cleveland, Buffalo and New York, in several of which the German cultural impact was not just enormous but domineering. As an editorial writer for the *Houston Post* noted at the outbreak of World War I, 'Germany seems to have lost all of her foreign possessions with the exception of Milwaukee, St Louis and Cincinnati.'[22]

Only a few German words naturalized into English date from the earlier period of immigration, notably *sauerkraut* (1776), *pretzel* (1824) and *dumb* in the sense of stupid (1825). Most Americanized German terms arose during or soon after the second wave: *to loaf* and *loafer* (1835), *ouch, bub* and *pumpernickel* (1839), *fresh* (in the sense of being forward; 1848), *kindergarten* (1852), *nix* (1855), *shyster* (probably from *Scheisse*, 'shit'; 1856), *check* (in the sense of a restaurant bill; 1868), and possibly *hoodlum* (from the Bavarian dialect word *hodalump*; 1872). Rather slower to assimilate were *delicatessen* (1889), *kaput* (1895), *fink* (from *Shmierfink*, a base character, literally 'a greasy bird'; 1892), *kaffeeklatsch* and *hockshop* (1903), and *scram* (1920). From German speakers too came the American custom of saying *gesundheit* ('health!') after a sneeze, *so long* upon departing, *and how* as an intensifier, and the practice of putting *fest* on the ends of many words – for example, *songfest*, *foodfest*, *slugfest* and *talkfest*.

Many German terms underwent some generally minor modifications of spelling to make them accord with English practice, so that *autsch* became *ouch*, *frech* became *fresh* (in the sense of impertinent), *krank* (unwell) became *cranky*, *zweiback* became *zwieback*, *Schmierkäse* became *smearcase*, and *Leberwurst* became *liverwurst*.

Equally productive, if rather less diffused through society, was Yiddish (from Middle High German *jüdisch diutsch*, 'Jewish German'), brought to America by eastern European Jews beginning in about 1880. Though based on German, Yiddish is written from right to left like Hebrew, and uses Hebrew characters. It originated in the early twelfth century in the Jewish ghettoes of central Europe. As the Jews dispersed through Europe they took Yiddish with them, enlivening it along the way with borrowings from Aramaic, Hebrew, various Slavic and Romance languages, and finally English. By the late nineteenth century it was the mother tongue of some eleven million people, a quarter of whom ended up in the United States.

As with the Germans, Jews came to America in well-defined but far more culturally distinct waves – first a small block of Sephardic Jews from Spain and Portugal (Sephardic means *Spaniard* in Hebrew) in the seventeenth and eighteenth centuries; then, from the 1820s to the 1880s, a much larger group of Ashkenazi Jews (named for the scriptural figure Ashchenaz) from elsewhere in western Europe, particularly Germany; and finally, from about 1880 to 1924, a tidal wave of eastern European Jews, especially from Poland and Russia.

Members of the first two groups were mostly educated and comfortably off, and they slipped relatively smoothly into American life. Many of the great names of American business and philanthropy – Guggenheim, Kuhn, Loeb, Seligman, Schiff,

Lewisohn, Morgenthau, Speyer – trace their origins to the first and more particularly second waves. Those in the final diaspora were by contrast almost universally ragged and poor. At least one-fourth could not read or write. To the 'uptown Jews', these new arrivals were something of an embarrassment. They referred to them as 'barbarians' or 'Asiatics', and regarded speaking Yiddish as a mark of poverty and ignorance.[23]

It was these poor eastern Europeans, however, who would more than any other group reshape America's concept of itself. They would create Hollywood, revivify the entertainment industry and provide many of America's most cherished creative talents, from the Marx Brothers to the composers George Gershwin and Irving Berlin. The latter two would get their start in the New York music district known as Tin Pan Alley (so called because of the cacophony of noise to be heard there), Gershwin with 'Swanee' and Berlin with the 1908 hit 'Yidl with Your Fiddle, Play Some Ragtime', a song that, in the words of the writer Marvin Gelfind, 'speaks volumes on the process called assimilation'.[24]

Among the Yiddish words that found their way to a greater or lesser extent into mainstream English were *to kibbitz, schmaltz* (literally 'chicken fat'), *schlemiel, schlock, keister* (rear end), *nosh, phooey, mashuggah* (crazy), *schmo* (a backward person), *schnozzle, to schlep, chutzpah, schikse* (a Christian female), *bagel, pastrami* and *glitch* (from *glitschen*, 'to slip'), plus a raft of expressions without which American English would be very much the poorer: *I should live so long, I should worry, get lost, I'm coming already, I need it like I need a hole in the head,* and many others.*

Many Yiddish terms convey degrees of nuance that make them practically untranslatable, except perhaps through humour, a quality never far off when Yiddish is under discussion. *Chutzpah*, for example, is usually defined in dictionaries as a kind of brazenness, but its subtleties cannot be better conveyed than by the

---

* It should be pointed out, however, that the closeness of German, Dutch and Yiddish often makes it impossible to ascribe a term positively to one camp. *Spook* and *dumb* could be either Dutch or German in origin, and *nosh, schlemiel* and *phooey,* among others, are as likely to have entered American English from German sources as Yiddish. More often than not, the influence most probably came from two directions simultaneously.

old joke about the boy who kills his parents, then begs mercy from the court because he has only recently been orphaned.

Such was the scale of immigration that by 1930 more than 35 per cent of white Americans were foreign born or had at least one foreign-born parent.[25] Confined as they often were to ethnic enclaves by a combination of economics, prejudice and convenience, it is a wonder that America didn't splinter into scores of linguistic pockets. But it did not, and for several reasons. First, as we have already seen, people moved on as assimilation and economic circumstances permitted. An area like that around Hester Street in New York might remain Yiddish-speaking for several generations, but the speakers were a constantly changing mass. For the most part, foreign immigrants couldn't wait to learn English and circulate in the wider world. Indeed many, particularly among the children of immigrants, refused to speak their ancestral tongue or otherwise acknowledge their ethnic grounding. In 1927, *Time* magazine pointed out, older Jews were complaining that the younger generation didn't understand Yiddish.[26] At about the same time H. L. Mencken was noting: 'In cities such as Cleveland and Chicago it is a rare second-generation American of Polish, Hungarian or Croatian stock who even pretends to know his parents' native language.'[27]

Children not only refused to learn their parents' language, but 'would reprove their parents for speaking it in front of strangers'.[28] As the historian Maldwyn Allen Jones has put it: 'Culturally estranged from their parents by their American education, and wanting nothing so much as to become and to be accepted as Americans, many second-generation immigrants made deliberate efforts to rid themselves of their heritage. The adoption of American clothes, speech, and interests, often accompanied by the shedding of an exotic surname, were all part of a process whereby antecedents were repudiated as a means of improving status.'[29]

'Every immigrant who comes here should be required within five years to learn English or leave the country,' barked Theodore Roosevelt in 1918. In fact, almost all did. Of the 13.4 million foreign-born inhabitants of the United States in 1930, all but 870,000 were deemed by census enumerators to have a workable grasp of English, and most of those who did not were recent arrivals or temporary residents (many Italians in particular came for a part of every year when there was no farm work to be had at home), or felt themselves too old to learn. Although most urban, non-native speakers of English could get by without English, most chose not to. There were to be sure troubling disparities. Only 3 per cent of German immigrants did not speak English in 1930, while almost 13 per cent of Poles and 16 per cent of Italians (rising to over 25 per cent for Italian women) existed in linguistic isolation, though within a generation those proportions would become negligible.[30]

Occasionally rearguard actions were fought. In 1890, when a law was introduced requiring English to be used exclusively in parochial schools in Milwaukee, the German community was so incensed that it turfed out the city's Republican administration and brought in a Democratic one. As late as the outbreak of World War I, Baltimore had four elementary schools that taught exclusively in German. Already, however, those trying to protect their linguistic heritage were fighting a losing battle.

All this is understandable in urban areas where it was necessary and desirable to venture out of the neighbourhood from time to time, and where mingling between various immigrant groups was inevitable. It doesn't so easily explain more isolated communities. At the turn of the century throughout the Midwest there existed hundreds of towns or clusters of towns inhabited almost exclusively by specific linguistic groups. Iowa, for instance, had Elk Horn (founded by Danes), Pella (by the Dutch) and the Amana Colonies (by Germans), among many others. In each of these places, the local populace was both homogeneous and sufficiently remote to escape the general pressure to become Americanized. Even if they learned English in order to listen to the radio and converse with outsiders, we might reasonably expect them to preserve their mother tongue for private use. In fact, almost without exception, they did not. By the 1930s in such towns English was not only the main language spoken but the only language spoken. Even those German immigrants who came to America with the intention of founding a *Kleindeutschland*, or Little Germany, in Texas or Wisconsin, eventually gave up the fight. Today it is unusual to find anyone in any such town who knows more than a few words of his ancestors' tongue. Clearly even here the desire to feel a part of the wider culture proved irresistible in the long term.

Only one group has managed to resist in significant numbers the temptations of English. I refer to the speakers of the curious dialect that is known generally, if mistakenly, as Pennsylvania Dutch. The name is an accident of history. From the early eighteenth century to almost the end of the nineteenth, *Dutch* in American English was applied not just to the language of Holland and its environs, but to much else that was bewilderingly foreign, most especially the German language – doubtless in confusion with the German word 'Deutsch'.

The Germans came to Pennsylvania at the invitation of William Penn, who believed that their ascetic religious principles fitted comfortably with his own Quaker beliefs. The German influx, eventually comprising about 100,000 people, or a third of Pennsylvania's population, was made up of a variety of loosely related sects, notably Mennonites, Schwenkenfelders, Dunkards, Moravians and Amish, but it was the Amish in particular who spoke the Palatinate dialect of High German that eventually evolved into the tongue that most know as Pennsylvania Dutch. To the Pennsylvania Dutch the language is called *Muddersrschprooch*. To scholars and the linguistically fastidious it is Pennsylvania German.

For a century and a half Pennsylvania German was largely ignored by scholars. Not until 1924, when Marcus Bachman Lambert published a *Dictionary of the Non-English Words of the Pennsylvania-German Dialect*, with just under 17,000 entries, did it at last begin to receive serious attention. Even now it remains relatively neglected as a topic of academic interest, which is a pity because few dialects provide a more instructive example of what happens to languages when they exist in isolation. As the linguist and historian C. Richard Beam has put it: 'In an age when there are billions of dollars available for trips to the moon and destruction abroad, it is very difficult to procure even a few hundred dollars to help finance the production of a dictionary of the language of the oldest and largest German language island on the North American continent.'[31]

Because it has always been primarily a colloquial, spoken dialect, very different in form and content from standard German,

Pennsylvania German presents serious problems with orthography. Put simply, almost any statement can be rendered in a variety of spellings. Here, for instance, are three versions of the same text:

> *Die Hundstage kumme all Jahr un bleibe sechs. . .*
> *De hoons-dawga cooma alla yohr un bliva sex. . .*
> *Die Hundsdaage kumme alle Yaahr un blwewe sex. . .*[32]

During its long years of isolation, Pennsylvania German has become increasingly distinct from mainstream German. Many words bear the unmistakable mark of English influence, others preserve archaic or dialectal German forms, and still others have been coined *in situ*. The drift away from standard German can be seen in the following:

PENNSYLVANIA GERMAN	STANDARD GERMAN	ENGLISH
aageglesser	Brillen	eyeglasses
bauersleit	Bauern	farmers
bauerei	Bauernhöfe	farms
elfder	elf	eleven
feierblatz	Kamin; Feuerplatz	fireplace
eensich ebbes	etwas; irgend etwas	anything
Febber	Februar	February
dabbich	ungeschickt	clumsy
alde daage	Alter	old age
Schtaagefensich	zick zack	zigzag
Grischtdaag	Weihnachten	Christmas
Nei Yarick	New York	New York

A striking feature of Pennsylvania German is its wealth of curiously specific terms. Notions and situations that other languages require long clauses to convey can often be expressed with a single word in Pennsylvania German. For example:

> *fedderschei* – the condition of being reluctant to write letters.
> *aagehaar* – an eyelash hair that grows inwardly and irritates the sclera.
> *dachdrops* – water dripping from a roof.
> *aarschgnoddle* – the globules of dung found on hair in the vicinity of the anus. (And, no, I cannot think why they might need such a word.)

At its peak in the nineteenth century Pennsylvania German was spoken in communities as far afield as Canada, the upper Midwest and the deep South. Today, according to Beam, it constitutes 'but the remnants of a unique German-American folk culture, so rapid has been the process of acculturation'.[33] Estimates for the current number of speakers range as high as 16,000 – Marckwardt in 1980 said that up to a quarter of the inhabitants of Lehigh, Lebanon and Berks counties in Pennsylvania still spoke it[34] – but the trend is implacably downward.

II

If one attitude can be said to characterize America's regard for immigration over the past two hundred years it is the belief that while immigration was unquestionably a wise and prescient thing in the case of one's parents or grandparents, it really ought to stop now. For two hundred years succeeding generations of Americans have persuaded themselves that the country faced imminent social dislocation, and eventual ruin, at the hands of the grasping foreign hordes pouring through her ports.

As early as the turn of the nineteenth century, Thomas Jefferson responded to calls for restrictions on immigration by asking, a trifle plaintively, 'Shall we refuse the unhappy fugitives from distress that hospitality which the savages of the wilderness extended to our fathers arriving in this land?' – though even he feared that immigrants with their 'unbounded licentiousness' would turn the United States into a 'heterogeneous, incoherent, distracted mass'.[35]

From the earliest days, immigrants aroused alarm and attracted epithets. For the most part, early nicknames for foreigners were only mildly abusive – for example, calling the Germans *cabbage-heads* or *krauts* (from their liking for sauerkraut) – or even rather backhandedly affectionate. This was particularly the case with the Irish, whose fondness for drinking and brawling and perceived lack of acquaintance with the higher mental processes inspired a number of mostly good-natured terms of derogation, so that a police station was an *Irish clubhouse*, a wheelbarrow was an *Irish buggy*, bricks were *Irish confetti*, an *Irish beauty* was a woman with two black eyes.

As time went on, however, the terms grew uglier and more barbed, and tended to cluster around harsh mono- or disyllables that were not so much spoken as spat: *chink, kike, dago, polack, spic, hebe*. Many of these had been floating around in English long before they became common in America. *Polack* was current in Elizabethan England and can be found in *Hamlet*. *Chink* appears to have been coined in Australia. *Sheeny*, a term of uncertain provenance, arose in the East End of London, where it was first noted in 1824. *Kike*, however, is an Americanism first recorded in 1917. It is thought to come from the *-ki* terminations on names like *Levinski*. *Bohunk*, probably a blend of *Bohemian* and *Hungarian*, is also of American origin and dates from the early 1900s. *Spic*, for Latin Americans, is said by Mencken to derive from 'no spik Inglis'. *Wop*, from *guappo*, a Neapolitan expression for a dandy or fop, was brought from Italy but took on its unseemly, more generalized shadings in the New World. (The idea that *wop* is short for 'without passport' is simply untrue.)

Geographical precision has never been a hallmark of terms of abuse. *Guinea* began, accurately, as a term to describe an African in the late eighteenth century, then attached itself to Italians in the 1880s. *Dago* originated as a shortening of *Diego* and was at first applied to Spaniards before becoming associated with Italians, Greeks, Mexicans and anyone else suspiciously foreign and swarthy in the 1880s, as did *greaser* (dating from as far back as 1836) and the more recent *greaseball*. Many others have mercifully fallen by the wayside, notably *skibby* for a Japanese (possibly, if somewhat mysteriously, from *sukebei*, 'lewdness'), and the even more obscure *gu-gu* for a Filipino, both once very common on the west coast.

Until the closing years of the nineteenth century America preserved most of its official racist animus for blacks and Indians, but in 1882 it added a new category when Chinese were expressly denied entry to the United States, and those already in the country were forbidden the rights and protections of citizenship. In 1907 the exclusion was extended to the Japanese. Throughout the early decades of this century, Orientals were compelled to attend segregated schools, and barred from owning property, providing landlords with considerable scope for abuse.[36] Into the 1950s, the immigration quotas for Asian countries were niggardly, to say the least: 185 for Japan, 105 for China, 100 each for Korea and the Philippines.

But beginning in the 1890s, as the flood of immigrants from the poorer parts of Europe turned into a deluge, racism became more sweeping, more rabid and less focused. Anti-immigrant fraternities like the American Protective Association and the Immigration Restriction League sprang up and found large followings, and books like Madison Grant's *The Passing of the Great Race* (which argued 'scientifically' that unrestricted immigration was leading to the dilution and degeneration of the national character) became best-sellers. William J. H. Traynor of the American Protective Association spoke for the mood of America when he argued against giving the vote to 'every ignorant Dago and Pole, Hun and Slav' and all the other 'criminal riffraff of Europe' that washed up on American shores.[37] Such sentiments appealed not only to the masses but extended even to people of considerable eminence. The Immigration Restriction League numbered among its supporters the heads of Harvard, Stanford, Georgia Tech, the University of Chicago and the Wharton School of Finance.[38]

Even Woodrow Wilson, who many would argue was as enlightened a President as there has been this century, could write in his *History of the American People* in 1902 that the recent immigrations had been characterized by 'multitudes of men of lowest class from the south of Italy, and men of the meaner sort out of Hungary and Poland' who collectively were endowed with neither skills nor energy 'nor any initiative of quick intelligence'. The Chinese, he added a trifle daringly, 'were more to be desired, as workmen if not as citizens'.[39]

When several Italian immigrants were lynched in New Orleans for associating with blacks, President Theodore Roosevelt made appropriate lamentations in public, but remarked in a letter to his sister that he thought it was really 'rather a good thing' and added derogatory comments about the tiresomeness of 'various dago diplomats' who had protested to him about the lynchings.[40] Even Margaret Sanger, the esteemed birth-control activist, was motivated not by a desire to give women more control over their destiny but merely by the wish to reduce the lower orders through the new science of eugenics. 'More children from the fit, less from the unfit — that is the chief issue of birth control,' she wrote.[41] Never before nor since have intolerance and prejudice been more visible, fashionable or universal among all levels of American society.

In 1907, to give vent to the growing concerns that America was being swept to oblivion by a tide of rabble, Congress established a panel called the Dillingham Commission. Its forty-two-volume report concluded essentially that immigration before 1880 had been no bad thing – the immigrants, primarily from northern Europe, were (by implication) industrious, decent, trustworthy, and largely Protestant, and as a result had assimilated well – while immigration after 1880 had been marked by the entrance into America of uneducated, unsophisticated, largely shiftless and certainly non-Protestant masses from southern and eastern Europe. It maintained that the Germans and Scandinavians had bought farms and become productive members of American society, while the second wave merely soaked up charity and acted as a drug on industrial earnings.

As evidence the commission pointed out that 77 per cent of arrested suspects in New York were foreign born, as were 86 per cent of those on some form of relief.[42] And the poor were not just overwhelmingly, but almost unanimously, of immigrant stock. When the commission investigators examined housing conditions in New York, they could not find a single case of a white native American living in a tenement. The commission concluded that immigrants from southern and eastern Europe had increased overall unemployment and depressed wages.

In fact, all evidence points in the opposite direction. It was *because* America had a base of low-wage, adaptable, unskilled labour that it was able to become an industrial powerhouse.[43] For over half a century American business had freely exploited its foreign-born workers, paying them appalling wages, dismissing them wholesale if they agitated for better pay or conditions, and replacing them with new supplies of compliant immigrants when necessary, and now it was blaming them for being poor and alienated. It failed to note that those who turned to crime or sought relief were only a small part of the immigrant whole, and that most were in fact loyal, productive, law-abiding citizens.

Fired by the oxygen of irrationality, America entered a period of grave intolerance, not just towards immigrants but towards any kind of anti-establishment behaviour. The Sedition Act of 1918 made it illegal, among much else, to make critical remarks about government expenditure or even the YMCA.[44] So low did standards of civil liberty fall that police not only routinely arrested people suspected of sedition, but even those who came to visit them in jail.

In 1917, in an effort to weed out unfit immigrants, a literacy test of sorts was introduced. An aspiring immigrant had to show that he was capable of reading at least thirty words – though, oddly, these words did not have to be English. Quite why a Croat who could read thirty words of Croatian was perceived to be better prepared for life in America than a fellow Croat who could not was never explained.

At the same time, the questions that were asked of immigrants at ports of entry became far more searching and insinuating. Arriving in America in 1921, G. K. Chesterton was astonished at the probing interview to which he had to submit. 'I have stood on the other side of Jordan,' he remarked later, 'in the land ruled by a rude Arab chief, where the police looked so like brigands that one wondered what the brigands looked like. But they did not ask me whether I had come to subvert the power of the *Shereef;* and they did not exhibit the faintest curiosity about my personal views on the ethical basis of civil authority.'[45] Finally, in 1924, a quota system was introduced and America's open-door policy became a part of history.

By this time, however, immigrants everywhere were proving the iniquity of the prejudice against them. The eastern European Jews in particular showed a regard for education and self-improvement that should have been seen as a model. By 1927, two-thirds of New York's 20,000 lawyers were Jewish,[46] and thousands more had built distinguished careers as academics, musicians, playwrights, journalists, doctors, composers, entertainers and in almost every other field of human endeavour. Having faced four decades of complaints that they did not work hard enough, Jews now found themselves accused of working too hard.

A quiet drive began to restrict Jewish admissions to law schools (echoing present-day concerns over Asian domination of institutions of higher learning) and a new expression entered the language, *five o'clock anti-Semitism,* by which was meant that people would work with Jews during the day, if they must, but wouldn't dream of socializing with them at night. For at least another three decades Jews would remain casually excluded from large parts of the American mainstream. Not until the 1960s could they hope to be admitted to non-Jewish country clubs, college fraternities and sororities, and other bastions of gentile life.

But the prejudice the Jews experienced paled when compared to that meted out to the most visible, least voluntary of all minorities: black Americans. It may come as a surprise to realize that blacks were one of the least numerous of immigrant groups to the United States, outnumbered by Swedes, Sicilians, Poles and almost every other national or ethnic block. Between 1505, when the first consignment of black slaves arrived in the Caribbean, and 1888, when slavery was finally outlawed in its last New World stronghold, Brazil, an estimated twelve million black Africans were transported across the Atlantic. The overwhelming majority, however, went to Brazil and the Caribbean. Just 5 per cent – no more than about half a million people – were imported into what was to become the United States.[47]

For obvious economic reasons, blacks were encouraged to propagate freely. As early as 1775, they accounted for 40 per cent of the population of Virginia, 30 per cent in North Carolina, Maryland and Georgia, and well over 60 per cent in South Carolina.[48]

Though the physical cruelties to which they were subjected have perhaps been somewhat inflated in the popular mind – most were at least passably fed and clothed by the standards of the day; it was after all in the slave-owner's interest to look after his property – the psychological humiliations to which they were subjected are immeasurable. It was not merely the imposition of involuntary servitude but the denial of even the most basic human dignities that made American slavery so singularly odious. Fischer reports how a visitor to Virginia 'was startled to see ladies buying naked male slaves after carefully examining their genitals'.[49] Female slaves were routinely regarded as sexual playthings for owners and their overseers. Scarcely a plantation existed that didn't have a sprinkling of *mulattos* (originally a Spanish term denoting a small mule), and visitors from outside the South were often taken aback at encountering a light-skinned slave bearing a more than passing resemblance to their host. (Sally Hemings, the slave woman who was almost certainly the long-standing mistress of Thomas Jefferson, was in fact his late wife's half-sister.)

Slaves were commonly wrenched from their partners – about a quarter ended up so separated – and mothers divided from their children. A typical advertisement of the time read: 'NEGROES FOR SALE. – A negro woman 24 years of age, and two children, one eight and the other three years. Said negroes will be sold separately or together as desired.'[50] In a thousand ways they were daily reminded of their subhuman status. As the words of a slave song had it:

> We bake de bread,
> Dey gib us de crust,
> We sif de meal,
> Dey gib us de huss . . .
> We skim de pot,
> Dey gib us de liquor
> An say dat's good enough for nigger[51]

Almost everywhere they were kept in a state of profound ignorance. Learning of any sort was assumed to be an invitation to insubordination. As Joel Chandler Harris had his fictional creation Uncle Remus say: 'Put a spellin-book in a nigger's han's, en right den an dar' you loozes a plowhand. I kin take a bar'l stave an fling mo' sense inter a nigger in one minnit dan all de schoolhouses betwixt dis en de state er Midgigin.'[52] In consequence, their awareness of the world beyond the plantation bounds was stupefyingly limited. Frederick Douglass recounted in his autobiography that until he secured his freedom he had never even *heard* of New York and Massachusetts.[53]

Even if they managed to secure their freedom, they scarcely enjoyed the fruits of democracy. By 1820 America had 233,000 freed blacks, but they weren't in any meaningful sense free. White workmen refused to work alongside blacks or to allow them apprenticeships, so their prospects of worthwhile employment, much less advancement, were exceedingly meagre. Iowa, Illinois and Indiana would not allow even free blacks to settle within their boundaries. Even where they were allowed to settle, blacks were subjected to constant indignities which they had to suffer in silence. Every white child knew that he could pelt a black person with a snowball without fear of reprisal. Even in the case of the most serious grievances, blacks were often denied the privileges of habeas corpus, trial by jury or even the freedom to testify in their own behalf. Almost nowhere were they allowed to testify against whites.

Though slavery was widely detested in the North, only a handful of idealistic eccentrics saw abolition as a prelude to equality of opportunity. Even Lincoln, in his debates with Stephen Douglas, made his position clear: 'I am not, nor ever have been, in favour of bringing about in any way the social and political equality of the white and black races . . . I am not, nor ever have been, in favour of making voters or jurors of negroes, nor of qualifying them to hold office, nor to intermarry with white people.'[54]

Most preferred to think of blacks as happy-go-lucky, childlike creatures who wanted nothing more from life than something good to eat and a chance to sing and dance. It appears never to have occurred to them that that was as much as the average freed black *could* hope for. The popular image was captured in the song 'Jim Crow', popularized by Thomas D. Rice in the mid-1830s:

> Come, listen all you gals and boys,
> I'se just from Tucky hoe;
> I'm goin' to sing a litle song,
> My name's Jim Crow.

What is remarkable is how durable this perception remained right up to modern times. Well into the 1940s, *Time* magazine was still commonly referring to blacks as 'pickaninnies' and revelling in news snippets in which black people fell down wells or otherwise came amusingly a cropper. Hollywood roles for blacks were largely limited to the shuffling, eye-rolling, perennially timorous and befuddled types as played by actors like Stepin Fetchit and Buckwheat Thomas. The 1950s saw the stereotype extended with television characters like Amos 'n' Andy and the faithful Rochester on the *Jack Benny Show*, while in the wider world of commerce almost the only black face one saw was the smiling countenance of Aunt Jemima, a fat and irrepressibly happy black woman who clearly saw no higher gratification in life than to fix pancakes for white folks. Elsewhere blacks simply didn't exist. Even a program like the *Andy Griffith Show*, set in the South, appeared to take place in a surreally all-white world.

On the few occasions when blacks were treated more seriously, it was almost always with a degree of patronizing ignorance that simply takes one's breath away. As late as 1949, the author of a nationally syndicated newspaper science column could solemnly inform his young readers that the American Negro was constitutionally incapable of pronouncing r's in words like 'cart' and 'horse' because 'his lips are too thick'. Almost no scholarly attention was devoted to black Americans. The few books that focused on them, like *The Negro in Africa and America* (1902) and *The Negro in American Life* (1926), took it as given that blacks were incapable, except in certain exceptional cases, of higher cerebral activity. Often, it was asserted that their distinctive speech habits were an inevitable consequence both of their impaired mental powers and of their physiology, as in this passage from *The Negro in American Life* discussing the Gullah dialect:

> Slovenly and careless of speech, these Gullahs seized upon the peasant English used by some of the early settlers . . . wrapped their clumsy tongues about it as well as they could, and, enriched with certain expressive African words, it issued through their flat noses and thick lips as . . . speech.[55]

And this, I urge you to bear in mind, was a scholarly work. Even the most eminent of linguistic scholars found it impossible to credit blacks with even the most modest capacity for linguistic innovation. In *The English Language in America* George Philip Krapp contended: 'American words brought into the language through the negroes have been insignificant in number. . . A few words like *juba*, a kind of dance, *banjo, hoodoo, voodoo, pickaninny*, exhaust the list of words of non-English origin.'[56] Of Gullah – now widely regarded as the richest, most expressive and most ethnically pure of all the Afro-American dialects in America – Krapp contended that 'very little of it, perhaps none, is derived from sources other than English'.

Almost every term of black speech was claimed to have its roots in English. *Jazz*, Krapp insisted, was an old English dialectal word. Another scholar went so far as to pronounce that *moke*, once a common word for a black person, came from the Icelandic *möckvi*, 'darkness'.[57] That even an eight-year-old child could see a certain implausibility in the idea of black Americans picking up and employing a term that had originated on a chilly island two thousand miles away didn't matter. What was important was that the credit had to go to some source other than the blacks themselves.

Not until a black academic named Lorenzo Dow Turner and a Swede named Gunnar Myrdal began studying black speech in the 1940s was it accorded serious, scholarly investigation. Turner and Myrdal quickly established that certain syntactical features of Gullah, a dialect still spoken by some 250,000 people on the Sea Islands off South Carolina and among neighbouring coastal communities, are clearly traceable to the languages of West Africa, and appear also in other New World patois as far apart as Brazil and Haiti, which clearly precludes British dialectal origins. Turner's *Africanisms in the Gullah Dialect* (1949) suggested that as many as 6,000 Gullah words showed signs of concordance with West African terms.[58]

Turner and Myrdal showed, among much else, that the Wolof *hipikat*, denoting a person who is attuned to his environment, literally 'has his eyes open', is the most plausible source for *hepcat* and *hip* and their many variants.[59] Other words almost certainly of ultimate African origin are *chigger, gumbo, banjo* (at first also spelled *banjou* or *bangy*), *jitter, cola, yam, zombie, juke, goober, tote, okra* and *boogie-woogie,* though many of these, like *banjo, chigger* and *gumbo,* reached America by way of the Caribbean, often after being filtered through an intermediate language.

Even Teddy Roosevelt's *speak softly and carry a big stick* appears to have its roots in a West African proverb. Likewise, 'Yankee Doodle Dandy' shows a striking similarity to a slave song from Surinam, which goes:

> Mama Nanni go to town
> Buy a little pony.
> Stick a feather in a ring,
> Calling Masra Ranni.[60]

Other terms that have been credited with African roots include *bogus, banana, gorilla, funky, phoney* and *jazz,* though in each instance the evidence is largely conjectural. *Jazz* is one of the most hotly disputed terms in American etymology. Among the suggested possibilities are that it comes from *Chaz,* the nickname of an early ragtime drummer named Charles Washington, or from *chasse,* a kind of dance step. Others have linked it to various African or Creole sources. In any case, its first use, among both southern blacks and whites, was to describe sexual intercourse. It wasn't until after World War I that it entered the wider world conveying the idea of a type of music. Quite a number of Afro-American terms contain some forgotten sexual association. *Boogie-woogie* appears originally to have signified syphilis. *Juke,* from the West African *dzugu,* 'wicked', originally carried that sense in English. Eventually it came to signify a brothel and then, by about 1930, a cheap tavern where lively music was played – a *juke joint. Jukebox* dates from 1937. *Blues,* a term popularized if not invented by one its greatest exponents, the cornet player W.C. Handy (his 'Memphis Blues' was written in 1910; 'St Louis Blues' followed in 1914), also originally had 'a strong sexual significance', according to Mencken, though he doesn't elaborate.[61] So, too, did *rock 'n' roll.*

A distinctive and long-standing feature of black speech was a tendency to apply food terms in a sexually euphemistic sense. Thus, *angel-food cake, custard pie* and other dishes often had a distinctly sexual connotation, especially in songs. When you realize that *shortening bread* was commonly used to describe sexual intercourse, the words of the well-loved song take on a whole new meaning:

> One turned over to the other an' said,
> 'My baby loves short'nin', short'nin',
> 'My baby loves short'nin' bread.'

The same applies to jelly roll, as in the lyrics

> Jelly roll, jelly roll ain't so hard to find,
> There's a baker shop in town makes it brown like mine.
> I got a sweet jelly, a lovin' sweet jelly roll.
> If you taste my jelly it'll satisfy your worried soul.

Among the many hundreds of neologisms created in America by blacks we find *to blow one's top, gimme five* for a handshake and *high five* for a congratulatory hand slap, *honky* (of unknown significance), *ragtime* (also obscure, but possibly arising from its ragged syncopation; it was first recorded in 1896), *right on, uptight, jive, be cool, bad mouth, bad* in the sense of good, *get down* in the sense of to attend to pleasures, and *cool* in the sense of being admirable.

Finally, a word needs to be said about descriptive terms for black people. *Negro* is Spanish and Portuguese for '*black*', and first noted in English in 1555. *Nigger* appeared in 1587 and was not at first a pejorative term but simply a variant pronunciation of *Negro*. *Sambo*, a Nigerian word meaning 'second son', was not originally pejorative either. Blacks were generally called *blacks* (or, more politely, *coloureds*) until the 1880s when *negro* became the preferred term. It wasn't usually capitalized until the 1930s. *Uncle Tom* comes of course from Harriet Beecher Stowe's popular novel *Uncle Tom's Cabin*, though its use in the general sense of a servile black hasn't been found earlier than 1922.

When the Going was Good: Travel in America

I

On 8 January 1815 General Andrew Jackson led American troops in a stormy rout of the British at the Battle of New Orleans. It was a decisive triumph – or would have been had there been anything to be decisive about. Unknown to the combatants on both sides, the War of 1812 had been amicably concluded over port and brandy two weeks earlier with the signing of the Treaty of Ghent. More than two thousand men died fighting a battle in a war that was over.[1]

I bring this up here to make the point that, throughout the early American period, communications were a perennial problem. If winds were unfavourable it could take months to cross the Atlantic. In December 1606, when John Smith and his party set off to found Jamestown, the winds proved so 'unprosperous', as he rather mildly put it, that it took them six weeks just to get out of sight of England. A good crossing, such as that of the *Mayflower* Pilgrims, would take eight or nine weeks, but crossings of six or seven months were by no means unknown.[2]

In such circumstances food rotted and water grew brackish. If the captain or shipowner was unscrupulous, the food was often rotten to begin with. Journals of the time are full of baleful remarks. 'What with the heat and dampness, even the biscuit was so full of worms that, God help me, I saw many wait until nightfall to eat the porridge made of it so as not to see the worms,' wrote one dismayed mariner.[3] Personal hygiene became an impossibility. Lice grew 'so thick that they could be scraped off the body'.[4] Occasionally circumstances would be so dire that sailors would refuse to put to sea and would 'strike', or lower, the sails to show their defiance, which explains why workers today who withhold their labour are said to be *on strike*.[5]

For mariners conditions were challenging enough, but for passengers unaccustomed to the perils of the sea the experience all too often proved unbearable. One ship sailing from Leyden to Virginia in the winter of 1618 set off with 180 people. By the time it reached the New World all but fifty had perished.[6] The passengers of the *Sea-Flower*, sailing out of Belfast in 1741, were so consumed with hunger that they ate their dead. Throughout the whole of the early colonial period, the problem with populating the New World wasn't so much one of finding people willing to go but of keeping them alive before and after they got there.

The Atlantic was an equally exasperating barrier to the spread of news. Rarely did a letter posted in Boston in November reach London before the following spring. In 1745 the Board of Trade in London wrote to the governor of North Carolina asking him, a trifle peevishly, why it hadn't heard from him for three years.[7] Even news of crucial import was frequently delayed. No one in America knew of the Stamp Act or its subsequent withdrawal for two months after both events. The Bastille was stormed in July 1789, but President Washington, newly inaugurated, didn't learn of it until the following autumn.

Within America matters were, if anything, worse. Often letters never found their destination and when they did it was not uncommon for a year to elapse before they received a reply. Letters routinely began with a summation of the fate of previous correspondence, as in this note from Thomas Jefferson, writing from Philadelphia in 1776, to William Randolph in Virginia: 'Dear Sir, Your's of August I received in this place, that of Nov. 24th. is just now come to hand; the one of October I imagine has miscarried.'[8]

There was good reason for the difficulty: until well after the time of the Revolution, America had virtually no highways worthy of the name. Such roads as existed were often little more than Indian trails, seldom more than fifteen inches wide and fraught with the obvious peril that you might at any time run into a party of Indians, not necessarily a thing you would wish for in the middle of the wilderness even in times of peace. One such trail was the Natchez Trace – *trace* here being used in the sense of something that describes a line – which covered the five hundred miles of risky nowhere between Nashville and Natchez. It was principally used by boatmen who would float freight down the Mississippi on rough rafts, sell their goods, break up the rafts for lumber and hike back. Even in the more built-up East, such roads as existed would routinely disappear at riverbanks or dissolve into a confusion of forks. Signposts, maps and other aids to the bewildered traveller were all but unknown. (The first book of road maps would not be published until 1789.) When Jefferson travelled from Virginia to Philadelphia for the second Continental Congress he had to twice employ guides to show him the way along particular stretches – and this on one of America's better-travelled routes.[9] Until well into the nineteenth century, it was as cheap to send a ton of goods across the Atlantic as it was to move it thirty miles overland.[10]

With no roads to speak of, people travelled from place to place within America by ocean-going coaster or, more often than not, didn't go at all. Samuel Adams did not set foot out of Massachusetts – indeed didn't mount a horse – until he was in his fifties, and there was nothing especially unusual in that.[11] In 1750, the whole of Massachusetts could boast just six passenger coaches.[12] In Virginia, according to a contemporary account, most people had never seen any four-wheeled vehicle but a wagon and many had not seen even that.[13]

In the circumstances, it is perhaps not surprising that American English became particularly rich in terms for unsophisticated rustics. *Yokel*, a word of uncertain provenance (it may come from the German *Jokel*, a diminutive of *Jakob*), entered American English in 1812. *Hick*, a shortening of *Richard*, is older still, dating from fourteenth-century England and common in America from its earliest days. Among other similar words were *hayseed, bumpkin, rube* (from *Reuben*), *country jake* and *jay* (which eventually gave us the term *jaywalker* – that is, an innocent who doesn't know how to cross a city street). *Hillbilly*, perhaps surprisingly, doesn't appear to have entered the language until 1904 and didn't become widespread until the 1930s. By 1905 such uninformed rustics were said to come from *the sticks*. The expression derives from a slang term used by lumbermen for a forest. More recent still is *boondocks*. It is a Philippines word for mountain and entered English only in 1944.

Until the closing years of the eighteenth century the only real roads in America were the sixty-two-mile-long Philadelphia and Lancaster Turnpike (*turnpike* is a British term dating from 1678, and so called because the way was blocked by a studded pole, or *pike*, which was turned to allow passage once a toll was paid), the Boston Post Road between Boston and New York, the Wilderness Road into the Kentucky territory blazed by Daniel Boone, and the Great Road connecting Philadelphia with the mouth of the Conestoga River. The covered wagons built to negotiate the Great Road were at first called freighters. Later they came to be known as Conestogas, after the Pennsylvania town where they were built. Coincidentally, the town also became famous for a distinctive torpedo-shaped cigar. It was called, naturally, the Conestoga cigar, but the name was soon shortened to stogy (or stogie), and, fittingly, became a favourite of the Conestoga drivers along the Great Road.[14] An unusual feature of Conestoga wagons was that they were built with their brakes and 'lazy boards' – a kind of extendable running-board – on the left-hand side. If there was a particular reason for putting them there, it has since been forgotten. With drivers compelled to sit on the left, they tended to drive on the right so that they were positioned near the centre of the road, which is why, it appears, Americans abandoned the British custom of driving on the left.

Though it surprises most people to hear it, roads in America are effectively a twentieth-century phenomenon. Instead of having a lot of roads, America fell into the habit of having a few roads but giving them lots of names. The great National Road, the first real long-distance highway in America, was also variously known as the Cumberland Road, the Great Western Road, Uncle Sam's Road, the Ohio Road, and the Illinois Road. Begun in 1811 in Cumberland, Maryland, it ran for 130 miles to Wheeling, West Virginia, and eventually stretched on across Pennsylvania, Ohio, Indiana and as far west as Vandalia, Illinois, which it reached in mid-century and then terminated, its function abruptly overtaken by steamboats and railways. Much of this road would become Highway 40, but not for another seventy years. For the moment, long-distance road travel in America was dead.

Such highways as existed were not only few and far between, but perilous, uncomfortable and slow. Early coaches (the word comes from *Kocs*, a town in Hungary where the first such carriages were built; how it then became attached to a person who trains football players and the like is a mystery) were decidedly short on comfort, largely because a seemingly obvious invention – the elliptical spring – occurred to no one before 1804 and didn't become common on vehicles until much later. The best roads, called corduroy roads because they were made of felled trees laid side by side giving a ribbed effect like corduroy, were torturous enough, but they were a rarity. Most were simply rough clearings through the wilderness. That perhaps doesn't sound too bad, but bear in mind that the technology of the time didn't allow the easy removal of tree stumps. Even on the great National Road, the pride of the American highway system, the builders were permitted to leave stumps up to fifteen inches high – slightly under knee height. Imagine if you will bouncing for day after day over rocks, fallen branches, and tree stumps in an unsprung carriage and you may get some notion of the arduousness of a long-distance trip in nineteenth-century America.

Something of the flavour of the undertaking is reflected in the candid name of the most successful of the stagecoach companies running along the National Road: the Shake Gut Line. (It was an age of colourful names. The Shake Gut's principal rival was the June Bug Line, so called because its rivals predicted that it would survive no longer than the average June bug. They were wrong.) Coaches not only shook their occupants mercilessly, but routinely overturned. In 1829, according to Paul Johnson, 'a man travelling from New York to Cincinnati and back reported the coach had been overturned nine times'.[15]

It is perhaps little wonder then that when railways (and to a lesser extent steamboats and canal barges) began to provide an alternative form of transportation, people flocked to them. Even so, early trains were also slow, uncomfortable and dangerous. Cars were connected by nothing more sophisticated than chains, so that they were constantly shunting into one another, jarring the hapless occupants. Front-facing passengers had the choice of sitting with the windows closed – not an attractive option in hot weather – or suffering the assault of hot cinders, jocularly called 'eyedrops', that blew in a steady stream back from the locomotive (a word coined in

1657 to describe any kind of motion, but first applied to railway engines in 1815). Fires, derailments and breakdowns were constant possibilities, and until late in the nineteenth century even the food was a positive hazard. Until 1868 when a new word and phenomenon entered the language – the dining-car – customers were permitted to detrain at way stations and given twenty minutes to throw a meal down their gullets. The proprietors of these often remote and God-forsaken outposts offered what food they could get their hands on – or, more often, get away with. Diners at Sidney, Nebraska, were routinely fed what most presumed to be chicken stew; in fact, its basic component was prairie dog.[16] Some said they were lucky to get that.

Despite the discomforts, the railways became hugely popular and offered many thousands of people their first chance to leave home. By 1835, according to one estimate, fifty times as many people were travelling by rail as had travelled by all other means put together just five years earlier. From virtually nothing in 1830, the mileage of American railways rose to 30,000 by 1860 – that is, more than all the rest of the world put together[17] – and to a staggering 200,000 by 1890. Rail travel so dominated American travel that for four generations *road* meant *railroad*.[18] What Americans now call roads were more generally known as *trails*, as in the Oregon and Santa Fe trails.

With the arrival of train travel, the stagecoach was instantly eclipsed, and little wonder. Trains were not only faster and increasingly more comfortable, but also cheaper. From coast to coast the trip took eight to ten days at an average speed of about 20 m.p.h. (rising to a giddy 35 m.p.h. on the faster stretches). The one-way fare from Omaha to Sacramento was $100 first class (plus $4 a night for a berth in one of the new Pullman sleepers), $75 for second class, $40 for third.

Pullman cars, originally Pullman Hotel-Cars, were named for George M. Pullman who developed them in 1865 and dining-cars in 1868. To accommodate his 12,000 workers, Pullman built a model community, Pullman, Illinois (now part of Chicago), where workers lived in company houses and shopped at company stores, thus ensuring that most of what they made returned to the company. That Pullman porters were nearly always black was not a result of enlightened employment practices, but a by-product of abysmal pay. The custom of calling porters 'George', whatever their name, was apparently taken from Pullman's own first name.[19]

Among railway terms that have passed into general familiarity were *caboose, iron horse, cow catcher, jerkwater town, to featherbed, to ball the jack, to ride the rails* and *to ride the gravy train*. A *gravy train* was a good run, either because it paid well or wasn't too taxing. Surprisingly it isn't recorded before 1945. *To featherbed*, meaning to employ more workers than necessary, is also recent. It isn't found before 1943. *Caboose* is much older. From the Dutch *kabuis*, it was used to describe various parts of a ship, notably the galley, long before it was appropriated by the railways. A *jerkwater town* was literally that – a place, usually desolate, where trains took on water from a trackside tank by jerking on a rope. *To ball the jack*, to travel quickly, even recklessly, is entirely uncertain. It may have some connection with *high ball*, a signal to proceed.

Two other terms more loosely associated with railway travel are *bum* and *hobo*. *Hobo* was first attested in a newspaper in Ellensburgh, Washington, in 1891, but no one has ever come up with a certain explanation of its etymology. Among the theories: that it is a contraction of 'homeward bound' or that it has something to do with the salutation 'Ho! Beau!', which sounds a trifle refined for vagrants, but in fact was a common cry among railway workers in the nineteenth century and would certainly have been familiar to those who rode the rails. *Bum* in the sense of a tramp appears to be a shortening of the German *Bummler*, a loafer and ne'er-do-well.

Though we tend to associate urban congestion with the automobile and the shortcomings of our own age, horse-driven traffic clogged cities long before cars came along. In 1864 New York City built two miles of underground tunnels through Central Park to try to keep things moving, and dubbed them *sub-ways*. The British still use *subway* in the sense of a subterranean passageway (or, a cynic might add, public housing for vagrants) but in America that sense lasted just twenty-nine years before being usurped by the new urban underground railways in 1893.[20] The automobile may have its drawbacks, but at least it doesn't normally attract flies or drop things you need to step around. The filth of horses was a constant problem for cities well into this century, one that we can barely imagine now. In 1900 some dedicated official in Rochester, New York, calculated that the manure produced by the city's 15,000 horses would in a year cover a one-acre square to a depth of 175 feet. Often kept in insanitary conditions and worked hard through all weathers, horses not only drew flies but dropped like them. At the turn of the century, 15,000 horses a year died on the streets of New York, 12,000 on the streets of Chicago.[21] Sometimes they were left for days. Between the flies, the manure and the steaming corpses, there was no mistaking that you were in a city.

Thus the advent of the cable-car and trolley-car was not just a boon but a kind of miracle. The cable-car was perfected by a Scottish immigrant named Andrew Smith Hallidie, who had something of a vested interested in its success: he ran a company that made cables. Cable-cars moved by gripping underground cables that were in constant motion. When a driver wished to stop he pulled a lever that disengaged the grippers. If for some reason the grippers would not disengage – and this appears to have happened quite a lot – the result was a runaway car, which would trundle along inexorably, mowing down anything too slow or insensible to get out of the way, until the power station could be alerted to shut down the entire system.[22] It was not, as you can imagine, altogether ideal. Even so, cable-cars were briefly very popular, though today San Francisco is the only American city where they still exist, and even there the system is a shadow of its former self. In 1900 the city had 110 miles of line and 600 cars; by 1980 it had a little over 10 miles of line and just 40 cars.

What rendered the cable-car obsolete was the trolley-car, or *trawley car* as it was sometimes spelled in the early days. The trolley-car was so called because the mechanism that connected the cars to the overhead wires was a troller, which in turn was ultimately from a British dialect word *troll*, meaning to move about. Trolley systems were easier to install and cheaper to run than any competing systems and in consequence they thrived. It is generally overlooked that the United States once had the finest system of public transportation in the world. At the turn of the century, Berlin had the most extensive streetcar network in Europe; but in America it would have come only twenty-second.[23] By 1922, the peak year, America had over 14,000 miles of streetcar track. The biggest system in the country was, you may be surprised to hear, that of Los Angeles.

Streetcars changed the way people lived. They opened up suburban life. The population of the Bronx went from under 90,000 to 200,000 in the years immediately after the introduction of the streetcar.[24] By 1902 New York streetcars alone were carrying almost one billion passengers annually. Cities became bigger, busier, more confusing and in consequence in the 1890s two new words entered the language: *rush hour* and *traffic jam*.

But streetcars also offered opportunities for pleasure. People were for the first time able to explore districts of their cities that they had only heard about. Realizing the possibilities, streetcar companies began building amusement parks at the end of the lines as a way of boosting revenue – places like Willow Grove Park, twelve miles from downtown Philadelphia and now, inevitably, the site of a shopping mall.

Despite their popularity, streetcars were seldom profitable. In 1921 America's 300 largest streetcar systems made a collective profit of $2.5 million – roughly $8,000 each – on an investment of $1.5 billion. With the rise of private car ownership and other forms of transport such as buses – or 'trackless trolleys', as they were sometimes called at first – their fate was sealed. Between 1922 and 1932 the number of streetcar miles in America almost halved. In that same decade, a company called National City Lines – a cartel made up of General Motors and a collection of oil and rubber interests – began buying up trolley lines and converting them to bus routes. By 1950 it had closed down the streetcar systems of more than a hundred cities, including those of Los Angeles, Philadelphia, Baltimore and St Louis. Its actions were unquestionably illegal and the company was eventually taken to court and convicted of engaging in a criminal conspiracy. The fine: just $5,000, less than the cost of a new bus.

II

Tempting as it is to blame a monolithic corporation for the downfall of public transportation in America, the real culprit was the car, or more specifically the nation's abiding addiction to it. No innovation in history has more swiftly captured the affections of humanity or more radically transformed the way the world looks, behaves and operates. Look at any urban scene and notice how totally our world is dominated by the needs of the car. Building, repairing, selling and servicing cars now accounts for between one-fifth and one-sixth of all economic activity in the nation. Yet only about a century ago, this marvel of the age didn't even have a name. Motorized vehicles have been around for longer than you might think – as early as 1770 a Frenchman named Nicholas Cugnot had a steam-powered behemoth called the Fardier lumbering through the streets of Paris at just over 2 m.p.h. (considerably less than walking speed) – but most authorities agree that the first real, working car was one devised by the German engineer Gottlieb Daimler in 1884. He called it a Mercedes, after his daughter. Unaware of Daimler's creation, another German, Karl Benz, invented a second and very similar car at almost the same time. But in fact by this time the concept of an automobile was already patented in America. A sharp patent lawyer named George B. Selden had had the prescience in 1879 to take out a patent on a largely notional vehicle he called a 'road engine'. Selden was first not because he was a gifted inventor or even an inspired tinkerer – indeed, he never built a working vehicle – but because he was an opportunist who shrewdly anticipated the limitless possibilities inherent in controlling the patent on this budding technology. As there was no money in 'road engines' in 1879, he managed by various legal manipulations to delay the issuance of the patent for sixteen years until the market was at last poised to take off, and thus was positioned to enjoy royalties for the next seventeen years on a technology to which he had made absolutely no contribution. (He didn't do a great deal for the honour of patent lawyers either. The law was changed soon after his patent expired.)

Only by merest chance do Americans call this central component of their lives an automobile. Scores of other names were tried and discarded before *automobile* hauled itself to the top of the linguistic heap. Among the other names for the early car were *self-motor, locomotive car, autobat, autopher, diamote, autovic, self-propelled carriage, locomotor, horseless carriage, motor buggy, stink chariot* (presumably coined by a non-enthusiast), and the simple, no-nonsense *machine*, which for a long time looked like becoming the generic term for a self-propelled vehicle. *Automobile*, a French word concocted from Greek and Latin elements, was at first used only as an adjective, not only to describe cars ('an automobile carriage') but also other self-propelled devices ('automobile torpedo'). By 1899 the word had grown into a noun and was quickly becoming the established general term for cars – though not without opposition. The *New York Times* sniffed that *automobile*, 'being half Greek and half Latin, is so near indecent that we print it with hesitation'.[25] Before the year was out, the word was being shortened to *auto*. *Car* was first applied to the automobile in 1896, and by 1910 it had more or less caught up *automobile* in popularity.

Although the early technological developments were almost exclusively German, it was the French who became the first big manufacturers of cars and thus gave us many of the words associated with motoring – *chassis, garage, chauffeur, carburettor, coupé, limousine* and of course *automobile* itself. *Chauffeur* was a term for a ship's stoker and as such was applied to drivers of cars in at least a mildly sarcastic sense. *Limousine* was originally a heavy shepherd's cloak from the Limousin region of France. The first chauffeurs, forced to sit in the open air, adopted this coat and gradually the word transferred itself from the driver to the vehicle. By 1902 it was part of the English language.[26]

The first car most Americans saw was one designed by Karl Benz, which was put on display at the 1893 Chicago World's Fair. Before the year was out, two brothers in Springfield, Massachusetts, Charles and J. Frank Duryea, had built America's first gasoline-powered car, and the country never looked back.

No technology in history has taken off more swiftly, more breathtakingly, than the car. And nowhere did it take off faster than in America. In 1898, there were not thirty working cars in the whole of the United States. Within a little over a decade there were not just 700 cars in America, but 700 car factories. In just the first four months of 1899 – just the first four months – American investors provided no less than $388 million of start-up capital for new automobile companies.[27]

They came from every walk of life. John F. and Horace E. Dodge had run a Detroit machine shop. David D. Buick made plumbing supplies. Studebaker was the world's largest producer of horse-drawn carriages. Pope, Winton and Rambler all started out as makers of bicycles. A striking number of the first manufacturers were from the Midwest and particularly from Michigan – Ransom Olds, creator of the Oldsmobile, from Lansing; David D. Buick and Henry Ford from Detroit; William C. Durant, founder of General Motors, from Flint – which helps to explain why Detroit became the Motor City. As well as the celebrated names of the early years like Packard, Duesenberg and Cord, there were scores of companies now almost entirely forgotten – Pathfinder, Marmon, Haynes, Premier, McFarland, Ricker (which held the world speed record of 26 m.p.h. in the late 1890s*), Maxwell, Briscoe, Lexington. Many of the early cars were named for explorers, reflecting the sense of adventure they imparted: De Soto, Hudson, La Salle and Cadillac (named for a French nobleman, Antoine de la Mothe Cadillac, who would almost certainly have been long forgotten except that he had the good fortune to found Detroit). But buyers could choose among a positive galaxy of names now sadly forgotten: the Black Crow, the Bugmobile, the Averageman's Car, the Dan Patch, the Royal Mail, the Lone Star, the Premier, the Baby Grand, the Hupmobile, the Locomobile.

It is not easy to conceive from this remove just how improbable was the success of the car. In 1900 cars were costly, unreliable and fearsome. 'You can't get people to sit over an explosion,' remarked one observer sagely. Being in control of several hundred pounds of temperamental metal was a frightening challenge that proved too much for many. On her first attempt to drive, Mrs Stuyvesant Fish, a wealthy Boston socialite, switched on the engine and promptly ran over a servant who had been stationed near by should she required assistance. As the man struggled dazedly to his feet, Mrs Fish threw the car into reverse and backed over him. Panicking, she changed gears and mowed him down a third time. At this Mrs Fish fled to the house in a pique and never went near a car again. I suspect the servant didn't either.

All the infrastructure necessary to support an automotive society – petrol stations, traffic signals, road maps, insurance policies, drivers' licences, parking lots – was entirely lacking in the first years of this century. Cars were not just unnecessary but, since there was

---

* This was nothing compared with the speeds achieved by steam-powered cars. The great Stanley Steamer reached 127 m.p.h. in 1906. Unfortunately steam cars also tended to be unreliable and to blow up.[28]

almost no place to go in them, effectively pointless. As late as 1905, America possessed not a single mile of paved rural highway. Such roads as existed were unmarked dirt tracks, which became swamps in the wet months and were hopelessly rutted for much of the rest. In many parts of the country even a dirt track would have been welcome. To drive through Nebraska or Kansas often meant to cross a trackless prairie.

Those who made long journeys were deemed heroic or insane, often both. In 1903, the year that the Ford Motor Company was incorporated, Dr Horatio Nelson Jackson of Vermont, accompanied by a mechanic named Crocker and a dog named Bud (who, like his companions, wore goggles throughout the trip), made the first transcontinental crossing by car in a two-cylinder, open-top Winton. It took them sixty-five days, but it made them heroes. For the most part, cars of the period simply weren't up to the challenge. Those who tried to drive through the Rockies discovered that the only way was to back up them; otherwise the fuel flowed away from their engines. Not only were there almost no decent roads but no prospect of them. The federal government long refused to provide highway funds, arguing that it was a matter for the states, and the states likewise showed the deepest reluctance to subsidize what might be a passing fad. In 1912, twenty of them spent not a penny on highway construction.

But the absence of highways didn't stop anybody. America's 8,000 motor vehicles of 1900 had jumped to almost half a million by 1910 and to 2 million by 1915. Infrastructure began to appear. Licence plates made their first appearance in 1901. Four years later, Sylvanus F. Bowser invented a workable gas pump and, with some prescience, called it a Filling Station (though the term would not become common for gas stations until the 1920s). In the same year, the Automobile Gasoline Company of St Louis began the first chain of gas stations – already people were casually shortening *gasoline* to *gas* – and people everywhere were singing Gus Edwards's 'In My Merry Oldsmobile':

> Come away with me, Lucille
> In my merry Oldsmobile,
> Over the road of life we'll fly
> Autobubbling you and I.

An exciting new vocabulary emerged. Not everyone could yet afford to go *autobubbling* (dated to 1900, a racy if short-lived term for a pleasure spin), but soon most people were bandying about expressions like *road-hog* (a term originally applied to bicyclists in 1893), *self-starter* (1894), *station wagon* (1904), *spark plugs* (1908), *joy ride* (1909), *motorcade* (1913), *car crashes* and *blowouts* (1915), *to step on the gas* (1916), *to jaywalk* (1917), *jalopy* (1924), *hitchhike* (1925) and *rattletrap* (1929).[29] As early as 1910 people were *parking* in order to *neck* or *pet* (words that date from the same period). As time went on, slightly more sinister linguistic aspects of motoring emerged. *Speeding ticket* entered the language in 1930, *double-parking* in 1931 and *parking meters* in 1935. (The first ones were in Oklahoma City.)

Some words came into the language so quickly that no one seems to have noticed where they came from. *Jalopy* – in the early days often spelled *jolopy, jaloopy* and in many other similar ways – is wholly unexplained. It just emerged. Much the same is true of *Tin Lizzie* (1915) and *flivver* (1920). *Flivver* was sometimes used in the general sense of being a failure before it became attached to Henry Ford's Model T. Mary Helen Dohan notes that 'human flivver' appeared in the novel *Ruggles of Red Gap* in 1917,[30] but that would appear merely to muddy the question of how it originated and why it became attached to a car that was anything but a failure. *Tin Lizzie*, Flexner asserts, arose because *Lizzie* was a common name for maids, and both maids and Model T's were black and made to look their best on Sundays.[31] If this is so, then it appears to be unattested. An alternative theory is that it may be connected in some way to *lizard*, a kind of sledge. Nobody knows.

The two million cars of 1915 rose to ten million five years later. By 1920 Michigan alone had more cars than Britain and Ireland. Kansas had more cars than France. Before the decade was half over, America would be producing 85 per cent of all the world's cars and the automobile industry, which hadn't even existed a quarter of a century earlier, would be the country's biggest business.

Most of the credit for this can go to a single person, Henry Ford, and a somewhat oddly named vehicle, the Model T. Ford always used initials for his early cars, but in a decidedly hit-and-miss manner. For reasons that appear to have gone unrecorded, he disdained whole sequences of the alphabet. His first eight models were the A, B, C, F, K, N, R and S before he finally produced, on 1 October 1908, his first universal car, the Model T. (When, nineteen years later, he ceased production of the Model T, he succeeded it not with the Model U, but with another Model A.)

By 1912, just four years after its introduction, three-quarters of the cars on American roads were Model Ts.[32] Ford is often credited with introducing the world to the concept of the moving 'assembly line' in 1913. Though the word may be his, the idea wasn't. For decades scores of other industries, from vegetable canning to meat wholesaling, had used assembly line methods, but had referred to them as 'continuous process manufacturing' or 'flow production'. Ford simply adapted the idea to a much larger manufacturing process.[33] With his revolutionary methods and by keeping the car basic – 'You can have any colour you want as long as it's black' was his oft-repeated quip – Ford cut the time it took to produce a Model T from fourteen man-hours in 1910 to just two man-hours in 1913,[34] and with it of course the price fell. The first Model T cost $850 and rose the next year to $950, but after that, with Ford's novel and wondrously efficient production lines and increasing economies of scale, the price fell continuously. By 1916 a new Model T cost as little as $345. Even so, that was far more money than most people could get their hands on. A new system of financing arose and with it came a raft of ominous new expressions: *instalment plan, time payments, one-third down, downpayment* and that perennial invitation to ruin, *buy now, pay later*.

A month before the first Model T was produced, another great name of the industry was born: General Motors. The company, which had begun life as the Flint Road Cart Company, was founded by William Crapo 'Billy' Durant, a mercurial figure described by one friend as 'a child in emotions, in temperament and in mental balance'. Durant knew nothing of engineering and was not a gifted innovator. Indeed he wasn't even a particularly astute businessman. He was simply a great accumulator. He bought companies indiscriminately, not just car makers, but enterprises that were involved with the automobile business only tangentially, if at all – companies like the Samson Sieve-Grip Tractor Company (which built tractors steered by reins on the dubious grounds that farmers would find them more horse-like) and a one-man refrigerator company that would eventually become Frigidaire. Many of his automotive acquisitions became great names – Buick, Oldsmobile, Cadillac, Chevrolet – but many others, like Cartercar, Sheridan, Scripps-Booth and Oakland, were never more than highly dubious. His strategy, as he put it, was to 'get every kind of car in sight' in the hope that the successes would outweigh the failures. They didn't always. He lost control of General Motors in 1910, got it back in 1916, lost it again in 1920. By 1936, after more bad investments, he was bankrupt with debts of nearly $1 million and assets of just $250.[35]

Many of his best people found his imperiousness intolerable and took their talents elsewhere. Walter Chrysler left to form the Chrysler Corporation. Henry and Wilfred Leland departed to create Lincoln (which later came back to the GM fold). Charles Nash went on to build Nash-Rambler. Others were dismissed, often for trifling transgressions. In 1911 Durant hired a Swiss mechanic/racing driver named Louis Chevrolet. Unfortunately for them both, Durant couldn't abide smoking. When, shortly after joining the company, Chevrolet wandered into Durant's office with a cigarette dangling from his lips, Durant took the instant decision that the only thing he liked about the Swiss mechanic was his name. He dismissed Chevrolet, who thence dropped from sight as effectively as if he had fallen through a trapdoor, but kept his melodic moniker and built it into one of the great names of automotive history. (Durant was also responsible for the Chevrolet symbol, which he found as a pattern on wallpaper in a hotel room in Paris. He carefully removed a strip, took it home with him and had his art department work it up into a logo.)

As the opening years of the twentieth century ticked by, two things became clear: America desperately needed better roads and they weren't going to be paid for with government money. Into this seeming impasse stepped Carl Graham Fisher, one of the most remarkable go-getters of his or any other age. A former bicycle and car racer (for a time he held the world speed record over two miles), founder of the Indianapolis 500 Speedway, hugely successful businessman, and perennial daredevil – he once rode a bicycle along a high-wire stretched between two of Indianapolis's tallest buildings to publicize a business venture – Fisher was, as you may surmise, something of a dashing figure. His fortune came from the Prest-O-Lites car headlight company – early cars didn't have sufficient oomph to run headlights, so these had to be powered, and purchased, separately – but his fame came from creating America's first coast-to-coast highway.

In 1912 Fisher proposed spending $10 million on a gravelled two-lane road from New York to San Francisco, and to raise the money through donations. Thousands of people sent in money – President Woodrow Wilson patriotically gave $5, though Henry Ford refused to cough up a penny – and by 1915 the pot was sufficiently full to make a start. Two problems soon became evident. The first was what to call the highway. A good name was important to galvanize support. Fisher's proposed name, the Coast-to-Coast Rock Highway, was apt but rather short on zip. Fisher toyed with the Jefferson Highway, the Ocean-to-Ocean Highway or the American Road before finally settling on the Lincoln Highway, which had a solid patriotic ring to it, even if it alienated many southerners. The second problem was that even with all the donations, there wasn't nearly enough to build the necessary 3,389 miles of highway. Fisher hit on the idea of constructing what came to be called 'seedling miles'. He would find a section of dirt road roughly midway between two towns and pave it. The idea of building a mile of good road in the middle of nowhere may seem odd, but Fisher reasoned that once people got a taste of smooth highway they would want the whole concrete banquet. Soon towns all along the route were enthusiastically raising funds to connect themselves to that tantalizing seedling mile. A new slogan arose: 'See America First.'

In 1923 the Lincoln Highway – the first transcontinental highway in the world – officially opened. For the next forty years, it hummed with life as a daily cavalcade of cars and trucks brought commerce and the intoxicating whiff of a larger, livelier world to the hundreds of little towns (it mostly avoided cities) standing along its pleasantly meandering route. Almost overnight it became, as the postcards proudly boasted, America's Main Street.

Eventually the federal government decided to make money available for interstate highways, though it continued to consider the matter such a low priority that it handed the task to the Secretary of Agriculture as something to do in his free time. With the help of federal money, other great roads were built: the Jefferson Highway from Detroit to New Orleans, the Dixie Highway from Bay City, Michigan, to Florida, the William Penn Highway across Pennsylvania. The Dixie Highway was yet another Fisher inspiration, though here the motivation had more to do with self-interest than patriotism. In the late 1910s, Fisher became seized with the idea that Miami Beach – or Lincoln, as he wished for a time to call it – would make a splendid resort.

The notion was widely held to be deranged. Florida was, as far as anyone knew, a muggy, bug-infested swamp a long way from anywhere. But Fisher envisioned a great utopian city linked to the outside world by his Dixie Highway. The costs and logistics of building a resort in a distant swamp proved formidable, but Fisher persevered and by 1926 had nearly finished his model community, complete with hotels, a casino, golf courses, a yacht basin and a lavish Roman swimming pavilion (which featured, a trifle incongruously, a Dutch windmill). Then a hurricane blew it all down. Barely had he absorbed this blow than the stock market crashed in 1929 and the market for vacation homes dried up. Miami Beach did of course become a success, but not for Carl Graham Fisher. He ended his years living in a modest house on a side-street in the city he had built from nothing.[36]

At about the same time that the tireless Fisher was tempting fate in south Florida, the Secretary of Agriculture in Washington was deciding it was time to bring some order to American roads. He introduced uniform road signs – the octagonal red stop sign, the cross for a railway junction and so on – and instituted the system of numbering for interstate roads that is still used today. North–south highways were given odd numbers, and east–west highways were given even numbers (with major transcontinental routes ending in multiples of ten). Names were ruthlessly abandoned. At a stroke, highways lost much of their romance. The Lincoln Highway, completed only two years before, became US Route 30. The great Dixie Highway became the uninspiring Route 25. The William Penn became Route 22. Probably the most famous highway of them all, Route 66, never suffered the indignity of being stripped of its name for the simple reason that it never had one. It was not begun until 1926, in the post-name era. Its humiliation would have to wait until 1985, when the federal highway department removed all the Route 66 shield signs along its 2,200 miles from Michigan Avenue in Chicago to Ocean Avenue in Santa Monica. Overnight this once great highway became a series of back highways and anonymous frontage roads.

III

As you would expect, it wasn't long before people outside the automobile business discovered that there was money to be made from America's growing tendency to take to the roads. In the mid-1920s a new expression entered the language: *the drive-in*.

The drive-in experience was not in fact exclusive to the automobile age. Around the turn of the century a brief craze arose among drugstores to provide kerbside soda-fountain service to buggies. But it took the long-range mobility of the internal combustion engine to really put the concept on its feet. The first modern drive-in is generally agreed to be the Pig Stand, a barbecue pit that was the brainchild of one Royce Hailey. It opened for business in September 1921 along the highway between Dallas and Fort Worth and was such a hit that soon there were Pig Stands all over the southern states and California. In 1924 a competitor called A&W, named for its founders, a Mr Allen and a Mr White, opened for business. Its main contribution to American culture was the invention of 'tray girls', who brought the food to patrons' cars, saving them the emotional upheaval of having to be parted even briefly from their surrogate wombs.[37]

Highways became lined with diners, roadhouses, greasy spoons (first recorded in 1925) and other meccas of cheap, breezy service. In the early 1930s, a survey of the highway between New York and New Haven revealed that there was on average a gas station every 895 feet and a restaurant or diner every 1,825 feet.[38] Every main highway had its famed establishments, like the Pig Hip Restaurant in Lincoln, Illinois, or the Cozy Dog Drive-In in nearby Springfield (whose proud boast it was to have invented corn dogs in 1949, though it called them 'crusty curs'), both on Route 66. Some of these establishments were so successful that they grew into national chains, like the Servistation Café in Corbin, Kentucky, on the Dixie Highway, founded in 1929 by

Harland Sanders* and which evolved into Kentucky Fried Chicken, or Dairy Queen, founded in Moline, Illinois, in 1945.

Though highway eating places were plentiful, there was about them a certain worrying unpredictability. In 1929 a young drugstore owner in Massachusetts named Howard Johnson decided that what America's motorists craved was a safe, reliable uniformity of eating. He hit on the idea of franchising as a quicker, less risky way of building a chain. By 1940, 125 Howard Johnson's restaurants stood along the eastern seaboard, two-thirds of them owned by franchisees, or *agents* as Johnson called them. Most of his establishments were built in a homy, neo-colonial style, with shutters on the windows, a rooftop cupola with a weather-vane, and upstairs dormers that had no function beyond lending the structure an air of cosy domesticity. Only the busy parking lot and bright orange roof – designed, naturally, to attract the attention of passing motorists – suggested that this was not the home of a well-heeled citizen. Johnson's main breakthrough was to standardize the restaurant business. His operating manual – what he called 'The Bible' – dictated everything from the number of French fries per portion to how high to pour the coffee in a cup (to within three-eighths of an inch of the top), an obsession with detail that was to be copied with even greater success by Ray Kroc of McDonald's, as we shall see in Chapter 20.

As motorists required frequent infusions of food, so they also needed a place to sleep from time to time. Throughout the late 1910s and early 1920s cabin camps or tourist courts – free-standing wooden huts, usually ranged in a semicircle and often given affectionately illiterate names like U Like Um Cabins, Kozy Kourt and Para Dice[39] – began to appear on the landscape until by 1925 there were some two thousand of them, generally charging $2 to $3 a night, a price with which downtown hotels couldn't compete. Variations on *cabin camp* and *tourist court* began to appear – *tourist camps, motor courts*, even at least one *autel* – but the first place to style itself a *motel* was the Milestone Mo-tel, on

---

* Not until the 1940s did Sanders pretend to be anything other than the Indiana farm boy fate had made him. But upon being made an honorary colonel by the cherishably named Governor Ruby Laffoon of Kentucky, he took the role to heart. He grew a goatee and ever after affected the manner and attire of a southern gentleman.

Route 101 in San Luis Obispo, California, which opened its doors on 12 December 1925. (It is still in business, though operating now as the Motel Inn.) The term itself first appeared a few months earlier in *Hotel Monthly* magazine, in the same article in which *motor hotel* made its debut.[40] By the 1940s, *motel* had largely driven out the older *court* and *camp* almost everywhere.

Very early on, it became apparent that not every customer was coming for a good rest. The FBI's ever-vigilant J. Edgar Hoover gravely announced that America's motels were 'assignation camps' and 'hotbeds of crime'.[41] That may have been overstating matters, but if they weren't hotbeds, they certainly had them. A rather sneaky study by Southern Methodist University sociology students of the comings and goings at Dallas motels over one weekend in 1935 found that of the two thousand customers who used the city's thirty-eight establishments most were registered under fictitious names and at least three-quarters were deemed to be having illicit sex. (What, one wonders, was the remaining one-quarter up to, and how did the researchers determine that it wasn't sex?) Terrific money was to be made in the 'hot bed' or 'Mr and Mrs Jones' trade, as it came to be known. One establishment was noted to have rented out a particular room no fewer than sixteen times in twenty-four hours, or once every ninety minutes (clearly they don't waste time in Dallas).

By 1948 America had 26,000 motels. Unfortunately, a good many of them were a shade sleazy. Kemmons Wilson, a wealthy Tennessee businessman, had been disappointed by the standards of motels he had encountered during a family vacation and decided to do something about it. In 1952 he opened a bright, clean, *respectable* establishment on Summer Avenue in Memphis, charging $4 for singles, $6 for doubles. Carefully avoiding the seedy connotations inherent in *motel*, he called it a Holiday Inn. Before long, Holiday Inns were going up at the rate of one every two and a half days. In 1954 Howard Johnson got in on the act, and soon big hotel chains like Hilton and Sheraton were pushing their way into the market.

But it was also a golden age for individually owned establishments – 'ma-and-pa motels' as they were known in the trade. The 1950s saw a wave of good-quality, privately owned motels, often L-shaped and generally built in the sleek style known as *moderne*.

Increasingly they offered swimming pools, air-conditioning, ice machines, king-size beds with soothing coin-operated Vibro-Matic massagers, and other luxuries that made them considerably nicer than most of their patrons' own homes. Often they were given names that were at least as soothing as the massagers: Sleepy Hollow, Restwell Motel, Dreamland Inn, Memory Lane Motel.

In 1925, at about the same time that tourist courts were evolving into motels, another venerable institution made its appearance on the American roadside: the Burma-Shave sign. Born in the early 1920s, Burma-Shave was a revolutionary product – the first brushless shaving cream that really worked – but before its distinctive signs began appearing along highways it was going nowhere. The name cannot have helped. Few people equated a country in Indochina with a smooth, close shave. (It was called Burma-Shave because it was a sequel to a liniment, Burma-Vita, which *did* contain ingredients from Burma, or at least from the Malay Peninsula.)

Then in 1925 one of the company's travelling salesman noticed that gas stations were increasingly announcing themselves to motorists with a series of strident signs: GAS AHEAD! CIGARETTES! EATS! STOP HERE! It seemed to work, and he put the idea to the head of the company. As an experiment Burma-Shave erected signs along two Minnesota highways near its headquarters. The first signs didn't have a jingle. In fact, they could hardly have been less catchy. One read: GOODBYE SHAVING BRUSH!/HALF A POUND FOR/HALF A DOLLAR/VERY FINE FOR THE SKIN/DRUGGISTS HAVE IT/CHEER UP FACE/THE WAR IS OVER/BURMA-SHAVE, which was not only a trifle wordy, but a bit odd in its sentiments since the war had in fact been over for the better part of a decade. By the early 1930s the company was at last beginning to find its *métier*, and offering passing motorists such droll entertainments as: SHAVING BRUSHES/YOU'LL SOON SEE 'EM/WAY DOWN EAST/IN SOME/MUSEUM/BURMA-SHAVE (1930); HE PLAYED/A SAX/HAD NO B.O./BUT HIS WHISKERS SCRATCHED/SO SHE LET HIM GO/BURMA-SHAVE (1933); HE HAD THE RING/HE HAD THE FLAT/BUT SHE FELT HIS CHIN/AND THAT/WAS THAT/BURMA-SHAVE(1934); WHEN CUTTING/WHISKERS/YOU DON'T NEED/TO LEAVE ONE HALF/OF THEM FOR SEED/BURMA- SHAVE (1934).

As Frank Rowsome, jun., has put it in his engaging history of the Burma-Shave signs, *The Verse by the Side of the Road*, humour in advertising in the Depression years 'was so scarce as to be virtually a trace element'.[42] Burma-Shave became the exception. Its signs were virtually guaranteed to hold the attention of passing drivers for an average of eighteen seconds – far longer than any other type of roadside ad could count on. They not only effectively popularized the product, but by promoting highway safety and other timely causes like War Bonds they gave the company an air of kindly altruism, as here: DON'T TAKE/A CURVE/AT 60 PER/WE HATE TO LOSE/A CUSTOMER; PAST/SCHOOLHOUSES/TAKE IT SLOW/LET THE LITTLE/SHAVERS GROW.

Unable to come up with a steady stream of new verses, the company began holding national contests, paying $100 for each winning entry. At its peak, it was receiving over 50,000 entries a year. A few were decidedly daring for the times: SUBSTITUTES/CAN DO/MORE HARM/THAN CITY FELLERS/ON A FARM. Others were distinctly morbid: HER CHARIOT/RACED AT 80 PER/THEY HAULED AWAY/WHAT HAD BEN HUR. Or HE LIT A MATCH/TO CHECK GAS TANK/THAT'S WHY/THEY CALL HIM/SKINLESS FRANK.

Sites were selected with great care. They had to be level, straight, and not cluttered with other signs. They were perfect for the Midwest, though in fact they appeared in every state but four: Arizona, Nevada, New Mexico and Massachusetts. The number of signs, and the fortunes of the company, both peaked in 1955. At 60 m.p.h. or more the signs became hard to read even when spaced further apart. They seemed old-fashioned. Rent and maintenance for the signs cost $200,000 a year by 1960, and, besides, the two- lane highways were increasingly out of the mainstream. In 1963 the last of the Burma-Shave signs were removed. America was no longer a nation of two-lane highways. A golden age was over.

IV

In 1919 the US Army sent a convoy of trucks cross-country from Camp Meade, Maryland, to San Francisco, just to see if it could be done. It could, but only just. The trip took two months at an average speed of less than 7 m.p.h. The young officer in charge of the convoy was Dwight D. Eisenhower. Thirty-five years later, as President of the United States, he appointed a committee to study America's transportation needs. As Kenneth T. Jackson has observed: 'The committee considered no alternative to a massive highway system, and it suggested a major redirection of national policy to benefit the car and the truck.'[43] This should have come as no great surprise; the chairman of the committee was on the board of directors of General Motors. In 1956, in response to the committee's urgings, Eisenhower signed into law the landmark Interstate Highway Act, inaugurating the construction of 42,500 miles of superhighway and kicking off an era when America would spend 75 per cent of its transportation funds on highways and a slightly less than munificent 1 per cent on mass transit for cities.

High-speed roads had already been around for some time by 1956. The first freeway (of sorts) was the fifteen-mile-long Bronx River Parkway, opened in the 1920s, with a speed limit of a then breakneck 35 m.p.h. The name parkway was significant. These roads were designed for leisure driving for the middle classes. Commercial vehicles were prohibited (and anyway bridge clearances were kept intentionally low to keeps trucks and buses from sneaking on to them). They were lavishly landscaped and endowed with graceful curves and wooded medians to enhance their aesthetics. Billboards, gas stations and other roadside detritus were ruthlessly excluded. They weren't so much highways as sylvan glades where you could exercise your car.

The great builder of parkways was Robert Moses, the New York City parks commissioner, who ironically never learned to drive a car. He presided over the construction of such roads as the Meadowbrook Parkway to Long Island, the Henry Hudson Parkway, and the Taconic Parkway through the Taconic River Valley. Built between 1940 and 1950, the Taconic was possibly the most beautiful American highway ever built, but already it was an anachronism. By 1950 Americans had stopped thinking of driving as something you did for fun. It was something you did to get to where you could have fun. For this new style of driving something new was needed: the superhighway.

One of the enduring myths of American travel is that the nation's superhighways were modelled on Germany's *Autobahnen*. In fact, it was the other way round. Dr Fritz Todt, Hitler's superintendent of roads, came to the United States in the 1930s, studied America's sparkling new parkways and went back to Germany with a great deal of enthusiasm and a suitcase full of notes. Most people's first contact with superhighways were the models of Norman Bel Geddes's hugely popular Futurama exhibit at the 1939 New York World's Fair. Designed to show the world as it would be – or as General Motors would like it to be – twenty-five years hence in 1964, the exhibit comprised a large layout of model towns, cities, and countryside, all linked by sleek multilane highways along which tiny cars glided with ceaseless speed and ease. It was remarkably prescient. (Futurama also had a linguistic impact. Before long American roadsides were graced with Shop-o-ramas, Fisheramas, a Kosherama or two, and at least one Striperama.)

Within a year, Bel Geddes's vision was made reality with the opening of the Pennsylvania Turnpike, running 160 miles from just west of Harrisburg to just east of Pittsburgh. Designed primarily to provide work for the unemployed during the Depression, it opened on 1 October 1940. For the first six months it had no speed limits. Motorists could drive the entire length in two and a half hours – half the time it had taken on the old Lincoln Highway – for a toll of $1.50. Features that would soon become familiar all over America – clover-leaf interchanges, long entrance and exit lanes, service areas – astounded and gratified the 2.4 million motorists who came to experience this marvel of the age in its first year.

Two months after the Pennsylvania Turnpike opened, and two thousand miles away, American motoring passed another milestone with the opening of the first true freeway in – it all but goes without saying – Los Angeles when the mayor cut a tape and a procession of cars filled with dignitaries (three of which crashed in the excitement) rolled on to the eight-mile-long Arroyo Seco Parkway. Despite the semi-bucolic name, the Arroyo Seco Parkway wasn't a parkway at all but a sleek, brutally purposeful, eight-lane artery designed to move high volumes of traffic at speed. Pleasure didn't come into it. The age of the *freeway* – a term coined by a lawyer named E. M. Bassett to distinguish this new kind of serious motorway from the poky, old-fashioned parkway – had begun. As if in recognition of this, the Arroyo Seco was soon renamed the

Pasadena Freeway. Ironically, it was intended to lure shoppers downtown, rather than help locals flee to the suburbs.

Conventional wisdom has it that Los Angeles's sprawl is a consequence of its extensive post-war freeway system. In fact, it was because the city was sprawling already that freeways were thought a practical way of connecting its far-flung parts. It sprawled because it had the finest public transportation network in America, if not the world, with over a thousand miles of rail and trolley lines.

Freeways in fact evolved slowly on the west coast, at least at first. As late as 1947, the whole of California had just nineteen miles of them. Then along came State Senator Randolph Collier, from the remote town of Yreka, as far from Los Angeles as you can get in California. For forty years he dominated the California highway programme, not just promoting the construction of freeways, but repeatedly blocking the funding of rail systems (which he called 'rabbit transport'). By the mid-1950s most Californians had no choice but to take to the freeways. Today one-third of all the land in Los Angeles is given over to the automobile, and the Los Angeles County Transportation Commission has a larger budget ($4.5 billion in 1991) than the city it serves.[44]

Soon every city had to have a freeway of its own, even if it meant scything through old neighbourhoods, as with Boston's destructive Downtown Artery, or slicing into a beauty spot like Fairmont Park with the Schuylkill (popularly known as the 'Sure-Kill') Expressway in Philadelphia. At one time there was even a plan to drive a freeway through New Orleans's French Quarter.

As the freeways remodelled cities, so the new interstates dealt a blow to the old two-lane highways that stretched between them. Had it not been for the distraction of World War II, America almost certainly would have had a network of superhighways much earlier. The idea was really the brainchild of Franklin Delano Roosevelt, who saw the construction of a national high-speed highway system as the ultimate public works project. By the 1950s, Eisenhower saw in it the additional virtue of enhancing America's defence capabilities. Bridge and tunnel clearances were designed not for trucks but for the movement of intercontinental ballistic missiles. During the quarter-century beginning in 1956, America spent $118 billion on interstate highways. It was, as Phil Patton has put it, the 'last programme of the New Deal and the first space programme'.[45]

In less than two decades, America's modern interstate highways drained the life from thousands of towns. No longer was it necessary – and before long often not even possible – to partake of the traditional offerings of two-lane America: motels with cherishably inane names like the Nite-E-Nite Motor Court and the Dew Drop Inn, roadside diners with blinking neon signs and a mysterious fondness for meat loaf and mashed potatoes, two-pump gas stations built in the cosy style of a rustic cottage. Today in western Nebraska the old Lincoln Highway, or Route 30, is so little used that grass grows in its cracks. At the state border with Wyoming, it disappears altogether, abruptly and unceremoniously buried beneath the white concrete of Interstate 80. Like Route 66, the Dixie Highway and other once great roads, it has become a fading memory, and what a sad loss that is.

What's Cooking?: Eating in America

To the first Pilgrims, the gustatory possibilities of the New World were slow in revealing themselves. Though the woods of New England abounded in hearty sustenance – wild duck and turkey, partridge, venison, wild plums and cherries, mushrooms, all manner of nuts and berries – and though the waters teemed with fish, the Pilgrims showed a grim reluctance to eat anything that did not come from their dwindling stockpile of salt pork (which they called 'salt horse'), salt fish and salt beef, hard tack (a kind of biscuit baked so hard that it became more or less impervious to mould, weevils and human teeth), dried peas and dried beans, 'almost preferring', in the words of one historian, 'to starve in the midst of plenty rather than experiment with the strange but kindly fruits of the earth'.[1] Or as another put it: 'The first settlers had come upon a land of plenty. They nearly starved in it.'[2]

Lobster was so plentiful that 'the least boy in the Plantation may both catch and eat what he will of them', but hardly any did. John Winthrop lamented in a letter home that he could not have his beloved mutton but only such impoverished fare as oysters, duck, salmon and scallops. Clams and mussels they did not eat at all, but fed to their pigs. To their chagrin the colonists discovered that English wheat was unsuited to the soil and climate of New England. The crops were repeatedly devastated by a disease called smut. For the better part of two centuries wheat would remain a luxury in the colonies. Even their first crop of peas failed, a consequence not so much of the challenges of the New England climate as of their own inexperience as farmers. With their food stocks dwindling and their aptitude as hunter-gatherers sorely taxed, the outlook for this small group of blundering, in-experienced, hopelessly underprepared immigrants was bleak indeed.

Fortunately, there were Indians to save them. The Indians of the New World were already eating better than any European. Native Americans enjoyed some two thousand different foods, a number that even the wealthiest denizen of the Old World would have found unimaginably varied. Among the delicacies unique to the New World were the white and sweet potato, the peanut, the pumpkin and its cousin the squash, the persimmon (or 'putchamin' as the first colonists recorded it), the avocado, pineapple, chocolate and vanilla, cassava (source of tapioca), chilli peppers, sunflowers and the tomato – though of course not all of these were known everywhere. Even those plants that already existed in Europe were often of a superior variety in the New World. American green beans were far plumper and richer, and soon displaced the fibrous, chewy variety previously grown in Europe. Likewise, once Europeans got sight and taste of the fat, sumptuous strawberries that grew wild in Virginia, they gladly forsook the mushy little button strawberries that had theretofore been all they had known. The Indians' diet was healthier, too. At a time when even well-heeled Europeans routinely fell prey to scurvy and watched helplessly as their teeth fell from spongy gums, the Indians knew instinctively that a healthy body required a well-balanced diet.

Above all, however, their agriculture had a sophistication that European husbandry could not begin to compete with. They had learned empirically to plant beans among the corn, which not only permitted a greater yield from the same amount of land but also replenished the nitrogen that the corn took away. As a result, while Europeans struggled even in good years to scrape a living from the soil, the Indians of the New World enjoyed a constant bounty. That a single tribe in New England had sufficient surpluses to support a hundred helpless, unexpected visitors for the better part of a year is eloquent testimony of that.

The Indians' single most important gift to the colonists – apart from not wiping them out – was corn. Corn began as a wild grass, probably in the Tehuacán Valley of central Mexico. Converting a straggly wild grass into the plump and nutritious foodstuff we know today was possibly the greatest of all precolonial achievements. Corn will grow almost anywhere, and by 1620 was a well-established crop throughout the New World. To the original colonists, 'corn' signified any common grain, as it still does in Britain. So they adopted the Spanish name *maize* (after a West Indian Taino word, *mahiz*). Since maize was in effect the only type of grain there was, 'corn' gradually came to signify it alone. Corn has been domesticated for so long – some seven thousand years – that it is now totally dependent on humankind for its continued existence. Left on its own, the kernels of each cob – its seeds – would be strangled by the husk. Even in colonial times it was a far more demanding plant than the colonists were used to. With their usual vexing ineptitude the first colonists tried sowing it by broadcast method, as they did with other grains, and were baffled that it didn't grow. It took the natives to show them that corn flourished only when each seed was planted in a mound and helped along with a little fish-meal fertilizer.

By the early seventeenth century, many New World foods were already known in Europe, though not necessarily to the early English colonists. The first Pilgrims may have heard of, but almost certainly had never tasted, two New World foods: the tomato and white potato. Nor did they get the opportunity in their new-found land since these plants were unknown to the eastern seaboard. The Indians of the east coast did, however, have the sweet potato, and for almost two centuries when Americans talked of potatoes that was what they meant.

The white potato had reached England, via Spain, in the sixteenth century but suffered a crippling setback when the queen's cook, with that knack for culinary misapprehension with which the English have long distinguished themselves, discarded the tubers and cooked the leaves. For well over a century, the white potato was grown strictly as an ornamental plant until Europeans at last began to appreciate its manifold possibilities as a foodstuff. The Irish developed a particular attachment to it, not so much because of its agreeable versatility as because it was one of the few plants that would prosper on Irish soil. Elsewhere in the British Isles it remained largely unknown. It made its first recorded appearance in the American colonies in 1719, in Boston, though it was not until a gentleman farmer in Virginia named Thomas Jefferson tried cultivating the white potato – which he called the Irish potato – that it began to attract any attention in America as a potential food. Jefferson also appears to have been the first American to serve French fried potatoes – rather a daring thing to do since it was generally accepted that the tubers were toxic and that the only way to avoid a long and agonizing death was to boil them mercilessly. Until well into the 1800s almost no one dared to eat them any other way. It appears that the whole of Europe's potato output at this time came from just two plants brought back by the Spanish; this lack of genetic diversity is very probably what led to Ireland's devastating potato blight in the nineteenth century, with obvious consequences for American immigration. The word *spud*, incidentally, comes from the kind of spade with which potatoes were dug out. Though the word itself dates from the Middle Ages, it became associated with potatoes only in the 1840s.

The history of the tomato (from *tomatl*, like so many other food words a Nahuatl term) in the New World is strikingly similar to that of the potato. It was carried to Europe from South America by the Spanish, widely regarded as poisonous, treated for two centuries as a decorative curiosity, and finally rescued from obscurity by the ever industrious Thomas Jefferson, who made the first recorded mention of it in North America in 1781. He referred to it as the *tomata*. Until well into the nineteenth century it was regarded as dangerously exotic on its native soil, though a degree of caution is understandable since the tomato is after all a member of the nightshade family.

The colonists were, however, well acquainted with a New World food that abounded along the eastern seaboard: the turkey. A not unreasonable question is how a native American bird come to be named for a country four thousand miles away. The answer is that when turkeys first appeared in England, some eighty years before the *Mayflower* set sail, they were mistakenly supposed to have come from Turkey. They had in fact come from Spain, brought there from Mexico by Hernán Cortés's expedition of 1519. Many other European nations made a similar geographical error in naming the bird. The French thought they came from India and thus called them chickens '*d'Inde*,' from which comes the modern French *dindon*. The Germans, Dutch and Swedes were even more specifically inaccurate in their presumptions, tracing the bird to the Indian city of Calicut, and thus gave it the respective names *Kalekuttisch Hün, kalkoen* and *kalkon*. By the 1620s, the turkey was so well known in Europe, and its provenance had so long been assumed to be the Near East, that the Pilgrims were astounded to find them in abundance in their new-found land. A similar linguistic misunderstanding obtained with another native American food, the Jerusalem artichoke, which is not an artichoke at all – indeed it doesn't even look like an artichoke – but rather is the root of the sunflower *Helianthus tuberosus*. Jerusalem is merely a corruption of the Italian word for sunflower, *girasole*.

Under the patient tutelage of the Indians, the colonists gradually became acquainted with, and even developed a fondness for, native products like pumpkins, at first generally called *pompions*, and squashes, which the colonists confusingly also called *pompions*. Pumpkin pie became a big hit after the Pilgrims were introduced to it at their second Thanksgiving feast in 1623, but the conventional spelling didn't become established until much later. As late as 1796, the first American cookbook – a slender volume with the dauntingly all-embracing title of *American Cookery, or the Art of Dressing Viands, Fish, Poultry and Vegetables, and the Best Modes of Making Pâtés, Puffs, Pies, Tarts, Puddings, Custards and Preserves and All Kinds of Cakes, from the Imperial Plumb to Plain Cake, Adapted to this Country and All Grades of Life, by Amelia Simmons: An American Orphan* – called the dish 'pumpkin pie'. Pumpkin pie was also called *pumpkin pudding* until the mid-1600s, pudding then suggesting a pie without a top crust.

The Indians introduced the colonists not only to new foods, but to more interesting ways of preparing them. Succotash, clam chowder, hominy, corn pone, cranberry sauce, johnnycakes, even Boston baked beans and Brunswick stew were all Indian dishes. In Virginia it was the Indians, not the white settlers, who invented Smithfield ham.[3] Even with the constant advice and intervention of the Indians the Puritans stuck to a diet that was for the most part resolutely bland. Meat and vegetables were boiled without pity, deprived of seasonings and served lukewarm. Peas, once they got the hang of growing them, were eaten at almost every meal, and often served cold. The principal repast was taken at midday and called *dinner*. *Supper*, a word related to *soup* (and indeed at the time still often spelled *souper*), was often just that – a little soup with perhaps a piece of bread – and was consumed in the evening shortly before retiring. Lunch was a concept yet unknown, as was the idea of a snack. To the early colonists, 'snack' meant the bite of a dog.

Johnnycake is sometimes said to be a contraction of *journey cake*, the idea being that it was a food packed for journeys, but since it is a kind of corn-bread and corn-bread patently is not a travelling food, the explanation is unconvincing. Another suggestion is that it is a corruption of *Shawnee cake*. As Ciardi notes, in New England it was called *jonakin* or *jonikin* long before it was called *johnnycake*, suggesting that *johnnycake* is a folk etymology based on some earlier, forgotten Indian term.[4] Two other travelling foods known to early Americans were pemmican and jerked beef. Despite the name, nothing is jerked to make jerked beef. The word comes from *charqui,* a Spanish adaptation of a Peruvian Indian word. Though the variant name *jerky* is etymologically closer to the Spanish original, it actually entered the language much later. *Jerked beef* was well established in the colonies by the early eighteenth century. *Jerky* is not attested before 1850. *Pemmican,* more straightforwardly, is from the Cree *pimikân.*

The Pilgrims naturally brought many Old World dishes with them, among them flummery (a sweet dish made of flour or cornstarch, sufficiently insipid to still be eaten in England, where it is called blancmange), dunderfunk (a kind of hard-tack hash fractionally enlivened with molasses), frumenty (a milky mush), hoe-cake (another kind of mush), and that mysterious compound of the Little Miss Muffett nursery rhyme, curds and whey. (For the record, curds are the coagulated residue of milk and whey the watery remains created while making cheese.) Curds were also used to make syllabub, another sweet dish.

Pudding signified not just a dessert (a word that had recently entered the language from France and was pronounced 'duh-*zart*') but a wider range of dishes, from black or blood pudding to hasty pudding (a cornmeal mush so named because it could be prepared quickly). Cranberries were at first also called *craneberries, cramberries* or *bounceberries* because you bounced them to see if they were fresh. *Fool,* as in gooseberry fool, meant clotted cream. *Duff,* as in plum duff, merely reflected a variant pronunciation of *dough.* Doughnuts, which the Puritans had discovered from the Dutch during their years in Holland, did not have the hole with which we associate them now, but were small balls – 'nuts' in the parlance of the time – of fried dough. They also ate doughboys, often spelled 'dowboys', a dumpling made of flour or cornmeal.

Until 1624, when the first shipment of cows reached Plymouth, the colony's supply of livestock consisted of only half a dozen goats, fifty pigs and about as many chickens, but by the mid-1630s matters were improving rapidly. By then, with the population of Massachusetts standing at more than 4,000, the colony could boast 1,500 cows, 4,000 goats and 'swine innumerable'. Cows primarily had a dairy role. For a very long while meat came almost exclusively in the form of pork – indeed, in the South 'meat' and 'pork' were used interchangeably.

As time moved on, the diet of the average American became heartier if not a great deal more appealing. In an environment where women devoted their lives to an endless, exhausting round of doing everything from weaving to making soap and candles to salting and pickling anything that could be preserved, it is hardly surprising that quality cooking was at a premium and that most people were, in the words of Thomas Jefferson, 'illy fed'. None the less, by the late eighteenth century, portions for almost everyone were abundant, and visitors from the Old World commonly remarked on the size of meals in even the humblest households. For the wealthier families, dishes were varied and, by earlier standards, exotic. The cookbook kept at Mount Vernon, written by George Washington's mother, tells us much about both the variety of foods eaten and their sometimes curious spelling and pronunciation, notably 'mushrumps', 'hartichocke pie', 'fryckecy of chicken', and 'lettice tart'.

By the time of the Revolution, the main meal was taken between two and four o'clock in the afternoon, and eaten in an order that strikes us today as a trifle odd. A typical meal might consist of salted beef with potatoes and peas, followed by baked or fried eggs, fish and salad, with a variety of sweets, puddings, cheeses and pastries to finish, all washed down with quantities of alcohol that would leave most of us today unable to rise from the table.[5] Meat was consumed in quantities that left European observers slack-jawed in astonishment. By the early 1800s the average American was eating almost 180 lb. of meat a year, 48 lb. more than people were consuming a century later, but fresh meat remained largely unknown because of the difficulty of keeping it fresh. Even city people often had chickens in the yard and a hog or two left to scavenge in the street. Until well into the nineteenth century visitors to New York remarked on the hazard to traffic presented by wandering hogs along Broadway. Even in the more temperate north, meat would go off in a day in summer, and milk would curdle in as little as an hour. Spoiled food was a daily hazard for the wealthy as much as for the poor. One guest at a dinner party given by the Washingtons noted with a certain vicious relish that the General discreetly pushed his plate of sherry trifle to one side when he discovered that the cream was distinctly iffy but that the less discerning Martha continued shovelling it away with gusto. Ice-cream was a safer option. It was first mentioned in America in the 1740s when a guest at a banquet given by the governor of Maryland wrote about this novelty which, he noted, 'eat most deliciously'.

Thomas Jefferson, thanks to his scrupulous – one might say obsessive – record-keeping (for eight years, while helping to run a new nation, he found time to track the first and last appearances on Washington market stalls of thirty-seven types of vegetable), has left us the most complete chronicle of the life of a farmer in colonial times, but also the least typical. As we have already seen with the tomato and potato, Jefferson was a tireless experimenter with foods and grew any number of plants that most Americans had never heard of, among them such exotica as eggplant, damson plums, Savoy cabbages, sugar beets, cauliflower, endive, chicory (which he called *succory*), broccoli, celery and a kind of squash called cymling. Only grapes of a sufficient calibre to make a palatable wine eluded him, to his unending despair.[6]

Other planters were less adventurous, but compensated with quantity. Diners at the finer homes were commonly offered eight or ten kinds of meat or fish, a galaxy of vegetables, and half a dozen desserts, all washed down with copious quantities of wine, porter, rum, beer or Madeira. Jefferson, in his first year in the White House, spent $2,800 – more money than many people saw in a lifetime – on wine alone.

For farmers, food was almost entirely home-grown. As late as 1787, even a prosperous yeoman farmer in New England might spend no more than $10 a year on all outside purchases. This might include a little tea or coffee, a good deal of salt and perhaps some molasses, but in all other respects he and his household were entirely self-sufficient.

By the mid-1800s many Americans were eating well enough to give foreign critics something new to be appalled at. A correspondent for *The Times* of London recorded with amazement a 'typical' American breakfast – 'black tea and toast, scrambled eggs, fresh spring shad, wild pigeons, pigs' feet, two robins on toast, oysters' – and that, he implied, was one of the lighter repasts.[7] If such breakfasts were eaten, and a touch of scepticism might not be misplaced here, they weren't eaten by everyone. The bulk of urban dwellers ate poorly, partly because their meagre wages didn't permit better, but also because such medical advice as filtered down to them suggested that most fresh foods were hazardous. Until the mid-nineteenth century, received wisdom had it that anyone reckless enough to consume an apple or pear or indeed almost any other vegetative product was all but asking for a speedy death at the hand of typhoid, dysentery or cholera.[8] During cholera epidemics city councils routinely banned the sale of fruits and salads, but even during comparatively safe periods most people thought it imprudent to feed almost any plant food (with the exception of a well-boiled potato) to the more susceptible members of the community, especially children, who of course most needed the vitamins. As a result, diseases associated with malnutrition stalked even the better-off families.

Milk, too, was widely regarded as perilous, though with some justification, since it spoiled quickly and was processed and delivered in a manner that owed little – in fact nothing – to modern standards of hygiene. Almost every family had a story of a member who had died of 'milksick' or 'the trembles' after drinking tainted milk.

As the nineteenth century progressed, diet evolved into two camps – the few who ate well and the many who did not – and class antagonisms were not long in emerging. The patrician New Yorker Martin Van Buren was ousted from the Presidency in 1840 in large part because one of his Whig opponents made a celebrated speech attacking Van Buren for serving such delicate and unmanly fare in the White House as strawberries, cauliflower and celery. (Van Buren gained a sort of vicarious revenge when at the subsequent inauguration the crusty William Henry Harrison refused to don an overcoat, contracted pneumonia and with alarming haste expired; his tenure as President was just thirty days, much of that spent unconscious.)

Gradually even poorer Americans became acquainted with a wider variety of fruits and vegetables, though the linguistic evidence shows that they weren't always quite sure what to make of them. For the potato alone, the *Dictionary of American English on Historical Principles* records such arresting nineteenth-century concoctions as potato custard, potato chowder, potato pone, potato pudding and even potato coffee. We can assume that most of these were consumed in a spirit of either experimentation or desperation and that most didn't survive long in the native diet.

Only a relative handful of new foods entered the American vocabulary in the nineteenth century, among them *pretzel* (1824), *pumpernickel* (1839), *liverwurst* (1869), *tutti-frutti* (1876) and *spaghetti* (1880). What changed was the *way* Americans ate. In particular they began to eat out. Before the 1820s, dining out was an activity reserved almost exclusively for travellers. Though it was possible to eat in hotels and taverns, there were no places dedicated to the public consumption of food for the mere pleasure of it, nor any word to describe them. Then in 1827 a new word and concept entered American English from France: *restaurant*.

It was in that year that two Swiss-born brothers, Giovanni and Pietro Del-Monico, opened a coffee and pastry shop in the Battery district of New York City. The enterprise was sufficiently successful that in 1831 they invited their nephew Lorenzo to join them. Though just nineteen and with no experience in catering, Lorenzo was born to culinary greatness. He did none of the cooking, but he did buy the food, and made a point of arriving before dawn at the city's main markets to acquire the best and freshest provisions, a practice now routine but at the time unheard-of. He transformed the Del-Monicos' pastry shop into America's premier restaurant (actually a series of restaurants: Delmonico's moved frequently and sometimes operated under as many as four roofs at once), bringing a dimension of elegance to American dining that it had theretofore lacked. Under the new, unhyphenated name Delmonico's, the restaurant introduced Americans to many unfamiliar dishes, ranging from artichokes and mayonnaise (named originally for the Minorcan port Mahón)[9] to fricasseed calf's head, and invented several as well, notably lobster Newburg, which began life as lobster à la Wenburg. It was so called in honour of an esteemed client, Ben Wenburg, until he disgraced himself through some unseemly (but intriguingly unspecified) altercation on the premises, and the dish was abruptly anagrammatized. A similar transformation happened with another Delmonico's creation, chicken à la Keene, named for one Foxhall Keene, which became over time (for reasons that appear to have gone unnoted) chicken à la king.

Inspired by Delmonico's example, restaurants sprouted all over. By the 1870s New York City alone had over five thousand restaurants, many of them, like La Maison Dorée, Louis Sherry's and Lüchows, of a standard comparable to the finest restaurants of Europe. With the new restaurants came new dishes, like Waldorf salad and eggs Benedict, both created at the Waldorf-Astoria in the 1890s. The latter was designed as a hangover cure for one Samuel Benedict, though how anyone with a hangover could face poached eggs swimming in hollandaise sauce and think it recuperative will for ever be a mystery to me.[10]

For many immigrants, and for the Italians in particular, the restaurant business became an attractive way to establish a foothold in the New World. *Trattorie* – family-run restaurants – became a feature on street corners in every large city, some of them growing into large and celebrated establishments like Mama Leone's and Sardi's in New York and Colisimo's in Chicago. Most, however, stayed small, like G. Lombardi's on Spring Street in New York, which would now be forgotten to history except that one of its early proprietors had the uncommon prescience in 1905 to introduce Americans to a dish for which they would develop an abiding addiction: the pizza.[11]

Many 'classic' Italian dishes are in fact New World creations. Chicken tetrazzini – chicken in a cream sauce on spaghetti – was named for the Italian soprano Luisa Tetrazzini but invented in New York. The caesar salad comes from Tijuana. It was devised by a restaurateur named Caesar Cardini who, so the story goes, whipped up the salad from leftover ingredients when a party of hungry guests descended on him late one night. Fettuccine primavera was born in the kitchen of New York's Le Cirque restaurant. Veal parmigiana, clams Posillipo, fettuccine Alfredo, even spaghetti and meatballs were all products designed to satisfy the American palate. 'By the 1950s,' as one writer has put it, 'Italian-American food was all but unrecognizable to visitors from Italy. A businessman from Turin might peruse a menu in an Italian restaurant in Chicago and not be able to decipher a single item.'[12]

A similar situation obtained with many other well-loved 'foreign' foods. Russian dressing is unknown to the Russians, as is the American variety of French dressing to the French. Vichyssoise was invented not in France but in New York in 1910, and Liederkranz cheese sprang not from Germany, or even from Austria or Switzerland, but from Monroe, New York, in 1892. (The name, meaning 'wreath of song', commemorates a local choral society.) Chilli con carne was unknown in Spain until introduced there from the New World. Salisbury steak has nothing to do with the English cathedral city (it was named for an American, Dr J. H. Salisbury), nor does Swiss steak have even the tiniest alpine pedigree. Chop-suey (based on the Cantonese word for miscellany) first saw light not in China but in San Francisco in the late 1800s, though the word itself does not appear in print until 1903. The fortune cookie was invented in Los Angeles in the second decade of this century. More recent still is chow mein, which first appeared in 1927, though the pidgin word *chow* dates in print from 1856 and the slightly more emphatic *chowchow* is first recorded in 1857.[13]

As America became increasingly urbanized, people took to eating their main meal in the evening. To fill the void between breakfast and dinner, a new and essentially American phenomenon arose: lunch. The words *lunch* and *luncheon* (often spelled *lunchon, lunchen, lunchion* or *lunching*) have been around in English since the late 1500s. Originally they signified lumps of food – 'a lunchen of cheese' – and may have come from the Spanish *lonja*, a slice of ham. The word was long considered a deplorable vulgarism, suitable only to the servants' hall. In America, however, 'lunch' became respectable, and as it dawned on opportunistic restaurateurs that each day millions of office workers required something quick, simple and cheap, a wealth of new facilities sprang up to answer the demand. In short order Americans got *diners* (1872), *lunch counters* (1873), *self-service restaurants* (1885), *cafeterias* (1890s), *automats* (1902), and *short-order restaurants* (1905).

The process began in 1872 in Providence, Rhode Island, when one Walter Scott loaded a wagon with sandwiches, boiled eggs and other such fare and parked outside the offices of the *Providence Journal*. Since all the restaurants in town closed at 8 p.m. he had no competition and his business thrived. Soon wagons began appearing all over. By the time Scott retired forty-five years later he had fifty competitors in Providence alone. They were called *lunch wagons*, which was odd: because they didn't come out until dusk, lunch was the one thing they didn't serve. When residents complained about having food served outside their houses, cities everywhere enacted ordinances banning the wagons. So the lunch wagon proprietors hit on the idea of moving their wagons to vacant lots, taking off the wheels and calling them restaurants, since restaurants were immune from the restrictions. By the 1920s several companies were mass-producing shiny, purpose-built restaurants known everywhere as *diners*. From a business point of view diners were an appealing proposition. They were cheap to buy and maintain. You could set them up in hours on any level piece of ground, and if trade didn't materialize you loaded them on to a flat-bed truck and moved them elsewhere. A single diner in a good location could make a profit of $12,000 a year – a lot of money in the 1920s. One of the more enduring myths of American eating is that diners were built out of old railway dining-cars. Hardly any were. They were just made to look that way.

The first place known to be called a *cafeteria* – though the proprietor spelled it *cafetiria* – was opened in Chicago in the early 1890s. The word came from Cuban Spanish and as late as 1925 was still often pronounced in the Spanish style, with the accent on the penultimate syllable. Cafeterias proved so popular that they spawned a huge, if mercifully short-lived, vogue for words of similar form: *washeteria, groceteria, caketeria, drugeteria, bobateria* (a place where hair was bobbed), *beauteria, chocolateria, shaveteria, smoketeria, hardware-ateria, garmenteria, furnitureteria* – even *casketeria* for a funeral home and the somewhat redundant *restauranteria*.

The automat – a cafeteria where food was collected from behind little windows after depositing the requisite change in a slot – was not an American invention but a Swedish one. In fact, they had been common in Sweden for half a century before two entrepreneurs named Horn and Hardardt opened one in Philadelphia in 1902 and started a small, lucrative empire.

Luncheonette (sometimes modified to *lunchette*) entered American English in about 1920 and in its turn helped to popularize a fashion for words with -*ette* endings: *kitchenette, dinette, usherette, roomette, bachelorette, drum majorette,* even *parkette* for a meter maid and *realtyette* for a female estate agent.[14]

The waitresses and hash slingers (an Americanism dating from 1868) who worked in these establishments evolved a vast, arcane and cloyingly jocular lingo for the food they served and the clients who ate it. By the 1920s if you wanted to work behind a lunch counter you needed to know that 'Noah's boy' was a slice of ham (since Ham was one of Noah's sons) and that 'burn one' or 'grease spot' designated a hamburger. 'He'll take a chance' or 'clean the kitchen' meant an order of hash, 'Adam and Eve on a raft' was two poached eggs on toast, 'cats' eyes' was tapioca pudding, 'bird seed' was cereal, 'whistleberries' were baked beans' and 'dough well done with cow to cover' was the somewhat laboured way of calling for an order of toast and butter. Food that had been waiting too long was said to be 'growing a beard'. Many of these shorthand terms have since entered the mainstream, notably 'BLT' for a bacon, lettuce and tomato sandwich, 'over easy' and 'sunny side up' in respect of eggs, and 'hold' as in 'hold the mayo'.

Eating out – usually quickly, cheaply and greasily – became a habit for urban workers and a big business for the providers. Between 1910 and 1925 the number of restaurants in America rose by 40 per cent. A hungry New Yorker in 1925 could choose from among 17,000 restaurants, double the number that had existed a decade before.[15] Even drugstores got in on the act. By the early 1920s, the average drugstore, it was estimated, did 60 per cent of its business at the soda fountain.[16] They had become in effect restaurants that also sold pharmaceutical supplies.

As the nineteenth century wore on and the American diet became consistently livelier, it inevitably sparked alarm among those who believed that sensual pleasures were necessarily degenerate. There arose mighty bands of men and women who believed with a kind of religious fervour that the consumption of the wrong foods would lead to the breakdown of the nation's moral fibre. One man went so far as to form a Society for the Suppression of Eating, which would appear to be taking matters about as far as they will go. Others were only slightly more accommodating to the need for sustenance. Typical of the breed was the Revd Sylvester Graham, who equated insanity with eating ketchup and mustard, and believed that the consumption of meat would result in the sort of hormonal boisterousness that leads men to take advantage of pliant women. Many believed him – so many indeed that by mid-century the nation was not only following his cheerless recipes, but many thousands of people were living in Graham boarding-houses, where his dietary precepts were imposed with rigour. Then there was Horace Fletcher, who gave the world the notion that each bite of food should be chewed thirty-two times. Though he had no standing as a nutritionist – he was an importer by trade – that didn't stop him from disseminating his theories in a phenomenally successful book, *The ABC of Nutrition*, published in 1903.

But the zenith of America's long, obsessive coupling of food with moral rectitude came with a Seventh Day Adventist doctor named John Harvey Kellogg who in 1876 took over the failing Western Health Reform Institute in Battle Creek, Michigan, renamed it the Medical and Surgical Sanitarium (though everyone soon knew it as the Battle Creek Sanitarium or simply the Kellogg) and introduced a regime of treatments that was as bizarre as it was popular. Possibly the two were not unconnected.

Patients who were underweight were confined to their beds with sandbags on their abdomens and forced to eat up to twenty-six meals a day. They were not permitted any physical exertion. Even their teeth were brushed by an attendant lest they needlessly expend a calorie.[17] The hypertensive were required to eat grapes and nothing else – up to 14 lb. of them daily. Others with less easily discernible maladies were confined to wheelchairs for months on end and fed experimental foods such as gluten wafers and 'a Bulgarian milk preparation known as yogurt'. Kellogg himself was a trifle singular in his habits. It was his practice to dictate long tracts on the evils of meat-eating and masturbation (the one evidently led to the other) while seated on the lavatory or while riding his bicycle in circles around the lawn. Despite – or very possibly because of – these peculiarities, Kellogg's 'Temple of Health', as he liked to call it, thrived and grew into a huge complex of buildings with such classy amenities as elevators, room service and a palm house with its own orchestra. Among its devoted and well-heeled patrons were Teddy Roosevelt and John D. Rockefeller.

Throughout much of his life, Kellogg nurtured a quiet obsession with inventing a flaked breakfast cereal. One night the process came to him in a dream. He hastened in his nightshirt to the kitchen where he boiled some wheat, rolled it out into strips and baked it in the oven. It was not only tasty but sufficiently unusual as to be without question good for you. Dr Kellogg's patients simply couldn't get enough of it. One of these patients was a young man named C. W. Post, who spent nine months at the sanitarium sitting listlessly and needlessly in a wheelchair before abruptly embracing Christian Scientism and fleeing. One thing Post took away with him was a profound respect for the commercial possibilities of Dr Kellogg's cereal. Unable to get a licence from Kellogg, he decided to make his own, and in a breathtakingly short time became one of America's wealthiest men. Among Post's inventions were *Grape-Nuts* (a curious name since it contained neither grapes nor nuts) and *Post Toasties*, or *Elijah's Manna* as it was known until 1908.

As it dawned on townspeople that breakfast cereals were awfully easy to make, imitators sprang up. Soon, it appears, almost everyone in town was at it. By the turn of the century at least forty-four companies in Battle Creek were churning out breakfast cereals with names like *Grip Nuts, Hello-Billo, Malt-Ho, Flake-Ho, Korn Kure, Tryabita, Tryachewa, Oatsina, Food of Eden* and *Orange Meat* (which, like Grape-Nuts, contained none of the implied ingredients).[18] Without exception these products were sold as health foods.* Each packet of Grape-Nuts contained an illustrated leaflet, *The Road to Wellville*, explaining how a daily dose of the enclosed toasted wheat and barley granules would restore depleted brain and nerve cells, and build strong red blood. For a short but deliriously exciting time fortunes were there for the taking. A Methodist preacher named D. D. Martin cooked up some healthful

---

* And compared with later cereals they certainly were. Kellogg's Sugar Smacks, introduced in 1953, were 56 per cent sugar.

goop on the kitchen stove, dubbed it *Per-Fo* and immediately sold the formula for $100,000. Curiously almost the only person in Battle Creek unable to capitalize on Kellogg's invention was Kellogg himself. Not until 1907, when he at last brought to market his cornflakes, did he begin to get the credit and wealth his invention merited.

Preoccupation with health-enhancing qualities became a theme for all manner of foods. Moxie, known for its soft drinks, was founded in 1885 as the Moxie Nerve Food Company of Boston, and Dr Pepper, founded in the same year, was so called not because the name was catchy but because it sounded sternly healthful. For a time, it seemed that no food product could hope to sell unless it dealt vigorously with a range of human frailties. Quaker Oats claimed to curb nervousness and constipation. Fleischmann's Yeast not only soothed frayed nerves and loosed the bowels, but also dealt vigorously with indigestion, skin disorders, tooth decay, obesity and a vague but ominous-sounding disorder called 'fallen stomach'. Fleischmann's kept up these sweeping claims – occasionally added to them – until ordered to desist by the Federal Trade Commission in 1938 on the grounds that there wasn't a shred of evidence to support any of them.[19]

Against such a background it is little wonder that Americans turned with a certain enthusiasm to junk food. The term *junk food* didn't enter the American vocabulary until 1973, but the concept was there long before, and it began with one of the great breakthroughs in food history: the development of a form of edible solid chocolate.

Though a New World food (the Mayas and Aztecs so prized it that they used cocoa beans as money), chocolate took a long time to become a central part of the American diet. Not until just before the Revolution did it become known in colonial America, and then only as a drink. At first chocolate was so exotic that it was spelled and pronounced in a variety of ways – *chockolatta, chuchaletto, chocholate, chockolatto* – before finally settling in the late eighteenth century into something close to the original Nahuatl Indian word, *xocólatl*. Chocolate came from the cacao tree, which somehow became transliterated into English as *cocoa* (pronounced at first with three syllables: *co-co-a*).[20] The chocolate bar was invented in England in the 1840s and milk chocolate in Switzerland some thirty years later, but neither became popular in America until Milton Stavely Hershey gave the world the nickel Hershey bar in 1903. (The price would stay a nickel for the next sixty-seven years, but only at a certain palpable cost to the bar's dimensions. Just in the quarter-century following World War II, the bar shrank a dozen times, until by 1970, when it was beginning to look perilously like an after-dinner mint, the bar was reinvigorated in size and the price raised accordingly.)

As is so often the case with American entrepreneurs, Milton Hershey was an unlikely success. His formal education ended with the fourth grade and he spent decades as a struggling, small-time candy maker before suddenly and unexpectedly striking it rich in middle age with caramels, a new sensation that swept the country in the late nineteenth century.

In 1900 he sold his caramel business for $1 million – this at a time when $10 was a good weekly wage – and turned his attentions to the still fairly novel process of making milk chocolate. This new venture was such a huge and instantaneous success that within three years he was able to embark on building his own model community, complete with streets named Chocolate Avenue and Cocoa Avenue, near his birthplace of Derry Church in central Pennsylvania. Among the names Hershey considered for the new town were Ulikit, Chococoa City, and Qualitytells, but eventually he decided on Hersheykoko. For reasons lost to history, the postal authorities refused to countenance the name and he was forced to settle on the more mundane, but unquestionably apt, name of Hershey. As well as the world's largest chocolate factory, the town of Hershey boasted several parks, a boating lake, a museum, a zoo, a professional ice hockey team and the usual complement of banks, stores and offices, all owned by Mr Hershey. Hershey ran the town as a private fiefdom. He prowled the streets looking for malingering municipal workers, whom he would instantly dismiss, and personally supervised (with a certain presumed keenness) the censoring of movies at the local bijou. But he also engaged in many charitable works, most notably the building of one of the world's largest orphanages for boys (and boys alone; orphan girls would have to look elsewhere) and endowing it with most of his fortune, some $66 million (today worth $1.7 billion).

The first true candy bar – that is, one containing ingredients additional to chocolate – was the Squirrel Brand peanut bar introduced in 1905. But the golden age of candy bars was the 1920s. Several classics made their début in that busy decade – the Oh Henry! and Baby Ruth bars in 1920, the Milky Way and Butterfingers in 1923, Mr Goodbar in 1925, Snickers in 1930. The Baby Ruth, originally called the Kandy Kake, was not, as is often supposed, named for the baseball player – in 1920 Babe Ruth had only just joined the New York Yankees and the bulk of his celebrity lay before him – but for the daughter of President Grover Cleveland. This bonny infant had indeed captured America's heart and gained the affectionate sobriquet Baby Ruth, but that had been more than twenty years earlier, so the choice of her nickname for a candy bar in 1920 was a trifle odd. Still, it was perhaps no odder than Oh Henry!, named for a fresh-faced youth whose droll quips to the girls at the George Williamson candy factory in Chicago provoked the constant cry, 'Oh, Henry!'

Among the many hundreds of other candy bars loosed on a willing nation during the decade were Big Dearos, Fat Emmas, the Milk Nut Loaf and the intriguing Vegetable Sandwich. Made of chocolate-covered vegetables it was sold with the solemn assurance that 'it will not constipate'. As might have been predicted, constipation was not a compelling consideration among America's children and the Vegetable Sandwich soon disappeared from the scene. Equally improbable, I would have thought, was the Chicken Dinner candy bar, so called because it was supposed to engender the feeling of well-being provided by a steaming roast chicken dinner. Though few people were able to make the leap of imagination necessary to equate a five-cent chocolate peanut roll with a well-balanced meal, the Chicken Dinner sold well and survived into the 1960s. Curiously, none of these products was known as a candy bar. The term is not recorded in print until 1943.

The 1920s saw the birth of many other well-loved snack foods, including such perennial mainstays of the American diet as the Good Humor bar in 1920, the Eskimo Pie a year later, Popsicles in 1924, Milk Duds in 1926, and Dubble Bubble Gum in 1928. This last was invented by Frank H. Fleer, whose earlier bubble gum, Blibber-Blubber, was something of a failure – it tended to dissolve in the mouth but to stick tenaciously to everything else, including Junior's face, when popped – but who had made a fortune with an earlier invention, Chiclets.

All of these, however, paled in comparison with a dietary behemoth that emerged from the shadows in the 1920s and took its place at the top of the table. I refer of course to the hamburger.

No one knows where the first hamburger was made. The presumption has always been that it came to America from Hamburg, Germany, in the same way that the frankfurter came from Frankfurt and that baloney hailed from Bologna. However, this overlooks the niggling consideration that Hamburg has never had any tradition of serving such a dish. Given its central role in the American diet, the evidence as to when the hamburger first appeared and why it was so called is vexingly uncertain, though there is no shortage of claimants for the title. Among the more insistent, if not necessarily most likely, contenders have been the towns of Seymour, Wisconsin, and Hamburg, New York, both of which claim to have been the birthplace of the hamburger in 1885. Seymour attributes the invention to one Charles Nagreen and unequivocally advertises itself as the 'Home of the Hamburger', though its supporters tend to grow quiet when asked to explain on what basis Nagreen chose to commemorate a distant German city. More plausible, on the face of it, would appear to be the claim of Hamburg, New York, whose proponents believe that it was the inspired creation of the brothers Frank and Charles Menches, who developed it at the Erie County Fair in 1885.

Unfortunately for both claims, the etymological evidence suggests an earlier birth for the name, if not the dish. There is some evidence to suggest that it may have appeared as 'Hamburg steak' on a Delmonico's menu as early as 1836 or 1837. The first undisputed sighting has been traced to the *Boston Journal* of 16 February 1884, which wrote in passing, 'We take a chicken and boil it. When it is cold we cut it up as they do meat to make a Hamburg steak.' As so often happens with first citations, the context makes it clear that by this time the dish was already well known. Unfortunately, it also indicates that it was a different dish from the one we know today, involving as it did beef cut up rather than ground, and eaten cold. What is certain is that the Hamburg steak was widely called *hamburger steak* by 1889 (the fist reference was in a newspaper in Walla Walla, Washington, suggesting that by this time it was eaten nationwide). That term in turn was being shortened to *hamburger* by 1901, by which time it had come to signify a patty of ground beef fried on a grill.

But it was still not a sandwich. It was, rather, a lump of ground beef served bare and eaten with a knife and fork. Who first had the idea of serving it in a bun is unknown and essentially unprovable, though once again there is no shortage of claimants. One such is Louis' Lunch of New Haven, Connecticut, which claims to have invented the true article in 1900, though some purists dismiss Louis' on the grounds that it served its burgers (indeed still does) on toasted bread rather than buns. Kaelin's Restaurant in Louisville, meanwhile, claims to have concocted and named the first cheeseburger in 1934, and I have no doubt that there are many other places around the country making similar heartfelt assertions. At all events, we can safely say that by about 1910 the object that we now know and venerate as the hamburger was widely consumed and universally known by that name. In its early years the hamburger was often regarded by short-order cooks as a convenient way of passing off old or doubtful meat, and by its consumers, in consequence, as an item to be approached with caution. Not until 1921, with the rise of two entrepreneurs in Wichita, Kansas, did the hamburger begin to take its first vigorous strides towards respectability. The men in question were a former insurance executive named E. W. 'Billy' Ingram and a short-order cook named Walter A. Anderson, and their brilliant stroke was to offer the world decent hamburgers using fresh meat. Not much fresh meat, mind you. Their steam-fried hamburgers cost a nickel and weren't much larger. Ingram and Anderson managed to squeeze eighteen hamburgers from a pound of ground beef, significantly less than one ounce each. None the less, people were soon flocking to their tiny cubicle, built of rock-faced concrete shaped vaguely, and a little preposterously, in the image of a castle. They called it White Castle because, they explained, *white* symbolized purity and cleanliness, and *castle* suggested permanence and stability.

Anderson and Ingram hit on three novelties that sealed their success and have been the hallmarks of fast-food service ever since. They offered a limited menu, which promoted quick service and allowed them to concentrate on what they were good at; they kept their premises spotless, which encouraged confidence in their hygienic integrity; and they employed a distinctive, eye-catching design for the building, which made it instantly recognizable from blocks away. Soon there were White Castles all over the country and a following throng of eager imitators – White Tower, White Diamond, Royal Castle and White Crest – some of which survive to this day. The age of fast food was with us, though no one would know it as such for another thirty years. The expression *fast food* first appeared in 1954. *Takeout food* was even slower to arrive; its first recorded appearance is not until 1962.[21]

Before we part temporarily from the delights of hand-held comestibles, two other linguistic novelties of the early 1900s need mentioning. The first is *hot dog*. Memorably defined by H. L. Mencken as 'a cartridge filled with the sweepings of abattoirs', the hot dog had been part of the American scene since the early 1800s, but had gone under the name of *frankfurter* or *wienerwurst* (literally 'Vienna sausage', and corrupted to *wienie* as early as 1867). The modern name didn't arise until a popular cartoonist named T. A. 'Tad' Dorgan drew a picture of a dachshund in an elongated bun in the early 1900s and the term caught on in a big way. It was also helped by the fact that the catch-phrase *Hot dog!* as a cry of delight or approbation was also sweeping the nation.

Dorgan was responsible for a slew of catch-phrases, among them *cat's pyjamas, yes man, skiddoo, you said it, drugstore cowboy* and *yes, we have no bananas*, which he had picked up from an Italian fruit-seller and used in one of his cartoons. It became a national catch-phrase (one wonders how anyone found a context in which to employ it) and was soon set to music loosely plagiarized from 'I Dreamt That I Dwelt in Marble Halls' and became a national sensation.[22] (It is striking how many words have come into American English through comic strips. *Heebie-jeebies, hot mama, hotsy-totsy, bodacious* and *horsefeathers* were all either coined or popularized by W. B. 'Billy' DeBeck in his comic strips involving the characters Barney Google and Snuffy Smith. *Hooligan* was popularised by the comic strip 'Happy Hooligan'. *Keeping up with the Joneses* was an expression inspired by a comic strip by I. Bacheller begun in 1911. 'Popeye' popularized *goon* and *jeep*.)

At about the time that the hot dog was taking its place in the language, another much-loved snack came to prominence: the ice-cream cone. Its invention is commonly traced to the 1904 St Louis World's Fair. According to one story (and there are many to choose from), a waffle vendor and ice-cream seller were stationed side by side on the grand concourse and discovered that if they combined their products they could not only produce an appealing and portable treat but one that also eliminated the trouble, expense and hygienic uncertainty of having to supply dishes and spoons. Unfortunately for this story, the ice-cream cone already existed in 1904. A patent had been taken out a decade earlier by an Italian-American named Italo Marchiony. The ice-cream cone may have become popular at the fair – though that in itself is by no means certain – but it wasn't invented there. In any case, the term is not recorded in general usage before 1909.

II

And on to drinking. One of the more enduring misconceptions concerning the Puritans in America is that they abjured alcohol. In fact, they liked a good drink or even a not-so-good one. One of the more popular tipples of early America, especially at weddings and other big social occasions, was sack posset, a concoction made by combining any handy intoxicant, usually ale or wine, with thick clots of curdled milk, which may explain why no one drinks it any longer. The *sack* in the name has nothing to do with a cloth container, incidentally. It is a corruption of the Latin *siccus*, meaning dry.

If colonial Americans were not adventurous eaters, they were happy to take their drinks from almost anywhere. The international pedigree of drinking terminology is evidenced by, among many others, *julep*, from the Arabic *julab*; *sangría* (often called *san garee* in eighteenth-century America), from the Spanish word for blood; *toddy* from Hindi *tārē* or *tārī*, a kind of palm tree sap; and *beer*, from the Germanic *bēor* (and ultimately from the Latin *bibere*, 'to drink').

The early colonists showed a particular fondness for blending odd ingredients – eggs with milk and beer, for instance – and employed a variety of names to describe the result: *mum, perry, switchel, metheglin, egg pop, balderdash* (from which comes our word for nonsense), *cherry bounce*, any number of *flips*, and *cock ale*. This last named – a somewhat less than beguiling mixture of chicken soup and beer – is sometimes cited as the source for *cocktail*. Though *cocktail* is indubitably an Americanism – its first known appearance was in a newspaper in Hudson, New York, in 1806 – its similarity to *cock ale* is probably coincidental. Cock ale was never a popular drink – even in that adventurous age few thought of chicken soup as a distinguished addition to the punch bowl – and there is no known link between the two words. So where then does *cocktail* come from? According to Flexner, the term 'almost certainly' evolved from the French *coquetier*, or egg-cup, after a New Orleans apothecary who dispensed concoctions in egg-cups. Other, more literal-minded observers suggest that it has some connection with the tail of a rooster, though quite why the tail of a rooster would suggest a potent beverage is anyone's guess. A more ambitious and almost certainly fanciful theory is that the cocktail was invented for the daughter of King Oxolotl VIII of Mexico. Her name was Xochitl, which the Spanish translated as Coctel.[23] The word also bears a striking, but apparently coincidental, resemblance to a word from the Krio language of Sierra Leone, *kaktel*, meaning a scorpion, a creature with a notorious sting in its tail. One possibility that seems not to have been considered by any authority, so far as I can tell, is that it might refer to a stiff drink's capacity to make one's tail cock up. Applied to horses, the word took on that sense in England at almost exactly the time that it first appeared in a drinking context in America. At all events for most of its early life *cocktail* didn't have the whiff of sophisticated refinement now associated with it. In the 1820s, a Kentucky breakfast was defined as 'three cocktails and a chew of terbacker'.[24]

Through most of the eighteenth century the principal strong drink in America was rum, a shortening of *rumbullion*, a word whose origins are entirely obscure. Towards the end of the century a new drink came along that rapidly displaced it – bourbon. Bourbon was a by-product of the Whisky Rebellion of 1791, when the federal government imposed a bitterly opposed tax on domestic rye whisky. In an effort to evade taxation, some two thousand distillers fled to Kentucky – which was not yet a state and thus, they hoped, not subject to the tax – and set up their stills there. When the rye crop failed, they turned as an expedient to corn and found to their gratification that it produced a drink of uncommon smoothness. They called it after the county in which they had settled, though in fact it was not bourbon as we now know it. It was only later, after the 1820s, that distillers took to ageing it in oak casks, a process that gives modern bourbon its agreeable colour and flavour. Although there is still a Bourbon County in Kentucky, none of the state's bourbon is produced there (at least not legally). To say that it was popular barely hints at its effect. By the 1830s, the average adult American was drinking six gallons of bourbon a year – twenty-four times more than today.

Saloon, in the sense of a place to drink, is not recorded until 1848, though, oddly, *saloon-keeper* goes back to the eighteenth century.[25] From the French *salon*, it originally signified any large hall or other public gathering place. *Bootleg*, first used in 1855, comes from the American West. According to Dillard, enterprising traders sold liquor illegally to the Indians by putting it in a flat bottle that they could slip into their boot.[26] I have no grounds to dispute this, but it does seem to me evident that the amount of liquor one could transport in this way would be hardly worth the bother. Certainly there must have been more commodious places to hide illicit alcohol on any wagon. I suspect the term may be metaphorical.

Rotgut, often shortened to *rot*, dates from 1819. Those who drank too much would get the *jitters*, or *shakes*. For a time strong drink was known as *jitter sauce*, and one who took to it too heartily was a *jitterbug*, a sense resurrected by Cab Calloway in 1934 for a type of dance music. Chronic drinkers faced the prospect of ending up on *skid road*, a term that comes from western logging camps, where logs were slid down a track called a skid road. Eventually the word was transferred to the shanty towns that grew up near by and, misheard by easterners, was transliterated into *skid row*.[27]

In response to the increasing sottishness of Americans, there arose a vigorous temperance movement in the early nineteenth century and with it a new word: *teetotal*. No one knows where the word comes from but, as ever, there is no shortage of theories. The most plausible is that it was simply a jocular way of emphasizing the 'total' in 'total abstinence'. It appears to have first been used at a New York temperance meeting in 1827 and was common in both Britain and America by the 1830s.

Booze is not recorded in America before 1890, in a *Webster's Dictionary,* which is surprising since the word has existed in the shadows of respectability since Chaucer's time. We can assume that it was used in America long before 1890, but just didn't find its way into print. *Manhattan, highball, hangover, daiquiri* and *gin rickey* are all also first attested in the 1890s. *Daiquiri* comes from Daiquirí, Cuba, where a potent form of rum was made. *Gin rickey* evidently commemorates a certain Col. Rickey, but beyond that the story grows vague. Equally murky is the derivation of *Tom Collins.* According to Mencken the drink was named for a 'distinguished bartender' though tantalizingly he gives no further clues as to the gentleman's identity.

Drinking terms then grow quiet for a time, but on 16 January 1920 three ominous terms became suddenly fixed in the American consciousness: *the Eighteenth Amendment, the Volstead Act* and *Prohibition.* The first was the Constitutional amendment that made the whole thing possible, the second the law that laid down the terms of punishment, and the third the generic term for the whole business. Considering its impact on American habits, Prohibition slipped into law with remarkable ease. As Frederick Lewis Allen put it: 'The country accepted it not only willingly, but almost absent-mindedly.'[28] Many, including quite a few in the temperance movement itself, were under the impression that Prohibition would affect only hard liquor and that milder tipples like beer would be safe. How wrong they were.

The new law had a devastating effect on restaurants, particularly at the classier end of the market. Deprived of bar earnings, many had no choice but to close down or to tempt fate by quietly offering bootleg liquor. In 1921, Delmonico's suffered the mortal humiliation of being noisily raided after an undercover agent attending an afternoon *thé dansant* was served something with more kick than tea. The restaurant eventually gave up the fight on 21 May 1923, just short of its hundredth birthday. The same fate befell scores of other famous establishments across the land.

Wine growers to their dismay were reduced to producing harmless grape concentrate, which of course almost no one wanted. They recovered their composure, and their fortunes, when they discovered that there was nothing illegal about pasting a prominent label on each bottle announcing boldly, 'WARNING: WILL FERMENT AND TURN INTO WINE', and providing step-by-step instructions on how a careless consumer might inadvertently convert this healthful beverage into something with the power to make his legs wobble. Sacramental wine, excluded from the strictures of the Eighteenth Amendment, also showed a curious leap in sales, with some cynics suggesting that not all of it – or even much of it – was ending up in devout stomachs. In the years 1925 to 1939 American wine consumption actually trebled, and California's vineyards expanded from less than 100,000 acres before Prohibition to almost 700,000 acres afterwards.[29]

Seldom has any law anywhere led to greater hypocrisy or been more widely flouted. People not only continued to drink, but in greater numbers than ever. Before Prohibition New York had 15,000 legal saloons; by the end of Prohibition it had over 30,000 illegal ones. Detroit had no fewer than 20,000 *speakeasies*, as illegal drinking establishments became rather curiously known. Boston was rather primmer with just 4,000 illicit watering holes, but that was four times the number of legal saloons in the whole of Massachusetts before Prohibition. Hardly anyone took the law seriously. In 1930, a journalist testified to the House Judiciary Committee that he had attended a lively party at a Detroit roadhouse where he had seen the Governor of Michigan, the chief of police of Detroit, and four circuit court judges drinking lavishly and enjoying the entertainment of a troupe of young ladies who were dancing the *hootchy-kootchy* (another new word of the age, based on the earlier *coochee-coochee*) without benefit of clothing. They couldn't even have been wearing *G-strings* since this device of minimal attire would not become known to strippers until 1936. Although the term is often said to have arisen as a jocular allusion to the thinness of the G-string on a violin, it actually has a more noble pedigree. In the nineteenth century it described the leather string Indians employed to hold up their loincloths and was spelled *geestring* (probably a folk translation of a more complicated, and now forgotten, Indian term).

All this is by way of reaching the point that Prohibition – or more correctly the Volstead Act – was a law without teeth. Congress appropriated just $5 million to enforce the act and employed just

1,520 agents to protect America's frontiers from smugglers – or one man for every twelve miles of border.[30] A small but curiously durable myth is that President Herbert Hoover stoutly defended Prohibition as 'a noble experiment'. In fact, he called it 'a great social and economic experiment, noble in motive and far-reaching in purpose', which isn't quite the same thing and actually falls considerably short of a ringing endorsement. He wasn't praising Prohibition itself, but merely the motives of those who had foisted it on the nation. In point of fact, by the election campaign of 1928, when Hoover made his utterance, Prohibition was an obvious disaster.

Prohibition may have been an inconvenience to drinkers but it enriched the vocabulary. *Bootlegger, speakeasy, hip flask* and many other terms associated with illicit behaviour became part of the common parlance. So, too, did the expression *the real McCoy*. Although often supposed to date from a much earlier period, it is a Prohibition catch-phrase. No one knows who or what this McCoy was – explanations range from its being the name of a now-forgotten but presumably talented bootlegger to its having some connection with opiates from Macao – but there is no documentary evidence to favour any particular claim.

The more sinister side of Prohibition also gave new meaning to such words as *gangster* (originally in the nineteenth century it denoted membership of political gangs, not criminal ones), *moll* (an old English term for a girl, which was given an unexpected boost as the word for a gangster's distaff sidekick), and *racket*, another English word dating back to 1812 in the sense of shady doings, but which had died out there and was resurrected in America in 1927. The growing importance of the car to criminals, as well as to everyone else, is reflected in *getaway car* and *to be taken for a ride*.

Brewers didn't have nearly as easy a time of it as wine-growers. In desperation they turned to producing a product they hopefully called *near-beer*, and soft drinks with names like *Howdy, Chero-Cola* and *Lithiated Lemon* (which would eventually evolve into 7-Up, so called because it came in seven-ounce bottles).

Soft drinks were already an old tradition in America having first appeared as flavoured soda water in Philadelphia in either 1825 or 1838, depending on which source you credit. Throughout the nineteenth century root beer, sarsaparilla, ginger beer, spruce beer and other non-intoxicating beverages became increasingly popular. However, it was not until 1886 that America got its quintessential soft drink when John Styth Pemberton, an Atlanta pharmacist and patent medicine man whose earlier, less inspired inventions had included Globe of Flower Cough Syrup and French Wine Coca, brewed up a concoction of cola nuts, coca leaves, caffeine and other similarly dubious condiments in an iron tub in his backyard, stirred it with a wooden oar from an old boat and called it *Coca-Cola*.

His bookkeeper, Frank Robinson, who was a dab hand at calligraphy, drew up the florid italic logo that Coke uses to this day. Pemberton viewed his invention not as the refreshing thirst-quencher that the world has come to love, but as an efficacious tonic for hangovers and other ills of the upper body.[31] (It was also discreetly hinted that it was a potent aphrodisiac.) Pemberton, alas, failed to see Coca-Cola's true potential. In 1887, he sold a two-thirds interest in the company for the curiously precise but decidedly short-sighted sum of $283.29. It took another Atlanta pharmacist, Asa G. Candler, to capitalize on Coca-Cola's true possibilities as a money-making refreshment. Just before the turn of the century he bought the formula from its new owners for $2,000 and with canny marketing converted his investment into a fortune. By 1919, when the company was sold again, this time to a consortium of Atlanta businessmen, Candler's $2,000 outlay had grown in value to $25 million.

Such success naturally encouraged imitation and soon American purchasers could try competing brands like Co Kola, Coke-Ola, Coke, Koke, Klu-Ko Kola, Afri-Cola, Okla-Cola, Carbo-Cola, Sola Cola, Pepsi-Cola and even Celery-Cola. Many copied not only Coca-Cola's famous name and italic logo, but also its distinctive bottle. Coke took them all to court. By 1926 it had resorted to law no fewer than seven thousand times to protect its trademark, including one fight that went to the Supreme Court. Not only did it destroy almost all its challengers, but in 1930 it won the exclusive right to its alternative name, Coke, making it the world's only successful product with two names.[32]

The one competitor it notably failed to quash was Pepsi-Cola, invented in 1898 by Caleb D. Bradham and so called because it was intended to combat dyspepsia. Despite going bankrupt twice in its formative years, PepsiCo is now actually a larger company than Coca-Cola thanks to its diversifications – it owns, among much else, Pizza Hut and Taco Bell, which is why you needn't bother asking for Coke there – and by having the good sense not to tamper with its formula as Coke did, with disastrous results, in 1985, when it introduced New Coke. (Marketing disasters are something of a tradition at Coke. It once launched Coca-Cola flavoured cigars, with results not unlike those that greeted New Coke.)

Despite its occasional setbacks Coke has long been a symbol of American culture in a way that Pepsi has never managed. As long ago as 1950, it inspired a word for the American cultural takeover of the planet: *Coca-Colonization*. Today, Coke is sold in 195 countries (giving it a bigger following than the United Nations, with 184) and is claimed to be the second most universally understood term in English, exceeded only by *OK* – an expression that conveniently carries us back to the nineteenth century and the start of the next chapter.

Democratizing Luxury: Shopping in America

In 1846 an Irish immigrant in New York named Alexander Stewart opened a business on Broadway called the Marble Dry-Goods Palace and in so doing gave the world a new phenomenon: the department store. Never before had a single enterprise tried to bring together such a range of merchandise under one roof. The business thrived and soon it covered a whole block on Broadway and had a staff of two thousand. Even that was not enough, however. In 1862 Stewart relocated to an eight-storey building near by, and renamed it A. T. Stewart's Cast-Iron Palace. It was, and for many years would remain, the largest retail operation in the world.

In its wake came scores of other similar emporia – Field, Leiter & Co. (later Marshall Field) in Chicago, Jordan Marsh in Boston, John Wanamaker's in Philadelphia, Hudson's in Detroit, R. H. Macy's, E. V. Haughwout's and Lord & Taylor in New York.

We don't know when people started calling them department stores. The term isn't found in print until 1893 (in *Harper's Magazine*), but, as so often, the context makes it clear that it was already widely used and understood: 'They [Brooklyn stores] compare favourably with the best and largest department stores of New York.'[1]

What is certain is that department stores transformed the shopping experience for millions of urban Americans. *Palace* was scarcely an exaggeration for these new establishments. They offered not only an unprecedented range of goods, but also levels of comfort, luxury and excitement previously unknown to consumers. Three things made this possible: the development of cast-iron architecture, allowing the construction of more open interiors, the arrival of the safety elevator, giving stores the option of expanding upwards, and, above all, the increasing prosperity of Americans.

Compared with previous retail establishments, these new bazaars were airy and spacious and marvellously self-contained. Almost from the start they boasted restaurants, tearooms, restrooms and other conveniences, eliminating the need to go elsewhere for anything. As early as the 1850s, Stewart's emporium was entertaining shoppers with fashion shows and organ recitals. You could, as millions remarked in wonder, spend a whole day there. But what truly distinguished department stores was that they were the first grand commercial enterprises that were open to everyone. In the words of Émile Zola, they 'democratized luxury'.[2] A secretary or clerk might live a lifetime in a city and not once enter a swanky hotel or restaurant, never see the inside of a concert hall or opera house, or venture into a fashionable milliner's. But such a person could experience something of the same intoxicating whiff of elegance and possibility in a department store, and mingle on equal terms with what was known in the business as *the carriage trade*, those wealthy enough to arrive in their own conveyances.

Department stores offered millions their first look at wonders of the age like the passenger elevator (the world's first permanent safety elevator was installed in the Haughwout Department Store in New York in 1857), electric lighting, public telephones, and escalators (the last so novel and giddying that some stores stationed nurses at the top to minister to those made light-headed by the experience). By the turn of the century the department stores' services were almost limitless. They had post offices, branch libraries, lost-and-found departments, hair salons, roof gardens, first-aid stations, information bureaus, 'silence rooms for nerve-tired shoppers', even their own in-store radio stations. They would sew on missing buttons, bandage a cut, amuse a lost child, answer any question – and all without charge. Some put on lectures, concerts and plays. Most provided demonstrations of new products. Shopping had become a social experience.

By 1900, Marshall Field was serving as many as 250,000

customers a day, and had become one of Chicago's biggest employers with a staff of 8,000. Wanamaker's in Philadelphia took orders twenty-four hours a day. Its Crystal Tea Room could handle 10,000 customers at a time. America had embraced with both arms *conspicuous consumption*, a term coined in 1899 by the sociologist Thorstein Veblen in his *Theory of the Leisure Class*, and much required ever since.

One man more than any other was responsible for the modern look of department stores. He was Harry G. Selfridge, a Wisconsin native who took a job as a stock boy with Marshall Field in 1879 and quickly rose through the ranks. One of his first acts was to take goods down from the high shelves and put them on counters and tables where customers could peer at them, touch them and, as critics noted, shoplift them (though this was by no means a new activity; *shoplifting* has been part of the English vocabulary since 1680). Among Selfridge's many other innovations were the bargain basement, annual sales, gift certificates, the practice of reminding customers how many shopping days were left till Christmas, the custom of keeping the ground-floor windows lighted at night, thus encouraging evening strollers to browse and plan their next day's shopping, and the now universal practice of putting the perfumes and cosmetics departments on the ground floor by the main entrance where they would sweeten the atmosphere and act as a magnet for passers-by.

Retiring from Marshall Field, Selfridge moved to Britain and at the age of fifty founded the London department store that bears his name. Though most British observers felt certain that such a crassly commercial undertaking would never succeed in London, it not only thrived but made Oxford Street into London's premier shopping thoroughfare. Selfridge was obsessively devoted to his store. He concerned himself with everything from the sharpness of sales clerks' pencils to the quality of their teeth. Something of his dedication to work is evidenced by a vacation he took in 1914. He left London by train on a Saturday morning and by noon the next day was on the skating-rink of a Swiss hotel. He skated vigorously for four hours, packed up his skates and stocking cap, caught a train back to London and was at his desk at 8 a.m. on the Monday morning. That was his idea of a holiday.

But with the death of his wife in 1918, something snapped inside him. He began to go nightclubbing, fell in with a pair of Hungarian-American vaudeville stars known as the Dolly Sisters and neglected his business. He bought racehorses, gambled and lost spectacularly at Monte Carlo, chartered aeroplanes to bring the Dollys cartons of ice-cream and breasts of chicken for their lapdog, bought a castle on England's south coast, at Highcliffe in Hampshire, and laid plans to build a 250-room, $15 million estate near by.

In ten years, he ran through $8 million. Unfortunately, not all of it was his. Unable to pay back the debts he owed to his own store – for a decade he and the Dollys had been helping themselves to whatever they fancied without troubling to pay for it – he was ignominiously retired from the Selfridge's board of directors and given a pension of $25,000 a year (later cut to $12,000 and then to $8,000), from which he was expected to pay back debts of $2 million. He lost his houses and his Rolls-Royce, took a small flat in Putney and travelled by bus. On 8 May 1947 he died nearly destitute and virtually forgotten, and how many times have we heard that story before?

Rather more successful at keeping his hands on his money was Frank W. Woolworth. Where Selfridge had created the bargain basement as a sideline – a useful way of generating money from otherwise unsaleable goods – Woolworth had the idea of building a store that was in effect nothing but a bargain basement. He opened the first Woolworth's store in Utica, New York, in 1879. Everything cost five or ten cents – a proposition scarcely less incredible then than it would be now. The store was immediately successful, and by 1900 Woolworth had fifty-nine stores with annual sales of over $5 million. By 1913, he was so rich that he was able to fund the construction of the $13.5 million Woolworth Building in New York with cash.[3] By then people everywhere were shopping at *bargain counters* (an expression first used in 1888) and *five and tens* or *five and dimes* (1905).

Actually, not everywhere. In the early 1900s, America was still a largely rural country. Farm families and small-town folk longed to consume and possess like everyone else, but for years there was no way to reach them. Then in 1872 an organization formally called the Patrons of Husbandry but better known as the Grange (an old English word, etymologically related to *grain* and signifying a farmstead) began offering a mail-order service to its members. It, too, was a huge hit and by the 1890s its catalogue contained over 24,000 items, bringing a new world of choice and possibility to thousands of rural consumers. The Grange eventually evolved into Montgomery Ward, but in the mean time it was overtaken by one of the most successful companies America has ever seen: Sears, Roebuck and Company.

Founded in 1886, the enterprise was named for its two original partners, Richard Sears and Alvah Roebuck, though the latter sold out in 1893. Sears's rise was little short of phenomenal. By 1900 it had surpassed the Grange in size and by 1906 it was so mammothly successful that it needed 2,000 workers to process the 900 sackloads of orders it received each day. Such was the volume of business that the railways, telegraph companies and Post Office all opened branch offices at the company's Chicago headquarters.[4] Sears's success is all the more remarkable when you consider that in its early days it was not terribly noted for scruples. In one early ad, it offered a sewing-machine at the exceptional price of $1. Customers who responded received a needle and thread.[5] In 1899 it ran ads offering, for the next sixty days only, a luxuriously upholstered sofa and two matching chairs for just ninety-five cents. Thousands sent in their orders – and received three pieces of doll's house furniture.

Despite these stunts, people became hugely devoted to Sears. In rural areas especially, they relied on Sears for everything from shoes to sewing-machines. By the early 1900s it was possible to buy a car (called, naturally, the *Sears*) or even a house and all its furnishings from the company. The bi-annual receipt of its catalogues was among the high points of the year. The people of one North Dakota town were so taken with the company that they renamed their community Seroco, for *Sears Roebuck & Co.*, and would have been more explicit had the US Postal Service let them.

The quarter of a century or so from 1885 saw the refinement of another venerable component of American retailing: the brand name. Although a few durable brand names date from even earlier – *Smith Brothers Cough Drops* from 1866, *Arm & Hammer Baking Soda* from 1867, *Ivory Soap* from 1878 – the closing years of the nineteenth century and opening years of the twentieth saw the birth of a positive blizzard of famous products: *Coca-Cola* (1886), *Log Cabin Syrup* (1887), *Aunt Jemima* pancake mix (1889), *Shredded Wheat* (1892), *Tootsie Rolls* and *Cracker Jack* (1896), *Jell-O* gelatin (1897), *Pepsi-Cola* (1898), *Fig Newtons* (1900), *Animal Crackers* (1902), *Post Toasties* (1904), *Planters Peanuts* (1906), *Sunkist* fruit (1907), and *Life Savers* (1911).

What made all this possible, in large part, was the development of secure packaging such as the National Biscuit Company's patented (and much misspelled) *In-er-Seal* wrap, which not only ensured freshness but also enabled manufacturers to turn from selling in bulk out of boxes and barrels to providing small, individualized packages. Often the packaging was all that stood between success and failure. Clarence Crane, the father of the poet Hart Crane, invented Life Savers in 1911, punching them out on a pharmacist friend's pill-making machine, but they were a flop because the mints quickly went stale inside their paper wrappers and tended to absorb the flavour of the glue with which the wrappers were sealed. Only after a New York businessman bought the company and began wrapping the mints in tin foil did Life Savers take off – and take off they did. In just over a decade his initial investment of $1,500 in the company had become worth $3.3 million.

As foods and other household products became individually wrapped and more conveniently transportable, it was only a matter of time before someone thought of a new way of selling them. In 1916 Clarence Saunders of Memphis, Tennessee, hit on a novel proposition that he patented under the name the *Self-Serving Store*.

The first well-known grocery store chain in America was the Great Atlantic and Pacific Tea Company, founded in 1859. As the name suggests, it began as a tea importer, but it was stocking groceries as early as 1865. By the outbreak of World War I, A&P, as it was by then known, had 2,000 stores all over America.[6] They were, however, stores of the old-fashioned type in which clerks fetched requested items from high shelves.

Clarence Saunders changed all that with his Memphis store. He called it a Piggly-Wiggly. When asked why he had given it such an odd name, he replied: '*That's* why – because it makes people curious!' Customers entered through a turnstile, picked up a basket, made their selections and eventually arrived at the 'settlement and checking' desk, where the selections were 'checked up' and wrapped. A reporter for the *New York Times*, clearly agog at this revolutionary concept, described how a customer 'rambles down aisle after aisle, on both sides of which are shelves. The customer collects his purchases and pays as he goes out.' The motivation behind the stores was not so much to provide a convenience for the customers as to deal with a shortage of clerks occasioned by World War I. It soon became evident, however, that shoppers liked being able to squeeze the bread and handle the soup cans, and the idea took off in a big way.

Saunders lost control of Piggly-Wiggly while playing the stock market in 1923 and devoted his remaining years to an even more ambitious, but ultimately hare-brained, scheme called *Keydoozle* (for which read: 'key does all') *Markets*, a kind of automated grocery store in which the customers would make their selections by inserting keys into slots beside a specimen product. Behind the scenes an absurd assortment of clattering machinery and flapping conveyor belts would sort the products and carry them, bagged and ready to take home, to the checkout counter. The system never really worked, and no more was heard of Clarence Saunders.[7]

In one important respect, Saunders's stores represented no advance on the old-style grocery stores. They were small, often no more than 1,500 square feet, with no more than three or four aisles. The credit for creating the first true supermarket is usually given to Michael Cullen, who opened a 'grocery warehouse' or 'food market' – he used either name freely – in Jamaica, New York, in 1930. It wasn't the first big food store in America. As early as 1923 San Francisco had a grocery store called the Crystal Palace with parking for 4,350 cars* and 68,000 square feet of retail space. However, Cullen did offer several features that would become standard in the business – evening opening, self-service, strident advertising, and a practically irresistible impulse to put a misspelled word in the title. He called it *King Kullen*. The first company to use the word *supermarket* in its title appears to have been Albers Super Mkts., Inc., of Cincinnati, which registered the

---

* Or so most books of retailing history say, though it seems an awfully large number. Many modern shopping centres can't take that many cars.

name in 1933.[8] The same decade saw the development of an appliance to help shoppers deal with the increasing volume of goods on offer: the shopping trolley. Although a grocery store in Houston had for years been offering its customers the use of children's wagons with a basket attached to help them manage their purchases, it wasn't until 1936 when a store owner in Oklahoma City named Sylvan Goldman invented the modern shopping trolley which he called a *basket carrier* that bulk-buying became a possibility. (At first, customers showed great reluctance to use the new contraptions. Only when Goldman employed half a dozen people to push the carts around all day, pretending to shop, did others begin to imitate them.)

In terms of numbers, supermarkets were relatively slow in taking off. As late as 1955, 95 per cent of America's 360,000 grocery stores were *mom and pop* corner businesses or medium-sized stores known as *superettes*. Although supermarkets accounted for just 5 per cent of grocery outlets, they already had half of America's food sales.[9] In most communities the days were numbered not only for mom and pop stores and superettes (though a few unexpectedly survive, such as the A-1 Superette off Waikiki Beach in Honolulu), but for bakeries, butchers, delicatessens and all kinds of other stores.

Supermarkets not only changed the way America shopped but the way America ate. As women increasingly went out to work, convenience foods took on an ever more important role. Frozen foods were developed by a small company called Birds Eye, which took its oddly unappetizing name from Clarence Birdseye, a naturalist from Gloucester, Massachusetts, who accidentally discovered the potential of flash-freezing food while out ice-fishing. The first Birds Eye frozen foods came on to the market in 1930, though they weren't called that. They were sold as *frosted foods* because it was thought that *frozen* would suggest flesh-burns and other spoilage. It quickly became apparent that people were even more baffled by *frosted* – they weren't sure if it meant *partially frozen* or even that the food was covered in some kind of icing – and *frozen food* it became. Birdseye's first range of frosted/frozen offerings consisted of a range of eighteen meats, three seafoods, two vegetables and three fruits. Suddenly in the middle of January America's housewives could, as the ads gushed, buy 'June peas as gloriously green as any you will next Summer'.[10]

Frozen prepared foods followed just before the outbreak of World War II. Baked beans were the first, rather improbable, offering, though soon you could get more exotic dishes like chicken à la king and lobster Newburg. The first frozen dinners were produced in 1945, for use by the army, and a year later the concept was offered to the public under the buckle-your-seatbelt name of *Strato Meals*. Another early competitor made *Frigidinners* before C. A. Swanson & Sons swept all before it with its *TV Brand Dinners*, launched in 1954.[11]

The phenomenon that made supermarkets bloom – namely, the rise of suburbia – was responsible for another development without which modern life for millions would be unendurable: the shopping mall.

Malls of a sort have been around for a long time. The first began as arcades (from the Italian *arcata*, 'arch') in Europe, starting with the Burlington Arcade in London in 1819 and soon followed by the Galeries Saint Hubert in Brussels and the cathedral-like Galleria Vittorio Emanuele II in Milan, which Mark Twain found so enchanting that he declared he would happily live in it for the rest of his life. It is still probably the most beautiful shopping centre in the world. The fashion soon spread across the Atlantic. By the 1830s, beginning with the Weybosset Arcade in Providence, Rhode Island, most large American cities could boast an arcade or two.

Arcades never became anything but an incidental feature in American retailing. For most Americans shopping implied department stores and smaller businesses inhabiting the ground floors of downtown office buildings. Often these went through certain linguistic vogues. *Cafeteria*, as we have already seen, spawned a host of like forms – *baketeria, bargainteria, camerateria* and so on. In the 1920s and '30s *-teria* gave way to *-orium: suitatorium, shavatorium, corsetorium, hairitorium, shoetorium, pantatorium*, even *hot-dogatorium*. These in turn were followed by brief fashions for *-rama* (*Shop-a-Rama*, etc.) and *-ette* (*washerette, superette, drugette*) before the infatuation with odd terminations ran its course in the 1950s.

As America spread into the suburbs, businesses naturally followed. Soon every residential area had a row of little businesses – a barber-shop, a corner grocery, a drugstore perhaps – standing beside popular streetcar stops as a kind of prototype shopping centre. These early assemblages of suburban stores were known variously as *shopping strips, string streets*, or *taxpayer blocks* (so called because they were often intended only as temporary improvements, the hope being that they would generate enough revenue to pay the taxes on the land until something grander could be erected).

Such was the proliferation of strips, triangles, squares and other collections of retailers that the argument over who built the first true shopping centre in America is all but unanswerable. As far back as 1907 a Baltimore businessman named Edward H. Bouton erected a development of six stores that was slightly set back from the street, with space for parking at the front, and which he called the Roland Park Shopping Center. The National Register of Historical Places recognizes Market Square, built in 1916 in Lake Forest, Illinois, as the first planned shopping mall.[12] Others give the honour to Country Club Plaza in Kansas City, built by J. C. Nichols in 1922 as part of a huge housing development. It was the first to contain a few areas exclusively for the use of pedestrians, though its layout was otherwise strictly conventional with the stores facing on to the street. Highland Park Shopping Village in Dallas, built in 1931, was the first to completely segregate shoppers and motorists by turning its back on the street. With the exception of the Roland Park Shopping Center, most of the early complexes were called neither *shopping centers* nor *malls*, but something rather cosier, usually incorporating in their titles the words *square* or *village*, as with the Highland Park Shopping Village, Suburban Square (built in 1928 in Ardmore, Pennsylvania), and Hampton Village (erected in St Louis in 1941).

The shopping centre was, however, essentially a 1950s phenomenon. By the close of World War II there were just eight shopping centres in America and as late as 1949 no more than a dozen. Then in 1950 came the Northgate Center in Seattle, followed the next year by Shoppers' World in Framingham, Massachusetts, and the floodgates opened. Shopping centres began to go up everywhere. Such was the rate of development that by 1956, *Business Week* was headlining a story 'Too Many Shopping Centers' and noting with alarm that in just two months of 1956 more shopping-centre space opened in America than in the eight preceding years.[13] In the generic sense for shopping centre, *mall* is not recorded until as late as 1967. The word has a curious history. It comes from a game popular in Europe in the sixteenth and seventeenth centuries. Called *palla a maglio* ('ball to mallet') in Italy and *pallemaille* in France, it became in England *pall-mall* (but pronounced 'pell mell'). The game involved knocking a wooden ball along a leafy alley and chipping it through a hoop – a sort of early hybrid of golf and croquet. By the mid-eighteenth century it had fallen out of fashion, but the name lives on in two London streets: Pall Mall and the parallel avenue called the Mall (which by analogy ought to be pronounced 'mell' but isn't). The Mall in particular became associated with aristocratic strolling. By 1784 *mall* had found a place in the American lexicon as a fashionable name for any green place suitable for perambulations, notably for the sweep of grass that features in the centre of Washington, DC.

The man responsible for the layout and ambience of the modern shopping centre was not an American but a Viennese named Victor Gruen, who had fled the Austrian *Anschluss* in 1938 and arrived in America with just $8 in his pocket. Within twelve years he had become one of the country's leading urban planners. Ironically, Gruen's intention was not to create a new and more efficient way of shopping but to re-create in America something of the unrushed café-society atmosphere of European city centres. Shopping centres – or *shopping towns*, as he preferred to call them – were to be gathering places for the neighbourhood, focal points of the community where people could stroll and meet their friends, dally over a coffee or an ice-cream and only incidentally shop. Gruen was convinced that he was designing a system that would slow suburban sprawl and tame the automobile. How wrong he was.

'We must sensitively observe the colourful, stimulating and commercially busy urban scenes in the market squares in Central European cities in order to understand the contribution to community life the open spaces in our new shopping towns can make,' he wrote in his 1960 book *Shopping Town USA*.[14] He 'systematized' the shopping centre and developed the idea of an anchor store at each extremity to encourage people to stroll from one to another. The idea was to get shoppers out of their cars and on to their feet. He insisted on having public gathering places at strategic spots – open areas with benches, fountains and perhaps a piece of sculpture or two to encourage social interaction and a sense of community.

In 1956, the year that the British novelist Aldous Huxley coined the much-needed term *spending spree*,[15] Gruen's utopian vision was given tangible shape with the construction of the Southdale Center in the Minneapolis suburb of Edina. Built at a cost of $20 million, it was the biggest shopping centre in the world, and the commercial wonder of its age. Reporters from almost every large newspaper and magazine in America came to marvel at its 10 acres of enclosed shopping area, 72 stores and 45 acres of parking with space for 5,200 cars. It became the model from which almost all other malls in America were cloned. Gruen followed Southdale with other malls in a similar vein – the Northland and Eastland shopping centres near Detroit, the Southland Shopping Center near Minneapolis, Valley Fair in San Jose, the Bay Fair Center in San Leandro, California, and the South Bay Shopping Center in Redondo Beach, California.

Shopping mall design became a science. At their conferences, mall planners bandied about new concepts like *Reilly's Law of Retail Gravitation* (essentially, the mix of stores necessary to keep people moving) and *optimal positional isochrones* (another way of saying that the best location for a shopping centre is near a highway interchange). No one any longer thought about the idea of encouraging people to linger or socialize. Benches were built without backs so that people *wouldn't* linger on them, and food court tables given just enough crampedness to induce a sense of discomfort after about ten minutes. Victor Gruen's vision of people sitting with cappuccinos, reading newspapers on gripper rods provided by a thoughtful management, or playing chess beside whispering fountains never materialized.

Shopping centres didn't just transform towns, they often effectively created them. In the late 1940s Paramus, New Jersey, was a dying little community with no high school, no downtown to speak of, and almost no industry or offices. Then two shopping centres were built along Route 4 – Macy's Garden State Plaza and Allied Stores' Bergen Mall. Within a decade Paramus's population had more than quadrupled to 25,000 and its retail sales had shot up from $5 million to $125 million. Much the same thing happened to Schaumburg, Illinois. In 1956 it had 130 people. Then two things happened: O'Hare became Chicago's main airport and the Woodfield Shopping Center, with over two million square feet of retail space, was opened. By 1978 Schaumburg's population had increased to 50,000 and it was on course to becoming the second biggest city in Illinois after Chicago by the turn of the century.[16]

As shopping centres blossomed, downtowns began to die. Between 1948 and 1954, at the height of America's post-war economic boom, downtown retailers in America's thirteen largest cities lost on average a quarter of their business.[17] One by one downtowns grew more lifeless as stores and offices fled to the suburbs. Hudson's Department Store in Detroit closed in 1981 after watching its annual sales fall from $153 million in 1953 to $45 million in its last year – the victim, ironically, of the automobile, the product that had brought Detroit its wealth.[18] Sears closed its flagship story on State Street in Chicago in 1983. All over America, where downtown department stores survived it was as a matter of pride or of tax breaks, and seldom one of commercial logic.

By the early 1980s America had 20,000 large shopping centres, which between them accounted for over 60 per cent of all retail trade. They employed 8 per cent of the workforce, nine million people, and were generating sales of $586 billion – 13 per cent of the nation's gross national product.[19] By 1992 the number of shopping centres had almost doubled again, and new malls were opening at the rate of one every seven hours. Four billion square feet of America's landscape was shopping centres, two-thirds of it built in the previous twenty years.[20] Shopping centres weren't just growing in numbers, but evolving into new types. One type was known as the *large regional center* – that is, a shopping centre with at least 400,000 square feet of shopping space, or more than most downtowns. There were almost 2,000 of these by 1990. Another type came to be known, somewhat ominously, as *power centers*, unenclosed developments, usually built in a U-shape around a central parking lot and containing at least one *category killer* store – a place like Toys 'R' Us or Circuit City selling a particular type of product in such volume and at such low prices as to deter any nearby competition.

Mall shopping had become America's biggest leisure activity. Mall of America in Minneapolis, the country's biggest mall with

4.2 million square feet of consumer-intensive space (though still considerably less than the world's biggest, the West Edmonton Mall in Canada with 5.2 million square feet), was forecast to attract more people than the Grand Canyon in its first year of business.[21] By the early 1990s Americans were spending on average twelve hours a month in shopping malls, more than they devoted to almost any activity other than sleeping, eating, working and watching television.[22]

And what of Victor Gruen, the man who had started it all? Appalled at what he had unleashed, he fled back to Vienna where he died in 1980, a disappointed man.

13

Domestic Matters

If the British disliked Americans for their use of English, they liked them no more for their habits. In book after book through the nineteenth century – William Cobbett's *A Years [sic] Residence in the Unites States of America*, Harriet Martineau's *Society in America*, Dickens's *American Notes,* Frances Trollope's *Domestic Manners of the Americans*, Frances Wright's *Views of Society and Manners in America,* Thomas Hamilton's *Men and Manners in America* – the British showed a strange and unfriendly preoccupation with American life and habits.

'In regard to the passengers,' wrote Thomas Hamilton in typical vein, 'truth compels me to say, that any thing so disgusting in human shade I had never seen. Their morals and their manners were alike detestable.'[1] William Cobbett offered the opinion that 'the natives are by nature idle, and seek to live by cheating'. Frances Trollope detested almost everything:

> The total want of all the usual courtesies of the table, the voracious rapidity with which the viands were seized and devoured, the strange uncouth phrases and pronunciation; the loathsome spitting, from the contamination of which it was absolutely impossible to protect our dresses; the frightful manner of feeding with their knives, till the whole blade seemed to enter into the mouth; and the still more frightful manner of cleaning the teeth afterwards with a pocket knife, soon forced us to feel that we were not surrounded by the generals, colonels, and majors of the old

world; and that the dinner hour was to be anything rather than an hour of enjoyment.'[2]

Americans, she felt, suffered from a 'universal deficiency in good manners and graceful demeanour'.

The haste and indelicacy of American dining habits was a constant theme. Isabella Lucy Bird noted in 1856: 'I cannot forbear mentioning the rapidity with which Americans despatch their meals. My next neighbour has frequently risen from his seat after a substantial and varied dinner while I was sending away my soup-plate.'

Robert Louis Stevenson, generally a sympathetic observer, was startled in North Platte, Nebraska, when a fellow diner asked another to pass a jug of milk and was turned upon in a fury and told there was a waiter for passing things. 'I only asked you to pass the milk,' replied the first man meekly. To which the second cried: 'Pass? Hell! I'm not paid for that business; the waiter's paid for it. You should use civility at table, and, by God, I'll show you how!' To Stevenson's considerable relief, and presumably that of the milkless fellow, the threat was not carried out, and the meal was concluded in silence.[3]

The widespread American habit of chewing tobacco and disposing of the excess juice by expectorating in the *approximate* direction of a brass spittoon also excited much comment. Both houses of Congress, Dickens recorded in *American Notes*, 'are handsomely carpeted; but the state to which these carpets are reduced by the universal disregard of the spittoon with which every honourable member is accommodated, and the extraordinary improvements on the pattern which are squirted and dabbled upon it in every direction, do not admit of being described.' (In fact, of course, he had just described them.)

To be sure, there was something in this. Americans did often lack certain refinements. Louis Philippe, the future king of France, reported with dismay during a trip through the States in 1797, that when he asked for a chamber-pot his host told him there were none but invited him to make free use of the window.[4] Even when they tried to haul themselves to a higher level of gentility, Americans often betrayed a certain misapprehension in regard to the conventions of society. A junior army officer named Nathaniel Tracy, charged with entertaining a visiting delegation of French officers, and being hazily aware of the peculiarities of French dietary habits, sent his men to a nearby swamp to gather a sackful of frogs, which were then boiled whole and served floating in a soup.

Only recently had Americans become generally acquainted with an appliance that had been around in Europe for some time: the fork. Before that, diners in the New World got by with knives (which often had two prongs on the end for spearing meat) and spoons. Because they were accustomed to using the right hand for both cutting food and raising it to the mouth, they developed the habit – curious to the rest of the world – of transferring the fork from left hand to right between actions.[5] But even as late as the mid-1840s, many Americans were still struggling with the concept, as *The Art of Good Behavior*, a best-selling etiquette guide of the day, tacitly acknowledged when it cautioned: 'If possible, the knife should never be put in the mouth at all.'

Having said this, the Europeans' own manuals of decorum – such as the French tome that instructed its readers: 'When the fingers are very greasy, wipe them first on a piece of bread'[6] – invite speculation as to the standards in their own dining salons.

What is certain is that until about the 1840s levels of hygiene and social sophistication did generally lag in America. Well into the nineteenth century, the bulk of Americans lived lives that were, in the words of one historian, 'practically medieval'.[7] Most Americans were by modern standards abysmally poor. A survey of Delaware farmers in 1800 found that only 16 per cent had a barn and only half had even one horse. A farmer who could not afford a horse was unlikely to invest much in hygienic niceties. Although several words associated with cleanliness first appeared in America at about the same time as they did in England – *bathing-house* in 1760, *bathing-room* in 1791 – the contexts almost always make clear that these were luxuries enjoyed only by the very rich.

Even among the middle classes bathing was a novel experience until well into the 1800s. At the turn of the century one Elizabeth Drinker noted in her diary that she had just had her first bath in twenty-eight years, and the tone with which she recorded the fact indicates that there was nothing particularly remarkable in allowing a quarter-century or so to pass between immersions.[8] Not until the 1820s did bath-tubs begin to be produced commercially, though for their first half-century they would be called *bathing-tubs*. *Bath-tub* is not recorded until 1870, when it appeared in a story by Mark Twain.

At about the time that bath-tubs first became commercially available, the toilet began its long, slow move indoors. At first it was generally installed in a small room separate from the bathroom, and was normally called the *water closet* in the British fashion, though there was a vogue – unfortunately short-lived if you ask me – for calling it a *quincy* after John Quincy Adams installed the first one in the White House. *Bathroom* is first noted in 1836, though *toilet paper*, intriguingly, isn't found before 1880. *Washroom* also first appeared in 1880 and had been further euphemized into *restroom* by 1900.

If America got off to a slow start in terms of civilizing comforts, by the 1840s it was racing ahead of Europe and the rest of the world – ironically at just about the time that British criticisms of American life were reaching full shriek. Department stores and restaurants brought a measure of democratic luxury and convenience to the middle classes that their European counterparts would not enjoy for at least half a century. American trains were plusher, faster and equipped with lavatories at a time when Europeans had to hope for either a strong bladder or a short trip, and her city streets were better lit at night. Above all, where America began to stand out was in the quality of its hotels.

In the sense of a place to stay for the night, the word is, rather surprisingly, an Americanism. In French, *hôtel* signified a grand structure (as in *hôtel de ville*, 'town hall'), but as early as the eighteenth century Americans were using it to describe hostelries.[9] America's first grand hotel was the City Hotel in Baltimore, built in 1826. Three years later Boston's Tremont House opened. Soon palatial hotels were opening all over the country – the Astor House in New York, the Burnet House in Cincinnati, the St Charles in New Orleans, the Maxwell House in Nashville.

These establishments led the way in the development of all manner of comforts – central heating, spring beds, elevators (New York's Fifth Avenue Hotel was the first hotel to get one, in 1859) and, towards the end of the century, electric lighting and telephones. Just as elevators made department stores possible, so too did they transform hotels. Previously rooms on the upper floors had to be let at a discount since few guests would wish to drag suitcases up and down several flights of stairs. Suddenly, thanks to elevators, rooms on the upper floors could be let at a premium. As the Otis Elevator Company's sales literature persuasively cooed, guests could now 'enjoy a purity and coolness of atmosphere, an extended prospect, and an exemption from noise, dust and exhalations of every kind'.[10] Even the most critical foreign observer was hard pressed to find complaint with American hotels. Anthony Trollope, the novelist son of Frances, was so impressed that he devoted a whole chapter of one of his travel books to this most marvellous of New World innovations.[11]

Homes, too, became notably better equipped with conveniences like furnaces and artificial lighting than those of Europe, though the severity of the American climate made comfort an elusive goal even among the wealthier classes. In January 1866, the business-man George Templeton Strong lamented that even with both his furnaces and all the fireplaces going he couldn't get the temperature in his house above 38 °F.[12] Even so, such matters are relative, and foreign observers continually remarked about the intolerable warmth and stuffiness of American households. The British consul-general in Massachusetts noted with quiet wonder that in the finer American houses 'an enormous furnace in the cellar sends up, day and night, streams of hot air, through apertures and pipes, to every room in the house' to the extent that 'casual visitors are nearly suffocated'.[13]

Summers could be equally unbearable. Not only was there no practical way of getting rid of the heat, but the lack of proper sanitary services in towns, and the proliferation of horses and other animals, meant that flies, mosquitoes and other insects thrived to an extent unthinkable today. At least, food could now be kept. By the 1840s many middle-class homes enjoyed the benefits of an icebox (an Americanism first recorded in 1839), and the ice industry was huge. By mid-century Boston alone was shipping out 150,000 tons of ice a year, some of it going as far as India and China.

Improved lighting remained a constant preoccupation. Until the late 1700s illumination was limited to tallow candles and whale oil, but both were inefficient – it would take a hundred candles to create as much light as a single modern light-bulb – and beyond the means of most households. Until the early 1800s the average American home existed in nearly total darkness once night fell. For the middle classes, illumination improved dramatically with the invention in 1783 of the Argand lamp (named for its Swiss creator), which had greater intensity and less flicker. The next step forward was the invention of kerosene by a Canadian, Abraham Gesner, in 1858, and by petroleum a year later.[14]

But the big transformation came with gas. Initially gas was used to light streets – Baltimore had gas-lamps as early as 1816, before Paris or Berlin – but the dirt, odours and volatility of gas meant it could not be safely relied on for domestic purposes until after the Civil War. Once these problems were dealt with, gas swept the nation. Each gas outlet, or *gasolier*, provided as much light as a dozen candles. By 1895, it was estimated, the average middle class home was twenty times better lit than it had been at mid-century.[15] Even cleaned up and made more stable, gas remained dirty and dangerous. It emitted unpleasant, potentially lethal fumes that required special vents to clear the air. Even in the best-ventilated homes the carbonic acid and smoke that seeped from them took a heavy toll on books, curtains, wallpaper and soft furniture, as well as the eyes, lungs and clothes of the inhabitants.

What was really needed was electricity, and not just for lighting but for scores of other appliances that Americans had the prosperity to buy if only the means existed to make them practical. Before electricity, labour-saving devices had about them a certain air of the ridiculous, most notably a rudimentary vacuum cleaner consisting of two bellows that the user wore like shoes. As the user plodded about the room, the exertions on the bellows created a suction action of sorts, which could be used to sweep up dust and crumbs. It was, as you might imagine, not terribly efficient. Simpler, quieter and far less exhausting was the carpet sweeper, an invention of the 1860s. Other offerings of the pre-electrical age were a gas-heated iron and an elaborate contraption called the 'Water Witch', which operated with pressurized water and which the makers boasted would not only vacuum the carpets, but could be employed to dry one's hair and massage aching muscles.[16]

In 1882, domestic electricity at last became a possibility when Thomas Edison began providing electricity on a commercial basis. By mid-decade 200 of New York City's wealthiest households were enjoying the illumination of 5,000 light-bulbs – or *electric lamps* as the Edison company called them. Only the very wealthiest could afford such an indulgence. A single bulb cost a dollar – half a day's earnings for the average working person – and cost up to twenty cents an hour to run.[17] Nor was household electricity a hit with everyone. After spending thousands of dollars and suffering much disruption to walls, floorboards and ceilings having electricity installed, Mrs. Cornelius Vanderbilt ordered every inch of it torn out when it was implicated (very possibly wrongly) in a small fire.[18]

Outdoors, however, it was another matter. Almost overnight America became the most illuminated country in the world. By the 1890s Broadway was already being described as 'the Great White Way' because of its dazzling lights (almost all of them advertising products). People came from all over just to see the lights, which included the world's first flashing sign, for Manhattan Beach and its hotels. Standing 50 feet high and 80 feet wide, the sign would light up line by line and then flash rhythmically before starting the cycle over again. It seemed a wonder of modern technology. In fact it was manually operated by a man in a rooftop shack.

In 1910 Broadway got a sign that *was* a wonder of electrical engineering. Rising the equivalent of seven storeys above the rooftop of the Hotel Normandie and incorporating 20,000 coloured light-bulbs, it offered in intricate detail the illusion of a 30-second chariot race, complete with cracking whips and flying dust. People were so agog over it that squads of police had to be assigned to the area to keep pedestrians and traffic moving lest the whole of Manhattan grind to a halt.[19] Almost as arresting were the lights of Luna Park on Coney Island. Two hundred thousand bulbs picked out ornamental patterns and the outlines of the towers and minarets at the amusement park, turning it literally into a night-time wonderland.[20] Even now it looks quite wonderful in pictures.

By 1896 electricity had become such an accepted part of life that people were familiarly referring to it as *juice*. But the expense held people back. In 1910 just one home in ten had electricity. By 1930, however, 70 per cent of American households, some 20 million homes, had electricity – more than the rest of the world combined. The proportion would have been higher still except that rural electrification took so long to complete. As late as 1946, barely half of American farm homes had electricity. (But then only a tenth had an indoor flush toilet.)

As electricity became more widely available, electrical products began to come on to the market. Singer introduced the first electric sewing-machine in 1889. The electric fan appeared in 1891, the electric iron in 1893, the electric vacuum cleaner in 1901, the electric stove – sometimes called a *fireless cooker* – in 1902, the electric washing machine in 1909, the electric toaster in 1910, and the electric dishwasher in 1918. By 1917 the American house-holder could choose between fifty types of electrical appliances – and eagerly did so. In that year, Americans spent $175 million on them.[21] Within a little over a decade, that figure would rise to no less than $2.4 billion a year.[22]

The new and fast-changing market for electrical appliances often gave small companies a chance to thrive. After General Electric turned down the idea of an automatic washing machine, a small outfit named Bendix, which had no experience of manufacturing household appliances, took up the idea and within a decade had become one of America's biggest manufacturers of appliances. Much the same happened with a small subsidiary of General Motors called Frigidaire, which saw an opening for domestic refrigerators and so successfully seized it that the name almost became generic.[23] The idea of the refrigerator might have been new but the word wasn't. It had existed in English since 1611, and had been used as a synonym for *icebox* since 1824.[24]

Refrigerators, rather surprisingly, were among the last common electrical appliances to catch on. Frigidaire began production in 1918, but the first models were ungainly and expensive. The cheapest cost $900 – as much as a good car. As late as 1921, just 5,000 were made in America. Then things took off. By 1931 a million refrigerators were being produced every year and by 1937, at the height of the Great Depression, the number was nudging 3 million.[25]

But no product was more successful than the radio. *Radio*, in the form of *radio-receiver,* entered the language in 1903. Earlier still there had been such specialized forms as *radiophone* (1881) and *radioconductor* (1898). As late as 1921 the *New York Times* was referring to the exciting new medium as 'wireless telephony'. Others called it a 'loud-speaking telephone' or simply a 'wireless'.

When a leading golf club, the Dixmoor, installed radio speakers around the course so that its members could listen to church services (honestly) while playing their Sunday morning round, it referred to the system simply as a 'telephone'. *Radio* in the sense of a means of communication and entertainment for the general public didn't enter the language until 1922 and it took a decade or so before people could decide whether to pronounce it *rādio* or *rădio*.

Until as late as 1920, all radio receivers in America were home-made. A crystal set involved little more than some wire, an oatmeal box, an earphone and a piece of crystal. The earliest commercial sets were bulky, expensive and maddeningly difficult to tune. The big breakthrough for radio was the Dempsey–Carpentier fight of 2 July 1921 – which is a little odd since it didn't actually involve a radio transmission, though it was supposed to.

It is difficult to conceive now how big an event like a heavyweight boxing fight could be in the 1920s, but the Dempsey–Carpentier fight was *huge* – so huge that the *New York Times* devoted virtually the whole of its first thirteen pages to reporting it (though it did find a small space on the front page to note the formal ending of World War I). The day before the fight, under the lead front-page headline 'Radio Phones to Tell Times Square of Fight', it noted that an operator at ringside in New Jersey would speak into a 'wireless telephone transmitter' and that his words would be transmitted instantly to halls in several cities and to crowds outside the New York Times Building on Times Square. Although the headline used the word *radio*, the article never did. On the day of the fight, ten thousand people jammed Times Square, but because of technical difficulties the radio transmitter wasn't used. A ticker-tape was pressed into service instead. Even so, most of the people in the crowd *thought* they were receiving their eyewitness account live by the miracle of radio from New Jersey.[26] The very notion of instant, long-distance verbal communication was so electrifying that soon people everywhere were clamouring to have a radio. (Dempsey knocked Carpentier out in the fourth round, incidentally.)

In just three years, beginning in 1922, over four million radio sets were sold, at an average price of $55. In 1922 only 1 home in 500 had a radio. By 1926, the proportion was 1 in 20, and by the end of the decade saturation was nearly total. Radio sales went from

$60 million in 1922 to almost $850 million by 1929.[27] Radio buffs pored over specialized magazines and formed clubs where they could swap tips and bandy about terms like *regenerative circuits, sodion tubes, Grimes reflex circuits, loop aerials, rotary sparks* and *neutrodynes*. Companies that made radios became monolithic corporations seemingly overnight. In one heady year the stock of Radio Corporation of America went from 85¼ to 549. By 1928 people could even listen to broadcasts in their cars after a little company called Motorola invented the car radio.[28]

The first broadcasters were ham operators using Morse code, but by the 1910s experimental stations were springing up all over. KDKA of East Pittsburgh, Pennsylvania, which was opened by Westinghouse in 1920, has the distinction of being the first true radio station in America, though the credit is sometimes given to a station without call letters operated by the San Jose College of Engineering and Wireless, which began regular transmissions of news reports and music to receivers set up in local hotel lobbies in 1909. The station eventually moved to San Francisco and became KCBS. Most of the early stations were distinctly amateurish. KDKA featured musical renditions by the chief engineer's young (and not notably gifted) sons. Another early Westinghouse station, WJZ of Newark, broadcast from a curtained-off area of the ladies' restroom at a Westinghouse factory, apparently because it was the quietest place in the building. To say that most of these early stations were low-powered would be to engage in riotous understatement. Many transmitters used less wattage than a single light-bulb.[29]

By the middle of the decade, however, radio was taking on a more professional air and even producing its first celebrities, like Harold W. Arlin of KDKA. For reasons that seem deeply un-fathomable now, Arlin and most other broadcasters developed the custom of donning a tuxedo for evening broadcasts, even though – patently – no one could see them.[30]

In 1926 RCA, General Electric and Westinghouse got together to form the National Broadcasting Company. (It actually comprised two networks, one known as the Red network, the other as the Blue.) A year later the Columbia Broadcasting System was born. At first some effort was made to bring higher values to radio. In the 1920s and early 1930s the government issued 202 licences for educational stations, but by 1936, 164 of those – some 80 per cent

– had closed down or become commercial. 'Accordingly,' in the ponderous words of a radio historian, 'in the critically formative first two decades of its utilization, the radio spectrum had only the most limited opportunity to demonstrate its capabilities for human resource enhancement.'[31]

If radio's resource enhancement capabilities were underutilized, they were as nothing compared with television once it got going. Most of us think of television as a comparatively recent development, but in fact in terms of its practical applications it is nearly as old as radio. It just took longer to get established. As early as the 1880s it was known in theory what was required to make a working television, though the necessary valves and tubes had yet to be invented.[32] The word *television* dates from 1907, but in the early days it went by a variety of names – *electric eye*, *iconoscope*, *electric telescope*, *televisor* or *radio vision*.

Unlike other technologies television was the result of work by numerous inventors in different places – Herbert Ives, Charles Jenkins and Philo T. Farnsworth in America, John Logie Baird in Britain, Boris Rosing in Russia. The first working television – that is, one that broadcast something more profound than silhouettes and shadows – was demonstrated by Charles Jenkins in Washington in 1925. Baird, a Scotsman, demonstrated a similar model, but with sound, four months later.

Television didn't attract much public notice until Bell Telephone demonstrated its new system in New York in April 1927. Shown on a screen just two inches high by three inches wide – slightly smaller than a pack of cigarettes – the broadcast consisted of a brief speech of encouragement from Washington by Secretary of Commerce Herbert Hoover, followed by some entertainment from the AT&T studio in Whippany, New Jersey – a vaudeville comic who first told some Irish jokes and then changed into blackface and told some 'darky' jokes. Sadly his jokes were not recorded. (It is curious that from its inception people instinctively grasped that this was a medium built for trivializing; when Baird demonstrated the first colour transmission in London in 1928 – yes, 1928 – his viewers were treated to the sight of a man repeatedly sticking out his tongue.)

The *New York Times* gave much of page 1 and almost the whole of page 20 to this big event under the headline:

FAR-OFF SPEAKERS SEEN
AS WELL AS HEARD HERE
IN A TEST OF TELEVISION

LIKE A PHOTO COME TO LIFE

HOOVER'S FACE PLAINLY
IMAGED AS HE SPEAKS
IN WASHINGTON

The reporter marvelled that 'as each syllable was heard, the motion of the speaker's lips and his changes of expression were flashed on the screen ... with perfect fidelity'. None the less, he considered television's prospects doubtful. Its future, 'if it has one, is thought to be largely in public entertainment – super-news reels flashed before audiences at the moment of occurrence, together with dramatic and musical acts shot on the ether waves in sound and picture at the instant they are taking place at the studio'.[33]

In 1928 Baird made the first transatlantic broadcast from a studio near London to one in Hartsdale, New York, and the following year the cumbersomely named W2XCW in Schenectady, New York, became the country's first 'regularly operating television station', though in fact its telecasts consisted of three thirty-minute programmes a week – usually just shots of an unidentified head talking, laughing or smoking – and of course there was almost no one to watch them. By the end of 1929 there were twenty-six stations in America, though only those that were supported by big corporations, such as W2XBS in New York (which evolved into WNBC), were destined to survive through the 1930s. There was no great impetus to promote the industry in America because of the lack of a market during the Great Depression and the government's refusal to allow commercials until 1941.

Many people got their first glimpse of television at the New York World's Fair in 1939. The *New York Times*, with its now standard lack of prescience, forecast that it would never be a serious competitor for radio because 'people must sit and keep their eyes glued on a screen; the average American family hasn't time for it'.[34]

The year 1939 also saw the first television sets go on sale to the public, but still there wasn't much to watch (unlike Britain where the BBC was celebrating its tenth anniversary). During the war years, America had just nine television stations in five cities – New York, Chicago, Philadelphia, Los Angeles and Schenectady – and just 7,000 sets on which to watch the meagre programming available. In the autumn of 1944, for instance, on Wednesday and Saturday nights there was no television at all in America. On Thursdays only CBS was on the air, with fifteen minutes of news followed by an hour of local programming where available and a half-hour show called *Missus Goes A Shopping*. On Sundays the American viewer could watch DuMont Labs' *Thrills and Chills* followed by *Irwin Shane's Television Workshop*, or nothing.[35]

With the end of the war, American TV was unleashed at last. By 1947, the number of television sets in American homes had soared to 170,000. In that same year a programme called *Puppet Television Theater* made its début. A year later it was renamed *Howdy Doody*, and television had its first hit.

As late as 1949, radio was still generating profits of over $50 million, while TV was making losses of $25 million.[36] But as the 1950s opened, television became a kind of national mania. As early as 1951, advertisers were cashing in on the craze. McGregor Sportswear took a full-page ad in *Life* to unveil its new sportswear range for go-ahead guys, 'Videos', which featured such televisually appropriate fare as the reversible 'Visa-Versa Jacket', 'the Host Tri-Threat Jacket,' the 'Durosheen Host Casual Jacket' and matching 'Durosheen Host Lounge Slacks', all expressly designed for wear in front of the TV. Soon people everywhere were buying folding tray-tables so they could eat their 'TV Dinners' while glued to the box. America was well on its way to becoming a nation of couch potatoes, though that expression would not of course be used for many years. (Its first appearance has been traced to the unlikely forum of *American Banker* magazine of 30 December 1980, but the context suggests that it was already current, at least in California.)[37]

By 1952, the number of sets had soared to 18 million, 105 times as many as there had been just five years earlier. The seminal date for television was Monday, 19 January 1953, the date on which Lucille Ball gave birth to 'Little Ricky' on national television (by happy coincidence she gave birth to the real Desi Arnaz, jun., on the same day). The nation was so enthralled it hardly noticed that

Dwight D. Eisenhower had been installed as President that afternoon.[38]

The first television networks were run by NBC, CBS, ABC (which had evolved from the NBC Blue radio network) and the now largely forgotten DuMont Labs, a leading electronics company of the 1930s and 1940s. As a television network it struggled for years – by 1955 it had just two shows on the air – and finally expired altogether in 1957, though the company itself, renamed Metromedia, lives on as a chain of television and radio stations.

Many early television programmes were simply lifted from radio. *The Lone Ranger, Sergeant Preston of the Yukon, Sky King, Meet the Press, Queen for a Day, Stop the Music* and *Gunsmoke* had all begun life as radio shows, though the transition to a visual medium often required alterations of cast. The squat and portly William Conrad, who played Marshal Matt Dillon on the radio, was replaced on TV by the more slender figure of James Arness. A more telling alteration was the adaptation of the popular *The $64 Question* from radio, but with the pay-offs raised a thousandfold, reflecting television's sudden, staggering wealth. The show became not just a hit but a phenomenon. When a Marine Corps captain named Richard S. McCutchen won the $64,000 pay-off, the story made the front page of the *New York Times*. Inevitably it spawned a legion of imitative quiz shows – *Dotto, Twenty-One, Tic Tac Dough, Name That Tune* (one of whose early contestants, Marine Major John Glenn, won $15,000 by naming twenty-five tunes), and the brazenly derivative *$64,000 Challenge*. Almost all relied on the formula of ending the shows with the winning contestant having to defer until the following week the agonizing decision of whether to take his or her winnings or press on at the risk of losing all, thereby ensuring a supply of eagerly returning viewers.

The difficulty was that contestants had an exasperating tendency to blow an answer late in the programme, thus precluding the possibility of an even more exciting return performance the following week. To get around the problem the producers of several shows hit simultaneously on a simple expedient. They cheated. Each week they supplied selected contestants – among them a respected minister from New Jersey – with the correct answers, which made the results rather easier to forecast.

Unfortunately they failed to consider that some contestants, having got a taste of success, would grow miffed when the producers decided that their reign should end. A contestant named Herbert Stempel blew the whistle on *Twenty-One* when its producers told him to 'take a dive', and soon contestants from several other quiz shows were sheepishly admitting that they too had been supplied with answers. And that was pretty much the end of such shows. None the less, the expression 'the $64,000 question' has shown a curious durability.

Perhaps not coincidentally, the boom years of the 1950s saw the development of another great electrical breakthrough: the home air-conditioner. Air-conditioning had been around for a long time. It was developed in 1902 by a twenty-year-old fresh out of Cornell University named Willis Carrier. As we have seen elsewhere, Carrier didn't call it an air-conditioner but an *apparatus for cooling air*. *Air-conditioner* was coined four years later by a North Carolina textile engineer named Stuart Cramer, who invented a device designed not to cool textile mills but to humidify them.[39]

By the 1920s air-conditioning was being widely used for specific applications – in hospitals and cinemas, for instance – but the considerable cost and the need for outsize ducts acted as a disincentive for its use in most homes and office buildings. Even in the late 1940s, a home air-conditioning unit – which Carrier called an 'Atmospheric Cabinet' – was as big as an upright piano and as noisy and as expensive to run as you would expect a piano-sized appliance to be. The development of small window models in 1951 made the industry take off. In 1952 sales of home units went from virtually nothing to $250 million, and they have never looked back. Today Americans spend $25 billion a year, more than the gross national products of some countries, just on the electricity to run their air-conditioners.

Three years after the window air-conditioner made its début, another durable household appliance entered the world: the microwave oven. The first was called the *Radarange*. It was large and bulky – it weighed over 700 lb. – required a lot of complicated cooling apparatus and didn't cook food very well. Renamed the *microwave oven*, the first consumer unit was produced in 1955 by Tappan, but the product and word didn't become familiar to most

Americans until the late 1960s when further improvements and advanced miniaturization of components – not to mention the increasing busyness of American women – made it at last a realistic proposition for home use.[40]

Such was the proliferation of gadgets and appliances that by the 1960s it was possible to perform almost any daily household task while scarcely rippling a muscle – from opening cans to brushing one's teeth to juicing an orange to carving a turkey. Instead of becoming more versatile and innovative, household appliances mostly just became more complex. Blenders accumulated a dazzling array of buttons. One had no fewer than sixteen buttons that the user could activate in an almost infinite selection of permutations, though, in the candid words of one executive, it still 'couldn't do much more than whip cream'. Labelling the buttons presented a linguistic as well as marketing challenge. A manufacturer, quoted in Susan Strasser's history of domesticity, *Never Done*, recalled that 'eight of us sat up two nights straight, trying to get words with five letters, each one sounding a bit higher than the other'.[41]

Perversely, this plethora of labour-saving devices didn't translate into greater leisure. The average 'non-working mother', as they are so inaccurately called, spends as much time doing housework now as fifty years ago – about fifty-two hours a week.[42] Although she has the benefits of countless appliances, the increased productivity they have brought her has been effectively offset by the larger size of modern houses, more wide-ranging lifestyles (her great-grandmother didn't run children everywhere in the family station wagon and her groceries were probably delivered) and more scrupulous standards of household cleanliness.

Leisure in any meaningful sense is actually quite a modern concept. *Sightseeing* didn't enter the language until 1847 and *vacation* not until 1878, and even then both were diversions for the well-off few. For millions of people a vacation was a once-in-a-lifetime indulgence that they experienced only on their honeymoon, or *bridal tour*, as it was often called until about 1900. *Honeymoon* has existed in English since 1546, but originally signified only the first month of marriage. It didn't become associated with a trip away from home until about the middle of the nineteenth century.

Weekend is an even more recent concept. The word was coined in 1879 in England, but didn't become part of the average American's vocabulary until as recently as the 1930s. Well into the 1900s most people worked a sixty-hour, six-day week and thus terms like *Monday-to-Friday* and *weekend* had no particular significance for them. The five-day, forty-hour week is often attributed to Henry Ford, but in fact it was introduced by the steel industry in 1923. Ford followed in 1926. Most of the rest of the nation didn't catch up until the Great Depression, when a shorter working week became a convenient way of dealing with falling demand.[43] Though nine-to-five had become the standard working day for most Americans by the early 1940s, the term *nine-to-fiver* isn't recorded before 1959.

Today, according to some studies, Americans work harder – or at least longer – than at any time since the forty-hour week became standard. According to Juliet B. Schor in *The Overworked American,* the amount of leisure time has fallen by almost 40 per cent since 1973[44] as people have been driven to seek overtime, take second jobs or simply show a zealous commitment to the workplace lest they find themselves the victims of *restructuring, premature retirement, coerced transition, constructive dismissal, skill mix redeployment* or any of the other forty or so euphemisms for being laid off that the managing editor of *Executive Recruiter News* reported in 1991.[45] (Of which Digital Equipment Corporation's *involuntary methodologies* was perhaps the most chillingly recondite.)

Across the economy as a whole, it has been estimated, the average American works 163 hours more per year today than two decades ago. Men are working 98 hours more, and women no less than 305 extra hours.[46] The burden is particularly heavy on working mothers who put in, on average, an eighty-hour week when cleaning, cooking and child care are included. Not surprisingly, nearly all the recent neologisms relating to work and the workplace are negative: *workaholic* (1968), *three o'clock syndrome* (i.e., the tendency to grow drowsy in mid-afternoon, 1980), *information overload* (1985), *sick building syndrome* (a feeling of general malaise generated by a poorly designed environment, first noted in *Industry Week* in 1983), *time squeeze* (1990), and so on.

According to Schor, the average American adult enjoys just sixteen and a half hours of leisure a week after disposing of work and household commitments – though it must be said such a claim appears dubious when you consider that other studies show that the average American also devotes over twenty-eight hours a week to watching television, spends three hours in shopping malls and presumably manages to find at least a few hours for sex, eating and socializing.

What is certain is that Americans work longer hours and more days than their counterparts in almost any other nation in the developed world. Principally as a result of shorter vacations and fewer national holidays, the average manufacturing employee in America puts in the equivalent of eight weeks a year more at the workplace than a manufacturing employee in France or Germany.[47]

Thanks to all that hard work, America as a nation produces twice the goods and services per person that it produced in 1948. Everyone in the country could, in principle at least, work a four-hour day or a six-month year and still maintain a standard of living equivalent to that enjoyed by our parents. Almost uniquely among the developed nations, America took none of its productivity gains in additional leisure. It bought consumer items instead.[48]

14

The Hard Sell: Advertising in America

I

In 1885 a young man named George Eastman formed the Eastman Dry Plate and Film Company in Rochester, New York.[1] It was rather a bold thing to do. Aged just thirty-one, Eastman was a junior clerk in a bank on a comfortable but modest salary of $15 a week. He had no background in business, but he was passionately devoted to photography and had become increasingly gripped with the conviction that anyone who could develop a simple, un-technical camera, as opposed to the cumbersome, outsize, fussily complex contrivances then on the market, stood to make a fortune.

Eastman worked tirelessly for three years to perfect his inven-tion, supporting himself in the mean time by making dry plates for commercial photographers, and in June 1888 he produced a camera that was positively dazzling in its simplicity: a plain black box just 6½ inches long by 3¼ inches wide, with a button on the side and a key for advancing the film. Eastman called his device the 'Detective Camera'. Detectives were all the thing – Sherlock Holmes had been born the year before – and the name implied that it was so small and simple that it could be used unnoticed, as a detective might.[2]

The camera had no viewfinder and no way of focusing. The *photographer* or *photographist* (it took a while for the first word to become the established one) simply held the camera in front of him, pressed a button on the side and hoped for the best. Each roll took a hundred pictures. When the roll was fully exposed, the anxious owner sent the entire camera to Rochester for developing.

Eventually he received the camera back, freshly loaded with film, and – assuming all had gone well – 100 small circular pictures, 2½ inches in diameter.

Often all didn't go well. The film Eastman used at first was made of paper, which tore easily and had to be carefully stripped of its emulsion before the exposures could be developed. It wasn't until the invention of celluloid roll film by a sixty-five-year-old Episcopalian minister named Hannibal Goodwin in Newark, New Jersey – this truly was the age of the amateur inventor – that amateur photography became a reliable undertaking. The Revd Goodwin didn't call his invention *film* but 'photographic pellicule', and, as was usual, spent years fighting costly legal battles with Eastman without ever securing the recognition or financial pay-off he deserved – though eventually, years after Goodwin's death, Eastman was ordered to pay $5 million to the company that inherited the patent.

In 1888 Eastman changed the name of the camera to 'Kodak' – an odd choice since it was meaningless, and in 1888 no one gave meaningless names to products, especially successful products. Since British patent applications at the time demanded a full explanation of trade and brand names, we know how Eastman arrived at his inspired name. As he crisply summarized it in his patent application: 'First. It is short. Second. It is not capable of mispronunciation. Third. It does not resemble anything in the art and cannot be associated with anything in the art except the Kodak.'[3] Four years later the whole enterprise was renamed the Eastman Kodak Company.

Despite the considerable expense involved – a Kodak camera sold for $25 and each roll of film cost $10, including developing – by 1895, over a hundred thousand Kodaks had been sold and Eastman was a seriously wealthy man. (A lifelong bachelor, he lived with his mother in a 37-room mansion with 12 bathrooms.) Soon people everywhere were talking about *snapshots*, originally a British shooting term for a hastily executed shot. Its photographic sense was coined by the English astronomer Sir John Herschel, who also gave the world the terms *positive* and *negative* in their photographic senses.[4]

From the outset Eastman developed three crucial strategies that have been the hallmarks of virtually every successful consumer-goods company since. First, he went for the mass market, reasoning that it was better to make a little money each from a lot of people rather than a lot of money from a few. He also showed a tireless, obsessive dedication to making his products better and cheaper. In the 1890s such an approach was widely perceived as insane. If you had a successful product you milked it for all it was worth. If competitors came along with something better, you bought them out or tried to squash them with lengthy patent fights or other bullying tactics. What you certainly did not do was create new products that made your existing lines obsolete. Eastman did. Throughout the late 1890s Kodak introduced a series of increasingly cheaper, niftier cameras – the Bull's Eye model of 1896, which cost just $12, and the famous, slimline Folding Pocket Kodak of 1898 – before finally in 1900 producing his eureka model: the little box Brownie, priced at just $1 and with film at 15 cents a reel (though with only six exposures per reel).

What set Eastman apart above all was the breathtaking lavishness of his advertising. In 1899 alone, he spent $750,000, an unheard-of sum, on advertising. Moreover it was *good* advertising: crisp, catchy, reassuringly trustworthy. 'You press the button – we do the rest' ran the company's first slogan, thus making a virtue of its shortcomings. Never mind that you couldn't load or unload the film yourself. Kodak would do it for you. In 1905 it followed with another classic slogan: 'If It Isn't An Eastman, It Isn't A Kodak.'[5]

Kodak's success did not escape other businessmen. In Detroit, Henry Ford carried the idea of mass marketing to the automobile industry, creating in the Model T a car that was within the purchasing power of almost everyone. He failed to follow Eastman's second precept, however, and milked his Model T for years longer than he should have, a mistake Ford's successors would spend decades rectifying. Others, however, saw the virtue in the idea of steady refinement and improvement. AT&T and Westinghouse, among others, set up research laboratories with the idea of creating a stream of new products, even at the risk of displacing old ones. Above all, everyone everywhere began to advertise.

Advertising was already a well-established phenomenon by the turn of the twentieth century. American newspapers had begun carrying ads as far back as the early 1700s and magazines had soon followed. (Benjamin Franklin has the distinction of having run the first magazine ad, seeking the whereabouts of a runaway slave, in 1741.)[6] By 1850 the country had its first *advertising agency*, the American Newspaper Advertising Agency, though its function was to buy advertising space rather than come up with creative campaigns. The first advertising agency in the modern sense was N. W. Ayer & Sons of Philadelphia, established in 1869. *To advertise* originally carried the sense of to broadcast or disseminate news. Thus a nineteenth-century newspaper that called itself *The Advertiser* meant that it had lots of news, not lots of ads. By the early 1800s the term had been stretched to accommodate the idea of spreading the news of the availability of certain goods or services. A newspaper notice that read, 'Jos. Parker, Hatter', was essentially announcing that if anyone was in the market for a hat, Jos. Parker had them. In the sense of persuading members of the public to acquire items they might not otherwise think of buying – items they didn't know they needed – advertising is a phenomenon of the modern age.

By the 1890s advertising was appearing everywhere – in newspapers and magazines, on *billboards* (an Americanism dating from 1850), on the sides of buildings, on passing streetcars, on paper bags, even on books of matches, which were invented in 1892 and being extensively used as an advertising medium within three years.

Very early on, advertisers discovered the importance of a good slogan. Ivory Soap's '99 44/100 per cent pure' dates from 1879. Schlitz has been calling itself 'the beer that made Milwaukee famous' since 1895, and Heinz's '57 varieties' followed a year later. Morton Salt's 'when it rains, it pours' dates from 1911, the American Florist Association's 'say it with flowers' was first used in 1912 and the 'good to the last drop' of Maxwell House coffee, named for the Maxwell House Hotel in Nashville, where it was first served, has been with us since 1907. (The slogan is said to have originated with Teddy Roosevelt, who pronounced that the coffee was 'good to the last drop', prompting one wit to ask, 'So what's wrong with the last drop?')

Sometimes slogans took a little working on. Coca-Cola described itself as 'the drink that makes a pause refreshing' before realizing, in 1929, that 'the pause that refreshes' was rather more succinct and memorable. A slogan could make all the difference to a product's success. After advertising its soap as an efficacious way of dealing with 'conspicuous nose pores', Woodbury's Facial Soap came up with the slogan 'The skin you love to touch' and won the hearts of millions.[7] The great thing about a slogan was that it didn't have to be accurate to be effective. Heinz never actually had '57 varieties' of anything. The catch-phrase arose simply because H. J. Heinz, the company's founder, decided he liked the sound of the number. Undeterred by considerations of verity, he had the slogan slapped on every one of the products he produced, which in 1896 was already far more than fifty-seven. For a time the company tried to arrange its products into fifty-seven arbitrary clusters, but in 1969 it gave up the ruse altogether and abandoned the slogan.

Early in the 1900s, advertisers discovered another perennial feature of marketing – the *giveaway* as it was called almost from the start. Consumers soon became acquainted with the irresistibly tempting notion that if they bought a particular product they could expect a reward – the chance to win prizes, to receive a free book (almost always ostensibly dedicated to the general improvement of one's well-being but invariably a thinly disguised plug for the manufacturer's range of products), receive a free sample, or a rebate in the form of a shiny dime. Typical of the genre was a turn-of-the-century tome called *The Vital Question Cook Book*, which was promoted as an aid to livelier meals, but which proved upon receipt to contain 112 pages of recipes all involving the use of Shredded Wheat. Many of these had a certain air of desperation about them, notably the 'Shredded Wheat Biscuit Jellied Apple Sandwich' and the 'Creamed Spinach on Shredded Wheat Biscuit Toast'. Almost all in fact involved nothing more than spooning some everyday food on to a piece of shredded wheat and giving it an inflated name. None the less, the company distributed no fewer than four million copies of *The Vital Question Cook Book* to eager consumers.

But the great breakthrough in twentieth-century advertising came with the identification and exploitation of the American consumer's Achilles heel: anxiety. One of the first to master the form was King Gillette, inventor of the first safety razor and one of the most relentless advertisers of the early 1900s. Most of the early ads featured Gillette himself, who with his fussy toothbrush moustache and well-oiled hair looked more like a caricature of a Parisian waiter than a captain of industry. After starting with a few jaunty words about the ease and convenience of the safety razor – 'Compact? Rather!' – he plunged the reader into the heart of the matter: 'When you use my razor you are exempt from the dangers that men often encounter who allow their faces to come in contact with brush, soap and barber shop accessories used on other people.'

Here was an entirely new approach to selling goods. Gillette's ads were in effect telling you that not only did there exist a product that you never previously suspected you needed, but if you *didn't* use it you would very possibly attract a crop of facial diseases you never knew existed. The combination proved irresistible. Though the Gillette razor retailed for a hefty $5 – half the average working man's weekly pay – they sold in their millions and King Gillette became a very wealthy man. (Though only for a time, alas. Like many others of his era, he grew obsessed with the idea of the perfectibility of mankind and expended so much of his energies writing books of convoluted philosophy with titles like *The Human Drift* that eventually he lost control of his company and most of his fortune.)[8]

By the 1920s advertisers had so refined the art that a consumer could scarcely pick up a magazine without being bombarded with unsettling questions: 'Do You Make These Mistakes in English?', 'Will Your Hair Stand Close Inspection?', 'When Your Guests Are Gone Are You Sorry You Ever Invited Them?' (because, that is, you lack social polish), 'Did Nature Fail to put Roses in Your Cheeks?', 'Will There be a Victrola in Your Home This Christmas?'* The 1920s truly were the Age of Anxiety. One ad pictured a former golf champion, 'now only a wistful onlooker', whose career had gone sour because he had neglected his teeth. Scott Tissues mounted a campaign showing a forlorn-looking businessman sitting on a park bench beneath the bold caption 'A Serious Business Handicap – These Troubles That Come From Harsh Toilet Tissue'. Below the picture the text explained: '65% of

---

* The most famous 1920s ad of them all didn't pose a question, but it did play on the reader's anxiety: 'They Laughed When I Sat Down, but When I Started to Play. . .' It was originated by the US School of Music in 1925.

all men and women over 40 are suffering from some form of rectal trouble, estimates a prominent specialist connected with one of New York's largest hospitals. "And one of the contributing causes," he states, "is inferior toilet tissue." ' There was almost nothing that one couldn't become uneasy about. One ad even asked: 'Can You Buy a Radio Safely?' Distressed bowels were the most frequent target. The makers of Sal Hepatica warned: 'We rush to meetings, we dash to parties. We are on the go all day long. We exercise too little, and we eat too much. And, in consequence, we impair our bodily functions often we retain food within us too long. And when that occurs, poisons are set up – *Auto-Intoxication begins.*'

In addition to the dread of auto-intoxication, the American consumer faced a positive assault course of other newly minted maladies – *pyorrhea, halitosis* (popularized by Listerine beginning in 1921), *athlete's foot* (a term invented by the makers of Absorbine Jr. in 1928), *dead cuticles, scabby toes, iron-poor blood, vitamin deficiency* (*vitamins* had been coined in 1912, but the word didn't enter the general American vocabulary until the 1920s when advertisers realized it sounded worryingly scientific), *fallen stomach, tobacco breath*, and *psoriasis*, though Americans would have to wait until the next decade for the scientific identification of the gravest of personal disorders – *body odour*, a term invented in 1933 by the makers of Lifebuoy soap and so terrifying in its social consequences that it was soon abbreviated to a whispered *BO*.

The white-coated technicians of American laboratories had not only identified these new conditions, but – miraculously, it seemed – had simultaneously come up with cures for them. Among the products that were invented or rose to greatness in this busy, neurotic decade were *Cutex* (for those deceased cuticles), *Vick's Vapo Rub, Geritol, Serutan* ('Natures spelled backwards', as the voice-over always said with somewhat bewildering reassurance, as if spelling a product's name backwards conferred some medicinal benefit), *Noxzema* (for which read: 'knocks eczema') *Preparation H, Murine* eyedrops and *Dr Scholl's Foot Aids.** It truly was an age

---

* And, yes, there really was a Dr Scholl. His name was William Scholl, he was a real doctor, genuinely dedicated to the well-being of feet, and they are still very proud of him in his hometown of LaPorte, Indiana.

of miracles – one in which you could even cure a smoker's cough by smoking, so long as it was Old Golds you smoked, because, as the slogan proudly if somewhat untruthfully boasted, they contained 'Not a cough in a carload'. (As late as 1953, L&M was advertising its cigarettes as 'just what the doctor ordered!')

By 1927 advertising was a $1.5 billion a year industry in the United States, and advertising people held in such awe that they were asked not only to mastermind campaigns but even to name the products. An ad man named Henry N. McKinney, for instance, named *Keds* shoes, *Karo* syrup, *Meadow Gold* butter and *Uneeda Biscuits*.[10]

Product names tended to cluster around certain sounds. Breakfast cereals often ended in -*ies* (*Wheeties, Rice Krispies, Frosties*); washing powders and detergents tended to be gravely monosyllabic (*Lux, Fab, Tide*). It is often possible to tell the era of a product's development by its ending. Thus products dating from the 1920s and early 1930s often ended in -*ex* (*Pyrex, Cutex, Kleenex, Windex*) while those ending in -master (*Mixmaster, Toastmaster*) generally betray a late 1930s or early 1940s genesis.[11] The development of *Glo-Coat* floor wax in 1932 also heralded the beginning of American business's strange and long-standing infatuation with illiterate spellings, a trend that continued with *ReaLemon* juice in 1935, *Reddi-Wip* whipped cream in 1947 and many hundreds of others since, from *Tastee-Freez* drive-ins to *Toys 'R' Us*, along with countless others with a *Kwik, E-Z* or *U* (as in *While-U-Wait*) embedded in their titles. The late 1940s saw the birth of a brief vogue for endings in -*matic*, so that car manufacturers had *Seat-O-Matics* and *Cruise-O-Matics*, and even fitted sheets came with *Ezy-Matic Corners*. Some companies became associated with certain types of names. DuPont, for instance, had a special fondness for words ending in -*on*. The practice began with *nylon* – a name that was concocted out of thin air and owes nothing to its chemical properties – and was followed with *Rayon, Dacron, Orlon* and *Teflon*, among many others, though in more recent years the company has abandoned the practice and moved into what might be called its *Star Trek* phase with such intergalactic compounds as *Tyvek, Kevlar, Sontara, Cordura, Nomex* and *Zemorain*.

Such names have more than passing importance to their owners.

If American business has given us more than our share of anxiety, we may draw some comfort from the thought that business has suffered anxiety of its own protecting the names of those products.

A certain cruel paradox prevails in the matter of preserving brand names. Every business naturally wants to create a product that will dominate its market, but if that product so dominates the market that the brand name becomes indistinguishable in the public mind from the product itself – when people begin to ask for a 'thermos' rather than a 'Thermos brand vacuum flask' – then the term has become generic and the owner faces the loss of its trademark protection. That is why advertisements and labels so often carry faintly paranoid-sounding lines like 'Tabasco is the registered trademark for the brand of pepper sauce made by McIllhenny Co.', and why companies like Coca-Cola suffer palpitations when they see a passage like this (from John Steinbeck's *The Wayward Bus*):

> 'Got any coke?' another character asked.
> 'No,' said the proprietor. 'Few bottles of Pepsi-Cola. Haven't had any coke for a month . . . It's the same stuff. You can't tell them apart.'[12]

An understandable measure of confusion exists concerning the distinction between patents and trademarks and between trademarks and trade names. A *patent* protects the name of the product and its method of manufacture for seventeen years. Thus from 1895 to 1912, no one but the Shredded Wheat Company could make shredded wheat. Because patents require manufacturers to divulge the secrets of their products and thus give rivals the opportunity to copy them, companies sometimes choose not to seek their protection. Coca-Cola for one has never been patented.[13] *Trademark* is effectively the name of a product, its *brand name*. *Trade name* is the name of the manufacturer. So *Ford* is a trade name, *Escort* a trademark. Trademarks apply not just to names, but also to logos, drawings and other such symbols and depictions. The MGM lion, for instance, is a trademark. Unlike patents, trademarks have indefinite protection in America.

For a long time, it was felt that this permanence gave the holder an unfair advantage. In consequence, America did not enact its first trademark law until 1870, almost a century after Britain and even then the American law was thrown out as unconstitutional by the Supreme Court. Lasting trademark protection did not begin for American companies until 1881. Today the number of trademarks on issue in America is something over 1 million, and is rising by about 30,000 a year.

A good trademark is almost incalculably valuable. Invincible-seeming brand names do occasionally falter and fade. *Pepsodent, Oxydol, Sal Hepatica* and *Burma-Shave* all once stood on the commanding heights of consumer recognition. For the most part, however, once a product establishes a dominant position in a market, it is exceedingly difficult to depose it. In 19 out of 22 product categories, the company that owned the leading American brand in 1925 still has it today – Nabisco in cookies, Kellogg's in breakfast cereals, Kodak in film, Sherwin Williams in paint, Del Monte in canned fruit, Wrigley's in chewing-gum, Singer in sewing-machines, Ivory in soap, Campbell's in soup, Gillette in razors. A well-established brand name has a sort of self-perpetuating power. As a 1991 article in *The Economist* noted: 'In the category of food blenders, consumers were still ranking General Electric second twenty years after the company had stopped making them.'[14]

An established brand name is so valuable that only about 5 per cent of the 16,000 or so new products introduced in America each year bear all-new brand names. The others are variants on an existing product – *Tide with Bleach, Tropicana Twister Light Fruit Juices* and so on. Among some types of product a certain glut is evident. At last count there were 220 types of branded breakfast cereal in America. In 1993, according to an international business survey, the world's most valuable brand was Marlboro, with a value estimated at $40 billion, slightly ahead of Coca-Cola. Among the other top ten brands were Intel, Kellogg's, Budweiser, Pepsi, Gillette and Pampers. Nescafé and Bacardi were the only foreign companies to make the top ten, underlining American dominance in brands.[15]

Huge amounts of effort go into choosing brand names. General Foods reviewed 2,800 names before deciding on *Dreamwhip*.[16] (And to put this in proportion try to think of just ten names for an artificial whipped cream.) Ford considered more than 20,000 possible car names before finally settling on *Edsel* – which proves that such care doesn't always pay – and Standard Oil a similar number before it opted for *Exxon*. Sometimes, however, the most successful names are the result of a moment's whimsy. *Betty Crocker* came in a flash to an executive of the Washburn Crosby Company (later absorbed by General Mills), who chose *Betty* because he thought it sounded wholesome and sincere and *Crocker* in memory of a beloved fellow executive who had recently died. At first the name was used only to sign letters responding to customers' requests for advice or information, but by the 1950s Betty Crocker's smiling, confident face was appearing on more than fifty types of food product, and her loyal followers could buy her recipe books and even visit her 'kitchen' at the General Foods headquarters.

Even greater efforts go into finding out why people buy the brands they do. Advertisers and market researchers bandy about terms like *conjoint analysis technique, personal drive patterns, Gaussian distributions, fractals,* and other such arcana in their quest to winnow out every subliminal quirk of American buying habits. They know, for instance, that 40 per cent of all people who move to a new address will also change their brand of toothpaste, that the average supermarket shopper makes fourteen impulse decisions in each visit, that 62 per cent of shoppers will pay a premium for mayonnaise even when they think a cheaper brand is just as good, but that only 24 per cent will show the same largely irrational loyalty to frozen vegetables. To preserve a brand name involves a certain fussy attention to linguistic and orthographic details. To begin with, the name is normally expected to be treated not as a noun but as a proper adjective – that is, the name should be followed by an explanation of what it does: *Kleenex facial tissues, Q-Tip cotton swabs, Jell-O brand gelatin dessert, Sanka brand decaffeinated coffee.* Some types of products – notably cars – are granted an exemption, which explains why General Motors does not have to advertise *Cadillac self-driving automobiles* or the like. In all cases, the name may not explicitly describe the product's function, though it may hint at what it does. Thus *Coppertone* is acceptable; *Coppertan* would not be.

The situation is more than a little bizarre. Having done all they can to make their products household words, manufacturers must then in their advertisements do all in their power to imply that they aren't. Before trademark law was clarified, advertisers positively encouraged the public to treat their products as generics. Kodak invited consumers to 'Kodak as you go', turning the brand name into a dangerously ambiguous verb. It would never do that now. The American Thermos Product Company went so far as to boast 'Thermos is a household word', to its considerable cost. Donald F. Duncan, Inc., the original manufacturer of the Yo-Yo, lost its trademark protection partly because it was amazingly casual about capitalization in its own promotional literature. 'In case you don't know what a yo-yo is. . .' one of its advertisements ran, suggesting that in commercial terms Duncan did not. Duncan also made the elemental error of declaring, 'If It Isn't A Duncan, It Isn't a Yo-Yo', which on the face of it would seem a reasonable claim, but was in fact held by the courts to be inviting the reader to consider the product generic.[17] Kodak had long since stopped saying 'If it isn't an Eastman, it isn't a Kodak.'

Because of the confusion, and occasional lack of fastidiousness on the part of their owners, many dozens of products have lost their trademark protection, among them *aspirin, linoleum, yo-yo, thermos, cellophane, milk of magnesia, mimeograph, lanolin, celluloid, dry ice, escalator, shredded wheat, kerosene* and *zipper*. All were once proudly capitalized and worth a fortune.

II

On 1 July 1941 the New York television station WNBT-TV interrupted its normal viewing to show, without comment, a Bulova watch ticking. For sixty seconds the watch ticked away mysteriously, then the picture faded and normal programming resumed. It wasn't much, but it was the first television commercial.

Both the word and the idea were already well established. The first *commercial* – the term was used from the very beginning – had been broadcast by radio station WEAF in New York on 28 August 1922. It lasted for either ten or fifteen minutes, depending on which source you credit. Commercial radio was not an immediate hit. In its first two months, WEAF sold only $550 worth of air-time. But by the mid-1920s, sponsors were not only flocking to buy air-time but naming their programmes after their products – *The Lucky Strike Hour, The A&P Gypsies, The Lux Radio Theater* and so on.[18] Such was the obsequiousness of the radio networks that by the early 1930s many were allowing the sponsors to take complete artistic and production control of the programmes. Many of the most popular shows were actually written by the advertising agencies, and the agencies seldom missed an opportunity to work a favourable mention of the sponsor's products into the scripts.

With the rise of television in the 1950s, the practices of the radio era were effortlessly transferred to the new medium. Advertisers inserted their names into the programme title – *Texaco Star Theater, Gillette Cavalcade of Sports, Chesterfield Sound-Off Time, The US Steel Hour, Kraft Television Theater, The Chevy Show, The Alcoa Hour, The Ford Star Jubilee, Dick Clark's Beechnut Show* and the arresting hybrid *The Lux-Schlitz Playhouse*, which seemed to suggest a cosy symbiosis between soapflakes and beer. The commercial dominance of programme titles reached a kind of hysterical peak with a programme officially called *Your Kaiser-Frazer Dealer Presents Kaiser-Frazer Adventures in Mystery*.[19] Sponsors didn't write the programmes any longer, but they did impose a firm control on the contents, most notoriously during a 1959 *Playhouse 90* broadcast of *Judgement at Nuremberg*, when the sponsor, the American Gas Association, managed to have all references to gas ovens and the gassing of Jews removed from the script.

Where commercial products of the late 1940s had scientific-sounding names, those of the 1950s relied increasingly on secret ingredients. Gleem toothpaste contained a mysterious piece of alchemy called GL-70. Consumers were never given the slightest hint of what GL-70 was, but it would, according to the advertising, not only rout odour-causing bacteria but 'wipe out their enzymes!'*

A kind of creeping illiteracy invaded advertising too, to the dismay of many. When Winston began advertising its cigarettes with the slogan 'Winston tastes good like a cigarette should',

---

* For purposes of research, I wrote to Procter & Gamble, Gleem's manufacturer, asking what GL-70 was, but the public relations department evidently thought it eccentric of me to wonder what I had been putting in my mouth all through childhood and declined to reply.

nationally syndicated columnists like Sydney J. Harris wrote anguished essays on what the world was coming to – every educated person knew it should be '*as* a cigarette should' – but the die was cast. By 1958 Ford was advertising that you could 'travel smooth' in a Thunderbird Sunliner and the maker of Ace Combs was urging buyers to 'comb it handsome' – a trend that continues today with 'pantihose that fits you real comfortable' and other grammatical manglings too numerous and dispiriting to dwell on.

We may smile at the advertising ruses of the 1920s – frightening people with the threat of 'fallen stomach' and 'scabby toes' – but in fact such creative manipulation still goes on, albeit at a slightly more sophisticated level. The *New York Times Magazine* reported in 1990 how an advertising copywriter had been told to come up with some impressive labels for a putative hand cream. She invented the arresting and healthful-sounding term *oxygenating moisturizers*, and wrote accompanying copy with references to 'tiny bubbles of oxygen that release moisture into your skin'. This done, the advertising was turned over to the company's research and development department, which was instructed to come up with a product that matched the copy.[20]

If we fall for such commercial manipulation, we have no one to blame but ourselves. When Kentucky Fried Chicken introduced 'Extra Crispy' chicken to sell alongside its 'Original' chicken, and sold it at the same price, sales were disappointing. But when its advertising agency persuaded it to promote 'Extra Crispy' as a premium brand and to put the price up, sales soared. Much the same sort of verbal hypnosis was put to work for the benefit of the fur industry. Dyed muskrat makes a perfectly good fur, for those who enjoy cladding themselves in dead animals, but the name clearly lacks style. The solution was to change the name to 'Hudson seal'. Never mind that the material contained not a strand of seal fur. It sounded good, and sales skyrocketed.

Truth has seldom been a particularly visible feature of American advertising. In the early 1970s, Chevrolet ran a series of ads for the Chevelle, boasting that the car had '109 advantages to keep it from becoming old before its time'. When looked into, it turned out that these 109 vaunted features included such items as rear-view mirrors, reversing lights, balanced wheels and many other such items that were considered pretty well basic to any car. Never mind; sales soared. At about the same time, Ford, not to be outdone, introduced a 'limited edition' Mercury Monarch at $250 below the normal list price. It achieved this by taking $250 worth of equipment off the standard Monarch.[21]

And has all this deviousness led to a tightening of the rules concerning what is allowable in advertising? Hardly. In 1986, as William Lutz relates in *Doublespeak*, the insurance company John Hancock launched an ad campaign in which 'real people in real situations' discussed their financial predicaments with remarkable candour. When a journalist asked to speak to these real people, a company spokesman conceded that they were actors and 'in that sense they are not real people'. [22] During the 1982 presidential election campaign, the Republican National Committee ran a television advertisement praising President Reagan for providing cost-of-living pay increases to federal workers 'in spite of those sticks-in-the-mud who tried to keep him from doing what we elected him to do'. When it was pointed out that the increases had in fact been mandated by law since 1975 and that Reagan had in any case three times tried to block them, a Republican official responded: 'Since when is a commercial supposed to be accurate?'[23] Quite.

In linguistic terms, perhaps the most interesting challenge facing advertisers today is that of selling products in an increasingly multicultural society. Spanish is a particular problem, not just because it is spoken over such a widely scattered area but also because it is spoken in so many different forms. Brown sugar is *azucar negra* in New York, *azucar prieta* in Miami, *azucar morena* in much of Texas, and *azucar pardo* pretty much everywhere else[24] – and that's just one word. Much the same bewildering multiplicity applies to many others. In consequence, embarrassments are all but inevitable.

In mainstream Spanish *bichos* means *insects*, but in Puerto Rico it means *testicles*, so when a pesticide maker promised to bring death to the *bichos* Puerto Rican consumers were at least bemused, if not alarmed. Much the same happened when a maker of bread referred to its product as *un bollo de pan* and discovered that to Spanish-speaking Miamians of Cuban extraction that means a woman's private parts. And when Perdue Chickens translated its slogan 'It takes a tough man to make a tender chicken' into

Spanish, it came out as a slightly less macho: 'It takes a sexually excited man to make a chick sensual.'[25]

Never mind. Sales soared.

The Movies

In 1877, in one of those instances of one thing leading to another, the railway tycoon Leland Stanford and a business crony were lounging with drinks on the veranda of Stanford's California stud farm when the conversation turned to the question of whether a galloping horse ever has all four hoofs off the ground at once. Stanford was so sure that it did – or possibly didn't; history is unclear on this point – that he laid his friend a bet of $25,000. The difficulty was that no matter how carefully you watch the legs of a galloping horse you cannot tell (particularly, we might suppose, when you have had a number of drinks on the veranda) whether the horse is at any point momentarily suspended in air. Determined to find an answer, Stanford called in his chief engineer, John D. Isaacs, who in turn summoned the services of the photographer Eadweard Muybridge.

Muybridge was a self-created exotic (his real name was the rather more plebeian Edward Muggeridge) and an accomplished landscape photographer, though in 1877 his fame rested chiefly on having managed to get himself acquitted of murdering his wife's lover in one of the more sensational cases of the age. Isaacs and Muybridge deployed twenty-four cameras along a racetrack and with the aid of trip-wires executed a series of photographs of a horse galloping past. This had two effects. It proved beyond question that a galloping horse *does* get all four hoofs off the ground, and for quite a lot of the time, and it marked the beginning of motion picture photography.[1]

Motion pictures of a type had been around since the late eighteenth century. Usually they involved cut-out silhouettes, pictures painted on discs or cylinders or some other such simple device, which could be back-lit and spun to throw a moving image on to a wall or screen. Despite their primitiveness these early devices went by a variety of scientifically impressive names: the *phenakistoscope*, the *animatoscope*, the *thaumatrope*, the *phantascope*, the *stroboscope*. Inspired by their linguistic inventiveness, Muybridge constructed a projector of his own and called it a *zoopraxiscope*. Soon other similar devices were flooding the market: the *mutascope*, the *kinematoscope*, the *kinematograph*, the *theatrograph*.

All of these had certain deficiencies, primarily that they relied on stringing together sequences of still photographs, a process that required either a lot of cameras or careful orchestration of movements on the part of the subjects. What was really needed was moving film. Thomas Edison saw himself as the man to provide it – or at least as the man to provide the man to provide it. He gave the task to a young Scotsman in his employ named W. K. L. Dickson. Dickson (who would later go on to found Biograph, one of the first Hollywood studios) studied the competitors' machines, considered the problem, and in short order devised an entire motion picture system, the first in the world (which perhaps makes him the true father of the movies). The camera was called a *kinetograph*, the projection device a *kinetoscope*, and the films thus made were *kinetophones*. (I mention them specifically because books of film history sometimes confuse them.) Nothing that Dickson came up with was particularly new. He essentially put together, albeit in an ingenious way, existing technologies.

Edison didn't envision kinetophone viewing as a shared, public experience, but rather as a home entertainment system – and one whose primary purpose would be to provide an extra, incidental use for his recently invented phonograph. Some of the early motion pictures even had sound. (What slowed the progress of sound movies wasn't the problem of synchronization but of amplification.) He suspected the whole thing would prove a passing fad, and had so little confidence in it that he decided against spending $150 on an international patent, to his huge eventual cost.[2]

The first public demonstration of Dickson's new system was on

14 April 1894, on Broadway in New York. Despite an admission charge of twenty-five cents, people lined up around the block for the chance to take a look at this marvellous new peep-show.[3] (The invention may have been new, but the word wasn't; *peep-show* had first been used in 1861 in reference to kinematoscope viewers.) Projected through fifty-foot loops of film, each kinetophone show lasted no more than a minute and sometimes as little as sixteen seconds, with obvious consequent limitations on narrative possibilities. That the camera which recorded the moving images weighed 500 lb. and was the size of a modern refrigerator acted as a further deterrent to adventurous scenarios. As a result, the first kinetophone films consisted of simple amusements: quick vaudeville turns, pratfalls, dancing bears and – something of a surprise hit – a brief but lively feature called *Fred Ott's Sneeze* (Fred Ott being an Edison employee), which has the distinction of being the first copyrighted motion picture.

The shortcoming of the kinetoscope was that it could be viewed by only one person at a time. Unwilling or unable to see its potential, Edison failed to exploit his head start and was soon left behind in the hunt for a projection system that would allow motion pictures to become a shared experience. Rival systems began to sprout up everywhere, particularly in Europe where there were no copyright problems thanks to Edison's miserly failure to secure a patent. In one of the more intriguing developments, an inventor named Louis Aimé Augustin le Prince briefly excited Paris in 1890 by demonstrating a fully developed system in which moving film was projected on to a screen to the delight and astonishment of an invited audience. Shortly after this acclaimed performance, le Prince left his house on some errand and was never seen again. Another inventor in Paris, one Jean Leroy, thereupon demonstrated a rival system, again to great acclaim, and likewise mysteriously vanished.[4]

Not until 1895 did anyone else crack the problems of projecting film. Then in quick succession came three workable systems, all developed independently. One was the *cinématographe*, invented by the brothers Auguste and Louis Lumière. From this evolved both the French and British words for the movies as well as such terms as *cinematography*, *cinematographer* and, much later, *Cinerama*. The word occasionally appeared in America in the early days, though usually spelled *kinema*. In Germany, meanwhile, the brothers Max and Émile Skladanowsky developed their *Bioskop*, anglicized in America to *Bioscope*. And in England Robert Paul invented the *Theatrograph* or *Animatographe*, which was as technically sophisticated as the other two, but failed to prosper and soon dropped from contention.

At last it dawned on Edison that there was money to be made in the film game. Unable to invent his own projection system, he did the next best thing. He bought one and claimed to have invented it. The system was in fact the invention of Thomas Armat. The only thing Edison invented was the name: *Vitascope*. Armat based his system on Edison's kinetophone, but improved it substantially. One improvement was the addition of a small reel that gave the film another loop. Called the *Latham loop* after its American inventors, the brothers Otway and Greg Latham, it didn't look much, but it transformed the history of the movies. Before the Latham loop, movies of more than a minute or so were impossible because the film would so often break. The Latham loop eased the tension on the film and in doing so made it possible to create films of more than a hundred feet. For the first time real movies, with plots, were possible.

The first public display of this new wonder was on 23 April 1896, as an added attraction between live shows at Koster and Bial's Music Hall on Thirty-fourth Street and Broadway (a site now occupied by Macy's).[5] Not having enough films of his own to show, Edison illegally copied some of the Lumière brothers' early works.[6] *Motion picture* was coined in 1891, but wasn't used much at first. The earliest movies were called *life portrayals* or *mechanically reproduced theatre entertainment*, though by the end of 1896 people were calling them *moving pictures* and by the early 1900s had shortened this almost everywhere to *movies* (though until as late as the 1920s people sometimes referred to them as *movie plays*). People who took the pictures were called *camerists*. *Cameraman* didn't occur to anyone until 1905.

The first real movie – that is, one with a story-line – was *The Great Train Robbery* by Edwin S. Porter, who had begun in the Edison studios in Paterson, New Jersey, as a general handyman and *camerist* before rising to become head of production. Running eleven minutes and containing fourteen scenes, *The Great Train*

Robbery was not only revolutionary in its sophisticated editing and pacing, but also in its content. It was both the first true movie and the first *western* – though that word wouldn't become general until about 1928; before that they were *cowboy movies* or *gun operas* – and the first to explore the exciting possibilities of violent crime.[7] It was a sensation. The excitement it generated and its sense of wondrous novelty are difficult to conceive now. When one of the characters fired a gun at the camera, many members of the audience gasped and recoiled. (This may not seem quite so ridiculous if you pause to consider your own response the first time you saw a 3-D movie.) A few even fainted. It became one of those things that simply everybody had to see.

Almost overnight movies went from being a craze to a compulsion. By 1905 people everywhere were flocking to *store theatres* (so called because they were usually set up in vacant stores) or *nickelodeons*, where viewers were treated to half an hour of escapism for a nickel. *Nickelodeon* had been used as a word for peep-show arcades since 1888, though the first purpose-built cinema, in Pittsburgh, styled itself not a nickelodeon, but a *Nicolet*. Within two weeks of the Nicolet's opening, people were flocking to the theatre from eight in the morning until midnight to see Edwin S. Porter's sensational *Great Train Robbery*, and the proprietors were clearing profits of $1,000 a week.

By 1906 there were a thousand nickelodeons all over America; by 1907 five thousand. Film was designed to run at a speed of sixteen frames per second, but nickelodeon operators quickly discovered that if they speeded things up a little they could get in more shows. For millions, attending the nickelodeon became a kind of addiction. By 1908 New York City's *movie theatres* – the word had been coined the year before; in 1914 it would be joined by *movie houses* – were clocking up 200,000 admissions every day, including Sundays when they were required by law to be closed. Many non-movie-goers considered the phenomenon alarming if not distasteful. This was partly because of the mildly *risqué* nature of some of the shows – within two weeks of Edison launching the first kinetophone parlour in 1894 some enterprising opportunist was offering a peep-show called *Doloria in the Passion Dance*, which was not terribly titillating by modern standards but was certainly a step up on *Fred Ott's Sneeze* – and partly because the movies attracted a disproportionate number of lower-class immigrants (for whom language problems often made other, more verbal forms of entertainment impractical), and anything that gave pleasure to lower-class immigrants was almost by definition suspect. But it was also because of something less specific – a vague sense that going to the pictures was somehow immoral and conducive to idleness – and authorities often had sudden, unprompted purges on the early movie houses, as in 1908 when New York Mayor George B. McLellan arbitrarily ordered shut all 550 of that city's establishments for no real reason other than that he didn't like them.[8]

The word *movies* even began to take on a slightly unsavoury tone. In 1912 a studio called Essanay invited fans to come up with a better name. The winning entry was *photoplay*. It never caught on as a word for the pictures, but it did become the name of a hugely successful magazine.[9] (Hollywood's curious disdain of the word *movies* is reflected in the decidedly inflated title of its most vaunted institution: the Academy of Motion Picture Arts and Sciences.)

As movies became increasingly sophisticated they developed an argot to describe the new production techniques – *close-up* (1913), *to pan* (1915), *fade-in* and *fade-out* (1918), *dissolve* (1920), *trailers* (early 1920s), and *captions* (1907), *subtitles* or *titles* (1913) for the frames of dialogue or explication that were inserted into the film at intervals to explain the action. Some were used so often that they passed into the language as stock phrases, notably 'comes the dawn' and 'meanwhile back at the ranch'.[10] *Trailers* were so called because in the early days they followed, or *trailed*, the main film. Many other movie words were taken from the stage. *Slapstick* was a vaudeville term. It described two sticks that were literally slapped together off-stage to accentuate an on-stage pratfall (*prat* being an old slang term for the buttocks). *Ham actor*, first recorded in 1875, alludes to the practice of lesser performers having to use ham fat rather than cold cream to remove their make-up. Soon a second-rate actor was known as a *hamfatter*; by 1902 he was just a *ham*. *Grips*, the term for scenery shifters, was also originally a theatrical term. They were so called because they gripped the sets and props when they moved them.

By 1925 the movies had become not only America's most popular form of entertainment, but its fifth biggest industry, and people everywhere dreamed of making it big in Hollywood. How a dusty, misnamed southern California hamlet that never had much to do with the making of movies became indelibly fixed in the popular consciousness as the home of the entertainment industry is a story that takes a little telling.

Let's start with the name. Hollywood never had any holly or even much wood to speak of. Originally called Cahuenga Valley, it was principally the site of a ranch owned by a Mr and Mrs Harvey Henderson Wilcox. The more romantic name came after Mrs Wilcox, on a trip back east, fell into a conversation with a stranger on a train and was so taken with the name of her new acquaintance's summer home, *Hollywood*, that she decided to rename the ranch. That was in 1887, and in the general course of things that would very probably have been that. Hollywood would have been an anonymous piece of semi-arid real estate waiting to be swallowed up by Los Angeles.

But between 1908 and 1913 something else happened. Many small independent film companies began moving to southern California, among them the Selis Company, the Nestor Film Company, Biograph and Mack Sennett's Keystone Studios (from which of course would eventually come the Keystone Kops movies). Partly they were drawn by the weather, which would permit year-round filming without a lot of expensive lighting. (Early 'studios', if it's not too much to call them that, were mostly in the open air, with even interior scenes shot on stages that had backdrops but no roofs.) More crucially, they were also trying to escape the threats, legal and physical, of the Motion Pictures Patents Company, a consortium of eight studios led (inevitably) by Thomas A. Edison. The MPPC had been trying for some years to gain monopoly control of the movie business and had developed increasingly aggressive tactics to encourage competitors to join the consortium and pay its hefty licensing fees. Its idea of exploratory negotiations was to send in a party of thugs with baseball bats. Hence the appeal of a locale two thousand miles away on another coast.

Only one of the studios actually set up in Hollywood, the Nestor Film Company in 1911. Locals were so upset at the sudden appearance of ramshackle film sets and the *louche* appearance of

actors that they enacted an ordinance forbidding the erection of
further studios. So in fact Hollywood has never really had a film
industry. The studios that began to dot the landscape in the
following years were all elsewhere – in Culver City, Edendale,
Boyle Heights, Burbank, Santa Monica, indeed almost anywhere
but Hollywood. As late as 1913, when Cecil B. de Mille filmed *The
Squaw Man* in a studio at the corner of Sunset Boulevard and Vine,
Hollywood was a country hamlet.[11] Hollywood Boulevard was
not yet so named – indeed it was just a dirt road. None the less, by
1915 *Hollywood* had become so generic as a term for the movie
business that neighbouring communities scrambled to associate
themselves with its magic. Ivanhoe and Prospect Park reincorpo-
rated as East Hollywood and Lankersheim became North
Hollywood.[12] Laurelwood, not to be outdone, transformed itself
into Studio City.

Beverly Hills, the other southern California name that most of us
automatically associate with the movies, and more particularly
with *movie stars* (a term coined in 1919), was likewise named on a
whim. It was christened in 1907 by a property developer, who
named his 3,200-acre housing development (although it had just
one house at the time) Beverly Hills after his hometown of Beverly,
Massachusetts. It became especially fashionable with the stars after
Mary Pickford and Douglas Fairbanks married in 1920 and moved
into a Beverly Hills mansion they called Pickfair.

In 1917 the Motion Picture Patents Company was declared an
illegal cartel and ordered to disband. It hardly mattered. By that
time, Hollywood (and from here on in I am using the term
generically) all but owned the movie business. It is a curious fact
that this most American of phenomena was created almost entirely
by non-Americans. Apart from Mack Sennett and Mary Pickford
(who were in any case both Canadian), the early studios were run
by a small band of men who had begun life from strikingly similar
backgrounds: they were all eastern European Jews, poor and
uneducated, who had left Europe in the same decade (the 1880s),
and had established themselves in the New World in mostly lowly
trades before they all abruptly – and instinctively, it seems –
abandoned their careers in the first decade of this century and
became seized with the opportunities to be found in the
nickelodeon business.

It is most odd, but consider: Louis B. Mayer of Metro-Goldwyn-Mayer was a scrap merchant from Lithuania. The Hungarian-born Adolf Zukor of Famous Players Studios was a janitor and later a furrier. Samuel Goldwyn of the Goldwyn Picture Company was a glove salesman from Warsaw. Carl Laemmle, founder of Universal, was a German who had run a clothing store in Oshkosh, Wisconsin. William Fox (real name Wilhelm Fried) was a Hungarian who worked in the garment industry before founding Fox Pictures. Joseph M. Schenk, creator of Twentieth Century Productions, was a Russian-born fairground showman and pharmacist. The Warner brothers – Albert, Harry, Jack and Sam – were from Poland and had worked at various, mostly menial jobs. None had any link to the entertainment industry. Yet in the first years of the century, as if answering an implanted signal, they all migrated to New York City and became involved in the nickelodeon business – some as owners of nickelodeon parlours, some as makers of films. In the second decade of the century, another signal appears to have gone off in their heads and they decamped *en masse* to Hollywood. Some understandable confusion exists concerning Samuel Goldwyn and Metro-Goldwyn-Mayer. Though his name accounts for the middle initial in MGM, Goldwyn was never part of the company. He sold out to the Metro studios and Louis B. Mayer in 1924, and was astonished to discover that they took his name with them – though that was no more than Goldwyn himself had done. The Goldwyn Picture Company was not in fact named for Goldwyn, but rather he for it. His real name was Schmuel Gelbfisz, though for his first thirty years in America he had called himself – perhaps a little unwisely – Samuel Goldfish. Goldwyn was a portmanteau of the names of the studio's two founders: Samuel Goldfish and Edgar Selwyn. It wasn't until 1918, tired of being the butt of endless fish-bowl jokes, that he named himself after his corporation. After the MGM takeover, he had to go to court to win permission to continue making movies under the Goldwyn name.

It would be putting it mildly to say that Goldwyn never entirely mastered the nuances of English. Though many of the expressions attributed to him are apocryphal – he never, for instance, said to a pretentious director who wanted to make a movie with a message: 'If you want to send a message call Western Union' – he did actually say 'I was on the brink of an abscess', 'Gentlemen, include me out', and 'You've bitten the hand of the goose that laid the golden egg'. Warned that a Broadway production to which he had acquired rights was 'a very caustic play', he shot back: 'I don't give a damn how much it costs.' And a close friend swore that once when they were walking on a beach and the friend said, 'Look at the gulls,' Goldwyn stopped in his tracks and replied in all seriousness, 'How do you know they're not boys?' He had a particular gift for mangling names. He always referred to Mervyn LeRoy as 'Moiphy' LeRoy, to Preston Sturges as 'Preston Sturgeon' and, to his unending annoyance, to Ernst Fegte as 'Faggoty'.[13]

Not just the studio chiefs, but directors, composers, art directors, musicians and actors were as often as not foreigners working in this quintessentially American medium. The 1938 movie *The Adventures of Robin Hood*, for instance, starred an Australian, Erroll Flynn, and an Englishman, Basil Rathbone, was directed by a Hungarian, Michael Curtiz, scored by a Czech, Erich Wolfgang Korngold, and had sets designed by a Pole, Anton Grot. Consider the backgrounds of just a few of those who made Hollywood pulse in its early years: John Ford (born Sean O'Fearna) was Irish, Greta Garbo Swedish, Charlie Chaplin, Alfred Hitchcock, Cary Grant and Stan Laurel English, William Wyler Alsatian, Billy Wilder Hungarian, Frank Capra Italian (at least by birth), Fred Zinnemann and Erich Von Stroheim Austrian, and Ernst Lubitsch German. Never has an industry been more international in its composition or more American in its output.

As the years passed studios endlessly formed and reformed. Mutual, Reliance and Keystone amalgamated into the Triangle Film Corporation, which, despite having America's three leading directors – D. W. Griffith, Mack Sennett and Thomas H. Ince – soon went under. RCA and the Keith Orpheum theatre chain teamed up to form RKO. Joseph Schenk's Twentieth Century Pictures and William Fox's Fox Film Corporation merged into Twentieth Century-Fox. Many more fell by the wayside: Star, Biograph, General Film and even the Edison Company. But Hollywood itself went from strength to strength, filling the world with a distinctively American mix of glamour, adventure and moral certitude.

If the stars hadn't changed their names already, the studios often did it for them to make them fit more neatly into the pleasantly homogenized heaven that was Hollywood. Names were changed for almost any reason – because they were too dull, too exotic, not exotic enough, too long, too short, too ethnic, too Jewish. Generally, it must be said, the studio bosses knew what they were doing. Who after all could imagine John Wayne as Marion Morrison or Judy Garland as Frances Gumm or Mary Pickford as dowdy Gladys Smith? Spangler Arlington Brugh is a name for a junior high school woodwork teacher; change it to *Robert Taylor* and you are already halfway to stardom. Archie Leach might pass muster as the kid who delivers groceries, but if you want a man of the world it's got to be *Cary Grant*. Doris Kappelhoff is the 200 lb. chocoholic who baby-sits your little brother; *Doris Day* dates the quarterback. Even little Mortimer Mouse had his name changed to Mickey just four years after his creation in 1923.

In the very early days of the movies stars hadn't had to change their names because they weren't allowed any, at least not as far as their fans were concerned. Until the second decade of the century actors and actresses weren't billed at all. For years Mary Pickford was known only as 'Little Mary' and Florence Lawrence as 'the Biograph girl'. Then, as producers realized that audiences were drawn by certain faces and even styles of film-making, they began billing not just the featured players, but also directors and even sometimes cameramen. The first actress to have her name changed for purposes of enhanced aura (*sex appeal* wouldn't come into general use until the 1940s) is thought to have been one Theodosia Goodman from Cincinnati. Seeking a persona better suited to her dark, exotic looks, someone at the William Fox Company in 1914 played around with the words *Arab* and *death* (goodness knows why those two) and came up with *Theda Bara*. Soon all the studios were at it. Among the stars who found immortality with someone else's name, we can count the following. (Their original names are on the right.)

Rudolph Valentino	Rodolpho d'Antonguolla
Joan Crawford	Lucille Le Sueur
Al Jolson	Asa Yoleson
Bert Lahr	Isidore Lahrheim
Paul Muni	Muni Weisenfreund
Gilbert Roland	Luis Antonio Damoso De Alonzo

Lauren Bacall	Betty Jean Perske
Tony Curtis	Bernard Schwarz
Jack Benny	John Kebelsky
Barbara Stanwyck	Ruby Stevens
Veronica Lake	Constance Ockleman
Susan Hayward	Edyth Marrener
Fredric March	Frederick Bickel
Don Ameche	Dominic Amici
Red Buttons	Aaron Chwatt
Ed Wynn	Isaiah Edwin Leopold
Melvyn Douglas	Melvyn Hesselberg
Kirk Douglas	Issur Danielovitch Demsky
Lee J. Cobb	Leo Jacoby
June Haver	June Stovenour
Rita Hayworth	Margarita Carmen Cansino
Ginger Rogers	Virginia McMath
Mickey Rooney	Joe Yule, jun.
Jane Wyman	Sarah Jane Faulks
John Garfield	Julius Garfinkle
June Allyson	Ella Geisman
Danny Kaye	David Daniel Kaminsky
Sterling Hayden	Sterling W. Relyea
Rock Hudson	Roy Scherer
Cyd Charisse	Tula Ellice Finklea
Troy Donahue	Merle Johnson
Anne Bancroft	Anna Maria Italiano
Jerry Lewis	Joseph Levitch
Dean Martin	Dino Crocetti
Tab Hunter	Andrew Arthur Kelm
Virginia Mayo	Virginia Jones
W. C. Fields	W. C. Dukinfield
Clifton Webb	Webb Parmelee Hollenbeck
Dorothy Lamour	Dorothy Kaumeyer
Heddy Lamarr	Hedwig Kiesler
Walter Matthau	Walter Mattaschanskayasky
Boris Karloff	William Pratt

And, no, I don't know why Boris Karloff was thought to be an improvement on Bill Pratt.

In 1926, two new terms entered the language: *Movietone* from the Fox studios and *Vitaphone* from Warner Brothers, and sound movies were on their way. Both employed music and sound effects, but not speech. The *talkies* (often also called the *speakies* in the early days) would have to wait till the following year and the release of *The Jazz Singer*, though even it was only partly speaking. The first all-talking film, a gangster feature called *The Lights of New York*, came in 1928, though such was the quality of sound reproduction that it came equipped with subtitles as well. With sound, movies became not only more popular but immensely more complicated to make.

As the industry evolved through the 1920s and '30s, still more words were created to describe the types of films Hollywood was making – *cliffhangers, weepies, sobbies, tearjerkers, spine- chillers, westerns, serials* – and to denote the types of roles on offer. A character who wept a lot was a *tear bucket*. An actress in a melodrama was a *finger-wringer*. A villain was of course a *baddie*. Many movie terms, particularly portmanteau words like *cinemaestro* and *cinemactress* and fractured spellings like *laff* and *pix*, originated or were widely popularized by the bible of the movie business, the newspaper *Variety*. Many were short-lived. *Oats opera* for a western, *clicko* for a success, *bookritic, eight ball* for a failure and many such others died in infancy. Scores of others have prospered in the wider world, notably *whodunit, tie-in, socko, rave* (for a review), *flopperoo, palooka* (a word of unknown derivation), *belly laugh, newscaster, to scram* and *pushover*.

Behind the scenes, the development of increasingly sophisticated equipment brought a rash of new terms: *scrims, flags, gobos, skypans, inky dinks, century stands, flying rigs, match boxes, lupes* and other arcane apparatus. A *gobo* is a type of black screen (no one seems to know why it is so called), a *skypan* is a big light, an *inky dink* a small one, and a *match box* one smaller still. A *scrim* is a type of light diffuser. Such sophisticated equipment brought with it strange and intriguing job titles: *focus pullers, juicers, Foley artists, gaffers, best boys, supervising drapes, inbetweeners, wranglers, post-punch supervisors, swing-gangs* and so on. *Gaffer* (a corruption of *godfather*, originally a sarcastic term for an old person) is the head electrician. *Best boy* is the chief electrician's chief assistant. *Juicers* are those who move electrical equipment around. The *Foley artist* is in charge of sound effects; he's the one who adds the 'toosh!' to punches and the 'gerdoings!' to ricocheting bullets. It is named for Jack Foley, one of the great sound recordists. *Supervising drape* is the person in charge of drapes, rugs and other such inanimate objects. An *inbetweener* is an animator's assistant – one who draws the frames between the main action frames. *Swing-gangs* are those who build or rebuild sets overnight. *Wranglers* handle the animals, or indeed any living creatures. 'Cockroach wrangler' has been recorded in the credits of at least one film. As you will have gathered, often the title is more impressive than the job, and nowhere perhaps more so than with the *post punch supervisor*, whose responsibility essentially is to look after the photocopying.

With so many exotic professions involved it is little wonder that the credits nowadays seem to roll on for ever. The longest credits yet, for *Who Framed Roger Rabbit?*, actually go on for just six and a half minutes. Even so, they managed to salute 763 creative artists, technicians and other contributors – and that was without mentioning Kathleen Turner, the voice of Jessica Rabbit, who opted not to be credited.

Huge amounts of effort and emotion go into deciding the order of billing for movie stars – whether the name goes above the title, whether it is larger than the title and by what percentage and so on. When Paul Newman and Steve McQueen starred in *The Towering Inferno*, the problem of which of these superstars was to enjoy top billing led to protracted negotiations between agents and producers. Eventually it was decided that Newman's name would take the left-hand, pole position, but would be positioned fractionally lower than McQueen's, a practice that has been followed and elaborated on to the point of tedium in movie posters and advertising materials ever since. In 1956, Otto Preminger appalled the Hollywood community by announcing *The Man With the Golden Arm* as 'A Film by Otto Preminger'. No one had ever displayed such audacity before, and few have failed to engage in it since. Occasionally a director is so miffed with the handling of a film in post-production that he demands to have his name removed. The Directors Guild hit on the convention of crediting such disowned movies to the fabled and wholly fictional Allen Smithee, who is thus responsible for such classics as *Ghost Fever, Student Bodies, Morgan Stewart's Coming Home, City in Fear*, a Whitney Huston video and some two dozen other efforts.[14] The ultimate in screen credits, though, was almost certainly the 1929 production of *The Taming of the Shrew*, starring Douglas Fairbanks and Mary

Pickford, which contained the memorable line: 'By William Shakespeare, with additional dialogue by Sam Taylor.'[15] Possibly the most choleric credit line appeared on the 1974 movie *The Taking of Pelham 123*, which concerned the hijacking of a New York subway train and finished with the closing line: 'Made without any help whatsoever from the New York Transport Authority.'

No discussion of the lexicon of Hollywood would be complete without at least a passing mention of the Oscars and how these golden statuettes got their name. Few terms in any creative field have engendered more varied explanations of an etymology. The most plausible story perhaps is that the figure was named by Margaret Herrick, a librarian at the Academy of Motion Picture Arts and Sciences, who said upon seeing the prototype, 'Oh, that reminds me of my Uncle Oscar' (whose surname, for the record, was Pierce).[16] But it must be said there are many other similar versions to choose from. What is certain is that the figure of a naked man with a long sword standing on a film can originated as a doodle by Cedric Gibbons, the MGM art director, and that the first one was awarded in 1929.

In 1949, after nearly half a century of continuous, seemingly unstoppable success, Hollywood's executives got a shock when movie attendances slumped from 90 million to just 70 million in a single year. Matters would grow increasingly more fearful for them as the 1950s unfolded and Americans abandoned the movie theatres for the glowing comforts of their own televisions. In desperation the studios tried to make the most of whatever advantages they could muster. One was colour. Colour movies had been possible since as far back as 1917, when a Dr Herbert Kalmus invented a process he called *Technicolor*. The first Technicolor movie was *Toll of the Sea*, made by MGM in 1922. But the process was expensive and therefore little used. In 1947, only about a tenth of movies were in colour. By 1954 well over half were. Hollywood studios also responded by forbidding their stars to appear on the new medium, and by denying television networks access to their library of films, until it gradually dawned on them that old movies generated money when shown on television and didn't when locked in vaults.

But what was needed was some new technique, some

blockbuster development, that television couldn't compete with. In September 1952 the world – or at least an audience at New York's Broadway Theatre – was introduced to a startling new process called *Cinerama*. Employing a curved screen, stereophonic sound and three projectors, it provided watchers with the dizzying sensation of being on a Coney Island roller-coaster or whizzing perilously through the Grand Canyon. People loved it. But Cinerama had certain intractable shortcomings, notably distractingly wobbly lines where the three projected images joined, and an absence of theatres in which to show it. It cost $75,000 to convert a theatre to Cinerama, more than most could afford. There was also the problem that the process didn't lend itself to narrative performances and the few Cinerama movies that were made, such as *This Is Cinerama, Cinerama Holiday,* and *Cinerama South Seas Adventure,* consisted mainly of a succession of thrills. In 1962, as a kind of last gasp effort to save the process (theatre owners who had invested heavily in the massive screens and projector systems naturally wanted to put them to use) two narrative films were made, *How the West Was Won* and *The Wonderful World of the Brothers Grimm,* but the problem of having to swivel your head to follow a conversation between characters separated by sixty feet of screen was one that audiences failed to warm to.

In the same year that Cinerama was born, the world was also given 3-D movies. The first was a film called *Bwana Devil,* apparently one of the worst movies ever made. The process involved slightly overlapping images which melded into a three-dimensional whole once the viewer donned special Polaroid glasses. Originally called *Natural Vision,* it enjoyed a huge if short-lived vogue – sixty-nine Natural Vision movies were made in 1953 alone – and people flocked in their millions to features like *The Creature from the Black Lagoon* and *The Charge at Feather River* for the dubious thrill of having barge poles thrust at them and, in one particularly memorable scene, having a character appear to spit in their faces. So promising did the process seem at first that many quite respectable films, notably Hitchcock's *Dial M for Murder,* were filmed in 3-D, though the fad was so short-lived that most, including *Dial M,* were released in the normal flat form.

Before long it was all but impossible to go to a movie that didn't involve some impressive-sounding new technical process. One after another came *Vistarama, Superscope, Naturama,* even *AromaRama* and *Smell-O-Vision,* in which, as you might surmise, the theatre was pumped full of appropriate odours at regular intervals. The problem was that the odours tended to linger and mingle in a perplexing manner, and the members of the audience situated nearest the smell dispensers weren't particularly gratified to find themselves periodically refreshed with a moist outpouring of assorted scents.

A year after Cinerama made its début, Twentieth Century-Fox came up with a slightly more sophisticated, and certainly less gimmicky, process called *CinemaScope,* which required just a single camera with a special anamorphic lens. The first Cinema-Scope picture was *The Robe.* CinemaScope screens were roughly double the width of a normal movie screen and were slightly curved to give some illusion of depth.[17] By 1955, just two years after its introduction, more than 20,000 cinemas throughout the world had installed the CinemaScope system.[18] Hollywood would live to fight another day.

Hoplock's amazing catch in the 1946 World Series

16

The Pursuit of Pleasure: Sport and Play

The abiding impression of life in Puritan New England is that it wasn't a great deal of fun. 'Sad-visaged people moving always with sober decorum through a dull routine of work unrelieved by play' is the traditional view expressed by the historian John Allen Krout in 1929.[1]

In fact, it wasn't quite like that. Though they could scarcely be described as libertines, the Puritans were not averse to pleasure. They smoked and drank, and enjoyed games and contests as much as anybody, particularly those involving physical challenges like foot-races and wrestling, or that honed necessary skills like archery. Increase Mather called recreation 'a great duty', and at Harvard College the students were not merely permitted but actively encouraged to take part in 'lawful' games.[2] And lawful is the operative word. What the Puritans didn't like were activities deemed to be an encouragement to idleness or ungodliness – and of these, it must be said, they found many. Among the amusements they forbade at one time or another were quoits, ninepins, bowls, stool-ball and even shuffle-board. Games involving dice and cards were entirely out of the question. Plays, entertainments, 'dancing and frisking' and 'other crafty science' were equally abhorrent to them. Maypoles were cut down and even Christmas was abjured. Smoking was acceptable only within certain well-prescribed bounds. Connecticut had a statute forbidding inhabitants from taking 'tobacco publiquely in the street, nor shall any take yt in the fyelds or woods'.[3] On Sundays, no recreation of any sort was permitted. Even going for a stroll was forbidden. Indeed, sitting quietly could land you in trouble. One hapless couple found themselves hauled before magistrates for no graver offence than being found 'sitting together on the Lord's Day, under an apple tree'.[4]

Oddly, none of this was inherent in Calvinist doctrine. Calvin himself was known to enjoy a lively game of bowls on a Sunday afternoon. Nothing in their pre-American experience had suggested that the Pilgrims would institute such an aggressive crackdown on fun.

To understand why this happened in New England, it is necessary to re-examine two commonly held conceptions about the Puritans. The first is the belief that they had come to America to establish freedom of religion. In truth, freedom of worship was the last thing they wanted. Having suffered years of persecution on their native soil, they desired nothing from America so much as the opportunity to establish an equally intolerant system of their own. The second misconception is the belief that the colonization of New England was primarily pious in its impulse. In fact, throughout the early period Puritans were decidedly – indeed, uncomfortably – in the minority. The great bulk of early pilgrims were attracted to America not by religious zeal but by the hope of a better life. Between 1630 and 1640, of the 16,000 immigrants to Massachusetts, only one in four was a Puritan.[5] Even on the *Mayflower*, the Saints had been outnumbered 61 to 41 by Strangers. Both of these considerations worked powerfully on the Puritan psyche. From the outset they became jealously possessive of their moral authority in the New World, and in consequence showed a decidedly neurotic preoccupation with activities that might be construed as a challenge to their pre-eminence.

But beyond this there was a practical side to their detestation of idleness. Building a community in a wilderness was a terribly earnest undertaking, and one that did not admit of much leisure. Yet many of the non-Puritan settlers showed a vexing inclination to down tools and engage in play on any convenient pretext. Thus, when on Christmas Day, 1621 (almost precisely a year after their landing), Governor William Bradford found a group of impious Strangers 'in the streete at play, openly; some pitching the barr and some at stoole-ball', and huffily took their implements from them, he was offended not merely by their celebration of a holiday not recognized by his sect, but at the wanton and dangerous frittering away of time and energy that might have been directed to securing their survival.

Such concerns were far from unique to New England. In Virginia, too, outsiders were often appalled at how little the inhabitants attended to their well-being and security. Thomas Dale, arriving with supplies in 1611, found the residents on the brink of extinction but playing at bowls. Soon after, the Virginia Assembly enacted restrictive laws very similar to those of New England, making it illegal to gamble, to be found incapacitated by drink, to fail to observe the Sabbath, even to dress 'in excess'. None of this was motivated by a desire to help them tread the narrow path to heaven, but rather by the need to bring order and discipline to a vulnerable community.

When a celebration was deemed in order, the Puritans were delighted to let their hair down. The first Thanksgiving feast went on for three full days and involved, in addition to copious eating and drinking, such diversions as stoneball, a game similar to croquet, and competitions of running, jumping, arm-wrestling, shooting and throwing.

No one knows quite when this first Thanksgiving took place, other than that it was sometime between the beginning of October and the first week of November 1621. Nor was it regarded as the start of an annual tradition. No Thanksgiving appears to have been held the following year, and the Plymouth colony would not begin regular celebrations until almost the end of the century. For the rest of New England, Thanksgiving didn't become an annual tradition until about the 1780s. For the nation as a whole, Thanksgiving wasn't a fixed holiday until President Lincoln so decreed it in 1863. The date he chose was 6 August. The following year it was moved, arbitrarily, to the last Thursday in November, where it has remained ever since, apart from a brief period during the Depression years when it was brought forward seven days to give stores an extra week of potential Christmas shopping.[6]

Christmas likewise got off to an erratic start in America, not least because the Puritans disdained it, regarding it (not altogether inaccurately) as a pagan festival. In 1659 they went so far as to ban it altogether, and it remained widely suppressed in New England into the 1800s.[7] Partly because of this interruption of tradition, Christmas as now celebrated is a mongrel accumulation of practices from many lands.

Gift-giving, which has no intrinsic connection with Christmas, was borrowed from Holland. From the Middle Ages, the Dutch had made a custom of giving presents to children on 6 December, St Nicholas's Day. St Nicholas was a shadowy figure from Asia Minor whose many kindly deeds included bestowing bags of gold on three young women who otherwise faced a life of prostitution. Over time these three bags evolved into three golden balls and became, by some complicated leap of logic, the three balls associated with pawnbroking. In the late eighteenth century St Nicholas and the presents that went with him were borrowed from the Dutch but transferred to the nearest Anglican holiday, 25 December. At the same time, the now wholly secular figure of Santa Claus became bizarrely bound up with *Christkindlein*, the Christ child, and thus took on the alternative designation *Kris Kringle*.

The Christmas tree and the practice of sending greeting cards arrived from Germany – they are often attributed to Queen Victoria's German consort, Prince Albert – and gradually became part of the Christmas tradition in the nineteenth century. The first mention of a Christmas tree in America is in 1846. Carols (etymologically related to *choral*), mistletoe, holly and the yule log all come from Britain, mostly as survivors of a pre-Christian past. (*Yule* itself is pre-Saxon Germanic and evidently commemorates a forgotten pagan festival.)

The American attitude towards Christmas and how to celebrate it was long ambivalent. On the one hand Macy's was staying open till midnight on Christmas Eve as far back as 1867 in order to deal with the clamour to buy presents. But on the other, the practice of decorating trees was so late in developing that even in 1880 a manufacturer of ornaments could persuade F. W. Woolworth to take no more than $25 of his stock. (Before the decade was out, however, Woolworth had upped the order to $800,000.)[8]

It may come as a surprise to learn that there are no official national holidays in America. One of the rights reserved to the states was the prerogative to declare holidays. The President can, with the assent of Congress, declare 'legal public holidays', but these apply only to the District of Columbia and federal employees. They have no formal sanction elsewhere.

If revelries were seldom given official blessing in America, they generally found private outlets. Though those who governed the early colonies tried almost everywhere to subdue the national impulse to engage in dissolute pursuits, they didn't often succeed. Cock-fighting, dog-fighting, bear-baiting, drinking to excess and gambling were available to those who wished to find them, and not just on scattered feast days. Horse-racing, too, was widely popular, especially in Virginia, though suitable venues that offered a level surface and a measure of privacy were not always easy to find. Outside Jamestown there existed a particularly favourable stretch of road a quarter of a mile long. It became so popular as a location of illicit races that it led to the breeding of a new strain of horse, the quarter-horse, which lacked stamina but could sprint at enormous speed for short distances.[9] Horse-racing would later endow the American vocabulary with a wealth of terms, among them *frontrunner, inside track, to win by a nose, sure thing, also-ran* and *bookie*, though some of these would have to wait some time before finding general acceptance. *Bookie*, for instance, isn't found in print before 1885.[10]

In the Appalachian region, wrestling – or *wrassling* – of a particularly brutal nature became popular early on and evidently stayed both brutal and popular up to this century. Many of those who settled the region hailed from northern England, home of Cumberland and Westmorland wrestling, a contest that is thought to date from Viking times and remains popular to this day at country fêtes and other such gatherings throughout the English Lake District and slightly beyond. In it, two men embrace in a standing position, and with occasional bursts of grunting exertion, mixed with longer periods of strategic stillness (during which a spectator could be excused for thinking that they had temporarily nodded off), try to throw each other to the ground. It was, and in England remains, a gentlemanly pursuit. In the more rough-and-tumble environment of Kentucky and Virginia, however, Cumberland and Westmorland wrestling evolved into something rather more aggressive. Competitors grew their thumbnails long and filed their teeth to a point the better to inflict damage. Anything was permissible – pulling hair, gouging eyes, biting, stomping on a windpipe – so long as it was done with bare hands.

Fischer recounts the story of a fight between two men – and if you are squeamish you might just want to flit your eyes to the next paragraph – in which the winner secured an early advantage by gouging his opponent's eyes from his head with his thumbs. 'The sufferer roared aloud, but uttered no complaint' and astonishingly refused to give up the fight, according to one eyewitness. Not until his opponent had additionally bitten off his nose and torn his ears from his head did he at last conclude that discretion and the loss of a usable face were the better part of valour.[11]

Naturally, large sums of money changed hands at these spectacles. The Puritan ethic notwithstanding, Americans evinced an irrepressible urge to wager from the earliest days. Early gambling pursuits gave us many terms that have since passed into general usage. *Tinhorn*, meaning cheap or disreputable, comes from a metal cylinder of that name used to shake dice in games like *chuck-a-luck* (or *chutter-luck*) and *hazard*. *Pass the buck* came from the custom of passing a buckhorn knife as a way of keeping track of whose turn it was to deal or ante, and thus it is etymologically unrelated to *buck* as a slang term for dollar. American gambling led to a broadening of *bet* into the wider language in expressions like 'you bet I do', 'you bet your life', and so on, which foreign observers commonly noted as a distinguishing characteristic of American speech by the early nineteenth century. Mark Twain told the story of a westerner who had to break the news of Joe Toole's death to his widow. 'Does Joe Toole live here?' the westerner asks, and when the wife answers in the affirmative, he says, 'Bet you he don't!'[12]

Among the favourite card games until about the time of the American Revolution were *whist* (a word of unknown derivation, but possibly related to *whisk*), *brag* (so called because of the bravado required of betters) and *muggins* (whence the term for a gullible person or victim of fate). But by the closing years of the century they were giving way to *faro*, a game first mentioned in Britain in 1713. Corrupted from *pharaoh* (a pharaoh was pictured on one of the cards of a faro deck; it later evolved into the king of hearts), faro was a dauntingly complicated game in terms of equipment, scoring, betting and vocabulary. Each card dealt had a

name of obscure significance. The first was the *soda card*, the
second the *loser,* and so on to the final card, the *hock*; hence the
expression *from soda to hock*, and also *to be in hock*.[13] Scoring was
kept track of on an abacus-like device called a *case*, from which is
said to come the expression *an open and shut case. To break even*
and *to play both ends against the middle* also originated in faro, as
did the practice of referring to counters as *chips* (previously they
had been called *checks*). Thus most of the many expressions
involving *chips – to cash in one's chips, to be in the chips,* a *blue-
chip investment –* owe their origins to this now forgotten game.[14]

Gradually faro was displaced by *poker*. Dispute surrounds the
origins of the name. The most plausible guess is that it comes from a
similar German game called *Pochspiel*, in which players who
passed would call, '*Poche*', pronounced 'polka'.[15] Others have
suggested that it may have some hazy connection to *poke* or *puck*
(an English dialectal word meaning to strike, whence the name of
the hard black disc used in ice hockey) or to the Norse-Danish
pokker, 'devil', from which comes the *Puck* of English folklore. At
all events, *poker* is an Americanism first recorded in 1848. In its
very early days the game was also commonly referred to as *poko* or
poka.

Among the many terms that have passed into the main body of
English from poker are *deal* in the sense of a transaction, *jackpot*,
penny-ante, to stand pat, and *just for openers. Jackpot* is of
uncertain provenance. The *jack* may refer to the card of that name
or to the slang term for money, or possibly it may be simply another
instance of the largely inexplicable popularity of *jack* as a
component with which to build words: *jackhammer, jackknife,
jackboot, jackass, jack-in-the-box, jack-o'-lantern, jack-of-all-
trades, jackrabbit, jackstraw, jackdaw, jackanapes, lumberjack*
and *car jack*. In none of these, so far as is known, does *jack* contain
any particular significance. People clearly just liked the sound of it.

According to Dillard, *ace, deuce* and *trey*, for *one, two* and *three*,
are also American, through the influence of French gamblers of
New Orleans. He may be right in the case of *trey*, but the first two
were in common use in Britain in the Middle Ages and may date
from Norman times. *Ace* comes ultimately from the Latin *ās*, a
basic unit of currency, and *deuce* from the Latin *duōs*, or 'two'. The
French gamblers of New Orleans did, however, give us another

venerable gambling term: *to shoot craps*. In New Orleans the game the English called *hazard* became known as *crabs*, which mutated over time into *craps*. It has no etymological connection to the slang term for faeces. The French were also ultimately responsible for *keno* (from *quine*, 'a set of five'), an early form of bingo that was once very popular, though it left no linguistic legacy beyond its name.

More productive in terms of its linguistic impact was a much later introduction to America, *bridge,* which arrived from Russia and the Middle East in the early 1890s. The word is unrelated to the type of bridge that spans a river. It comes from the Russian *birich*, the title of a town crier. Among the expressions that have passed from the bridge table to the world at large are *bid, to follow suit, in spades, long suit* and *renege*.[16]

At about the time that bridge was establishing itself in America, a native-born gaming device was born: *the slot machine*. Slot machines of various types were produced in America as early as the 1890s, but they didn't come into their own until 1910 when an enterprising firm called the Mills Novelty Company introduced a vending machine for chewing-gum, which dispensed gum in accordance with flavours depicted on three randomly spinning wheels. The flavours were cherry, orange, and plum – symbols that are used on slot machines to this day. Each wheel also contained a bar reading '1910 Fruit Gum', three of which in a row led to a particularly lavish payout, just as it does today. Also just as today a lemon in any row meant no payout at all – and from this comes *lemon* in the sense of something that is disappointing or inadequate. The potential of slot machines for higher stakes than pieces of chewing-gum wasn't lost on the manufacturers and soon, converted to monetary payouts, they were appearing everywhere that gambling was legal, though no one thought to call them *one-armed bandits* until the 1950s.[17]

Partly in response to the popularity of gambling, a pious young New Englander named Anne Abbott invented a wholesome alternative in 1843: *the board game*. Board games like chess and checkers had of course been around for centuries and in almost all cultures, but never before had anyone devised a competitive entertainment in which players followed a path through a representation of the real world. Abbott intended the game not just as an amusement, but as an aid to upright living. Called *The Mansion of Happiness*, it required competitors to travel the board in pursuit of Eternal Salvation, avoiding such pitfalls along the way as Perjury, Robbery, Immodesty, Ingratitude and Drunkenness. The idea of moving a playing piece along a route beset with hazards was hugely novel in 1843, and not only made Abbott a tidy sum but also inspired a flock of imitators.

One was a young man named Milton Bradley, who produced his first hit, *The Checkered Game of Life*, in 1860. Also morally uplifting, it was clearly inspired by, if not actually modelled on, Abbot's elevating divertissement. Bradley's most original stroke, however, came when he devised a way of packing eight separate games, among them checkers, chess, backgammon and dominoes, into a small, easily portable box, which proved a hit with soldiers during the Civil War.

Rather more innovative was George Swinton Parker, founder of the second great name of the American games industry, Parker Brothers. Born into a venerable but declining family in Salem, Massachusetts, Parker loved the idea of board games, but hankered for a reward more immediately gratifying than future salvation. In 1883, aged just sixteen, he created a game called *Banking* in which the object was to speculate one's way to wealth. A new games-playing ethos was born, one that seized the imagination of Americans. As the writer Peter Andrews has put it: 'Instead of the most pious player reaping the most joy in the next world, the smartest player got the most money in this one.'[18]

With two of his brothers, Parker built the family firm into the biggest games company in the world. Parker himself invented more than a hundred games – or, more accurately, more than a hundred variations of essentially the same game. Almost always they were built around some world event or technological break-through that had recently seized the popular imagination. Among his more popular creations were *Klondike*, *Pike's Peak or Bust*, *The Motor Carriage Game*, *War in Cuba*, *The Siege of Havana* and *The Philippine War* (death and destruction proving nearly as irresistible to games players as accumulating a pile of fantasy money).

But the game that secured the company's fortunes was not invented by Parker or anyone else connected with the company. It was created during the early years of the Depression by one Charles Darrow, an unemployed salesman from Germantown, Pennsylvania, who sketched out the prototype on a piece of oilcloth spread out on his kitchen table. He called his game *Monopoly*. In 1933 Darrow submitted the game to Parker Brothers in the hope that the company would manufacture it on a large scale. The Parker Brothers executives dutifully tried the game but weren't impressed. They concluded that it had '52 fundamental errors'. For one thing there was no finishing-line, no visible ultimate goal. The idea of going around the board again and again struck them as faintly absurd. Then there was all this confusing business of mortgages and variable rents. All in all, the rules were too complicated and the game took too long to play. Clearly it would never sell, and they politely turned him down.

Undaunted, Darrow made up some games himself and took them to Wanamaker's Department Store in Philadelphia, where they became a small sensation. When Parker Brothers learned of this, they decided to give the game a try on an experimental basis. In the first year, Monopoly sold a million sets, a figure unknown in the world of games, and it has remained the best-selling board game in America ever since. His faith in the game vindicated, Darrow retired to an estate in the country, where he grew orchids and counted his money.

Monopoly was the great craze of the early 1930s, but crazes had been a feature of American life since the 1820s when the word unexpectedly took on the sense of a sudden widespread mania. (Previously it had signified something cracked or broken.) The curious thing about crazes is that they are usually invented elsewhere but taken up in America with such enthusiasm and panache as to make them seem native born. Such was the case with one of the great nineteenth-century crazes, roller skating, a pastime invented in Holland and introduced to America in 1863.

While Europeans were juddering unsteadily along cobbled streets, Americans were building vast skating palaces like the Casino in Chicago and the Olympian Club Roller Skating Rink in San Francisco. Such places could accommodate up to a thousand skaters at a time on their polished ash and maple floors. Often they had their own orchestras, playing tunes to which the audience could perform the latest, American-invented steps like the

Philadelphia Twist, the *Richmond Roll,* the *Picket Fence* and the *Dude on Wheels.*

Much the same happened with the bicycle. Before an Englishman named J. I. Stassen coined the term *bicycle* in 1869, two-wheeled vehicles had gone by a variety of names: *velocipedes, dandy horses, draisines* and *boneshakers. Boneshakers* was particularly apt. Early bikes ran on wooden wheels, had wooden saddles and of course ran over much less smoothly paved surfaces. Early models were propelled either by pushing the feet along the ground or by means of a complicated treadle mechanism. Most came without brakes. They were, in short, neither safe nor comfortable. But they were hugely popular.

Soon people everywhere were getting in on the mania for *wheeling,* as it was known. Cycling quickly developed its own complex terminology. The more energetic adherents went in for *scorching* or *freewheeling* (sometimes shortened by the linguistically debonair to *freeling*). Scorchers who showed a selfish disregard of others were known as *road hogs.* Such was their capacity to startle or surprise other road users – one popular model was called the *Surprise* – that in some places laws were passed requiring cyclists not simply to slow down and dismount when approaching a horse, but to lead it to safety before continuing.[19]

As early as 1882 people were referring to them familiarly as *bikes.* Such was the popularity of the sport that in 1885 a playing-card company in Cincinnati was inspired to try to cash in on the craze, which is how *Bicycle* brand playing-cards came about. By the mid-1880s cycling seemed to be as popular as a sport could get, but in 1888 came the invention of the pneumatic tire by the Scotsman John Dunlop, and other developments like lighter frames, handbrakes, gears and safety chains, and biking moved on to a higher plane of popularity.

A large part of bicycling's popularity was that it was one of the few exhilarating enjoyments permitted to women, though some authorities worried that perhaps it was too exhilarating. The *Georgia Journal of Medicine and Surgery* for one believed that cycling was unsuitable for females because the movements of the legs and the pressure on the pelvis of the saddle were bound to arouse 'feelings hitherto unrealized by the young maiden'.[20] The *Wheelman* magazine defended bicycling as a healthy pursuit for women, but added this ominous warning to its female readers: 'Do not think of sitting down to table until you have changed your underclothing.'

By 1895 ten million bicycles crowded America's roads, and manufacturers were producing a vast range of vehicles with jaunty, buy-me names like the *Sociable*, the *Quadrant*, the *Rudge Triplet Quadricycle,* and the *Coventry Convertible Four in Hand*. The craze looked set to run and run, but less than a decade later most people had packed up their bikes for ever, having lost their hearts entirely to the greatest of all American passions, the automobile.

The first two decades of the twentieth century were a period of relative calm in the world of crazes, but in the 1920s America made up for lost time. Among the phenomena that gripped the nation in that lively decade were dance marathons, flag-pole sitting competitions (the champion was one Alvin 'Shipwreck' Kelly who maintained his perilous perch atop a Baltimore flagpole for twenty-three days and seven hours), beauty contests, coast-to-coast car races, coast-to-coast foot-races known as *bunion derbies*, and miniature golf.

Miniature golf – at first called *dwarf golf* – was born in 1927 when a developer named Garnet Carter built a resort hotel called Fairyland on Lookout Mountain in Tennessee and added a miniature links complete with mechanical hazards. He intended it as a diversion for children, but to his astonishment the adults soon drove the mites off. Realizing that there must be something in this, Carter formed a company called Tom Thumb Golf and began producing factory-built courses. In just three years 25,000 Tom Thumb courses were erected across America.[21]

At home, three other forms of amusement entered the American vocabulary in the period. One was *mahjong* (or *mah-jongg*), a game from China that swept the nation beginning in 1922. Mahjong – the name is Mandarin for 'house sparrow', from a figure on the most important piece – was particularly fashionable among the *smart set* (a term roughly concurrent with the birth of the game in America). People paid up to $500 for their mahjong sets – more than the cost of a Model A Ford. Some even redecorated rooms of their houses in the Chinese style and invested in silk robes for themselves and their guests to help the mood along. For a decade or so, you couldn't hope to move in society if you didn't know the difference between a *South Wind* and a *Red Dragon*, or failed to comprehend cries of 'Pung!' 'Chow!' and 'Broke the wall!'[22]

Rather less fashionable but no less influential was *ouija*. (The name is a portmanteau of the French and German words for 'yes'.) Ouija, in which devotees place their hands on a small pointer that glides across the board picking out letters and numbers in response to questions, was invented sometime in the nineteenth century (accounts vary considerably both to year and place) but found a ready following in America in the 1920s, to such an extent that the *Baltimore Sun* appointed a Ouija Editor. As a popular entertainment ouija had faded by the 1940s, though occasionally it popped back into popularity and even sometimes into the news, as in 1956 when the descendants of an heiress named Helen Dow Peck discovered to their horror that she had left her considerable fortune to a John Gale Forbes – a person of whom she apparently knew nothing – because his name had been revealed to her during a session with a ouija board almost forty years before. Fortunately for the descendants, no such person could be found and they got to keep the money.[23]

The final component of this home entertainment trio of the 1920s was the one that proved the most durable: *the crossword puzzle*. At first called a *word-cross*, the crossword puzzle was invented in 1913 by an Englishman employed by the *New York World* newspaper, but it didn't catch on in a big way until a small publishing company called Simon and Schuster published a crossword puzzle book in 1924. As with mahjong and ouija, it quickly became a national passion, to such an extent that the Baltimore and Ohio Railroad put dictionaries in its passenger compartments for the benefit of crossword-addicted travellers – but unlike the first two its popularity has never faltered. Today solving crossword puzzles remains the most popular sedentary amusement in America besides watching television.

At about the same time that crossword puzzles, ouija boards and mahjong were seizing America's attention, baseball became known as *the national pastime*, though it had effectively been that for the better part of a century.

No one knows where or when baseball was first played. It has often been suggested that the game evolved from the English children's game rounders. Baseball and rounders do have un-questionable similarities – in both the batter hits a pitched ball and then sprints around a base path – but the difficulty is that the *Oxford English Dictionary* can find no citation for rounders before 1856, by which time baseball as both a sport and a name was firmly established in American life. (No one seems to have explored the possibility that rounders may in fact be derived from baseball.)

What is certain is that baseball's antecedents go back to well before the *Mayflower*. Cricket, played since the sixteenth century in England and commonly in America until the nineteenth, appears to be the grandfather of all bat and ball games, but many others followed in both Britain and America over the next two centuries – *tipcat* (or *kitcat*), *bittle-battle*, *stick ball*, *one old cat*, *two old cat*, *three old cat*, and *base* or *base-ball*, among others.* All involved the same principles of striking a ball with a stick or paddle and trying to traverse a defined path before being caught or thrown out by the fielding side. The first mention of baseball is found not in America but in Britain, in a children's book called *A Pretty Little Pocket Book, Intended for the Amusement of Little Master Tommy and Pretty Miss Polly*, published in London in 1744.[24] But ball games by this time were already well rooted in America. The first mention of a bat in the context of American play is in 1734, and there are many references throughout eighteenth-century America to ball games and their implements. The Boston Massacre, for instance, was provoked in part by someone waving a tipcat bat in a threatening manner at the British troops, and soldiers at Valley Forge are known to have passed the time in 1778 by 'playing at base'.[25]

By the early nineteenth century, ball games in America appear to have settled for the most part into a general form known as *town ball*, which came in two similar versions, *the Massachusetts game* and *the New York game*. The diverse etymologies of baseball terminology – *innings, shortstop, outfielder* and so on – indicate that the modern game arose not as an outgrowth of any particular sport but by borrowing and absorbing elements from a variety of

---

* Cricket derives its curious name from an old French word, *criquet*, describing the sound made by a ball striking wood. The insect the cricket also gets its name from *criquet*.

games. The question is, who was responsible for melding these disparate elements into a unified game?

The traditional answer is Abner Doubleday. According to David Hackett Fischer, 'Doubleday appears to have codified one of many sets of rules before 1840.' Fischer notes that Doubleday did not invent baseball, but, he adds, 'neither was his association mythical, as some revisionists have suggested'.[26]

In fact, it was entirely mythical.

Responsibility for the Doubleday legend rests ultimately with Albert Goodwill Spalding, who was an outstanding ball player and an astute businessman but an undiscriminating historian. After a brief but distinguished baseball career, Spalding opened a sporting goods store in Chicago, which grew into one of the world's largest manufacturers of sports equipment. By 1903 he was a very wealthy man and a figure of godlike authority among baseball followers.

In that same year – the year that also saw the first modern World Series, the Wright Brothers' first flight and the invention of the Model A car – Henry Chadwick, editor of the respected *Baseball Guide*, wrote a short history of the game in which he traced its probable origins to rounders and cricket. The patriotic Spalding was mortified at the thought that baseball might not be an all-American invention. After stewing over the matter for two years, in 1905 he appointed a six-man commission to look into the question. The commission was guided by A. G. Mills, president of the National League and, it so happened, a friend for thirty years of the recently deceased Abner Doubleday. In 1907 the commission issued a report in which it stated without substantiation that the game was created by Doubleday at Cooperstown, New York, in 1839. When pressed for details, Mills revealed that he had heard the story from 'a reputable gentleman' named Albert Graves, whose word he had accepted without question. (Graves would shortly end up in a lunatic asylum.)

To anyone who looked into the matter even slightly, it was obvious that the story didn't hold water. For one thing, Doubleday was not at Cooperstown in 1839, but at West Point, and in any case his family had left Cooperstown in 1837. At his death, Doubleday had left sixty-seven diaries and not once in any of them did he mention baseball. Finally, if Mills's story is to be believed, never in their thirty years of close friendship had Doubleday thought to mention to Mills that he had invented the game from which Mills was making his living.[27]

In so far as baseball can be said to have a founder, it is Alexander Cartwright, a member of the New York Knickerbocker Club who in 1845 drew up a set of rules based on the form of town ball known as the New York game. In its rudiments Cartwright's version of the game was very like that of today. It incorporated nine-player teams and an infield in the shape of a diamond with bases ninety feet apart. Three strikes made an out, and three outs concluded a team's at-bat.

But in its details the game that Cartwright and his immediate successors played was replete with differences. For one thing, fielders could put out opponents by catching the ball on the first bounce as well as on the fly, or by hitting them with the ball as they ran (an option that no doubt brought fielders the most pleasure if not the most outs). They wouldn't wear protective gloves until the 1890s. Before that they caught balls barehanded or sometimes in their hats. The pitcher stood much closer to the batter than now, threw with an underhand delivery, and was required to keep offering pitches until the *batter* (an Americanism of 1824) found a pitch he liked. Until as late as 1887 he had to put the pitch where the batter instructed him to.[28]

Batters were at first also known as *strikers*, and after 1856 as *batsmen*. The catcher – sometimes called a *catcher-out* – stood up to fifty feet behind home plate and would remain cautiously out of range of foul tips until the development of the catcher's mask in the 1890s. The *umpire*, a term first noted in a baseball context in 1856, also stood (or often sat) safely out of the way along the first base line. In those days the umpire's judgement was trusted even less than now. Important matches also had a referee, whose job was simply to judge the umpire. (*Umpire*, incidentally, is one of those many words in which an initial *n* became attached, like a charged particle, to the preceding indefinite article. In Middle English, one was 'a noumpere', just as an apron was at first 'a napron'.)

Uniforms were strikingly different, too. Cartwright's Knickerbocker Club, for example, wore uniforms of white shirts, blue trousers and straw boaters, making them look more like the lounging aesthetes in Manet's *Déjeuner sur l'herbe* than gutsy, knockabout athletes. In fact, they often were more like aesthetes than athletes. The early teams were intended as exclusive fraternal organizations for the upper crust, which is why to this day we call them *clubs*. Often the games were largely incidental to the social gathering afterwards. Then two things happened: competition between clubs grew more prickly and intense, and the game spread to the masses, where it became evident that manual labourers often enjoyed certain advantages in terms of strength and endurance over stockbrokers and junior executives. At first, working men played in their own leagues – working men's matches on Boston Common often began at 5 a.m. so as not to interfere with the players' working day – but before long the gentlemen's teams began quietly recruiting them as paid ringers. Baseball began to lose its wholesome glow as words like *hippodroming* (throwing a game for a bribe) and *revolving* (jumping teams to secure better pay) entered the parlance of the game.

In 1859, when the National Association of Base Ball Players was formed (the national in the title was a trifle ambitious since all the clubs were from greater New York), it insisted on amateurism and gentlemanly behaviour. It got neither. As early as 1860, the Brooklyn Excelsiors were paying a salary to a fastball pitcher named Jim Creighton while the New York Mutuals were charging an admission of ten cents to their matches and dividing the takings among themselves. Fair play was not always on-hand either. At least one crucial game was decided when the owner of one team had his dog frighten off an outfielder chasing a fly ball.

By 1869 America had its first forthrightly professional team, the Cincinnati Red Stockings, who racked up a record of fifty-seven wins, no loses and one tie during the year, and played before crowds of as many as 15,000 people.[29]

As baseball became increasingly professional, various leagues and alliances formed – including one called, a trifle redundantly, the League Alliance. In 1877 the National Baseball League, the first true major league, was formed.[30] The American League followed in 1901, though it had its roots in the old Western League. Among the early professional teams were the *Philadelphia Athletics, Troy Haymakers, Brooklyn Atlantics, Detroit Wolverines, Washington Olympics, Hartford Dark Blues* and *Cleveland Spiders,* who in 1899 earned the distinction of having the worst record ever notched up by a professional baseball team: 20–134. New York alone had the *Mutuals, Highlanders, Harlems, Gothams, Putnams,* and *Eagles*. Often the place-name meant little. Hartford played the 1877 season in Brooklyn. Often, too, if a team was out of a pennant race (so called because the competition was at first literally for a pennant), it didn't bother to make road trips towards the end of the season. Even when the opponent showed up, it wasn't always worth the bother. For their last game of the 1881 season, the Troy Haymakers had a paying attendance of just twelve.

Teams endlessly formed and reformed. Many faded away. Others evolved new identities – sometimes a series of new identities. The Chicago Cubs began life in 1876 as the *White Stockings* (the name was later appropriated by a rival cross-town team) and between 1887 and 1905 went by a variety of official and unofficial nicknames – the *Colts, Black Stockings, Orphans, Cowboys, Rough Riders, Recruits, Panamas, Zephyrs* and *Nationals* – before finally settling down as the Cubs in 1905. A Brooklyn team began calling itself the *Bridegrooms* after four of its players were married in the same summer, but eventually that name metamorphosed into *Dodgers* – or, more specifically, *Trolley Dodgers*. The name referred not to the players, but to the intrepid fans who had to dodge across a series of trolley lines to reach the ballpark safely. The *Pittsburgh Alleghenys* became the more alliterative if not geographically apposite Pirates. The *Boston Beaneaters* became the Boston Braves. The Boston Red Stockings were known alternatively as the *Pilgrims* or *Somersets* before they returned to their roots as the Red Sox.

The first *World Championship Series* began in 1884 and was being shortened to *World Series* by 1889. It was a ludicrously inflated title. Not only was the series not global, it wasn't even representative of the United States. In 1903 there was no team in the major leagues south of Washington, DC, or west of St Louis – a pattern that would remain unchanged until the 1950s, when the rapid rise of air travel prompted a western exodus.[31]

During its long adolescence in the nineteenth century, baseball generated a vast vocabulary. Among the terms that are still current: *walk* for a base on balls and *goose egg* for a zero (1866), *double play* (1867), *bullpen* (1877), *bleachers* (1882), *raincheck* (1884), *southpaw* (1885), *charley horse* (1888), *fan* in the sense of supporter (1890s), *double-header* (1896), and *to play ball* in the sense of to co-operate (1901). But this is only the barest sampling. An exhaustive list would run to several pages. For *hit* alone well over a hundred terms have been recorded – *Texas Leaguer, squib, nubber, banjo, stinker, humpie, drooper,* and so on.[32]

Only sometimes do we know the derivation of these terms. *Southpaw* has been attributed to Charles Seymour of the *Chicago Times,* because pitchers at the city's old West Side ballpark faced west, and thus a left-hander would stand with his throwing arm on his south side. *Bleachers* has been credited to another Chicago sports-writer, who applied it to those unfortunates who had to sit in an uncovered portion of grandstand and thus were 'bleached' by the sun.[33] Mencken traces *charley horse* to a player named Charley Esper of the Baltimore Orioles, who 'walked like a lame horse', but Flexner points out that the term was in use six years before Esper started playing.[34] *Banjo hit,* dating from 1925, was coined by the appealingly named Snooks Dowd of the Jersey City Giants, and evidently alludes to the plinking banjo-like sound made by a poorly hit ball. A *raincheck* was – indeed, still is – another name for a ticket stub. If the game was rained out in the first five innings, the customer could gain free admission to any later match by presenting his raincheck. Hence, the use of the term in the general sense of a deferred get-together.

Other terms are much less certain. *Bullpen,* for the warm-up area where spare pitchers sit, is often said to have arisen because that is where ads for Bull Durham tobacco were placed. But the story owes more to folk mythology than to any documentary evidence. The bullpen is at least as likely to be so called because of its similarity to the place where bulls are kept. At all events, the first reference to it, in the *Cincinnati Enquirer* in 1877, is not to an area where pitchers were confined, but to a place where fans were herded. Not until 1910 did it come to signify a warm-up area for pitchers. *Fans* in the sense of enthusiasts is presumed to be a shortening of *fanatics,* but the conclusion is only speculative. Mencken suggests that it may come from *fancy,* as in *to fancy someone's chances.* In the early days, in any case, supporters weren't called fans but *cranks,* presumably because they cranked up the home team with their cheering.

Baseball remains one of the most fertile grounds for inventive wordplay in American life. Among the more notable – and on the face of it more bewildering – recent neologisms are *to dial 8* for a home run and *Linda Ronstadt* for a good fastball. *Dial 8* comes from the practice among hotels of requiring customers to dial 8 for a long-distance line. *Linda Ronstadt*, more complicatedly, is an allusion to her song 'Blue Bayou', the significance of which becomes less puzzling when you reflect that a good fastball 'blew by you'.

During the long period that baseball was developing from a gentleman's recreation to the national pastime, another sport was shaping up to challenge its unquestioned pre-eminence. I refer to the sport that Americans insist on calling *football* (an odd choice since kicking features only incidentally in its play). As a term *football* has existed in English since 1486, before America was even known about. In its early days it primarily signified an annual competition in which the inhabitants of neighbouring English villages would try to kick or shove an inflated animal bladder between two distant points. Eventually in a more organized form it evolved into two principal sports, *rugby* (after the English school of that name where it was first played in 1864) and *soccer* (from British university slang and current only since 1891).

In its earliest manifestations in America, football wasn't so much a sport as legalized mayhem, very like the village sport of medieval England. Beginning at Yale in about 1840 it became customary for freshmen to take on upperclassmen in a vast, disorderly shoving match at the epicentre of which was a makeshift ball. After one such match, the *New York Post* fretted: 'Boys and young men knocked each other down, tore off each other's clothing. Eyes were bunged, faces blacked and bloody, and shirts and coats torn to rags.' Appalled at the injuries and disorder, Yale and Harvard banned the sport in the 1860s.

Students turned their attention away from the annual brawls and took up rugby instead. At first they used the English rules, but gradually they evolved forms of their own – even if they kept much of the terminology, like *offside, fair catch, halfback* and *scrimmage* (or *scrummage,* from an English dialect word for a tussle, and now shortened in the rugby world to *scrum*). Even with the imposition of some sense of order, play remained undisciplined and dangerous. In 1878 Walter Camp, a Yale student who appears to have been regarded as something of a deity by both his peers and mentors (and not without reason; one of the Yale teams he led outscored its opponents 482–2 over the course of one season and 698–0 in another), proposed several rules to bring a greater maturity to the game. The principal ones were that teams be limited to eleven players and that each side be granted three chances – or *downs* – to advance the ball five yards. This led to the painting of white lines at five-yard intervals, which by 1897 had inspired the term *gridiron* for a football field.

By about 1880 football and rugby had permanently parted ways in America, and by 1890 Yale was regularly attracting crowds of 40,000 to its football games. Some things had still to change. The centre didn't snap the ball with his hands, but kicked it back to the quarterback with his foot. Not until 1904 did a touchdown score more than a field goal. The forward pass wasn't written into the rules until 1906.[35] Even then no one really understood its possibilities. When it was used, which was rarely, it involved a quarterback lobbing a short pass to a stationary receiver, who would then turn and run with the ball. Not until 1913 did Gus Dorais, the Notre Dame quarterback, and his team-mate Knute Rockne come up with the idea of hitting a receiver on the run. In doing so, Notre Dame beat Army 35–13 and entered the realms of legend, at least on the sports pages.

Even with Camp's refinements American football remained violent and dangerous. In 1902 twelve American players died. In 1905 the number rose to seventy-one. To make matters worse, schools began to hire professional players. 'One man played, under various pseudonyms, at nine schools over a period of thirteen years,' Page Smith notes.[36]

Professional football grew up in mining and factory towns in the early 1900s, and the team names tended to reflect local industries, as with the *Pittsburgh Steelers* and *Green Bay [Meat] Packers*. Professional football was slow to establish itself. As late as 1925 the New York Giants franchise was purchased for just $500. Not until the 1950s and the age of television did professional football attract a huge and devoted following.

Although football has spawned a vast internal vocabulary – *T-formation* (1931), *play-off* (1933), *handoff* and *quarterback sneak* (early 1940s), to name just four – surprisingly few football terms have entered mainstream English. Among the few: *to blindside, cheap shot, game plan,* and *jock* for an athlete (from *jockstrap* for protective wear, and ultimately from a sixteenth-century English slang term for the penis).[37]

At the time that football was rising to eminence in colleges, another perennially popular sport was taking shape. In the fall of 1891, a young Canadian named James Naismith had just joined the staff of the International YMCA Training School in Springfield, Massachusetts, where he was instructed to devise an indoor game that didn't involve bodily contact, would not result in damage to the gym, and in which every player had a chance to get in on the action. The game he invented was basketball – or *basket ball* as it was called until about 1912. Naismith hung peach baskets at either end of the gym and used a soccer ball for play. The first game, in December 1891, involved two teams of nine men each and was not exactly a barn burner. The final score was 1–0.[38]

As an off-season recreation, basketball took off in a big way, largely because it was so cheap and easy to set up. Within three years, a company was producing balls specifically for the sport and many of the nuances of play had already evolved. For instance, in 1893 came the free throw – or *free trial for goal* as it was at first called. Five players to a side became standard in 1895, but the names of the positions – centre, two forwards and two guards – weren't fixed until the 1920s. By 1907, basketball was being called *the cage game. Cager*, whose continued currency is very largely the result of its convenience to writers of headlines, is first attested in 1922 in a newspaper in Ardmore, Oklahoma.

Oddly, although peach baskets were soon replaced by nets, until 1912 it didn't occur to anyone to cut a hole in the bottom of them. Until then it was necessary for someone to climb a ladder and retrieve the ball after each score.

Scores remained low for years. During the first National Invitational Tournament at New York in 1934, New York University beat Notre Dame 25–18, and Westminster beat St John's 37–33. Not until the evolution of the *jump shot* in the 1930s and *hook shot* in the 1940s and above all the *fast break* in the 1950s did the sport take on some real pace.

Many YMCA teams evolved into the first professional teams, notably the *Celtics*, who were formed in 1915 and came not from Boston but from New York. But financing was always a problem and teams often had to resort to desperate expedients to keep from going under. One early team, to secure sponsorship, called itself the *Fort Wayne Zollner Pistons*. It was named for a Fred Zollner who, as you will have guessed, manufactured pistons. Professional basketball didn't really get going until the formation in 1949 of the National Basketball Association, created by the merger of two smaller leagues. Like football, professional basketball was essentially a child of television, and, like football, it has had surprisingly little influence on American English. In fact, if you discount occasional figurative applications for a few expressions like *slam dunk*, *air ball* and *full-court press*, it has had none at all.

Of rather more interest linguistically is one of the more ancient of popular pastimes: golf. The game and many of the terms associated with it are of Scottish origin, among them *bunker, tee, divot, niblick, duffer, links* and *golf* itself. The word, of uncertain origin though possibly from the Scottish dialect word *gowf*, meaning to strike or hit, was first recorded in 1457. Variant spellings suggest that until fairly recent times it was pronounced with the *l* silent.

Golf came to America surprisingly early. As far back as 1786, just ten years after the Declaration of Independence, Charleston had a place that styled itself a golf club, and Savannah got one in 1795, though there is no evidence that golf was actually ever played at either. Certainly neither had anything remotely describable as a course. In any case, both were defunct by the second decade of the nineteenth century. The first real golf course in North America was that of the Royal Montreal Golf Club, formed in 1873. The first in the United States was the Foxburg Golf Club, in Pennsylvania, founded in 1887.

Though the game is Scottish, many of the terms are American, notably *par,* which dates from 1898. *Par* of course signifies the score a good player should make on a given hole. Before *par* became current the word used was *bogey*, an old Scottish word for a ghost or spirit. The notion was that each player was scoring against a hypothetical bogey man. However, in 1898, the rubber golf ball was invented and quickly displaced the old gutta-percha balls. (*Gutta-percha*, for the record, comes from a Malay word meaning 'strip of cloth'.) Because the new balls travelled further, one less stroke was required on average on each hole. *Par* therefore came to signify the new notional number of strokes required, and bogey was preserved for the old number of strokes. Gradually as gutta-percha balls disappeared altogether, *bogey* came simply to mean one stroke over par.[39]

Birdie, signifying one stroke under par, comes from a nineteenth-century American slang term meaning excellent. Both it and *eagle,* an Americanism meaning two strokes under par, became common in the 1920s.[40] In the same decade golf became associated with two rather odd items of clothing. The first was *knicker-bockers,* a nonce word coined by Washington Irving in 1809 for his *Knickerbocker's History of New York* (which wasn't actually called that; the formal title was *History of New York from the Beginning of the World to the End of the Dutch Dynasty, by Diedrich Knickerbocker*). By means that escape rational explanation, the word attached itself first to women's underwear (which are to this day called *knickers* almost everywhere in the English-speaking world but North America), and then, by a further dazzling flight, to the shortened trousers favoured by golfers in the 1920s, and whose continued existence appears to be the odd and, I would have thought, little encouraged quest of Mr Payne Stewart. Golf knickers further begat another short-lived item of apparel, the *plus fours,* so called because they were four inches longer than knickers.[41]

Finally, before we put the world of sports behind us, note should be taken of the recent controversy over the offensiveness of many team nicknames to American Indians. In 1992, a movement called the National Coalition on Racism in Sports and the Media was formed, partly to protest against the use of nicknames like *Braves, Redskins,* and *Indians.* In the view of Clyde Bellecourt, director of the American Indian Movement, 'calling the team the Washington Redskins is like calling them the Washington Negroes or the Washington Blackskins'.[42]

In defence of *Cleveland Indians,* it has been noted that the team name actually commemorates a Native American, Louis F. 'Alex' Sockalexis, a Penobscot Indian who had been one of the team's star players in the 1890s and for whom the Cleveland Indians named themselves in 1914, the year after his death. But the argument doesn't wash with some activists. As one put it, 'In that case, they should call themselves the Cleveland Sockalexises.'

A few colleges and high schools have changed their team

nicknames from *Mohawks* or *Hurons* to something more innocuous and less emotive, and one newspaper, *The Oregonian* of Portland, announced in 1992 that it would no longer publish Indian-related nicknames, explaining that they tended to 'perpetuate stereotypes that damage the dignity and self-respect of many people in our society'.[43]

At the time of writing, however, no professional team was seriously contemplating a name change.

Of Bombs and Bunkum: Politics and War

I

When, in about 1820, a Congressman named Felix Walker was accused of speaking drivel – which, evidently, he was – he replied that he was speaking to the people of Buncombe County, North Carolina, his district. Almost immediately his congressional colleagues began referring to any political claptrap as *speaking to Buncombe*. Soon the phrase had spread beyond Washington and was being abbreviated to *buncombe*, often re-spelled *bunkum*, and eventually was further contracted to *bunk*. *Debunk*, a back-formation, came later still, in 1927. *Bunkum* in turn begat *hokum* – a blend of *hocus* and *bunkum*. Thus with a single fatuous utterance the forgotten Felix Walker managed to inspire half a page of dictionary entries.[1] In doing so, Walker touched on a central paradox of American political rhetoric – namely, that while politicians may mostly spout *hot air* (in its metaphorical sense an Americanism of the 1840s), they also constantly refresh the language.

A few American political terms have considerable venerability. *Caucus*, from an Algonquian word for *counsellor*, dates from the early seventeenth century, and as such is one of the oldest of surviving Americanisms. *Mugwump* (at first often spelled *mugquomp*), another Algonquianism, followed soon after, making its first recorded appearance in 1643. For two hundred years it retained its original sense of a chief or leader before abruptly shifting in the 1880s to describe a political maverick. (The oft quoted definition is that a *mugwump* is someone who sits with his *mug* on one side of the fence and his *wump* on the other.) *Favourite son* was first used of Washington as far back as 1789 and *administration* was coined by him soon after.

But the golden age of American political terminology was the nineteenth century. Of the perhaps two hundred terms that gained some measure of currency in that tumultuous century, a good number were sufficiently useful to be still with us today, among them *spoils system, lobbyist, split ticket, party ticket, dyed-in-the-wool, office seeker, dark horse, lame duck, slate, standard-bearer, gag rule, straw vote, party machine, filibuster, slush fund, gubernatorial, junket* in the sense of a trip at government expense, *bandwagon* in the sense of a movement or fashion to climb aboard, *landslide* for a victory, *to dodge the issue, to electioneer, to campaign, to gerrymander, to be in cahoots with, to logroll, to stump, to run, to muckrake, to mend fences, to whitewash,* and *to keep the ball rolling* (so said because in the 1840 presidential campaign a ten-foot leather ball bearing that slogan was rolled from town to town in support of William Henry Harrison).[2]

One of the first of these terms to enter common parlance was *gerrymander*. Meaning to redraw electoral boundaries to favour a particular party, it dates from 1812 and was named for Massachusetts Governor Elbridge Gerry (shortly to become Vice-President under James Madison), whose Jeffersonian party engaged in some audacious cartographic manipulations to preserve its grip on the state assembly. Noticing that one district in Essex County had a vaguely reptilian shape, the artist Gilbert Stuart sketched on a head and legs and called it a salamander. 'No, a *gerrymander*!' cried an onlooker, and the term stuck. A small, overlooked aspect of the term is that we all mispronounce it. Gerry spoke his name with the hard *g* of *Gertrude* rather than the soft *g* of *Gerald*.[3]

In the following decade two other durable political terms arose, both in the New York state capital, Albany. One was *spoils system*, inspired by the expression 'to the victor belong the spoils', which has a nice classical ring to it but in fact was first uttered by an otherwise forgotten New York legislator named William E. Marcy.[4] Also in Albany at about the same time arose the much-needed term *lobbyist* for someone who hung around the capitol lobby seeking favours of passing legislators. (They hung around the lobby because they weren't allowed into the legislative chambers.)

Several other terms were borrowed from abroad. The custom of describing politicians as belonging to the *left, right* or *centre* of prevailing political sentiment came into American usage in about 1840 from Britain, though the British had in turn borrowed it from France, where it originated in 1789 as a by-product of the revolution. The terms reflect the seating arrangements of the French National Assembly, where it was customary for the more radical commoners to sit to the left of the President while the more conservative clergy and nobility filled the seats to the right. In neither Britain nor America did the terms reflect actual seating arrangements, but they proved convenient labels.[5]

Also from Britain came *dark horse* and *lame duck*, though neither had a political significance before America got its hands on them. *Dark horse* was coined by Benjamin Disraeli in his novel *The Young Duke* (1831). Though he was a politician himself, he meant it only in a horse-racing context. In America by the 1860s it was being extended to the political sphere. *Lame duck* originated in the eighteenth century as a London stock market term for a defaulter. It reached America with that sense around 1800, but by mid-century had been usurped by politicians to describe someone serving out a term of office and awaiting the arrival of his successor. In its political sense the term was reintroduced to Britain from America, but there it took on, and has retained, the sense of a politician who is incompetent, powerless or weak.

The oddest and certainly the most historically complicated foreign borrowing is *filibuster*. It began as the Dutch *vrijbuiter*, a pirate. To English speakers *vrijbuiter* naturally yielded *freebooter*.* But *vrijbuiter* was beyond the command of Spanish tongues. They converted the word to *filibustero*. The French then borrowed it as *filibustier*. From one of these, or both, the English reborrowed it as *filibuster*. Thus by 1585 *vrijbuiter* had given English two words with the same meaning. *Freebooter* went no further, but *filibuster* had a busy career ahead of it in American politics. First, still bearing something of its original sense, it came to

---

* The *boot* in *freebooter* has nothing to do with footwear. It comes from an old German word, *būte*, 'exchange', which also gave us *booty*.

describe Americans who formed private armies with a view to taking over Central American countries, for which there was a short but persistent fashion in the 1850s (the idea of manifest destiny rather going to some people's heads).

One of these hopeful militants was a character named William Walker. Born in 1824 in Tennessee, Walker was an extraordinary prodigy. He graduated *summa cum laude* from the University of Nashville at the age of just fourteen, and by the time he was twenty-five he had qualified as both a doctor and a lawyer, and somehow had also found time to edit a newspaper in New Orleans, take part in the California gold rush and engage in three duels, all of which becomes slightly more remarkable when you realize that he was also very small – little larger than a modern jockey. Despite his diminutive dimensions, Walker was clearly a leader of men. In 1853 he raised and armed forty-five recruits and set off with them for Baja California with the aim of capturing its mineral resources and simultaneously endowing its people with the benefits of American civilization, whether they wanted it or not.

The enterprise failed, but Walker had found his calling. Over the next seven years he divided his time between raising armies and finance, and sallying forth on a series of increasingly ambitious expeditions. Though he had some successes – he took over Nicaragua for about a year – ultimately each foray ended in defeat.

Finally in 1860, after a rout in Honduras, Walker surrendered to the British navy. To his astonishment, his captors did not repatriate him to America as had always happened before, but turned him over to the Honduran authorities, who promptly took him and his co-conspirators to a town square, lined them up before a firing-squad and brought to a close their lives and the fashion for private revolutions.[6] *Filibuster*, however, did not die with them. By the mid-1850s it was being used in Congress to describe any vaguely disruptive debating tactic, and by the 1880s had settled into its present sense of a wilful delaying action designed to thwart the passage of a bill.

Still other words might have filtered out into the world at large except that Congress in its early days was remarkably unforthcoming about its doings. Senate debates were kept secret until 1794, and reported only sketchily after that for several decades. The House of Representatives attracted more attention, partly because it was more open in its dealings but also because well into the nineteenth century it was regarded as the more prestigious chamber. Not until well into the nineteenth century did the Senate begin to take on an air of pre-eminence, for the simple reason that the House, reflecting the growth of American population, began to become very crowded – by 1860 it had 243 members, by 1880 332 – while the Senate remained comparatively compact and thus more exclusive and clubby. The men who made the Senate famous – Daniel Webster, Henry Clay and John C. Calhoun – would very probably have been in the House had they been born a generation earlier.[7]

At all events, the public enjoyed no right of access to congressional debates until as late as 1873, when the *Congressional Record* was at last created. Contrary to common belief, the *Record* even now does not constitute a full, verbatim transcription of all the debates in Congress. Speeches are frequently edited before being placed in the *Record*, and indeed the *Record* sometimes contains speeches that were never given at all. It has, in the words of Daniel Boorstin, 'no more than the faintest resemblance to what is actually said' in Congress.[8]

The nineteenth century also marked a busy time for political parties as alliances endlessly formed and reformed, often around a single issue like slavery or immigration. Political parties in America effectively date from the period immediately after the drafting of the Constitution, when the two main sides formed into loose associations. Those in favour of the Constitution pulled off something of a linguistic coup by dubbing themselves *Federalists*. In fact, the term would more accurately have described those who were against the Constitution and wished to revive the Articles of Confederation. Deprived of the term, this faction became known by default as the *Antifederalists*, which was not only inaccurate but had a negative ring to it that the more positive-sounding Federalists were delighted to exploit.[9] Saddled with a misleading name, the Antifederalists began, confusingly, sometimes to call themselves *Democrats*, sometimes *Republicans*, and sometimes *Democrat-Republicans*.[10]

A succession of party names briefly blazed and faded in the nineteenth century, like matches struck in a darkened auditorium – a not inapt metaphor since that is how one of the more memorably known parties got its name. I refer to the *Equal Rights Democrats*, who were known to everyone as the *Loco-Focos*, and so called because when one of their meeting halls was plunged into darkness by saboteurs the adherents continued with the aid of the new sulphur matches called *locofocos*.[11] No less memorable were the *Know-Nothings* – not the sort of name that would seem to inspire confidence in their capacity to lead. Officially called the *American Party*, it was as much a secret society as a political body and got its name from the reply members were instructed to give when asked to elucidate the party's aims: 'I know nothing.' Despite the obvious shortcomings of trying to attract a national following when you won't tell the world what you are up to, the Know-Nothings proved immensely popular among anti-immigrant, anti-Irish and anti-Catholic zealots, and for a time threatened to overtake the young Republican Party as a lasting political force in America.[12]

Among the other parties or sub-parties that passed through the busy scene that was the 1800s were the *Butt-enders, Roarers, Huge Paws, Copperheads, Ringtails, Ball-rollers, Barnburners, Anti-Masons, Free Soilers, Anti-Nebraskans, Anti-Renters, Pro-Bank Democrats, Constitutional Union Party* and *People's Party* – though many of these appellations, it should be noted, were bestowed by antagonists and weren't necessarily used by the adherents themselves.

The watershed year for political parties was 1836 when two sides coalesced into pro- and anti-Andrew Jackson factions. The pro-Jacksonites styled themselves *Democrats*. On the anti side, *National Republicans, Anti-Masons* and *Pro-Bank Democrats* rallied to the resuscitated name *Whigs* – a decidedly odd choice since during the Revolutionary War *whig* had designated a person who supported the British cause, and thus had long had a whiff of treachery about it. Despite its long-standing currency in both Britain and America, *Whig* is of mysterious origins. The *Oxford English Dictionary* says only that it 'probably' comes from *Whiggamores*, a term applied to the members of a military expedition against Scottish insurgents in Edinburgh in 1648, but no explanation as to the source of Whiggamores is adduced.

The Jackson Democrats remained Democrats after 1836, but the Whigs had further turmoil, and eventual dissolution, to face. In the 1850s the party splintered into an unhappy plethora of factions with names like the *Conscience Whigs* (those who were against slavery), the *Cotton Whigs* (those who were for), and the *Barnburners* (from a comic parable about an obstinate Dutch farmer who rid his barn of rats by burning it down). In 1855, the Whigs emerged from this internecine squabbling as *Republicans*, and thus have they remained. The respective symbols of the two main political parties – the elephant for the Republicans, the donkey for the Democrats – were the creation of Thomas Nast, the cartoonist who also gave human form to Uncle Sam.[13]

In this century, new political terms have been fewer in number, but no less resourceful. Among those that have arisen in the world of politics since 1900 and found a role in the wider world are *smoke-filled room*, *grass roots*, *pork barrel*, *square deal*, *new deal*, *keynote speech*, *off the record*, *egghead*, *brain trust* and countless, mostly short-lived words ending in *-gate*: *Koreagate*, *Lancegate*, *nannygate*, *Quakergate*, *Hollywoodgate* and *Irangate*, all of course inspired by *Watergate*. Even Britain has had its *Camillagate*.

Pork barrel had its roots in the 1800s. Throughout that century *pork* was a common political shorthand term for any kind of dubious abundance (it evidently alluded to the fattiness of pork). Early in this century, for reasons unknown, the term grew into *pork barrel*, and became particularly associated with federal largesse that a Congressman or Congresswoman managed to bring back to his or her home state.

Off the record was coined by the New York politician Al Smith in 1926. *Egghead* arose during the 1952 election campaign. It appears to have been inspired by Adlai Stevenson, or more precisely by Stevenson's dome-like pate, and by late in the year was in common currency as a flip synonym for an intellectual.

The century has also seen any number of slogans and catch-phrases emanate from political circles, from Teddy Roosevelt's 'speak softly and carry a big stick', to Woodrow Wilson's 'little group of wilful men' and 'to make the world safe for democracy', to Coolidge's 'the business of America is business', to Truman's 'the buck stops here', to Kennedy's 'ask not what your country can do for you, but what you can do for your country'. Some much quoted twentieth-century political phrases are actually mythical, however. Hoover never said 'prosperity is just around the corner', and he never used the expression 'a chicken in every pot' – though the

Republican Party almost did in advertisements for him during the campaign of 1928. It headed its ads with 'A Chicken for Every Pot', though even it acknowledged in the text that the expression was already old enough to be considered 'proverbial'.

One Washington term that has existed officially only since the early years of this century is, surprisingly, *White House*. On the original plans, the building was described only as 'the Palace'. No one knows when people started calling it the White House – but, oddly, it appears to have been before it was painted white. From 1800, when John Adams became its first resident, to 1814, when the British ransacked and partly burned it, the building was of unadorned grey Virginia freestone. Only after the British had vandalized it was the decision taken to paint it white to cover the smoke stains. So it is a little odd that people were calling it the White House as early as 1810. In any case, the name didn't become official until Theodore Roosevelt began printing it on the executive mansion stationery sometime after 1901.

Only in comparatively recent times, incidentally, has the White House become an unapproachable fortress. As late as the Harding era (1921–3) the public was allowed to picnic on the White House lawn or even wander over and peer through the windows of the Oval Office.[14] Harding himself sometimes answered the White House front door.[15]

II

And so to military matters.

There is an old joke that goes: 'Dear Diary: Today the Hundred Years War started.' The fact is that most wars didn't get the name by which we know them until the nineteenth century. The American Revolution wasn't normally called that until the nineteenth century. It was the *War for Independence*, or simply the *War with Britain*. The Civil War was at the time of its fighting more generally called the *War Between the States* by southerners and the *War of the Rebellion* by northerners. World War I for obvious reasons wasn't so called until there was a World War II. (It was the *Great War*.) *World War II*, although the term was commonly applied, didn't become official until the war was nearly over. Roosevelt didn't like *either World War II* or *Second World War*. Throughout its early years, he called it – a trifle melodramatically – the *War for Survival*, then shortly before his death started referring to it as the *Tyrants' War*. Other names that were commonly attached to it were *War of World Freedom*, *War of Liberation* and the *Anti-Nazi War*. In 1945, the question of a formal name was put to Secretary of War Henry L. Stimson. His choice, *World War II*, was formally adopted by President Truman.[16]

Battles, too, often went by a variety of names, particularly those of the American Civil War. Ulysses S. Grant didn't refer to the *Battle of Shiloh* but of *Pittsburg Landing*. To the North it was *Bull Run*, but to the South it was *Manassas*. The northern *Antietam* was the southern *Sharpsburg*, as the southern *Murfreesboro*, *Perryville* and *Boonsboro* were to northerners respectively *Stone River*, *Chaplin Hills* and *South Mountain*.[17]

Wars are always linguistically productive, though military slang and terminology, like armies themselves, tend to be continuously replaced with fresh recruits. In consequence, battlefield terms usually either survive more or less indefinitely – *bomb* dates from 1582, *grenade* (from *pomegranate* and ultimately from *Granada*) from 1532 – or else fade from the vocabularies of all but military historians.

Almost all that survives from the period of the American Revolution, apart from the (mostly mythical) slogans and catch-phrases discussed already in Chapter 3, is a single song: 'Yankee Doodle Dandy'. It was the most popular tune of the day, sung by both sides with lyrics that chided the other. No one knows who first sang it or when, though the mocking tone of the words in the best-known version suggests British authorship:

> Yankee Doodle came to town,
> riding on a pony,
> stuck a feather in his cap,
> and called it macaroni.

If you have ever wondered why Yankee Doodle called the feather in his cap *macaroni*, the answer is that *macaroni* was a slang term of the day for a fop. The feather in his cap possibly alluded to the habit of colonial soldiers, who often had no uniforms, of sticking a feather or piece of paper in their caps as a means of distinguishing themselves during battle.

The War of 1812 gave us, again as we have already seen, the 'Star-Spangled Banner' and Uncle Sam, plus *conscript* as both a noun and a verb, and two catch-phrases of some durability: 'Don't give up the ship' and 'We have met the enemy and they are ours.' Both belong to Admiral Oliver Hazard Perry, and come from a naval engagement on Lake Erie. 'Don't give up the ship' was the slogan emblazoned on a pennant flying from Perry's vessel (in point of fact, Perry *did* give up the ship, but accuracy seldom matters when a really good phrase is involved), and 'We have met the enemy and they are ours' were the words with which he communicated his triumph to his commander-in-chief.[18]

Not until we get to the Civil War period do we at last begin to encounter strictly military terms that have passed into wider usage. Among the Civil War neologisms that are still with us are *KP* (for *kitchen police*), *AWOL* (*absent without leave*), *pup-tents* (originally known as *dog-tents*), and, rather surprisingly, *doughboy* and *grapevine* in the context of rumours. *Doughboy* appears to have been first applied to Union soldiers during the 1860s. (The earliest reference is found in the memoirs of George Armstrong Custer in 1867, but the context indicates that it was already widely known.) The origins are entirely mysterious. Since early colonial times small fried cakes had been known as *doughboys*, and the word may betoken a similarity in appearance between these cakes and the buttons on cavalry soldiers' uniforms, but it is no more than a guess. At all events, the term faded from sight after about 1870 and didn't catch on again until World War I.[19] *Grapevine*, or *grapevine telegraph*, as a notional medium for the transmission of rumours, is equally mysterious. It was widely used during the Civil War, usually with the sense of a wholly unreliable rumour, but what precisely inspired it is unknown.

We have been conditioned by Hollywood to think of Union soldiers dressed identically in blue and Confederate troops in grey. In fact, for the first year or so of the war most soldiers wore the uniforms of their state militias, which came in any number of colours. Troops from Iowa and Wisconsin, for instance, wore grey uniforms that were very like the official Confederate outfits, leading to endless confusion on the battlefield. After the North lost the first battle of Bull Run partly because Union troops failed to fire on an advancing contingent of Virginia militia, mistaking them for

northern allies, the War Department rushed into production
hundreds of thousands of standard uniforms. These were manufactured with an old process employing recycled woollen fibres and
known as *shoddy*. Because the uniforms were poorly made and
easily came unstitched, *shoddy* came to denote any article of
inferior quality. The system of producing uniforms *en masse* also
led, incidentally, to the introduction of standard graduated sizes, a
process that was carried over to civilian life after the war.[20]

One myth of the Civil War period is that *hooker* for a prostitute
arose from the camp followers of General Joseph Hooker. It is true
that the cadres of sexual entrepreneurs who followed Hooker's
men from battlefield to battlefield were jocularly known as
Hooker's Division or *Hooker's Reserves*, but *hooker* itself predates
the Civil War. It was first noted in 1845 in reference to a section of
New York, *Corlear's Hook*, also known as *The Hook*, where
prostitutes congregated.[21]

One term that did spring to prominence during the Civil War,
though again of greater antiquity, was the *Mason-Dixon line*. It
had been laid out a century earlier by the English surveyors Charles
Mason and Jeremiah Dixon, who were brought to America in 1763
to resolve a long-standing border dispute between Pennsylvania
and Maryland. Though we tend to think of the Mason-Dixon line
as a straight east–west demarcation, a good quarter of it ran
north–south. It was only coincidentally that it delineated the
boundary between slave and non-slave states. Had it not been for
this, the line would very probably have been forgotten, which
would have been unfortunate because it was one of the great
scientific feats of its age. Mason and Dixon were not merely
surveyors but accomplished astronomers and mathematicians, and
their achievement in drawing an accurate line across 244 miles of
wilderness had a measure of heroism and scientific scrutiny not
easily appreciated today. To the dismay of historians, Mason's
careful notes of his four years' work disappeared for almost a
century. Then in 1860 they turned up – no one knows how or why
– two thousand miles from where they had last been seen, on a
rubbish heap in Nova Scotia, where they were about to be
burned.[22]

A final, incidental linguistic legacy of the war between the states
was the term *sideburns*, named for the Union commander Ambrose

E. Burnside, whose distinctive mutton-chop whiskers inspired a fashion and became known as *burnsides*. Within a decade the syllables had been transposed, but quite how or why is anyone's guess.

After its brief flurry of creativity during the Civil War, military terminology then grows quiet for nearly half a century. *Roughriders,* from the Spanish–American War, *limey* for a British sailor, and *leathernecks* for Marines (so called because for a decade in the late nineteenth century they wore a uniform with a leather lining in the collar; it was said to be excruciatingly uncomfortable)[23] effectively exhaust the list of neologisms from the period 1870–1917.

But the outbreak of global hostilities with World War I prompted an outpouring of new terms, many of which are with us yet. Among the words or expressions that entered the common argot during the period are *dog tags, chowhound* and *chowtime, convoy, dawn patrol, dogfight, eyewash, to go west* (actually much older, but not widely used before about 1918), *stunt, shellshock, gadget, to scrounge, booby trap, foxhole, brass hat,* MP for military police, *civvies* for civilian clothes, *draftee, pipe down* as a call for quiet (it originated in the nautical use of pipes to announce changes of watch and the like) and *to swing the lead.*[24]

From the British came *bridgehead, ack-ack, blimp, tank* and, rather unexpectedly, *basket case* for a severely wounded combatant. *Blimp* arose from its official designation: 'Dirigible: Type B-Limp', and *ack-ack* was a slang shortening of *anti-aircraft*, based on British telephonic code for the letters *AA*.

From the Germans came *zeppelin* (named for Count Ferdinand von Zeppelin, its designer), *black market* (from German *Schwarzmarkt*) and *Big Bertha* for an outsized gun. As was their custom, the Germans had named the gun after the wife of the head of Krupp Steel, the manufacturer, and with a certain lack of delicacy had called it not *Big Bertha* but *Fat Bertha*. Quite how Frau Krupp received this signal honour is not known.

From France, meanwhile, came *parachute, camouflage* (rather oddly from *camouflet*, meaning 'to blow smoke up someone's nose', a pastime that appears on the linguistic evidence to be specific to the French) and *barrage* (from *tir de barrage*) in the sense of concentrated artillery fire. *Barrage* already existed in English with the meaning of a barrier across a waterway, but previously had been pronounced to rhyme with *disparage*.[25]

Somewhat surprisingly, World War II was considerably less prolific of new terminology than World War I once you strip out those terms like *Lend Lease, VE Day* and *Luftwaffe* that are now used primarily in a historical context. Among the relatively few terms to come to prominence during the period and to live on after the war were *bazooka, blackout, GI, liberty* for shore leave, *pin-up girl, Mae West* for an inflatable jacket, *task force, jeep, blitzkrieg, flak, fascism, gestapo, kamikaze, displaced person, blockbuster* (originally a bomb sufficiently powerful to destroy an entire city block, and later of course appropriated by the entertainment industry), the expression *the greatest thing since sliced bread* and, not least, a robust and inventive use of the word *fuck*. One of the last named's offshoots is *snafu*, often said to be an abbreviation of 'situation normal, all *fouled* up', but don't you believe it. Once there were many more in like vein – namely, *tuifu* ('the ultimate in fuck-ups') and *fubar* ('fucked up beyond all recognition'). The use of *fucked* as a general descriptive ('this engine is completely fucked') appears also to be a legacy of World War II.

Several World War II words, it will be noted, were foreign creations. *Blitzkrieg* (literally 'lightning war'), *flak* (a contraction of *Fliegerabwehrkanone*, 'anti-aircraft gun') and *gestapo* (from *Geheime Staatspolizei*, 'Secret State Police') are of obvious German derivation. Also from Nazi Germany came one of our more chilling phrases, *final solution* (German *Endlösung*) coined by Reinhard 'The Hangman' Heydrich. *Fascism* dates from long before the war – from 1919, in fact, when Benito Mussolini launched the *Fascismo* movement in Italy – but came to prominence only in the period just before the war. It comes from the Latin *fasces*, 'bundle', and alludes to a bundle of rods that was used both as a tool of execution and a symbol of authority in imperial Rome.[26] *Kamikaze* is of course Japanese. It means 'divine wind', and commemorates a timely typhoon that routed a Mongol seaborne attack early in Japan's history.

Among the native-born terms that are not self-evident, *bazooka* was called after a comical stage prop – a kind of home-made trombone – used by a popular comedian named Bob Burns, and *GI* stands for *general issue*, the initials stamped on all military property. No one knows quite when *GI* was first applied to soldiers, but *GI Joe* can be dated with certainty. He first appeared in the 17 June 1942 issue of *Yank*, the armed forces newspaper, in a cartoon drawn by Dave Berger.[27]

Jeep, as a concept if not as a word, slightly predates America's involvement in the war. In 1941, just before Pearl Harbor, the Army introduced a sturdy vehicle for negotiating rough terrain. The jeep was actually not a very good vehicle. It was heavy, difficult to manoeuvre, devoured oil, had a chronically leaky water pump and cylinder head, and could run continuously for no more than four hours. But something about its boxy shape and go-anywhere capabilities earned it instant and widespread affection. No one knows how it got its name. The most common, and seemingly most plausible, explanation is that it is taken from the letters *GP*, short for *General Purpose*. The problem is that *General Purpose* was never officially part of its title, and doesn't appear on any documents associated with it. The Army with its usual gift for clunky appellations termed it a *truck, quarter ton, four-by-four*. More puzzlingly, the prototype for the jeep was generally known – for reasons now lost – as a *peep*. Mencken stoutly maintains that *jeep* comes from the Popeye the Sailor comic strip written by EC Segar.[28] It is true that a character named Eugene the Jeep appeared in the strip as early as March 1936, though no one has ever explained how, or more pertinently why, that character's name would have been applied to a four-wheel-drive vehicle. What is certain is that Segar did give the world another useful word at about the same time, *goon*, named for simian-like characters in the strip.

Towards the end of the war, a slogan, often accompanied by a cartoon drawing of the top half of a face peering over a fence or other barrier, mysteriously began appearing wherever the US Army went. The slogan was 'Kilroy was here'. No one has any idea who this Kilroy was. The figure at whom the finger is most often pointed is James J. Kilroy, an inspector of military equipment in Quincy, Massachusetts, who was said to have chalked the three famous words on crates of equipment that were then dispatched to the far corners of the world. Others attribute it with equal assurance to a Sergeant Francis Kilroy of the Army Air Transport Command, who would also have had the opportunity to place his name on boxes of supplies and munitions. But the theories are manifold. One desperately imaginative scholar has even interpreted it as an anti-authoritarian *Kill Roi,* or 'Kill the King'.*

One of the more striking fashions to grow out of World War II was a military affection for acronyms and other such shortenings. The practice had begun in earnest in civilian life during the New Deal years of the 1930s when combinations like *TVA, WPA, OPA* and *PWA* (respectively, *Tennessee Valley Authority, Works Progress Administration, Office of Price Administration* and *Public Works Authority*) became a part of everyday life. The military took it up with a passion once the world went to war, and devised not only alphabet soup acronyms like *OSRD-WD* (*Office of Scientific Research and Development, Western Division*), *ICWI* (*Interdepartmental Commission on War Information*), and *JMUSDC* (*Joint Mexican-US Defence Commission*), but also novel hybrids like *ComAirSoPa* (for *Commander of Aircraft for the South Pacific*) and *Seabees* (out of *CBs,* from the Navy's *Construction Battalion*). Occasionally these things had to be rethought. When it was realized that nearly everyone was pronouncing the abbreviation for the Commander-in-Chief of the US Fleet in the Pacific, *CinCUS,* as 'sink us', it was hastily amended to the more buoyant-sounding *ComInCh.*[29]

Oddly, one of the things World War II didn't leave Americans with was a memorable song. Almost every other war had, from 'Yankee Doodle' of the Revolution to 'John Brown's Body' and the 'Battle Hymn of the Republic' of the Civil War, to World War I's 'Over There'. Most World War II songs by contrast seemed to be begging for instant obscurity. Among the more notably forgettable titles to emerge in the early days of fighting were 'They're Going to Be Playing Taps on the Japs', 'Goodbye, Mama, I'm Off to

---

* It is curious how often we have lost track of the inspiration behind our eponymous words. We have already seen that no one knows who the real McCoy was. Equally, most authorities agree that there must have been a Mr Lynch who provided the inspiration for the word describing the abrupt termination of life without the inconvenience of a fair trial, and candidates almost without number have been suggested for this dubious honour. Indeed, it can appear that almost anyone named Lynch who had a position of authority anywhere in America between 1780 and 1850 has been mentioned as a candidate at one time or another. In fact no one knows who he was or what he did to earn his morbid immortality. It has even been suggested that Lynch may not be a person at all, but a creek in South Carolina favoured by locals for impromptu executions.

Yokohama', 'Let's Knock the Hit Out of Hitler', 'Slap the Jap Right Off the Map', and 'When Those Little Yellow Bellies Meet the Cohens and the Kellys'. Only one achieved anything like permanence in the popular consciousness – and that as a catch-phrase rather than a song. It was based on the supposedly real-life story of a naval chaplain, William A. McGuire, who reportedly climbed into the seat of an anti-aircraft gun at Pearl Harbor after the gunner had been killed and began knocking Japanese planes from the sky as he cried the famous words: 'Praise the Lord and pass the ammunition.' In fact, as a bemused McGuire told the world after the song became a hit, he had never said any such thing, and indeed had never even fired a gun. All he had done was help lift some boxes of ammunition.[30]

On 6 August 1945 President Harry S Truman announced to the nation: 'Sixteen hours ago an American airplane dropped one bomb on Hiroshima, an important Japanese army base. That bomb had more power than 20,000 tons of TNT. It is an atomic bomb.' It was the first time that most people had heard the term. In the following years many other words connected with splitting the atom would become increasingly familiar to them: *nuclear, fission, fusion, radiation, reactor, mushroom cloud, fallout, fallout shelter, H-bomb, ground zero,* and, unexpectedly, *bikini* for a two-piece swimsuit designed by Louis Reard, a French couturier, in 1946, and named for the Bikini Atoll in the Pacific, where America had just begun testing atomic bombs.

The dropping of atomic bombs on Hiroshima and Nagasaki marked the end of one war and the beginning of another: the cold war. The cold war may not have generated a lot of casualties, but it was none the less the longest and costliest war America has ever fought. War was unquestionably good for business – so good that in 1946 the president of General Electric, Charles E. Wilson, went so far as to call for a 'permanent war economy'. He more or less got his wish. Throughout the 1950s America spent more on defence than it did on anything else – indeed, almost as much as it did on all other things together. By 1960, military spending accounted for 49.7 per cent of the federal budget – more than the combined national budgets of Britain, France, West Germany and Italy.[31] Even America's foreign aid was overwhelmingly military. Of the

$50 billion that America distributed in aid in the 1950s, 90 per cent was for military purposes.

Cold war, the term that justified these gargantuan outlays, has often been attributed to the newspaper columnist Walter Lippmann. In fact, the expression was first used by the statesman Bernard Baruch at a speech in Columbia, South Carolina, in 1947, though credit for its coinage belongs to his speech-writer, Herbert Bayard Swope.[32] Out of the cold war came two other durable expressions – *iron curtain* and *the domino theory*. The domino theory – the idea that if one nation fell to Communism others would topple in its wake – was first used by the newspaper columnist Joseph Alsop in 1954, though it didn't become popular until the Vietnam War a decade later. *Iron curtain* is commonly attributed to Winston Churchill in an address he made in Fulton, Missouri, in 1946, but in fact the term had been in existence in the sense of an imaginary barrier since 1819, and had been used in political contexts since the 1920s.

The cold war, or more specifically the Cuban missile crisis, also brought to prominence *hawk* and *dove*, though again both had been around for some time. *Dove* had been the symbol of peace for centuries, and *hawk*, in the context of military belligerence, had been coined by Thomas Jefferson in 1798 in the expression *War Hawk*. What was new was the conjoining of the terms to indicate a person's militaristic leanings.

On the field of battle, the Korean War pitched in with a number of terms, among them *demilitarized zone* and its abbreviated form, *DMZ* (originally signifying the disputed area along the 38th parallel dividing Korea into North and South), *brainwash* (a literal translation of the Mandarin *hsi nao*), *chopper* for a helicopter, *honcho* (from Japanese *hancho*, 'squad leader') and *hooch* (from Japanese *uchi*, 'house'), which was at first used to describe the place where a soldier kept his mistress.

Several of these words were resurrected for the war in Vietnam a decade later, though that conflict also spawned many terms of its own, among them *free-fire zone, clicks* for kilometres, *grunt* for a soldier (first used dismissively by Marines, but taken on with affection by infantrymen), *search-and-destroy mission, to buy the farm,* meaning to die in combat, *to frag* (to kill a fellow soldier, usually an officer, with a hand grenade or *fragmentation device*;

hence the term) and a broad variety of telling expressions for the Vietnamese: *slope, gook, dink, zip, slant, slant-eye* and *Charlie*, though many of these – like *slant-eye* and *gook* – were older terms recently revived. *Charlie* as an appellation for Vietcong arose because VC in radio code was *Victor Charlie*.

Among the more sinister terms to catch the world's attention during the war in Vietnam were *Agent Blue, Agent Orange, Agent Purple* and *Agent White* (for types of *defoliants* – another new word – used to clear fields, destroy crops and generally demoralize and destabilize inhabitants of hostile territory), and *napalm*, from *naphthene palmitate*, which had much the same intent and effect. Though it first became widely known during the Vietnam War, *napalm* was in fact invented during World War II.

The military affection for clumsy acronyms found renewed inspiration in Vietnam with such concoctions as *FREARF* (for *Forward Rearm and Refuel Point*), *SLAR* (*Side-Looking Airborne Radar*), *FLAR* (*Forward-Looking Airborne Radar*) and *ARVN* (pronounced 'arvin') for the *Army of the Republic of South Vietnam*. One of the more arresting, if least reported, of the Vietnam era acronyms was *TESTICLES*, a mnemonic for the qualities looked for in members of the Second Ranger Battalion, namely *teamwork, enthusiasm, stamina, tenacity, initiative, courage, loyalty, excellence* and a *sense of humour*.

But where the war in Vietnam really achieved semantic distinction was in the creation of a vast heap of euphemisms, oxymorons and other verbal manipulations designed to create an impression of benignity and order, so that we got *pacification* for eradication, *strategic withdrawal* for retreat, *sanitizing operation* for wholesale clearance, *accidental delivery of armaments* for bombing the wrong target, *to terminate with extreme prejudice* for a political assassination, and many, many others.

The Gulf War, despite its merciful brevity, was also linguistically productive. Among the new formations it inspired were *clean bombing* (i.e., with pinpoint precision), *guest* for a prisoner of war, *headquarters puke* for a junior officer whose responsibilities keep him safely away from the front, *Nintendo effect* (that is, to become desensitized to destruction through watching films of bombing raids that resemble video games of destruction), *Airwing Alpo* for in-flight rations on fighter aircraft, the *smart bomb*, and *mother of* all, signifying ultimate, as in 'mother of all tanks', 'mother of all wars', etc.[33]

Finally, one of the most recent of military neologisms is also one of the most poignant: *ethnic cleansing,* signifying the removal or eradication of a portion of the indigenous population of an area. Apparently coined by Russian observers, it is a product of the war in the former Yugoslavia, and was first reported in English in the 9 July 1991 issue of *The Times.*

18

Sex and Other Distractions

In 1951 the proprietor of the Hi Hat Lounge in Nashville, Tennessee, purchased a life-size photograph of a naked young woman lying on a fluffy rug, and proudly hung it behind his bar. Even by the relatively chaste standards of the day it was not a terribly revealing picture – only her posterior was exposed to view – and probably nothing more would have come of it except that one day an electrician arrived to do some work and recognized the woman in the photograph as his wife, which surprised him because she had never mentioned that she was doing nude modelling for a local photographer.

The electrician took the Hi Hat to court, and for a short while the matter became first a local and then a national sensation. With the eyes of America on him, Judge Andrew Doyle ruled that as art the photograph was perfectly acceptable, but that as a bar-room decoration it was 'unquestionably obscene'. He suggested – apparently seriously – that one of the city's art galleries might like to take it over. In other words, if displayed in a darkened bar where it would be seen by no one but grown-up drinkers, the picture was held to be salacious and corrupting. But if placed in a public forum where anyone of any age could view it, it could be regarded as a local treasure.[1] And no one anywhere appears to have thought this odd.

I bring this up here to make the point that America's attitudes towards questions of public and private morality have long been a trifle confused. For this, as for so much else, we can thank the

Puritans. As early as 1607, *puritanical* had come to mean *stern, rigid, narrowly moral*, and the view has been steadily reinforced ever since by history texts and literary works like Hawthorne's *Scarlet Letter* and Longfellow's *Courtship of Miles Standish*.

The Puritan age was, to be sure, one in which even the smallest transgressions – or even sometimes no transgressions at all – could be met with the severest of penalties. Adultery, illegitimacy and masturbation were all at times capital offences in New England. Almost any odd occurrence darkened Puritan suspicions and fired their zeal for swift retribution. In 1651, when the wife of a Hugh Parsons of Springfield, Massachusetts, complained that her husband sometimes threw 'pease about the Howse and made me pick them up', and occasionally in his sleep made 'a gablings Noyse',[2] the town fathers saw at once that this was witchcraft and hanged him from the nearest gibbet.

Equally unlucky was George Spencer of New Haven, Connecticut. When a one-eyed pig was born in the town, the magistrates cast around for an explanation and lighted on the hapless Spencer, who also had but one eye. Questioned as to the possibility of bestiality, the frightened Spencer confessed, but then recanted. Under Connecticut law to convict Spencer of bestiality required the testimony of two witnesses. So keen were the magistrates to hang him that they admitted the pig as one witness and his retracted confession as another.[3]

But in many other ways colonial New England was not as simon pure (the expression comes from a play of 1718 by Susanna Centlivre called *A Bold Stroke for a Wife*, and involving a character named Simon Pure) as we might think. Just half a century after the *Mayflower* Pilgrims landed on Massachusetts's shores, Boston was 'filled with prostitutes', and other colonial centres were equally well equipped with opportunities for sexual licence. Despite its modest size, Williamsburg, capital of Virginia from 1699 to 1779, contained three brothels (though curiously none of these have been incorporated into the sanitized replica community so popular with visitors today).[4]

Sex among the Puritans was considered as natural as eating, and was discussed about as casually, to the extent that 'the writings of the Puritans required heavy editing before they were thought fit to print even in the mid-twentieth century'.[5] Premarital intercourse was not just tolerated but effectively encouraged. Couples who intended to marry could take out something called a *Pre-Contract* – in effect, a licence to have sex. It was the Puritans, too, who refined the curious custom of *bundling*, or *tarrying* as it was just as often called, in which a courting pair were invited to climb into bed together. Though the practice appears to have originated in Wales, it was sufficiently little known in Britain to have become a source of perennial wonder for British visitors to New England up to the time of the American Revolution and somewhat beyond. As one seventeenth century observer explained it:

> When a man is enamoured of a young woman, and wishes to marry her, he proposes the affair to her parents; if they have no objection they allow him to tarry the night with her, in order to make his court to her. After the young ones have sat up as long as they think proper, they get into bed together, also without pulling off their undergarments in order to prevent scandal. If the parties agree, it is all very well; the banns are published and they are married without delay. If not they part, and possibly never see each other again; unless, which is an accident that seldom happens, the forsaken fair proves pregnant, and then the man is obliged to marry her.[6]

In fact, more underclothes were yanked off than the chronicler dared to consider, and pregnancy was far more than 'an accident that seldom happens'. Up to a third of bundling couples found themselves presented with a permanent souvenir of the occasion. Nor did it necessarily mark the advent of a serious phase of a relationship. By 1782, bundling was so casually regarded, according to one account, that it was 'but a courtesy' for a visitor to ask the young lady of the house if she cared to retire with him.

Although never expressly countenanced, fornication was so common in Puritan New England that at least one parish had forms printed up in which the guilty parties could confess by filling in their names and paying a small fine. By the 1770s about half of all New England women were pregnant at marriage.[7] In Appalachia and other back-country regions, according to one calculation, 94 per cent of brides were pregnant when they went to the altar.[8]

Not until the closing quarter of the eighteenth century did official attitudes to sex begin to take on an actively repressive tinge with the appearance of the first *blue laws*. The term originated in Connecticut in 1781 because, it is often said, the state's laws concerning personal morality were printed on blue paper,[9] though other sources say that it was the church laws that were given the blue treatment.[10] Whichever was the case, no one knows why blue was thought an apt colour for such laws. More pertinently, I can find no evidence of anyone's ever having seen a law printed on blue paper. It may simply be our curious tendency to equate blueness with extreme moral rectitude, as in the expressions *blue nose* and *blue stocking*. *Blue nose* is said to have begun as a jocular nineteenth-century New England term for the fishermen of Nova Scotia, whose lives on the frigid waters of the north Atlantic left them with permanently discoloured hooters. More prosaically, it may simply refer to a type of potato associated with that maritime province. In either case, how the term then came to be attached to a person of puritanical bent is anyone's guess. (Very possibly the two are not connected.)

Blue stocking, for a woman of pedantry and attendant lofty mien, is more easily explained. It comes from the *Blue Stocking Society*, a name derisively applied to a group of intellectuals who began meeting at Montagu House in London in about 1750. Although the congregation was mostly female, the inspiration for the pejorative name appears to have been a male member, one Benjamin Stillingfleet, who wore blue worsted stockings instead of the customary black silk hose, a mode of dress so novel as to be considered both comical and slightly *risqué*. And speaking of *risqué*, why off-colour jokes are called *blue* is another mystery, but it may be connected to the eighteenth-century slang use of blue meaning *to blush*.

Seventeenth- and eighteenth-century users of English, Puritan and non-Puritan alike, had none of the problems with expressive terms like *belly*, *fart* and *give titty* (for *to suckle*) that would so trouble their Victorian descendants. Even the King James Bible contained such subsequently indecorous terms as *piss, dung* and *bowels*.[11] But as the eighteenth century gave way to the nineteenth, people suddenly became acutely – and eventually almost hysterically – sensitive about terms related to sex and the body. No one knows exactly when or why this morbid delicacy erupted. Like most fashions, it just happened. In 1818 Thomas Bowdler, an

Edinburgh physician, offered the world an expurgated version of Shakespeare's works suitable for the whole family, and in so doing gave the world the verb *to bowdlerize*. Bowdler's emendations were nothing if not thorough. Even the most glancing reminder of the human procreative capacity – King Lear's 'every inch a king', for example – was ruthlessly struck out. His sanitized Shakespeare was such a success that he immediately embarked on a similar treatment of Gibbon's *Decline and Fall of the Roman Empire*, which had been completed only a quarter of a century before but already needed careful scrubbing. But Bowdler's fastidious editing didn't inaugurate the change of mood. It merely reflected it.

Even before Bowdler began scratching away at the classics people were carefully avoiding emotive terms like *legs, blouse* and *thigh*. By the time Bowdler's *Family Shakespeare* appeared, *belly buttons* had become *tummy buttons*, *breast* had become *bosom*, and *underwear* had become *nether garments* or *small clothes* (and later *unmentionables*).

Though the practice began in Britain, it found its full flowering in America, where soon the list of proscribed words extended to the hundreds. Any word with an unseemly syllable in it like 'cock' or 'tit' became absolutely unutterable, so that words like *titter, titbit, cockerel* and *cockatoo* – all still unobjectionable in Britain – either disappeared from the American vocabulary or were altered to a more sanitised form like *tidbit, rooster* or *roach*. There is at least one recorded instance of *coxswain* being changed to *roosterswain*. Even *bulls* became *male cows*. Before the century was half over, the list of unspeakable words in the United States had been extended to almost any anatomical feature or article of apparel associated with any part of the human form outside the head, hands and ankles. *Stockings*, for instance, was deemed 'extremely indelicate' by Bartlett in 1850; he suggested *long socks* or *hose* as more comely alternatives. Even *toes* became humiliating possessions, never to be mentioned in polite company. One simply spoke of *the feet*. After a time *feet* too became unendurably shameful, so that people didn't mention anything below the ankles at all. It is a wonder that discourse didn't cease altogether.

Anxiety stalked every realm of life. It may be apocryphal that some families dressed their piano legs in little skirts to avoid moral distress to visitors, but it is certainly true that chamber-pots came with a crocheted cover to serve as a baffle so that anyone passing without would not hear the unseemly tinkle of the person passing within.[12] It wasn't just the noise that was baffled. Visitors from abroad found the neurotic lengths to which euphemism were carried deeply mystifying. It was not enough in America merely to avoid mentioning an object. A word had to be found that would not even hint at its actual function. Unable to bring themselves to say *chamber-pot* or even *commode*, Americans began to refer to the vessel as a *looking glass*, with obvious scope for confusion, not to say frustration, for anyone who sought the former and was given the latter.

Foreign visitors almost unfailingly ran aground in the shallow waters of American sensibilities. Frances Trollope noted the case of a German who stopped a roomful of conversation, and found himself being brusquely hustled from the house, for innocently pronouncing the word *corset* in mixed company. Elsewhere she discussed how a rakish young man tried to tease from a seamstress the name of the article of attire she was working on. Blushing hotly, the young lady announced that it was a frock, but when the young man pointed out that there wasn't nearly enough material for a frock she asserted it was an apron. Pressed further, she claimed it was a pillowcase. Eventually, she fled the room in shame and tears, unable to name the object. It was in fact a blouse, but to have uttered the word to a man would have been 'a symptom of absolute depravity'.

For women in particular, this rhetorical fastidiousness was not just absurd but dangerous. For much of the nineteenth century, *ankles* denoted the whole of a woman's body below the waist, while *stomach* did similar service for everything between the waist and head. It thus became impossible to inform a doctor of almost any serious medical complaint. Page Smith notes a typical case in which a young woman with a growth on her breast could only describe it to her physician as a pain in her stomach.[13]

Physical examinations were almost unknown. Gynaecological investigations in particular were made only as a last resort, and then usually in a darkened room under a sheet. One doctor in Philadelphia boasted that 'women prefer to suffer the extremity of danger and pain rather than waive those scruples of delicacy which prevent their maladies from being fully explored'.[14] Death, in other words, was to be preferred to immodesty. Given the depths of medical ignorance, it was probably just as well that the medical men kept their hands to themselves. Such was the lack of knowledge in regard to female physiology that until the closing years of the nineteenth century it was widely believed that the touch of a menstruating woman could turn a ham rancid. (The *British Medical Journal* ran a lively correspondence on the matter in 1878.)[15] Nor was it just male doctors who were profoundly innocent. As late as 1901, in a book entitled *What a Young Wife Ought to Know*, Dr Emma Drake was informing her readers that during pregnancy they might experience uncomfortable feelings of arousal. This, she explained frankly, was 'due to some unnatural condition and should be considered a disease'.[16]

Not surprisingly, sexual ignorance was appalling. On the eve of her wedding, the future novelist Edith Wharton asked her mother what would be expected of her in the bridal chamber. 'You've seen enough pictures and statues in your life,' her mother stammered. 'Haven't you noticed that men are made differently from women?' and with that closed the subject.[17]

Those who sought enlightenment from sex manuals were left little wiser. The two best-selling guides of the day were *What a Young Boy Ought to Know* and *What a Young Girl Ought to Know*, both written by a clergyman named Sylvanus Stall. Despite the books' titles Stall was at pains to make sure that his young readers should in fact know nothing. To deal with the inevitable question of where babies come from, he suggested parents memorize the following roundabout answer:

> My dear child, the question you have asked is one that every man and woman, every intelligent boy or girl and even many very young children have asked themselves or others – whence and how they came to be in the world. If you were to ask where the locomotives and the steamship or the telegraph and the telephone came from, it would be wisest, in order that we might have the most satisfactory answer that we should go back to the beginning of these things, and consider what was done by George Stephenson and Robert Fulton, by Benjamin Franklin and Samuel Morse, by Graham Bell and Thomas Edison toward developing and perfecting these useful inventions.

So there you have it, my child – they come from eminent inventors. But no, Stall then abruptly switches tack and launches into a discussion of corn-stalks and their tassels, with oblique references to Papa and Mama Shad, birds and eggs, oaks and acorns, and other such natural processes, but without so much as a hint as to how any of them manage to regenerate. Then, as a kind of cooling-down exercise after all this heady candour, he provides a brief sermon.

For young men, the great anxiety was *masturbation*, a term coined in a British medical journal in 1766 in an article entitled 'Onanism: A Treatise on the Disorders Produced by Masturbation'. The origins of the term are puzzling. The *Oxford English Dictionary* says that it comes from the Latin *masturbārī*, but then calls that a term of 'unkn. origin'. The verb form *masturbate* didn't arise until 1857, but by that time the world had come up with any number of worrisome-sounding alternatives – *selfish celibacy, solitary licentiousness, solitary vice, self-abuse, personal uncleanliness, self-pollution* and the thunderous *crime against nature*. By whatever name it went, there was no question that indulgence in it would leave you a juddering wreck. According to Dr William Alcott's *A Young Man's Guide* (1840) those who succumbed to temptation could confidently expect to experience, in succession, epilepsy, St Vitus's dance, palsy, blindness, consumption, apoplexy, 'a sensation of ants crawling from the head down along the spine' and finally death.[18]

As late as 1913 the American Medical Association published a book that explained that *spermin*, a constituent of semen, was necessary for the building of strong muscles and a well-ordered brain, and that boys who wasted this precious biological elixir would turn from 'hard-muscled, fiery-eyed, resourceful young men' into 'narrow-chested, flabby-muscled mollycoddles'.[19]

For women, ignorance was not just confined to matters sexual. Conventional wisdom had it that members of the fair sex should not be exposed to matters that might tax their fragile and flighty minds. Even as enlightened an observer as Thomas Jefferson believed that females should not 'wrinkle their foreheads with politics' or excite their susceptible passions overmuch with books and poetry, but rather should confine themselves to 'dancing, drawing, and music.'[20]

Recounting the difficulties of trying to bring a liberal education to young women, Emma Willard, founder of the Troy Female Seminary, the first true American girls' school, noted how parents had covered their faces and fled a classroom 'in shame and dismay' when they found one of the pupils drawing a picture of the human circulatory system on a blackboard.[21]

If by some miracle a woman managed to acquire a little learning, she was not expected to share it with the world. An influential manual, *A Father's Legacy to His Daughters*, cautioned its young readers, 'If you happen to have any learning, keep it a profound secret, especially from the men.'[22] When in 1828 Fannie Wright gave a series of public lectures, the nation's press was at first shocked and then outraged. A newspaper in Louisville accused her of committing 'an act against nature'. The *New York Free Enquirer* declared that she had 'with ruthless violence broken loose from the restraints of decorum'. The *New York American* decided that she had 'ceased to be a woman' by her actions.[23] No one objected to the content of the lectures, you understand, merely that it was issuing from the mouth of a female.

The tiniest deviation from conventional behaviour earned the rebuke of newspapers. In 1881 the *New York Times* editorialized against the growing use of slang by women, with the implication that it bespoke a dangerous moral laxity, and cited as an example the shocking expression 'What a cunning hat'.[24]

Yet – and here is the great, confusing paradox of the age – at the very time that these repressive currents were swirling around, many women were stepping forward and demanding to be heard with a vigour and boldness that would not be repeated for a century. The women's movement of the nineteenth century grew out of a huge thrust for social change that gripped America like a fever between about 1830 and 1880. Scores of new ideas seized the popular consciousness and found huge, fanatical followings: *utopianism, spiritualism, populism, vegetarianism, socialism, women's suffrage, black emancipation, tax reform, food reform, communalism, mysticism, occultism, second adventism, temperance, transcendentalism*. People dipped into these social possibilities as if pulling sweets from a bag. One group called for 'free thought, free love, free land, free food, free drink, free medicine, free Sunday, free marriage and free divorce'. Another, styling itself the

Nothingarians, rallied behind the cry 'No God, no government, no marriage, no money, no meat, no tobacco, no sabbath, no skirts, no church, no war and no slaves!' As Emerson wrote to Carlyle in 1840: 'We are all a little wild here with numberless projects of social reform. Not a reading man but has a draft of a new Community in his waistcoat pocket.'

Typical of this new spirit of experimentation was a commune called Fruitlands started in 1843 by A. Branson Alcott and some followers. For various fashionable reasons, the members of the Fruitlands community rejected meat, cheese, tea, milk, coffee, rice, woollen clothing, leather shoes, and manure. One particularly zealous adherent refused to eat any root that pushed downwards 'instead of aspiring towards the sun'. The colony lasted less than a year. Things went well enough during warm weather, but at the first sign of winter frost, it broke up and the members returned to their comfortable homes in Boston.

For women, the social ferment presented an opportunity to take part for the first time in public debate. It began with a few lectures, usually to other women in private homes, on subjects like abolition and education. By mid-century women were appearing on public platforms and speaking not just for abolition or vegetarianism or transcendentalism, but for their own interests.

Two of the most outspoken were the sisters Tennessee Claflin and Victoria Claflin Woodhull, who jointly ran a successful New York stockbroking firm and published a popular magazine, *Woodhull and Claflin's Weekly*, which espoused a variety of utopian schemes and engaged in an early form of 'outing' when it exposed the affair of the preacher Henry Ward Beecher and Elizabeth Tilton, the wife of one of his parishioners. Curiously, they didn't attack him for this, but praised him for his 'immense physical potency' and 'amativeness'.

Woodhull was particularly – and in the context of the times breathtakingly – forthright in her demands for free love. 'If I want sexual intercourse with one or one hundred men I shall have it,' she thundered. 'And this sexual intercourse business may as well be discussed . . . until you are so familiar with your sexual organs that a reference to them will no longer make the blush mount to your face any more than a reference to any other part of your body.'[25]

As a way of asserting their new-found sense of independence, many women took to wearing *bloomers,* an article of clothing named for Amelia Bloomer, a postmistress in upstate New York and a leading temperance lecturer. Bloomer did not invent bloomers but merely popularized them. Bloomers could hardly have been more modest. They were a sort of voluminous pants, not unlike those worn by modern baseball players, worn under a short skirt or smock – 'like a stratosphere balloon with two hot dogs peeping out at the bottom', as one historian has put it – and they freed women from the horrible constraints of corsets and bodices. They were decorous and they made eminent sense, but predictably they aroused huge agitation, and from pulpits to newspaper editorials they were fulminated against as graceless at best, lascivious at worst. It was not until much later that *bloomers* came to signify a woman's underclothing.

Pressing the fight for woman's suffrage, Woodhull ran for President in 1872 as the candidate of the Equal Rights Party. (Her running mate was the freed slave Frederick Douglass.) Soon afterwards, she moved to England, married an aristocrat, got religion and recanted almost everything. She devoted much of the energies of her later years to trying to persuade newspapers to throw out their files of her earlier utterances.

By this time, however, others had rushed to fill the vacuum created by her departure. The forthrightness with which many of these early feminists put their views seems astonishingly out of keeping with our usual perception of the age. Angela Heywood launched a spirited campaign for free love in which she made the universal acceptance of the word *fuck* a central tenet. Why should she be compelled to use the term 'generative sexual intercourse' in her lectures? she repeatedly asked. 'Three words, 27 letters, to define a given action . . . commonly spoken in one word of four letters that everybody knows the meaning of.'[26]

No less unexpectedly, the most vociferous exponents of free love and other radical practices were to be found not in Boston or New York, but out on the prairies in places like Iowa, Kansas and Illinois. The most radical freethinking newspaper, *Lucifer,* was based in Valley Falls, Kansas. It is worth noting, however, that even among the most committed bastions of libertarianism sexual enlightenment was a sometimes elusive quality. Even here it was widely believed that masturbation dangerously 'thinned the blood and destroyed vital energy'. Many in the free love movement supported uninhibited sexual intercourse between men and women not because of its inherent virtues, but simply because it prevented masturbation.[27]

Never before nor since, in short, has there been a more confused and bewildering age. To read on the one hand the *New York Times* castigating women for saying 'what a cunning hat' and on the other Angela Heywood publicly arguing for the right to say 'fuck', it is all but impossible to believe that we are dealing with the same people in the same country in the same century.

Much the same paradox obtained with sex. In no other time in history has sex been so rampantly suppressed or so widely available. In 1869 it was estimated that Philadelphia had 12,000 prostitutes, and Chicago 7,000. No estimates appear to have been made for New York, but it is known that the city had over 620 brothels. For the less adventurous there was a huge stockpile of *pornography* (from Greek terms meaning literally 'harlot writing' and coined in England in 1854) in both words and pictures.

Many terms associated with illicit sex are very old. *Bordello* (from an Old French word for a small hut), *brothel* (from the Old English *brēothan*, meaning derelict), *whore* (another Old English word), *strumpet, harlot, bawdy house* and *street walker* all comfortably predate the Pilgrims. Throughout the nineteenth century prostitutes were also commonly known as *flappers*, a term resurrected for fast girls in the 1920s, and *gay women* or *gays*. How *gay* then became attached to homosexuals is uncertain. We know approximately when it happened – the late 1960s – but no one appears to know why or by what reasoning. No less mysterious is one of the more unattractive epithets for homosexuals, *faggot*. In its homophobic sense, the term is an Americanism first recorded in 1905, but beyond that almost nothing is known. In England, *faggot* and its diminutive *fag* have had a multiplicity of meanings, from a slang term for a cigarette, to feeling fatigued, to being burned at the stake. The American usage may come from the schoolboy term *fag*, designating a boy who serves as a kind of slave for a more senior fellow, toasting his crumpets, fetching his slippers and, in the right circumstances, assisting him through that sexual delirium known as puberty. But puzzlingly there is no indication of *fag* ever having denoted a homosexual in Britain, and no one has ever posited a convincing explanation for the term's transmission to America.

Among other Americanisms connected with sex we find *red light district* from the 1890s (it comes, as you might guess, from the practice of burning a red light in the front window of a brothel); *hustler* from 1900; *floozie, trick, to be fast and loose,* and *cat house* from the early 1900s; *john* for a prostitute's customer, and *call girl*, both from the 1930s.[28]

Inevitably, all the loose talk of promiscuity and sexual assertiveness, and the growing availability of *smut* (an English dialect word related to *smudge*, and first recorded in 1722) in all its many forms brought forth a violent reaction. It was personified most vigorously in the beefy shape of Anthony Comstock, one of the most relentless hunters-down of vice America has ever produced.

A former salesman and shipping office clerk, Comstock had little education – he could barely read and write – but he knew what he didn't like, which was more or less everything, including even jock-straps. As founder and first secretary of the Society for the Suppression of Vice, he lobbied vigorously for a federal law against obscenity. The difficulty was that the Constitution reserved such matters for the states. The federal government could involve itself only in regard to interstate commerce, chiefly through the mail. In 1873 it passed what came immediately to be known as the Comstock Act. Described as 'one of the most vicious and absurd measures ever to come before Congress', it was passed after just ten minutes of debate. In the same year Comstock was appointed Special Agent for the US Post Office to enforce the new law, and he went to work with a vengeance.

In a single year, Comstock and his deputies impounded 134,000 lb. of books, 14,200 lb. of photographic plates, almost 200,000 photographs and drawings, 60,300 miscellaneous articles of rubber, 31,500 boxes of aphrodisiacal pills and potions, and 5,500 packs of playing-cards.[29] Almost nothing escaped his ruthless quest to suppress vice wherever it arose. He even ordered the arrest of one woman for calling her husband a 'spitzbub', or rascal, on a postcard.

By 1915 it had become Comstock's proud boast that his efforts had led to the imprisonment of 3,600 people and caused 15 suicides. Among those trampled by his zeal was one Ida Craddock, whose book *The Wedding Night*, a work of serious literature, had been found obscene by a jury that had not been allowed to read it.

Comstock's efforts were in the long run largely counter-productive. His merciless bullying earned sympathy for many of his victims, and his efforts at suppression had an almost guaranteed effect of publicising the attacked object beyond the creator's wildest dream, most notably in 1913 when he turned his guns on a mediocre painting by Paul Chabas called *September Morn* – which featured a young woman bathing naked in a lake – and made it a national sensation. Before the year was out practically every barber-shop and gas station in the country boasted a print.

Strangely, the one thing the Comstock Act did not do was define what constituted lewd, obscene or indecent material. Congress happily left such judgements to Comstock himself. Not until 1957 did the Supreme Court get around to considering the matter of obscenity, and then it was unable to make any more penetrating judgment than that it was material that appealed to 'prurient interests' and inflamed 'lustful thoughts'. In effect it ruled that obscenity could be recognized but not defined – or as Justice Potter Stewart famously put it: 'I know it when I see it.'[30] In 1973 the court redefined obscene works as those that 'appeal to the prurient interest, contain patently offensive conduct, and lack artistic, literary, political or scientific value'. It was left to local communities to interpret these values as they wished.

Problems of definition with regard to obscenity are notoriously thorny. In 1989, following criticism of the National Endowment for the Arts for funding exhibitions of controversial works by Robert Mapplethorpe and André Serrano, US Senator Jesse Helms produced a bill that would deny federal funding for programmes deemed to be obscene or indecent. The bill was interesting for being a rare attempt to provide an omnibus definition of what constituted the obscene. Among the proscribed subjects were works of art 'including but not limited to depictions of sadomasochism, homo-eroticism, the exploitation of children, or individuals engaged in sex acts; or material which denigrates the objects or beliefs of the adherents of a particular religion or non-religion; or material which denigrates, debases, or reviles a person, group or class of citizens on the basis of race, creed, sex, handicap, age or national origin'. At last America had a bill that stated the precise boundaries of acceptability. Unfortunately, as critics pointed out, it was also full of holes.

Quite apart from the possibilities for abuse inherent in open-ended phrases like 'including but not limited to' and 'a particular religion or non-religion', the law if followed to the letter would have made it illegal to provide funding for, among much else, Shakespeare's *Merchant of Venice, The Bacchae* by Euripides, *The Clouds* by Aristophanes, operas by Wagner and Verdi, and paintings by Rubens, Rembrandt and Picasso. It would even have made it illegal to display the Constitution, since that document denigrates blacks by treating them as three-fifths human (for purposes of determining proportional representation). The bill was rejected and replaced by one prohibiting 'obscene art', again leaving it to others to determine what precisely obscene might be, and trusting that they would know it when they saw it.

State laws regarding obscenity and morality are equally – we might fairly say ridiculously – prone to ambiguity. Two things are notable about such state laws: first, how intrusive they are, and, second, how vague is the language in which they are couched. Many go so far as to proscribe certain acts (for example, oral sex) even between consenting adults, even sometimes between husband and wife. Most states have laws against fornication and even masturbation lying somewhere on their books, though you would hardly know it, such is the evasive language with which the laws are phrased. One of the most popular phrases is 'crime against nature' (though in California it is 'the infamous crime against nature' and in Indiana 'the abominable and detestable crime against nature'), but almost never do they specify what a *crime against nature* is. An innocent observer could be excused for concluding that it means chopping down trees or walking on the grass.

Many others have laws against 'self-pollution', but again without providing a definition of what is intended by the expression. Occasionally statutes include a more explicit term like *sodomy* or *masturbation,* but often this serves only to heighten the uncertainty. Indiana, for instance, has a law, passed in 1905, which reads in part: 'Whoever entices, allures, instigates or aids any person under the age of twenty-one (21) years to commit masturbation or self-pollution, shall be deemed guilty of sodomy.'[31] If, as the law implies, masturbation and self-pollution are not the same thing, then what exactly *is* self-pollution? Smoking a cigarette? Failing to bathe regularly? Whatever it may be, in Indiana at least as late as the 1950s you could spend up to fourteen years in prison for it.

In those few instances where states have tried to be more carefully explicit in their statutes, they have usually ended up tying themselves in knots. Kansas, for instance, gave itself a law that made adultery in the form of vaginal intercourse illegal, but not when it involved deviant sex acts. What is certain is that most people have broken such a law at one time or another. The sex researcher Alfred Kinsey, not normally a man to make light of such matters, once remarked only half jokingly that, with what he knew from his surveys, 85 per cent of the people of Indiana should be in prison and the other 15 per cent were anaemic.

The difficulty of course is that acceptable behaviour, not just in sex but in all things, is a constantly changing concept. Just consider the matter of beards. In 1840, Americans had been beardless for so long – about two hundred years – that when an eccentric character in Framingham, Massachusetts, grew a beard he was attacked by a crowd and dragged off to jail. Yet by the mid-1850s, just a decade and a half later, there was scarcely a beardless man in America. From 1860 to 1897, every American President was bearded. Or consider hemlines. In 1921, when hemlines began to climb to mid- calf, Utah considered imprisoning – not fining, but imprisoning – women who wore skirts more than three inches above the ankle. Virginia, shocked at the other extreme, introduced a bill that would make it a criminal offence to wear a gown that displayed more than three inches of throat. Ohio decided to leave women unmolested, but to go to the heart of the matter and punish any retailer found guilty of selling a garment that 'unduly displays or accentuates the female figure'.[32] Such outrage wasn't reserved just for female attire. As late as 1935, any male venturing on to the beach of Atlantic City with a bare chest faced arrest for indecency.[33]

In short, standards of acceptability constantly change. A period of repression is almost always followed by a spell of licence. The ferociously restrictive age of Anthony Comstock, which drew to a close with his death in 1915, was immediately followed by a period of relative abandon. Not only did hemlines climb to shocking heights, but young people, made suddenly mobile by the availability of cars, took to partying until all hours, drinking bath-tub gin, and engaging in heavy sessions of *necking* and *petting* – activities that had always existed of course but had only recently acquired such explicit labels. Other newly minted terms of the period – *bedroom eyes; playboy; tall, dark and handsome* – betray a frankness that could not have been expressed ten years earlier.

Nothing better captured the new spirit of sexual boldness, or the inevitable backlash against it, than the movies. After their cautious start, movies in the period 1915–20 became wildly daring by the standards of the day. Studios cranked out a succession of pictures with provocatively enticing titles like *Virgin Paradise, Red Hot Romance, The Fourteenth Lover, Her Purchase Price, Flesh and the Devil* and *White Hot Stuff*.[34] One lurid poster promised viewers a motion picture featuring 'neckers, petters, white kisses, red kisses, pleasure-mad daughters, sensation-craving mothers . . . the truth – bold, naked, sensational'.[35] Even historical epics got the treatment. *Helen of Troy* was advertised as 'an A.D. Mamma in a B.C. town'.[36] A very few, like the 1918 movie *A Man's World*, did contain brief nudity, and others certainly implied rampant sex, but for the most part the hottest thing was the poster.

In 1921, with Hollywood rocked by scandal – it was the year of the Fatty Arbuckle case and the death in sexually questionable circumstances of a director named William Desmond Taylor – and with thirty-seven states and hundreds of municipalities threatening to come up with a confusion of censorship codes, Hollywood acted. It formed a body known as the Motion Picture Producers and Distributors of America, Inc., and appointed Will H. Hays, Postmaster General under President Warren G. Harding and a former chairman of the Republican Party, as its first head. Hays was a non-smoking, non-drinking Indiana Presbyterian whose pinched face had extreme moral rectitude written all over it. (Though, like many others in the Harding administration, his probity did not extend to financial dealings. He was happy to receive and adroitly launder hundreds of thousands of dollars in illegal campaign contributions.) At a salary of $100,000 a year, Hays became the moral watchdog of America's movies.

In 1927, the Hays Office, as it was immediately if informally known, issued a famous list of 'Don'ts and Be Carefuls'. The list consisted of eleven proscribed acts, such as 'excessive or lustful kissing', and twenty-six acts to be handled with extreme caution. In 1930 this was superseded by a much more comprehensive Production Code, which would remain the bible of film production for half a century. The code decreed several broad principles – that pictures should be wholesome, that the sympathies of the audience should never be 'thrown to the side of crime, wrong-doing, evil or sin' – and scores of specific strictures. It forbade the uttering on screen not just of every common swear word and racial epithet, but such dramatically useful terms as *eunuch, floozy, louse* (the Hays Office helpfully suggested *stinkbug* as an alternative), *guts, in your hat, nuts, nerts, cripes, hellcat, belch* and even, remarkably, *virtuous* (on the presumption that it was a too explicit reminder that some people weren't). *Liar* was permitted in comedies but not in dramas, and *travelling salesman* could be used but not in a context involving a farmer's daughter.[37] *Lord*, even in reverential contexts, had to be changed to *Lawsy*. One of the more indestructible myths concerning the code is that it decreed that when a man and woman were shown in bed together the man must always have at least one foot on the floor. It said no such thing. However, it did touch on almost everything else. As one movie historian has put it, 'it prohibited the showing or mentioning of almost everything germane to the situation of normal human adults'.

Even the word *it* in the wrong context could be considered dangerously suggestive. In 1931 the Hays Office ordered Samuel Goldwyn to change the name of his comedy *The Greeks Had a Word for It* to *The Greeks Had a Word for Them*. In much the same spirit the title of a Joan Crawford movie was changed from *Infidelity* to *Fidelity*. Three years later, when Goldwyn bought the rights to Lillian Hellman's play about lesbianism, *The Children's Hour*, Hays told him that he could by all means make it into a movie, as long as it didn't have anything to do with lesbians and he didn't call it *The Children's Hour*. The movie was made without lesbians and with the title *These Three*.[38]

Occasionally, producers could preserve a line through trade-offs. David O. Selznick managed to save Clark Gable's famous, and at the time shocking, 'Frankly, my dear, I don't give a damn' in

Gone With the Wind – a line not in the original script, incidentally – by sacrificing 'May your mean little soul burn in hell for eternity.'[39] But for the most part films became sensationally cautious, and would remain so into the 1960s.

As late as 1953, the main character in *Gentlemen Prefer Blondes* was not permitted to say 'Bottoms up' when quaffing a drink. In the Broadway production of *The Seven-Year Itch* the main character commits adultery, but in the 1955 movie Tom Ewell could only agonize over the dangerous temptation of it. *Captain's Paradise*, a 1952 British comedy in which Alec Guinness played a sea captain with wives in two ports, was allowed to be released in America only after the producers added an epilogue admonishing the audience not to try such a thing themselves.[40] Even Walt Disney was forbidden from showing a cow with udders.[41]

Finally in 1968, with the Production Code almost universally ignored, it was abandoned and a new system of ratings was introduced. Originally films were rated, in order of descending explicitness, *X, R, M* and *G. M* was later changed to *GP* and later still to *PG. XXX*, or *Triple-X*, though favoured by owners of *porno theatres* (an Americanism of 1966), never had official standing.

Newspapers and magazines had no regulatory body equivalent to the Hays Office, but it wasn't necessary because they were almost always prepared to exercise a rigorous self-censorship. In 1933, when there was a breakthrough in the treatment of syphilis, most papers were at a loss as to how to tell their readers. Most fell back on the conveniently vague term *social disease*. An innocent reader could well have concluded that it involved handshaking. As late as 1934, the *New York Times* would not allow *syphilis* or *venereal disease* to besmirch its pages even in serious discussions.[42]

As late as 1943, when a husband's homosexuality was a factor in a sensational murder trial, few newspapers could bring themselves to describe his affliction. One described the man as having 'indications of an abnormal psychological nature'.[43] Rape was commonly euphemized to *assault*, as in the famous – but probably apocryphal and certainly undocumented – story of an attacker who 'repeatedly struck and kicked his victim, hurled her down a flight of stairs and then assaulted her'.

Because of social strictures against even the mildest swearing, America developed a particularly rich crop of euphemistic expletives – *darn, durn, goldurn, goshdad, goshdang, goshawful, blast, consarn, confound, by Jove, by jingo, great guns, by the great horn spoon* (a nonce term first cited in the *Biglow Papers*), *jo-fired, jumping Jehoshophat* and others almost without number – but even these cautious epithets could land people in trouble as late as the 1940s. Mencken notes how a federal judge in New York threatened a lawyer with contempt for having the impertinence to utter 'darn' in his court. *Esquire* magazine found itself hauled into court by the Postmaster General in 1943 for daring to print *backside, behind* and *bawdy house* in various issues. It wasn't even necessary to say a word to cause offence. During World War II, an anti-German song called 'Der Fuehrer's Face' was banned from the nation's airwaves because it contained a Bronx cheer.

Television too had a self-imposed code of ethics. As early as 1944, when Norma Martin and Eddie Cantor sang a duet called 'We're Having a Baby, My Baby and Me', and accompanied it with a little hula dance, the cameraman was ordered to blur the image.[44] On an early talk show, when the English comedian Beatrice Lillie jokingly remarked of belly dances that she had 'no stomach for that kind of thing', it caused a small scandal. In the early 1950s, after an Arkansas Congressman with the God-fearing name of Ezekiel C. Gothings held hearings on sex and violence on television, the networks adopted their own code which essentially decreed that nothing immoral would appear on America's airwaves.[45]

Thus in 1952, when Lucille Ball became pregnant, the term wasn't permitted. She was *expecting*. Nor was it just sex that prompted censorship. In 1956, when Rod Serling wrote a script about a black youth in Mississippi who is murdered after whistling at a white woman, the producers of *US Steel Hour* enthusiastically went along with the idea – so long as the victim wasn't black, wasn't murdered and didn't live in the deep South.

Books by comparison showed much greater daring. *Fucking* appeared in a novel called *Strange Fruit* as early as 1945, and was banned in Massachusetts as a result. The publishers took the state to court, but the case fell apart when the defence attorney arguing for its sale was unable to bring himself to utter the objectionable word in court, in effect conceding that it was too filthy for public consumption.[46] In 1948 Norman Mailer caused a sensation by including *pissed off* in *The Naked and the Dead*. Three years later,

America got its first novel to use four-letter words extensively when James Jones's *From Here to Eternity* was published. Even there the editors were at sixes and sevens over which words to allow. They allowed *fuck* and *shit* (though not without excising about half of such appearances from the original manuscript) but drew the line at *cunt* and *prick*.[47]

Against such a background dictionary makers became seized with uncertainty. In the 1960s the *Merriam-Webster Dictionary* broke new ground by including a number of taboo words – *cunt, shit* and *prick* – but lost its nerve when it came to *fuck*. Mario Pei protested the omission in the *New York Times* but of course without once mentioning the word at issue. To this day America remains to an extraordinary degree a land of euphemism. Even now the US State Department cannot bring itself to use the word *prostitute*. Instead it refers to 'available casual indigenous female companions'.[48] Producers of rape-seed are increasingly calling it *canola*, lest the first syllable offend any delicate sensibilities, even though *rape* in the horticultural sense comes from *rāpa*, Latin for 'turnip'.[49]

Despite the growing explicitness of books and movies, in most other areas of public discourse – notably in newspapers, radio and local and network television – America remains perhaps the most extraordinarily cautious nation in the developed world. Words, pictures and concepts that elsewhere excite no comment or reaction remain informally banned from most American media.

In 1991 the *Columbia Journalism Review* ran a piece on the coverage of a briefly infamous argument between Pittsburgh Pirates Manager Jim Leyland and his star player Barry Bonds. It examined how thirteen newspapers from around the country had dealt with the livelier epithets the two men had hurled at each other. Without exception the papers had replaced the offending words with ellipses or dashes, or else had changed them to something lighter – making 'kissing your ass' into 'kissing your butt', for instance. To an outside observer there are two immediately arresting points here: first, that 'kissing your ass' is still deemed too distressingly graphic for modern American newspaper readers, and, secondly, that 'kissing your butt' is somehow thought more decorous. Even more arresting is that the *Columbia Journalism Review*, though happy to revel in the discomfort at which the papers had found themselves, could not bring itself to print the objectionable words either, relying instead on the coy designations 'the F-word' and 'the A-word'.

Examples of such hyperprudence are not hard to find. In 1987 the *New York Times* columnist William Safire wrote about the expression *cover your ass* without being able to bring himself to record the phrase, though he had no hesitation in listing many expressive synonyms: *butt, keister, rear end, tail*. In the same year, when a serious art-house movie called *Sammy and Rosie Get Laid* was released, Safire refused to name the film in his column (the *New York Times* itself would not accept an ad with the full title). Safire explained: 'I will not print the title here because I deal with a family trade; besides, it is much more titillating to ostentatiously avoid the slang term.'[50] Pardon me? On the one hand he wishes to show an understandable consideration for our sense of delicacy; but on the other he is happy to titillate us – indeed, it appears to be his desire to *heighten* our titillation. Such selective self-censorship would seem to leave American papers open to charges of, at the very least, inconsistency.

In pursuit of edification, I asked Allan M. Siegal, assistant managing editor of the *New York Times*, what rules on bad language obtain at the paper. 'I am happy to say we maintain *no* list of proscribed expressions,' Siegal replied. 'In theory, *any* expression could be printed if it were central to a reader's understanding of a hugely important news development.' He noted that the *Times* had used *shit* in reports on the Watergate transcripts, and also *ass, crap* and *dong* 'in similarly serious contexts, like the Clarence Thomas sexual harassment hearings'.

Such instances, it should be noted, are extremely exceptional. Between 1980 and July 1993, *shit* appeared in the *New York Times* just once (in a book review by Paul Theroux). To put that in context, during the period in review the *Times* published something on the order of 400 million to 500 million words of text. *Piss* appeared three times (twice in book reviews, once in an art review). *Laid* appeared thirty-two times, but each time in reference to the movie that Safire could not bring himself to name. *Butthead* or *butthole* appeared sixteen times, again almost always in reference to a particular proper noun, such as the interestingly named pop group *Butthole Surfers*.

As a rule, Siegal explained, 'we wish not to shock or offend unless there is an overweening reason to risk doing do. We are loath to contribute to a softening of the society's barriers against harsh or profane language. The issue is nothing so mundane as our welcome among paying customers, be they readers or advertisers. Our management truly believes that civil public discourse is a cherished value of the democracy, and that by our choices we can buttress or undermine that value.'[51]

One consequence of the American approach to explicit language is that we often have no idea when many of our most common expressions first saw light since they so often go unrecorded. Even something as innocuous as *to be caught with one's pants down* isn't found in print until 1946 (in the *Saturday Evening Post*), though it is likely that people were using it at least a century earlier.[52] More robust expressions like *fucking-A* and *shithead* are effectively untraceable.

Swearing, according to one study, accounts for no less than 13 per cent of all adult conversation, yet it remains a neglected area of scholarship. One of the few studies of recent years is *Cursing in America*, but its author, John Benjamins of North Adams State College in Massachusetts, had to postpone his research for five years when his dean forbade it. 'I was told I couldn't work on this and I couldn't teach courses on it, and it wouldn't be a good area for tenure,' Adams said in a newspaper interview.[53] 'The minute I got tenure I went back to dirty words.' And quite right, too.

Wing dining, somewhere over France, 1929

The Road from Kitty Hawk

The story is a familiar one. On a cold day in December 1903, Orville and Wilbur Wright, assisted by five locals, lugged a flimsy-looking aircraft on to the beach at Kitty Hawk, North Carolina. As Wilbur steadied the wing, Orville prostrated himself at the controls and set the plane rolling along a wooden track. A few moments later, the plane rose hesitantly, climbed to about 15 feet and puttered along the beach for 120 feet before setting down on a dune. The flight lasted just twelve seconds and covered less ground than the wing-span of a modern jumbo jet, but the airplane age had begun.

Everyone knows that this was one of the great events of modern technology, but there is still a feeling, I think, that the Wrights were essentially a pair of inspired tinkerers who knocked together a simple contraption in their bike shop and were lucky enough to get it airborne. We have all seen film of early aircraft tumbling off the end of piers or being catapulted into haystacks. Clearly the airplane was an invention waiting to happen. The Wrights were just lucky enough to get there first.

In fact, their achievement was much, much greater than that. To master powered flight, it was necessary to engineer a series of fundamental breakthroughs in the design of wings, engines, propellers and control mechanisms. Every piece of the Wrights' plane was revolutionary, and every piece of it they designed and built themselves.

In just three years of feverish work, these two retiring bachelors from Dayton, Ohio, sons of a bishop of the United Brethren Church, had made themselves the world's leading authorities on aerodynamics. Their home-built wind tunnel was years ahead of anything existing elsewhere. When they discovered that there was no formal theory of propeller dynamics, no formulae with which to make comparative studies of different propeller types, they devised their own. Because it is all so obvious to us now, we forget just how revolutionary their concept was. No one else had thought of putting the propeller at the front of the craft where it could pull, rather than pushing from the back, or recognized that a propeller is in effect a vertical wing. No one else was even within years of touching them in their mastery of the aerodynamic properties of wings. Their warping mechanism for controlling the wings was such a breakthrough that it is still 'used on every fixed-wing aircraft that flies today'.[1] As Orville noted years later in an uncharacteristically bold assertion, 'I believe we possessed more data on cambered surfaces, a hundred times over, than all of our predecessors put together.'[2]

Nothing in their background suggested that they would create a revolution. They ran a bicycle shop in Dayton. They had no scientific training. Indeed, neither had finished high school. Yet, working alone, they discovered or taught themselves more about both the mechanics and science of flight than anyone else had ever come close to knowing. As one of their biographers put it: 'These two untrained, self-educated engineers demonstrated a gift for pure scientific research that made the more eminent scientists who had studied the problems of flight look almost like bumbling amateurs.'[3]

They were distinctly odd. Pious and restrained (they celebrated their first successful flight with a brief handshake), they always dressed in business suits with ties and starched collars, even for their test flights. They never married, and always lived together. Often they argued ferociously. Once, according to a colleague, they went to bed heatedly at odds over some approach to a problem. In the morning, they each admitted that there was merit in the other's idea and began arguing again, but from the other side. However odd their relationship, clearly it was fruitful.

They suffered many early setbacks, not least returning to Kitty Hawk one spring to find that a promising model they had left behind had been rendered useless when the local postmistress had stripped the French sateen wing coverings to make dresses for her daughters.[4] Kitty Hawk, off the North Carolina coast near the site of the first American colony on Roanoke Island, had many drawbacks – monster mosquitoes in summer, raw winds in winter, and an isolation that made the timely acquisition of materials and replacement parts all but impossible – but there were compensations. The winds were steady and generally favourable, the beaches were spacious and free of obstructions, and above all the sanddunes were mercifully forgiving.

Samuel Pierpont Langley, the man everyone expected to make the first successful flight – he had the benefits of a solid scientific reputation, teams of assistants, and the backing of the Smithsonian Institution, Congress and the US Army – always launched his experimental planes from a platform on the Potomac River near Washington, which turned each test launch into a public spectacle, and which then became a public embarrassment as his ungainly test craft unfailingly lumbered off the platform and fell nose first into the water. It appears never to have occurred to Langley that any plane launched over water would, if it failed to take wing, inevitably sink. Langley's devoted assistant and test pilot, Charles Manly, was repeatedly lucky to escape with his life.

The Wright brothers by contrast were spared the pestering attention of journalists and gawkers and the pressure of financial backers. They could get on with their research at their own pace without having to answer to anyone. And when their experimental launches failed, the plane would come to an undamaged rest on a soft dune. They called their craft the Wright Flyer – named, curiously enough, not for its aeronautical qualities but for one of their bicycles.

By the autumn of 1903, the Wright brothers knew two things: that Samuel Langley's plane would never fly and that theirs would. They spent most of the autumn at Kitty Hawk – or more precisely at Kill Devil Hills, near Kitty Hawk – readying their craft, but ran into a series of teething problems, particularly with the propeller. The weather, too, proved persistently unfavourable. (On the one day when conditions were ideal they refused to fly, or do any work, because it was a Sunday.) By 17 December, the day of their breakthrough, they had been at Kitty Hawk for eighty-four days, living mostly on beans. They made four successful flights that day, of 120, 175, 180 and 852 feet, lasting from twelve seconds to just under a minute. As they were standing around after the fourth flight, discussing whether to have another attempt, a gust of wind picked up the plane and sent it bouncing across the sand-dunes, destroying the engine mountings and rear ribs. It never flew again.

Because it occurred so far from the public gaze, news of their historic achievement didn't so much burst on to the world as seep out. Several newspapers reported the event, but often with only the haziest idea of what had taken place. The *New York Herald* reported that the Wrights had flown three miles, and most other papers were similarly adrift in their details.

Many of those who had devoted their lives to achieving powered flight found it so unlikely that a pair of uneducated bicycle makers from Dayton, working from their own resources, had succeeded where they had repeatedly failed that they refused to entertain the idea. The Smithsonian remained loyal to Langley – he was a former assistant secretary of the institution – and refused to acknowledge the Wrights' accomplishment for almost forty years.

The Wrights' home town, Dayton, was so unmoved by the news that it didn't get around to giving them a parade until six years later. Unperturbed, the brothers put further distance between themselves and their competitors. By 1905, in an improved plane, they were flying up to twenty-four miles, and executing complicated manoeuvres, while staying aloft for almost forty minutes. Only the tiny capacity of the plane's fuel tank limited the duration of their flights.[5] The next year they received their patent, but even it was not the ringing endorsement they deserved. It credited them only with 'certain new and useful improvements in Flying-machines'.

The Wright brothers seemed unbothered by their lack of recognition. Although they made no secret of their flying, they also offered no public demonstrations, and hence didn't attract the popular acclaim they might have. Indeed in 1908, when the more publicity-conscious Glenn Curtiss flew over half a mile at Hammondsport, Connecticut, many assumed that that was the first flight.

In 1914, long after Langley himself was dead, the Smithsonian allowed Curtiss to exhume Langley's airplane, modify it significantly and try to fly it in order to prove retroactively that the Wrights had not been the first to design a plane capable of flight. With modifications that Langley had never dreamed of, Curtiss managed to get the plane airborne for all of five seconds, and for the next twenty-eight years the Smithsonian, to its eternal shame, displayed the craft as 'the first man-carrying aeroplane in the history of the world capable of sustained free-flight'.[6]

The original Wright Flyer spent twenty-five years under dust-sheets in a Dayton shed. When no institution in the United States wanted it, it was lent to the Science Museum in London and displayed there from 1928 to 1948. Not until 1942 did the Smithsonian at last accept that the Wrights were indeed the inventors of powered flight, and not until forty-five years after their historic flight was the craft at last permanently displayed in America.

The Wright brothers never called their craft an *airplane*. The word was available to them – it had existed in America for almost thirty years and, as *aeroplane*, in Britain for even longer. (*Aeroplane* was first used in 1869 in a British engineering magazine to describe a kind of aerofoil used in experiments.) In the early days there was no agreed term for aircraft. Langley had called his contraption an *aerodrome*. Others had used *aerial ship* or *aerial machine*. The Wright brothers favoured *flying machine*. But by 1910 *airplane* had become the standard word in America and *aeroplane* in Britain.

Flying and its attendant vocabulary took off with remarkable speed. By the second decade of the century most people, whether they had been near an airplane or not, were familiar with terms like *pilot, hangar, airfield, night flying, cockpit, air pocket, ceiling, takeoff, nosedive, barnstorming, tailspin, crack-up* (the early term for a crash), *bail out* and *parachute*. Pilots were sometimes referred to as *aeronauts*, but generally called *aviators,* with the first syllable pronounced with the short *ă* of *navigator* until the 1930s.

In 1914 *airlines* entered the language. The first airlines were formed not to carry passengers but mail. Pan American Airways began by ferrying mail between Key West and Havana. Braniff, named for its founder, Tom Braniff, covered the south-west. Other early participants were United Aircraft and Transport Corporation, which would eventually become United Airlines, Pitcairn Aviation, which would evolve into Eastern Air Lines, and Delta Air Lines, which had begun as a crop-dusting service in the South. *Airmail* was coined in 1917, and *airmail stamp* followed a year later.

Early planes were dangerous. In 1921 the average pilot had a life expectancy of 900 flying hours.[7] For airmail pilots, flying mostly at night without any proper navigational aids, it was even worse. While an airmail pilot on the St Louis–Chicago run, Charles Lindbergh staked his life on a farm boy in Illinois remembering to put on a 100-watt bulb in his backyard each night before he went to bed. It is little wonder that of the first forty pilots hired to carry air mail for the government thirty-one died in crashes. Lindbergh himself crashed three planes in a year.

Largely because of the danger, flying took on a romance and excitement that are difficult to imagine now. By May 1927, when Lindbergh touched down at Curtiss Field on Long Island for his historic flight across the Atlantic, the world had become seized with a kind of mania about flying and was ready for a hero. Lindbergh was just the person.

In recent months, six aviators had died attempting to cross the Atlantic, and several other groups of pilots at or around Curtiss Field were preparing to risk their lives in pursuit of fame and a $25,000 payoff called the Oteig Prize. All the other enterprises involved teams of at least two men, and muscular, well-provisioned, three-engined planes. And now here was someone who had flown in from out of nowhere (and had incidentally set a coast-to-coast speed record in the process) who was aiming to fly the ocean alone in a frail, single-engined mosquito of a plane. That he had lanky boyish good looks and an air of innocence made him ideal, and within days America and the world were gripped by a Lindy hysteria. On the Sunday after his arrival, 30,000 people showed up at Curtiss Field hoping to get a glimpse of this untried twenty-five-year-old hero.

That Lindbergh was a one-man operation worked in his favour. Where others were fussing over logistics and stocking up with survival rations, he bought a bag of sandwiches at a nearby lunch counter, filled up his fuel tank and quietly took off in the little plane named the Spirit of St Louis (so called because his backers were from there). He departed at 7.52 a.m. on 20 May 1927, and was so loaded down with fuel that he flew most of the distance to Nova Scotia just fifty feet above the ocean.[8] Because a spare fuel tank had been bolted on to the nose, Lindbergh had no forward visibility. To see where he was going, he had to put his head out the side window. Thirty-four hours later, at 10.22 at night, he landed at Le Bourget airfield outside Paris. One hundred thousand people were there to greet him.

To the French he was *Le Boy*. To the rest of the world he was *Lucky Lindy* – and he was lucky indeed. Though he did not know it, the night before he had taken possession of the plane, one of the workmen fuelling it had lost a piece of hose in the tank. Since a piece of hose could easily foul the fuel lines, there was no option but to take it out. The workman had cut a six-inch hole in the tank, retrieved the hose and surreptitiously patched the hole with solder. It was a miracle that it held throughout the turbulent Atlantic crossing.

Lindbergh was by no means the first person to cross the Atlantic by air. In May 1919, eight years earlier, a US Navy plane had crossed from Newfoundland to Lisbon, though it had stopped in the Azores en route. A little less than a month after that, John Alcock and Arthur Brown of Great Britain flew from Newfoundland to Ireland, the first non-stop flight. Lindbergh flew 1,500 miles further, and he did it alone, and that was enough for most people. Indeed, most didn't want to be reminded that Lindbergh was not the first. When 'Ripley's Believe It or Not', a popular newspaper feature, noted that some twenty other people (including those in dirigibles) had crossed the Atlantic by air before Lindbergh, its offices were inundated with 250,000 angry letters.

Never before in modern history had anyone generated such instant and total adulation as Lindbergh. When he returned to America, the parade in his honour produced more confetti than had been thrown to greet the returning troops after World War I. New York City gave him the largest dinner that had ever been put on for a private citizen. The New York Stock Exchange even closed for the day. Such was the hysteria that attached itself to Lindbergh that when his mother went to have her hair done in Washington, it took twenty-five policemen to control the mobs.[9]

The immense excitement and sense of possibility that Lindbergh's solo flight generated helped to usher in the age of passenger travel. Within two years most of the airmail lines were carrying passengers, and others, like American Airways (later Airlines), National Airlines Taxi Service, and Northwest Airways Company, were rushing to join the market. Lindbergh himself helped to found what is generally credited as the first true passenger airline. Formed in 1929, it was called Transcontinental Air Transport, or TAT, but was commonly known as the Lindbergh Line. In July of that year, using Ford Tri-Motor planes, TAT began the first long-distance passenger services across America, and in so doing introduced concepts that are still with us: flight attendants (only men were employed at first), lavatories, meals on board, and individual reading lights. Three months later the first in-flight movies were introduced. It also took the very bold – at the time almost unthinkable – decision not to carry parachutes.

Because of a paucity of suitable airports and certain vexing limitations of the Ford Tri-Motors, not least an inability to clear any but the smallest mountains, passengers flew only about two-thirds of the total distance. Westward-bound travellers began with an overnight train ride from New York's Pennsylvania Station to Columbus, Ohio. There, safely past the Alleghenies, they boarded the first plane. It flew at about 2,500 feet and at a top speed of 100 m.p.h., stopping in Indianapolis, St Louis, Kansas City, Wichita and Waynoka, Oklahoma. At Waynoka, passengers boarded yet another train to carry them past the Rockies to Clovis, New Mexico, where a plane was waiting to take them on to Los Angeles via Albuquerque, and Winslow and Kingman, Arizona. The whole undertaking was, by modern standards, drafty, uncomfortable and slow. Altogether the trip took forty-eight hours – though that was twenty-four hours faster than the fastest train. As a reward for their bravery, and for paying an extravagant $351.94 for a one-way ticket, every passenger was given a solid-gold fountain-pen from Tiffany's.[10]

Planes were unpressurized and unventilated. For many passengers, breathing at the higher altitudes was difficult. Often the rides were so rough that as many as three-quarters of the passengers became *airsick* (another new word of the age). Even the celebrated aviator Amelia Earhart was seen diving for the *airbag* (yet another).

For pilots there were additional difficulties. The Ford Tri-Motor, called with wary affection the *Tin Goose* by airline crews, was a challenging plane to fly. One of its more notable design quirks was that the instruments were mounted *outside* the cockpit, on one of the wing struts, and frequently became fogged once airborne.[11]

Almost from the start TAT was dogged with misfortune. Six weeks after services began, a Los Angeles-bound plane crashed in bad weather in New Mexico, killing all eight passengers. Four months later, a second plane crashed in California, killing sixteen. People began to joke that *TAT* stood for 'Take a Train'. In between these two crashes came another – that of Wall Street, when shares plummeted on Black Monday, 29 October, marking the start of the Great Depression. TAT's potential market all but dried up.

TAT lost almost $3 million in its first year and was taken over by Western Air Express, which itself evolved into Transcontinental and Western Air – TWA. (The name Trans World Airlines was the product of a later, more expansive age.) Within a year, it had slashed the one-way fare to just $160 (though there were no more free pens) and introduced the first *stewardess*. (Her name was Ellen Church and she chose the job title herself.)

On 21 October 1936, just nine years after Lindbergh's daring flight, Pan Am inaugurated regular passenger flights across the Pacific from San Francisco to Manila, with refuelling stops at Honolulu, Midway, Wake and Guam. Three years later, the airline also offered the first scheduled flights across the Atlantic, to Marseilles via the Azores and Lisbon, aboard its Flying Clippers, four-engine, twenty-two-passenger Boeing flying boats. Ocean flights inspired an ominous new term, *point of no return*, which first appeared in the *Journal of the Royal Aeronautics Society* in 1941, and quickly moved into the language in various figurative senses.

The logistics of Pan Am's Pacific operations were formidable. Wake and Midway were uninhabited, so everything needed on the islands, from pancake batter to spare engines, had to be shipped in. Three complete hotels were built in San Francisco, dismantled, shipped to Midway, Wake and Guam, and there reassembled. By September 1940, Pan Am had extended its Pacific operations, and was advertising flights to New Zealand in just four and a half days. If pressed for time, travellers could instead settle for Midway – 'an ideal choice for those who seek a restful, carefree South Seas atmosphere' – which could be reached in just two days. What the advertisements didn't say was that Midway was a desolate heap of sand and that the few lonely people stationed there spent most of their time shooting rats. In any case, a little over two years later, Midway became a rather less desirable holiday spot when it became the focus of the first great battle of the war in the Pacific.

Despite the risks and discomfort, the number of airline passengers soared. Between 1930 and 1940 the number of air travellers went from 417,000 to over 3 million.[12] World War II naturally acted as a brake on the growth of the airlines, but it also had the benefit of producing huge advances in long-distance aviation, which the airlines were quick to exploit with the return of peacetime. By 1947 Northwest Orient Airlines was boasting a flying time from Chicago to Shanghai of forty-one hours, and from New York to Tokyo of just thirty-nine hours, on its wondrous Stratocruisers, which offered every comfort. Because hotel stops were no longer necessary, they came equipped with beds known, almost inevitably, as *Skysleepers*. Six years later Pan Am introduced transatlantic jet services, and beds became a thing of the past as the faithful Stratocruiser gave way to the Boeing 707. Instead of names, planes increasingly had numbers – a not insignificant loss to the romance of air travel. (Having said that, Boeing had used numbers since its first commercial plane, the 247, which carried just ten passengers.)

Jet travel sprinkled the language with new words: *jet-hop* (1952), *jetport* (1953), *jet set* (1960), *jet lag* (1966), and *jet fatigue* and *jet syndrome* (alternative words for the more durable *jet lag*, both coined in 1968). Also in 1968 came an entirely new type of passenger plane named for, of all things, a circus elephant that had lived a century earlier. I refer of course to the *jumbo jet*.

The jumbo became a feature of travel when introduced into service by Pan Am on 21 January 1970. (The first flight, from Kennedy Airport to Heathrow, took off seven and a half hours late because of an engine problem.) The plane's formal name was the Boeing 747, so called because ever since the 707, Boeing's jetliners had been numbered in increments of ten in the order in which they came off the drawing-board. Interestingly, the feature that makes the jumbo instantly recognizable, its hump, came about because

Boeing feared the plane would not be a success. The feeling in the early 1960s when the plane was being designed was that supersonic jets were just around the corner and that they would quickly render jumbos obsolete as passenger carriers. The decision was taken therefore to design them so that they could easily be converted into freighters. By putting the cockpit out of the way up in a hump, freight could be loaded through the aircraft's nose.

That the most successful commercial aircraft in history should be called after a circus elephant is an obvious oddity. People are sometimes surprised to learn that Jumbo the elephant wasn't called that because he was big, but rather that big things are called *jumbo* because of him. In fact, when he was given his name – it is a shortening of *mumbo jumbo*, a term for a West African witch-doctor, which found a separate usefulness in English as a synonym for *gibberish* – he was just a baby, only recently arrived at London Zoo. No one had any idea that he would grow to become the largest animal ever kept in captivity.

Most Americans became familiar with Jumbo when P. T. Barnum, the circus impresario, bought the elephant from London Zoo in 1884, a scandal that outraged millions of Britons, and began exhibiting him all over America. Barnum's handbills depicted Jumbo as absolutely enormous – one showed a coach and horses racing through his legs, with plenty of clearance. In fact, Jumbo was nothing like that tall. Though indisputably the largest elephant ever measured, he was no more than eleven feet seven inches in height. (Barnum was seldom troubled by considerations of accuracy. One of his other lasting creations, the 'wild man from Borneo', was in fact a native of Paterson, New Jersey.)[13]

None the less, thanks to Barnum's tireless and inventive promotion, the name Jumbo became associated with largeness, and before long people were buying jumbo cigars, jumbo suitcases, jumbo portions of food, and eventually travelling on jumbo jets. Jumbo's American career was unfortunately short-lived. One night in September 1885, after Jumbo had been on the road for only about a year, he was being led to his specially built boxcar after an evening performance in St Thomas, Ontario, when an express train arrived unexpectedly and ploughed into him, with irreversible consequences for both elephant and train. It took 160 men to haul Jumbo off the tracks. Never one to miss a chance, Barnum had

Jumbo's skin and bones separately mounted, and thereafter was able to exhibit the world's largest elephant to two audiences at once, without any of the costs of care or feeding. He made far more money out of Jumbo dead than alive.

1946

New... from the tires down!

New as nuclear fission and twice as powerful – that's the new, newer, newest, all-new Bulgemobile!!

Welcome to the Space Age: The 1950s and Beyond

In 1959, in one of those delvings into the future that magazines found so satisfying at the time, *Newsweek* presented this confident scenario for the lucky housewife of 1979: 'Waking to cool 1970-style music from a tiny phonograph built into her pillow, the housewife yawned, flicked a bedside switch to turn on the electronic recipe-maker, then rose and stepped into her ultrasonic shower.'

Among the many things *Newsweek*'s soothsayer failed to foresee was that by 1979 the housewife would be an endangered species. What the world got instead were words like *workaholic, drive-by shootings, crack cocaine, AIDS, repetitive stress injury, gridlock* and *serial killer*. We're still waiting for the ultrasonic shower.

If *Newsweek* surveyed the future in 1959 from a somewhat optimistic perspective, we can hardly blame it. In the 1950s life in the United States was about as good as it gets. World War II had not only ended the Great Depression and decked America with honour, but had laid the groundwork for an economic boom almost beyond conceivable proportions. Where the war had reduced much of Europe and Asia to rubble, exhausted national exchequers, destroyed industries, and left millions homeless or even stateless, America was intact. Her twelve million returning servicemen and women came home to a country untouched by bombs. In 1945 the country had $26 billion worth of factories that had not existed when the war had started, all but $6 billion of which could be converted more or less immediately to the production of non-military goods: cars, televisions, refrigerators, tractors, processed foods, steel girders, you name it. And America, uniquely among nations in 1945, had money to spend – more than $143 billion in War and Savings Bonds alone.[1] The stage was set for the greatest consumer boom in history.

By the early 1950s most American homes had a telephone, television, refrigerator, washing machine and car – items that would not become standard possessions in Europe and Japan for years. With just 6 per cent of the earth's population and 7 per cent of its land area, the United States by the mid-1950s was producing and consuming 40 per cent of total global output – nearly as much as the rest of the world put together.[2] What is particularly notable is how self-contained America was in this period. Throughout the 1950s, imports amounted to no more than 3.2 per cent of *gross national product* (an Americanism coined in 1946 by the economist Simon Kuznets, who won a Nobel Prize for his efforts) and direct exports to no more than 4.7 per cent. America became the richest country in the world without particularly needing the rest of the world.

It did so partly by being massively more efficient than its competitors. General Motors, with 730,000 employees, made a profit in 1966 of $2.25 billion. To equal this figure it would have been necessary to combine the total profits of the forty largest firms in France, Britain and Germany, which together employed about 3.5 million people. American companies grew bigger than some countries. General Electric's sales in 1966 exceeded the gross national product of Greece. Ford was a bigger economic entity than Austria or Denmark. IBM generated more turnover than Sweden, Belgium or Spain. And General Motors was bigger than them all.

In short, life in post-war America was bounteous, secure and infinitely promising. The economy was running at full throttle, jobs and wages were plentiful, and stores bulged with consumer goods of a richness and diversity that other nations could simply gape at. America had truly become, in the words of John Kenneth Galbraith's 1958 book, *the affluent society*. Only two things clouded the horizon. One was the omnipresent possibility of nuclear war. The other was a phenomenon much closer to home and nearly as alarming. I refer to teenagers.

Teenagers, it hardly needs saying, had always been around, but only recently had they become a recognized presence. So little had they been noticed in the past that *teen-ager* had entered the language only as recently as 1941. (As an adjective *teen-age* had been around since the 1920s, but it wasn't much used.) But in the heady boom of the post-war years, America's teenagers made up for lost time. Between 1946 and 1960, when the population of the United States rose by about 40 per cent, the number of teenagers grew by 110 per cent as America underwent a massive *baby boom* (though that term would not be coined until 1978, in an article in the *New Yorker*).[3]

By the mid-1950s teenagers were not just everywhere, but disturbingly so. To their elders they seemed almost another species. They dressed sloppily, monopolized the phone and bathroom, listened to strange music, and used perplexingly unfamiliar terms – *wheels* for a car, *square, daddyo, far out, beat, cool* and *coolsville, what a drag, bad news, big deal, chick, neat* and *neato, gone, real gone*. They had a particularly rich supply of words for the culturally underendowed: *loser, creep, weirdo, square, drip*, and the much missed *nose-bleed*. Any stupid joke, particularly if voiced by one's immediate relatives, was met with a pained expression and a withering 'hardeeharhar.' They seemed to take pride in appearing demented and even created a word for the condition: *kooky* (probably modified from *cuckoo*). Movies like *Rebel Without a Cause* and *The Wild One*, and books like *On the Road* and *The Catcher in the Rye* showed America's youth to be disaffected, wilful, irrational and possibly dangerous. One prominent psychologist, Robert Linder of Baltimore, gravely announced in a series of lectures that young people 'were suffering from a form of collective mental illness',[4] suggesting that he may have had a touch of it himself.

An ominous new term, *juvenile delinquency*, began to fill news pages and excite comment. *The Blackboard Jungle*, a 1955 movie that dealt with delinquency and other manifestations of youthful angst, was thought so sensational that Clare Booth Luce, America's ambassador to Italy, led a campaign to forbid its being shown abroad lest people get the wrong impression about America. Apparently she was not worried that they might instead conclude that America no longer believed in freedom of expression. The movie's theme tune, 'Rock Around the Clock', was for most non-teenagers their first experience of the music known as *rock 'n' roll*, a term popularized by a Cleveland disc jockey named Alan Freed, who had studied classical trombone before taking to the airwaves, where he introduced his listeners to the music of Chuck Berry, Fats Domino and other such exotics. He first began referring to the music as *rock 'n' roll* in 1951, though among black Americans the expression was older, having originally been applied to sex and later to dancing.

Above all, what separated America's teenagers of the 1950s from previous generations was that they were rich. By mid-decade, as one historian has noted, 'America's 16.5 million teens were buying some 40 per cent of all radios, records and cameras, more than half the movie tickets, and even 9 per cent of all new cars. Altogether they were worth over $10 billion a year to the economy.'[5]

Much of their wealth came from, and often returned to, another phenomenon of the age, the hamburger joint, which provided employment for thousands of teenagers and a haunt for most of the rest. Though the hamburger had been part of the American diet for half a century, it underwent a kind of apotheosis in the 1950s. As late as 1950, pork was still the most widely eaten meat in America, and by a considerable margin, but over the next two decades the situation was reversed. By 1970 Americans were eating twice as much beef as pork, nearly a hundred pounds of it a year, and half of that in the form of hamburgers. One company more than any other was responsible for this massive change in dietary habits: McDonald's.

The story as conveyed by the company is well known. A salesman of Multimixers named Ray Kroc became curious as to why a small hamburger stand on the edge of the desert in San Bernardino, California, would need eight Multimixers – enough to make forty milk-shakes at a time, more than any other restaurant in America could possibly want to make – and decided to fly out and have a look. The restaurant he found, run by the brothers Maurice and Richard McDonald, was small, only 600 square feet, but the burgers were tasty, the fries crisp, the shakes unusually thick, and it was unquestionably popular with the locals. Kroc at this time was fifty-two years old, an age when most men would be thinking of slowing down, but he saw an opportunity here. He bought the McDonald's name and began building an empire. The implication has always been that the original McDonald's was an obscure, rinky-dink operation in the middle of nowhere, and that it was only the towering genius of Ray Kroc that made it into the streamlined, efficient, golden-arched institution that we know and love today. It wasn't entirely like that.

By 1954, when Kroc came along, the McDonald brothers were already legendary, at least in the trade. *American Restaurant* magazine had done a cover story on them in 1952, and they were constantly being visited by people who wanted to see how they generated so much turnover from so little space. With sales of over $350,000 a year (all of it going through one busy cash register) and profits above $100,000, McDonald's was one of the most successful restaurants in America. In his autobiography, Kroc makes it sound as if the McDonald brothers had never thought of franchising until he came along. In fact, by the time he visited them they had a dozen franchised operations going.

Almost everything later associated with the McDonald's chain was invented or perfected by the brothers, from the method of making French fries to the practice of trumpeting the number of hamburgers sold. As early as 1950, they had a sign outside announcing 'Over 1 Million Sold'. They even came up with the design of a sloping roof, red and white tiled walls and integral golden arches – not for the San Bernardino outlet but for their first franchise operation, which opened in Phoenix in 1952, two years before Kroc came along.

The McDonalds were, in short, the true heroes of the fast-food revolution, and by any measure they were remarkable men. They had moved to California from New Hampshire (or possibly Vermont; sources conflict) during the depression years, and opened their first drive-in restaurant in 1937 near Pasadena. It didn't sell hamburgers. Then in 1940 they opened a new establishment at Fourteenth and E Streets, at the end of Route 66, in San Bernardino in a snug octagonal structure. It was a conventional hamburger stand, and it did reasonably well.

In 1948, however, the brothers were seized with a strange vision. They closed the business for three months, fired the twenty carhops, got rid of all the china and silverware, and reopened with a new, entirely novel idea: that the customer would have to come to a window to collect the food rather than have it brought to the car.

They cut the menu to just seven items – hamburgers, cheeseburgers, pie, crisps, coffee, milk and pop. Customers no longer specified what they wanted on their hamburgers but received them with ketchup, mustard, onions and pickle. The hamburgers were made smaller – just ten to a pound – but the price was halved to fifteen cents each.

The change was a flop. Business fell by 80 per cent. The teenagers on whom they had relied went elsewhere. Gradually, however, a new type of clientele developed, the family, particularly after they added French fries and milk shakes to the menu, and even more particularly when customers realized that the food was great and that you could feed a whole family for a few dollars. Before long McDonald's had almost more business than it could handle.

As volume grew, the brothers constantly refined the process to make the production of food more streamlined and efficient. With a local machine-shop owner named Ed Toman they invented almost everything connected with the production of fast food, from dispensers that pump out a precise dollop of ketchup or mustard to the Lazy Susans on which twenty-four hamburger buns can be speedily dressed. They introduced the idea of specialization – one person who did nothing but cook hamburgers, another who made shakes, another to dress the buns, and so on – and developed the now universal practice of having the food prepared and waiting so that customers could place an order and immediately collect it.

The parallels between the McDonald brothers and Wright brothers are striking. Like the Wrights, the McDonald brothers never married and lived together in the same house. Like the Wrights, they had no special interest in wealth and fame. (The McDonalds' one indulgence was to buy a pair of new Cadillacs every year on the day that the new models came out.) Both sets of brothers were single-mindedly devoted to achieving perfection in their chosen sphere, and both sets created something from which others would derive greater credit and fame. The McDonald brothers had just one distinction that set them apart from the Wrights. They dreaded flying, which presented a problem in keeping tabs on their expanding empire. So when Ray Kroc came along and offered to form a partnership in which he would look after the franchising side of the operation, they jumped at his offer.

Kroc was, it must be said, a consummate seller of franchises. By 1961, the year he bought the brothers out for $2.7 million, there were two hundred McDonald's restaurants, and the company was on its way to becoming a national institution. Kroc achieved this success in large part by making sure that the formula of the original San Bernardino McDonald's was followed everywhere with the most exacting fidelity. His obsession with detail became legendary. He dictated that McDonald's burgers must be exactly 3.875 inches across, weigh 1.6 ounces and contain precisely 19 per cent fat. Big Mac buns should have an average of 178 sesame seeds. He even specified, after much experimentation, how much wax should be on the wax paper that separated one hamburger patty from another.

Such obsessiveness made McDonald's a success, but it also led to the creation of a culture that was dazzlingly unsympathetic to innovation. As he recounted in his autobiography, when a team of his most trusted executives suggested the idea of miniature outlets called MiniMacs, Kroc was 'so damned mad I was ready to turn my office into a batting cage and let those three guys have it with my cane'.[6] Their failing, he explained, was to think small. One could be excused for concluding that their failure was to think at all.

As an empire builder Kroc had no peer, but as a dietary innovator his gifts were modest. As one of his biographers has noted: 'Every food product he thought of introducing – and the list is long – bombed in the marketplace.'[7] In consequence McDonald's menu is essentially a continuing testament to the catering skills of the founding brothers. The relatively few foods that have been added to the menu since 1954 have usually been invented by franchisees, not by headquarters staff, and have often drawn liberal inspiration from the creations of competing chains. The *Big Mac*, introduced nationwide in 1968, was invented and named by a franchisee in Pittsburgh named Jim Delligatti, though it was certainly similar to, if not actually modelled on, a two-patty, triple-deck sandwich created by the Big Boy chain in California fourteen years earlier. The *Filet-O-Fish* was thought up by a franchisee in a Catholic section of Cincinnati who wanted something to offer his customers on Fridays, but essentially it is just a large fishfinger in a bun. The *Egg McMuffin*, originally called the *Fast Break Breakfast*, came when a franchisee in Santa Barbara developed the prototype, but again it echoed a rival's product, an eggs Benedict breakfast roll from the Jack-in-the-Box chain.

None the less, the McDonald's formula has clearly worked. In an average year, all but 4 per cent of American consumers will visit a McDonald's at least once. Thirty-two per cent of all hamburgers, 26 per cent of all French fries, 5 per cent of all Coca-Cola, and nearly a fifth of all meals taken in a public place are eaten at a McDonald's. McDonald's buys more beef and potatoes and trains more people than any other organization, the US Army included. It is the world's largest owner of real estate. In 1994 it had 13,000 restaurants in 68 countries serving 25 million customers daily.[8] So international a commodity has the Big Mac become that since 1986 *The Economist* magazine has used the cost of a Big Mac in various world cities as a more or less serious basis for an index comparing the relative value of their currencies.

McDonald's, like so much else of modern American life, from the supermarket to the shopping mall, was a creature of the two great phenomena of the post-war years: the car and the suburbs. Together they transformed the way Americans live.

Suburbs were hardly new in the 1950s. The word dates from as far back as 1325, and both *suburbia* and *suburbanite* have been current since the 1890s. Before the American Revolution most cities had their suburbs – places like Harlem, New York, and Medford, Massachusetts – but they weren't dormitory communities in the modern sense. Until about 1850, a suburb was defined as 'an undifferentiated zone outside the city limits'.[9] They were largely self-contained communities, and often the sites of noxious enterprises that were ill suited to the confined spaces of cities.

Of necessity, most people in colonial America lived densely packed together in cities – in 1715 Boston's 15,000 inhabitants shared just 700 acres of land – and went almost everywhere on foot. Walking was such an unquestioned feature of everyday life that until 1791, when William Wordsworth coined the term *pedestrian*, there was no special word to describe someone on foot. (Interestingly, *pedestrian* in the sense of dull or unimaginative is significantly older, having been coined in 1716.)

Not until the development of the steam passenger ferry in the 1830s did the possibility of retiring at night to a home in a separate (if invariably close by) community begin to take root. The passenger ferry transformed a few places like Tarrytown, Stony Point, and Brooklyn, New York, but the expense, limited carrying capacity and slow speed of ferries kept their overall effect slight. The history of suburban living in America really begins with the railways. Starting with Naperville, Illinois, in 1857, railway suburbs began to pop up everywhere. Orange and Secaucus, New Jersey, Oak Park, Lake Forest and Evanston, Illinois, Scarsdale, New York, Darien and Fairfield, Connecticut – these and hundreds of other communities were either created or wholly transformed by the railways. Even California, a state not normally associated with railways, spawned a number of such communities, notably San Rafael and Pomona.[10] As railway suburbs grew, two new words entered the language, *commute* and *commuter,* both Americanisms and both first recorded in 1865.[11]

The growing popularity of the railway suburbs inspired an entirely new type of community: the model suburb. As the name suggests, model suburbs were purpose-built communities, primarily for the well-to-do. Where railway suburbs had grown willy-nilly, often absorbing existing communities, the model suburbs were built from scratch, and offered not just handsome residential streets, but everything else their well-heeled citizens could require: parks, schools, shopping districts and eventually country clubs. (The Country Club, built in the Boston suburb of Brookline in 1867, appears to have provided both the name and the model for this most suburban of social centres.) Among the more venerable of model suburbs are Beverly Hills, California, Shaker Heights, Ohio, and Forest Hills, New York.

The development of the streetcar in the closing years of the nineteenth century provided a new boost and a measure of democratization to suburban living with the rise of streetcar suburbs, which pushed cities further into the countryside and offered the prospect of fresh air, space and escape from the urban hurly-burly for millions of office and factory workers and their families.

Even taken together all these early types of suburbs never added up to more than a peripheral feature of American life. Two factors conspired in the 1940s to make the suburbanization of the country complete. The first was the need for cheap, instant housing immediately after the war. The second was the rise of the automobile in the early 1950s.

In 1945 America needed, more or less immediately, five million additional houses as war-deferred marriages were consummated and millions of young couples settled down to start a family. The simplest and cheapest solution was for a developer to buy up a tract of countryside within commuting distance of a city and fill it with hundreds – sometimes thousands – of often identical starter homes. The master of the art was Abraham Levitt, who began scattering the eastern states with his Levittowns in 1947. By making every home identical and employing assembly-line construction techniques, Levitt could offer houses at remarkably low cost. At a time when the average house cost $10,000, Levitt homes sold for just $7,900, or $65 a month, with no down payment, *and* they came equipped with major appliances.

Soon housing developments were going up along the edges of every city. By 1950, one-quarter of Americans lived in suburbs. Ten years later the proportion had risen to one-third. Today over half of Americans live in suburbs – more than in cities, farms and rural communities combined.

As people flocked to the suburbs, jobs followed. Between 1960 and 1990, five of every six jobs created in America's thirty-five biggest metropolitan areas were in the suburbs. Instead of pouring into the cities by day to work, millions of Americans hardly went into the cities at all. In the thirty years from 1960, the number of people who commuted across county lines – in effect, lived in one suburb and worked in another – tripled to over 27 million.[12] The suburbs had taken over.

As early as 1955, the phenomenon was noticed by the writer A.C. Spectorsky, who coined the term *exurbia* for this new kind of community that was emotionally and economically independent from the metropolis that had spawned it, but it was not until 1991, when a *Washington Post* reporter named Joel Garreau wrote a book called *Edge City*, that this vast transition in living patterns gained widespread notice.

To qualify as an edge city by Garreau's definition, a community must have 5 million square feet of office space, 600,000 square feet of shopping, and more people working there than living there. America now has more than 200 edge cities. Los Angeles and New

York have about two dozen each. Almost all have been created since 1960, and almost always they are soulless, impersonal places, unfocused collections of shopping malls and office complexes that are ruthlessly unsympathetic to non-motorists. Many have no pavements or pedestrian crossings, and only rarely do they offer any but the most skeletal public transport links to the nearby metropolis, effectively denying job opportunities to many of those left behind in the declining inner cities. About one-third of all Americans now live in edge cities, and up to two-thirds of Americans work in them.[13] They are substantial places, and yet most people outside their immediate areas have never heard of them. How many Americans, I wonder, could go to a map and point to even the general location of Walnut Creek, Rancho Cucamonga, Glendale, Westport Plaza, Mesquite or Plano? Anonymous or not, they are the wave of the future. In 1993, nineteen of the twenty-five fastest-growing communities in the United States were edge cities.

If affordable housing was the first thing most returning GIs wanted in 1945, then without question a car was the second. As late as 1950 some 40 per cent of American households still did not have a car, but that would change dramatically in the next decade as the automobile became not just a convenience of modern life but, for millions, a necessity. In the period 1950–80, America's population rose by 50 per cent, but the number of cars quadrupled, until the number of cars far exceeded the number of households (because of two-or-more-car families).[14]

In keeping with America's confident new age of materialism, cars grew bigger, flashier and more powerful in the post-war years. The man behind it all was one Harley J. Earl, a long-time General Motors designer whose fascination with the Lockheed P-38 Lightning fighter aircraft of World War II led him to put outsize tail fins on the 1948 Cadillac. The next year, racy portholes called *venti-ports* appeared on Buicks. The year after that Studebaker produced the sleek, bullet-nosed Champion DXL, which actually *looked* like a plane, and the race was on. By the mid-1950s every car maker was turning out huge, flashy, grinning-grilled, multi-toned, chrome-heavy, monstrously tail-finned road beasts that were the hallmark of the decade – cars that looked, in the words of one observer, as if they should light up and play. The style was called the *Forward Look*.

Cars were given names that suggested that these things were not just powerful, but barely under control – *Firedome V8, Thunderbird, Tempest, Comet, Fury, Charger* – and they came with features that promised a heady mix of elegance, comfort and fingertip control. Impressive-sounding features had been part of the car salesman's armoury for some time – as early as 1940 De Soto was boasting a model with 'Fluid Drive Simplimatic Transmission' – but it was really the development of powerful V-8 engines, a direct spinoff of World War II technology, that allowed car makers to provide lots of gadgetry and gave the marketing people the scope to scramble for technological hyperbole. Some actively suggested aeronautic qualities, like the 1955 Buick which came with *RSVP* (short for 'Really Sensational Variable Pitch') *propeller blades*. As the ads explained, these changed their pitch 'like the propellers on an air liner, and what that does to getaway from a standing start – or for a safety-surge when it's needed out on the highway – is something you can only believe from firsthand experience'. Others, like the Thunderbird with its *Trigger-Torque Power* and *Speed-Trigger Fordomatic Transmission*, sounded as if they might have the capacity to shoot down rival motorists. The next year Thunderbird added *Cruise-O-Matic Transmission*, presumably so that the driver could keep both hands on the gun.

By 1956 cars had features that all but promised lift-off. Chryslers came with *PowerFlite Range-Selector, Torque-Flight Transmission, Torsion-Aire Suspension* and *Super-Scenic Windshield*. The Packard offered *New Torsion-Level Ride* and *Twin Ultramatic Transmission*, while the Chevrolet Bel-Air had a hold-on-to-your-hats feature called a *Triple-Turbine TurboGlide*. Mercury, misreading the market, could offer nothing zippier than *Dream-Car Design* and *Seat-O-Matic Dial* that remembered the driver's favoured position, and paid heavily for its technological timidity with lost sales.

The height of this techno-excess came in 1957 when Packard produced a 145-horsepower Super Eight model, which came equipped with everything but a stewardess. The vaunted features included *Prest-O-Justment Seats, Flite-Glo Dials, Comfort-Aire Ventilation, Console-Key Instrument Panel* and *Push-Button*

Control Wrinkle-Resistant RoboTop Convertible Roof. Unfortunately it drove like a tank. Five years later, Packard was out of business.

The irony in this is that virtually none of the modern improvements to cars, such as disc brakes, fuel injection, front-wheel drive, torsion bars and the like, were invented in America. Detroit was more concerned with gloss and zip than with genuine research and development, and within twenty years it would be paying for this lapse dearly.[15]

In 1955, into the midst of this battlefield of technological hyperbole and aerodynamic styling, came a car so ineptly named, so clumsily styled, so lacking in panache that it remains almost forty years later a synonym for commercial catastrophe. I refer, of course, to the wondrous Edsel.

It is hard to believe now what high hopes Ford, its dealers and most of America had for this car when it was announced to the world. After the Ford Company's huge success during its first two decades, it began to falter dangerously, largely because of Henry Ford's extreme reluctance to offer six-cylinder engines or models with a few curves and a dash of styling. It fell behind not only General Motors, but even Walter Chrysler's Plymouth. By the 1950s Ford desperately needed a success. A new mid-sized car seemed the best bet. General Motors had not introduced one since the La Salle in 1927 and Chrysler not since the Plymouth in 1928. Ford's most recent effort at a breakthrough vehicle had been the Mercury way back in 1938.[16] The time was right for a new, world-beating car. In 1952 Ford began work on a secret project it called the *E car*.

Huge care was taken with choosing a name. Ford's advertising agency, Foote, Cone and Belding, drew up a list of 18,000 suggestions, and Ford staff added a further 2,500. The poet Marianne Moore was commissioned to come up with a list of names, and offered such memorable, if unusable, suggestions as the *Mongoose Civique*, the *Utopian Turtletop*, the *Pluma Piluma*, the *Pastelogram*, the *Resilient Bullet*, the *Varsity Stroke* and the *Andante con Moto*.

All of these were carefully whittled down to a short-list of sixteen names. On 8 November 1956 an executive committee met to make the final choice. After much discussion it reduced the list to four favoured names: *Corsair, Citation, Ranger* and *Pacer*. Then, for reasons that are much disputed (largely because no one wished afterwards to be actively associated with the choice) the panel members opted for a name not on the list: *Edsel*.

It was named for Edsel Ford, Henry and Clara Ford's only child, who in turn had been named for Henry Ford's best friend. The name had been considered once before, but had been discarded when consumer research showed that almost everyone thought it sounded like the name of a tractor or plough.

Having signally botched the name, the company went on to botch the design and production of the car. The chief stylist of the Edsel was Roy A. Brown, jun. By all accounts Brown's initial design was a winner,* but excessive tampering – in particular the imposition of a grille that has been variously likened to a horse collar or toilet seat – doomed it. There was also the consideration that the Edsel was not very well made. The publicity department's plan was to have seventy-five automotive writers drive identical green and turquoise Edsel Paces from Detroit to their home-town dealers. But when the first Edsels rolled off the assembly line they were so riddled with faults that Ford had to spend an average of $10,000 apiece – twice the cost of the car – getting them road-worthy. Even then it managed to have just sixty-eight cars ready by launch day.[17] A further setback occurred when the Edsel made its public début on a live national television special and wouldn't start.

Edsel had the most expensive advertising promotion of any product up to that time, but the company could hardly give the cars away.[18] Two years, two months, $450 million and 110,847 Edsels later, Ford pulled the plug, and the Edsel became part of history.

But the automobile as a component of American life went from strength to strength. By 1963 one-sixth of all American businesses were directly connected with the car in one way or another.[19] The production of cars consumed 20 per cent of American steel, 30 per cent of glass and over 60 per cent of the nation's rubber.[20] By the 1970s, 94.7 per cent of American commuters travelled to work by car. About half had no access to any form of public transportation. They had to drive to work whether they wanted to or not. Most in

---

* Brown had gained his reputation in the company by designing a stunning concept car called the *Lincoln Futura*. It never went into production, but it did eventually find greater glory – as television's Batmobile.

fact wanted to. Today the car has become such an integral part of American life that the *maximum* distance the average American is prepared to walk without getting into a car is just six hundred feet.

Despite the nation's attachment to the car, relatively few motoring terms have entered the general lexicon in the post-war years. Among the few: *gridlock*, coined in 1971 but not in general usage until about 1980; *fast lane* in a metaphorical sense ('life in the fast lane') in 1978; *drive-by shooting* in 1985; and *jump start* in a metaphorical sense ('jump start the economy') as recently as 1988. And that is about it.

What increasingly changed were the types of cars Americans drove. Until the early 1970s, with the exception of the Volkswagen Beetle and a few incidental European sports cars, American cars were overwhelmingly American. (In 1954, for instance, of the 7.2 million new cars sold in America, only 50,000, well under 1 per cent, were imports.) But then things changed as Japanese manufacturers entered the market. *Made in Japan*, which in the 1950s had been a joke term synonymous with shoddiness, took on an ominous sense of reliability and efficiency. Japanese car makers that few Americans had heard of in 1970 were by 1975 household names.*

American car makers, so invincible only a decade before, suddenly seemed worryingly inept. They continued churning out heavy, often unreliable, *gas-guzzlers* (an Americanism of 1969) in overstaffed factories that were massively uncompetitive compared with the lean production techniques of the Japanese. By 1992 the American car industry was losing $700 million a month. Even those who patriotically tried to *buy American* (an expression that gained widespread currency in the late 1970s) often couldn't. Of the $20,000 purchase price of a Pontiac Le Mans in 1991, $6,000 went to South Korea, $3,500 to Japan, and between $100 and $1,500 each to suppliers in Germany, Taiwan, Singapore, Britain,

---

* In case you have ever wondered, the following are the derivations of the more popular Japanese car names: *Honda,* named for the company's founder, Soichiro Honda; *Isuzu,* named for the Isuzu River; *Mitsubishi,* Japanese for 'three stones,' which feature on the family crest of the founder; *Nissan,* Japanese for 'Japan Industry'; *Suzuki,* named for the founder, Suzuki Michio; *Toyota,* named for the founder, Sakicki Toyoda, and not, as many stories have it, because the early models looked like 'toy autos'.[22]

Ireland and Barbados.[22] By 1988 imports, primarily of cars but also of cameras, televisions, radios and much else in which America had once been self-sufficient, accounted for over 13 per cent of America's gross national product, and the country's annual trade balance had grown to $150 billion – about $600 for every man, woman and child in the country.

By 1990 America's sense of declining economic prowess generated a volume of disquiet that sometimes verged on the irrational. When a professor of economics at Yale polled his students as to which they would prefer, a situation in which America had 1 per cent economic growth while Japan experienced 1.5 per cent growth, or one in which America suffered a 1 per cent downturn but Japan's fell by 1.5 per cent, the majority voted for the latter. They preferred America to be poorer if Japan were poorer still, rather than a situation in which both became more prosperous.

Years before America suffered the indignity of watching its industrial advantage eroded, it experienced a no less alarming blow to its technological prestige. On 26 August 1957 the nation was shaken to the core to learn that the Soviet Union had successfully launched a satellite called *Sputnik* (meaning 'fellow earth traveller'). Never mind that Sputnik was only about the size of a beachball and that it couldn't do anything except reflect light. It was the first earthbound object hurled into space. Editorial writers, in a frenzy of anxiety, searched for a scapegoat and mostly blamed the education system (a plaint that would be continually refined and applied to other perceived national failings ever after). Four months later America rushed to meet the challenge with the launch of its own Vanguard satellite.[23] Unfortunately the satellite rose only a few feet off the launchpad, tipped over and burst into flames. It became known, almost inevitably, as the *Kaputnik*. A little over three years later, America suffered further humiliation when the Soviets launched a spaceship, *Vostok*, bearing the cosmonaut Yuri Gagarin, which made a single orbit of Earth and returned safely. A week later, Cuban exiles, with American backing, launched the disastrous Bay of Pigs invasion of Cuba, and were routed. Never had America's stock sunk so low in the world.

The country's response was not entirely unlike that of the Yale economics students mentioned above. Without any idea of what the payback might be other than in glory, the country embarked on the most expensive scientific enterprise ever undertaken on the planet with the single ultimate goal of landing a man on the moon before the Soviet Union did. On 20 July 1969 the goal was achieved when Neil Armstrong stepped from his Apollo 11 spacecraft and became the first person to walk on the moon. America was back on top.

The heady first decade of the space programme created, or significantly rejuvenated, a clutch of words, among them *re-entry, lift-off, blast-off, mission control, A-OK, thrust, launchpad, orbit, gantry, glitch* (first recorded outside a Yiddish context when spoken by John Glenn in 1966), and *astronaut*. What is perhaps most interesting is how many space terms predate the space age, thanks for the most part to the world's abiding love for science fiction. Among the words that took flight long before any space traveller did we find *astronaut* (1880), *space ship* (1894), *space suit* (1924), *rocket ship* (1928), *star ship* (1934), *space station* (1936), *blast-off* (1937) and *spaceman* (1942).[24]

The space race did have many technological spinoffs, not least in the development of communications satellites and even more particularly in the advance of computing. So universal have computers become in offices, banks, stores and homes that it is easy to forget just what a recent development they are. Though the word was coined in 1872, for a type of adding machine, as late as 1956 there were no more than two dozen computers in the nation. In the following two decades their numbers multiplied vastly, but even in 1976, the year Apple Computer was founded, there were still perhaps no more than 50,000 computers in the world. A decade later, that many were being built every day.[25]

One of the first popular investigations into computers appeared in March 1961 when *Life* magazine ran an article, 'The Machines Are Taking Over', about the new phenomenon. In a tone of chirpy awe, the author noted how a room-sized 'robot' (a word he used throughout the story) had transformed the efficiency of the Braun Brothers sausage factory in Troy, Ohio. When fed a stack of punch cards telling it what cuts of meat were available, this device 'hummed softly, its lights flickered, and it riffled the deck of cards over and over again'. After just thirty-six minutes of technological pondering, it spewed out the optimum recipe for making bologna: '24 pounds of cow meat, 24 of beef, 103 of beef cheeks, 150 of beef plate, 30 of neck bone meat, 24 of picnics, 65 of neck trimmings, 10 of trim conversion, 20 of rework from previous batches'. That was *all* it did. It couldn't handle accounts or billing, or monitor the company's heating and electricity. Thirty-six minutes of intense thinking about beef cheek and neck trimmings, and it retired exhausted till the next day.

It doesn't seem a terribly impressive performance now, but just five years earlier, Braun Brothers would have needed several million dollars and a separate building to house the computer power necessary to calculate the best use of beef plate, trim conversion and the other delectable constituents of a well-made bologna. At just $50,000, the Braun Brothers computer was a snip.

The same article went on to note how a computer in Glendale, California, was programmed with the 500 words most frequently used by Beatnik poets and told to create its own poems. Typical of the genre was 'Auto-Beatnik Poem No. 41: Insects', which included these lines:

> All children are small and crusty
> And all pale, blind, humble waters are cleaning,
> A insect, dumb and torrid, comes of the daddyo
> How is a insect into this fur?

The reporter noted that when several of these poems were read to an unsuspecting audience at a Los Angeles coffee-house, many listeners 'became quite stirred up with admiration'.[26]

Though the computer is a comparatively recent entrant into daily life, some of the terminology associated with it goes back half a century or so. *Computer bugs* dates from the 1940s. There is, it appears, a literal explanation behind the term. In 1945 a huge US Navy computer broke down. Its operators searched in mystification for a cause until they found a moth crushed between the contact points of an electrical relay switch. After that whenever a computer was down, it was said to need *debugging*.[27] *Bit* (a contraction of *b*inary dig*it*) was coined at about the same time, though its offspring, *byte* (eight bits for the technically unaware), dates only from 1964, and was apparently chosen arbitrarily.[28]

Equally arbitrary is the *Winchester disk drive* (first recorded in print in 1973). It doesn't commemorate any person or place, but was simply the code-name under which IBM developed the technology.

Computers have spawned many technical languages – *Assembler, Pascal, C, C++, OLE, Lisp, Ada, Fortran, Cobol, Algol, Oberon*, and others almost without number – and these in turn have generated a huge vocabulary. But for the lay-person searching for linguistic excitement the computer world is pretty much a dead planet. Though computer terminology runs to many thousands of words, the great bulk coined in the past twenty years, probably more than half are merely elaborations on already existing words (*port, format, file, copy, array*), and those that are original to the field are almost always dully and self-evidently descriptive of their function (*microprocessor, random access memory, disk driver, database*). A slight exception is the operating system known as *DOS*. It originated as *Q-DOS* (a play on *kudos*), and stood, rather daringly, for *Quick and Dirty Operating System*. When Microsoft bought the firm in 1981, it changed the name to the more staid *MS-DOS*, for *Microsoft Disk Operating System*.[29] That is about as lively a computer story as you will find.

Among the few computer terms that have seeped into general usage are *word processor* and *word processing* (both coined in 1970 but not current outside technical journals before 1977), *hacker* (1975, presumably from the image of one hacking through a thicket of passwords, as with a machete), *hardware* and *software* (coined in the mid-1960s, in general usage by the mid-1970s), and *computer virus* (coined by an American researcher named Fred Cohen in 1984).

Thanks largely to the computer and other new technologies, the English language is growing by up to 20,000 words a year.[30] Though most of these new terms are scientific, technical or of otherwise specialized application, many hundreds flow into the main body of English each year. The third edition of the *American Heritage Dictionary*, published in 1992, contained 10,000 words, about 5 per cent of the total, that had not existed twenty years before. The second edition of the *Random House* unabridged dictionary, published in 1987, underwent an even more extensive change, with 50,000 new words and 210,000 of its 315,000 entries revised or updated. Such is the accumulation of new formations that 'dictionaries are going to have to come out every six to eight years rather than every ten to keep up with the [new] vocabulary', an editor of the *AHD* said in an interview.[31]

Among the many hundreds of words that have entered English in the last decade or so, one starkly stands out: *AIDS*. Short for *Acquired Immune Deficiency Syndrome*, it was coined in 1982, but didn't enter the general consciousness until about 1985. Previously it had been called *GRID*, for *Gay-Related Immune Deficiency*, but the name was changed – and, it must be said, the world's attention perked up – after it was found to be infecting heterosexuals, particularly haemophiliacs. The name for the active agent in AIDS, the *Human Immunodeficiency Virus*, or *HIV*, was coined in May 1986 by a committee of virologists after a year in which the virus had gone by two names: *LAV* and *HTLV3*.

Before we leave the space age, one small rhetorical curiosity, which oddly failed to attract much attention at the time, needs mentioning. I refer to the utterance of Neil Armstrong when he became the first person to set foot on the moon. As millions of people watched, Armstrong sombrely announced: 'That's one small step for man, one giant leap for mankind.' The sentence was reprinted in thousands of headlines the next morning, but in the excitement of his achievement no one seems to have noticed the tautology of it. According to the historian Richard Hanser, Armstrong was astonished and dismayed upon his return to his native planet to find that he had been misquoted everywhere. What he had said was, 'That's one small step for *a* man, one giant leap for mankind.' The indefinite article had been lost in transmission.[32]

A more thorny issue is whether, in light of developments of recent years, he should have engaged in such manifestly gender-biased speech. But that is another chapter.

American English Today

I

Few issues in America have soaked up more ink and excited more passion in recent years than the debate over education standards. Falling test scores, a perceived decline in literacy, and the frankly abysmal performance of American students compared with those of other nations, have all generated much journalistic hand-wringing.

Troubling indicators of educational failure are not hard to find. In a comparison of proficiency in mathematics among sixth formers from fifteen nations, the United States came twelfth in geometry and calculus and fourteenth in advanced algebra. (Hong Kong came first and Japan second in all three. England and Wales came third or fourth in all three.) In a similar comparison, American thirteen-year-olds did slightly better, though only slightly. Set against students from nineteen other countries, the US pupils came sixteenth in geometry, twelfth in algebra and tenth in arithmetic.[1] The conclusion commonly drawn from this is that poor standards of education and economic decline go hand in hand. In 1992 Yoshio Sakurachi, the speaker of Japan's lower house of Parliament, stirred a brief but vocal controversy when he attributed America's poor economic performance to illiteracy among its workforce. One-third of American workers, Sakurachi declared, could not read. Many Americans were outraged by his utterances, not so much because they were inaccurate as because a Japanese had had the impertinence to express them.

In fact, no one knows how many Americans are illiterate.

Defining literacy is a complicated matter. The US Department of Education divides literacy into three categories – prose literacy (as in books and newspapers), document literacy (as on order forms and tax returns) and quantitative literacy (involving the sort of mathematical skills necessary to calculate a 15 per cent tip, say) – and further breaks down each category into four levels, thus giving Americans twelve quite distinct ways in which to be literate or not. At the simplest level of prose literacy, according to the department's criteria, a person should be able to write a simple declarative sentence describing the kind of job he or she wants. On this basis, 96.1 per cent of adult Americans are literate – a creditable, if not especially outstanding, performance compared with other nations. But at a slightly more demanding level of prose literacy – being able to read a leading article in a newspaper and briefly summarize its contents – the level of reading competence in America falls to 78.9 per cent. Put another way, slightly more than one American adult in five cannot read a newspaper effectively.[2]

By even the most conservative estimates, America has at least twenty million adults who cannot read well enough to understand the instructions on a medicine bottle or add and subtract with sufficient competence to tally a cheque-book.[3] Probably the figure is much worse. Noting a 'national tendency to graduate anyone who occupies a desk long enough', the journalist Jonathan Maslow quotes a woman in Jackson, Mississippi, who told him: 'I went through twelve years of school and two years of community college without ever learning to read, and passed with flying colours.'[4]

Signs of a national failure to educate students to even a basic level are not hard to find. In Mississippi, almost half of the adults do not have a high school diploma. One-third of the people in Kentucky aged twenty-five or older are functionally illiterate.[5] Throughout the country, large employers like Ford, Motorola and IBM routinely spend huge sums teaching their workers the basic skills that schools failed to impart. Just among private employers, the market for remedial reading textbooks is worth $750 million a year[6] – good news for publishers, but hardly a source of pride for anyone else.

Any number of culprits have been cited for this national

embarrassment. Some have blamed the shortness of American school days (six hours on average) and school years (175 to 180 days – only slightly shorter than England and Wales with 190).[7] Others blame the states for neglecting the central role of education. In contrast to most other countries, public education is not the preserve of central government in the US. Standards of attainment and levels of funding are set by each state, and many, particularly in the deep South, have historically shown a less than wholehearted commitment to raising the levels of either. Until as recently as 1982 in Mississippi school attendance was not even mandatory. Previously each year up to six thousand children in Mississippi did not bother to start school.[8]

Still others attribute the decline in learning to a lack of encouragement and attention at home, as parents increasingly have become absent through work or divorce. The economist Victor Fuchs has calculated that parents in white households spend on average ten fewer hours per week with their children than they did in 1960. In black homes the decline has been even greater at twelve hours.[9]

Almost everyone cites television as a primary or secondary factor. Without question, American children watch a lot of TV. The average child aged two or older spends four hours a day, about a quarter of his or her waking time, plugged to the box. By the time they are eighteen, American children have been exposed to no fewer than 350,000 commercials.[10]

Alarmed by such figures, Congress in 1990 introduced the Children's Television Act, mandating that stations show programmes with some educational value. The result, alas, was not better programming but more creative programme descriptions. One station described *GI Joe* as 'a pedagogical tool' that 'promoted social consciousness' and familiarized children with 'the dangers of mass destruction'. Another described *Chip 'n' Dale Rescue Rangers* as a valuable demonstration of 'the rewards of team effort'. *The Flintstones*, meanwhile, was found to promote initiative and family values. A few stations did provide some more demonstrably educational programmes, but a survey found that the great bulk of these were shown before 7 a.m. 'After that,' as *The Economist* noted drily, 'the stations got down to the scholarly stuff.'[11]

While there is no doubt something in all of these considerations, it should also be noted that it is easy to give a distorted impression of educational performance. Consider the matter of the American sixth formers who did so poorly on maths tests. What almost all commentators failed to note is that secondary education in America is, for better or worse, very different from that of most other countries. To begin with, the American system does not encourage – or often even permit – sixth-form students to specialize in a core discipline like science, maths or languages. Moreover, American high schools are open to all young people, not just those who have demonstrated academic proficiency. That England and Wales came third or fourth in all the maths tests is, it may be argued, less a testament to the far-sightedness of the British education system than to the rigorousness with which the less apt are excluded. Yet it was against high-flyers such as these that the American students were in virtually every case being compared.

The fact is that by most measures the American educational system is not at all bad. Almost 90 per cent of Americans finish high school and a quarter earn a college degree – proportions that put most other nations to shame. For minorities especially, improvements in recent years have been significant. Between 1970 and 1990 the proportion of black students who graduated from high school increased from 68 per cent to 78 per cent.[12] America is educating more of its young, to a higher level, than almost any other nation in the world.

There is of course huge scope for improvement. Any nation where twenty million people can't read the back of a cornflakes box, or where almost half of all adults believe that human beings were created sometime in the past ten thousand years,[13] clearly has its educational workload cut out for it. But the conclusion that American education is on a steep downward slope is, at the very least, unproven.

II

Early in 1993 Maryland discovered that it had a problem when someone noticed that the state motto – *Fatti maschii, parole femine* ('Manly deeds, womanly words') – was not only odd and fatuous, but also patently sexist. The difficulty was that it was embossed on a lot of expensive state stationery, and engraved on buildings and monuments, and anyway it had been around for a long time. After much debate, the state's legislators hit on an interesting compromise. Rather than change the motto, they decided to change the translation. Now when Marylanders see *Fatti maschii, parole femine*, they are to think, 'Strong deeds, gentle words.'[14] Everyone went to bed happy.

Would that all issues of sensitivity in language were so easily resolved. In fact, apart from the perceived decline of educational standards, almost nothing in recent years has excited more debate or awakened a greater polarity of views than the vaguely all-embracing issue that has come to be known as *political correctness*.

Since 1991, when the term appears to have sprung wholly formed into the language, journals and newspapers have devoted much space to reports that have ranged for the most part from the mildly derisive to the openly antagonistic. Some have treated it as a kind of joke (a typical example: a *Newsweek* report in 1991 that pondered whether restaurant customers could expect soon to be brought a *womenu* by a *waitron* or *waitperson*), while others see it as something much graver. Under leading headlines like 'The New Ayatollahs' (*US News & World Report*), 'Politically Correct Speech: An Oxymoron' (*Editor & Publisher*) and 'The Word Police' (*Library Journal*), many publications have assayed the matter with a mixture of outrage and worry.

Most of the arguments distil down to two beliefs: that the English language is being shanghaied by people of linguistically narrow views, threatening one of America's most valued constitutional freedoms, and that their verbal creations are burdening the nation with ludicrously sanitized neologisms that are an embarrassment to civilized discourse.

Two authors, Henry Beard and Christopher Cerf, have made much capital (in every sense of the word) out of these absurdities with their satirical and popular *Official Politically Correct Dictionary and Handbook*, which offers several hundred examples of absurd euphemisms designed to free the language of the slightest taint of bias. Among the examples they cite:

differently hirsute for bald, *custody suite* for a prison cell, *chemically inconvenienced* for intoxicated, *alternative dentation* for false teeth, and *stolen nonhuman animal carrier* for milkman. What becomes evident only when the reader troubles to scan the notes on sources is that almost all of these excessively cautious terminologies, including those just listed, were made up by the authors themselves.

This might be excused as a bit of harmless, if fundamentally pointless, fun except that these entries have often been picked up by others and transmitted as gospel – for example in a 1992 article in the *Nation,* which referred to the 'grotesque neologisms' of the political correctness movement, and included several examples – *involuntarily domiciled* for homeless, *vocally challenged* for mute – that in fact never existed before Beard and Cerf concocted them as amusing padding for their curious book.[15]

Most of the genuine examples of contrived neologisms that the authors cite are in fact either justifiable on grounds of sensitivity (*developmentally challenged* for mentally retarded), widely accepted (*date rape, pro-choice*), never intended by the creator to be taken seriously (*terminological inexactitude* for lie), the creations of jargon-loving bodies like sociologists or the military (*temporary cessation of hostilities* for peace), drawn from secondary sources of uncertain reliability (*personipulate* for manipulate, taken from another book on political correctness, but not otherwise verified), or become ridiculous only when given a barbed definition (suggesting that *wildlife management* is a common euphemism for 'killing, or permitting the hunting, of animals').

What remain after all this are no more than a few – a very few – scattered examples of genuine ridiculousness by extremist users of English, mostly from the women's movement and mostly involving the removal of 'man' from a variety of common terms – turning *manhole* into *femhole, menstruate* into *femstruate,* and so on.

I don't deny that there is much that is worthy of ridicule in the PC movement – name me a sphere of human activity where there is not – and I shall cite some questionable uses presently, but it seems to me that this is a matter that deserves rather more in the way of thoughtful debate and less in the way of dismissive harrumphing or feeble jokes about waitrons and womenus.

All too often overlooked in discussions of the matter is that at the root of the bias-free language movement lies a commendable sentiment: to make language less wounding or demeaning to those whose sex, race, physical condition or circumstances leave them vulnerable to the raw power of words. No reasonable person argues for the general social acceptance of words like *nigger, chink, spazz* or *queer*. Virtually everyone agrees that such words are crass, insensitive and hurtful. But when the argument is carried to a more subtle level, where intolerance or contempt is merely implied, the consensus falls to pieces.

In 1992 *US News & World Report*, in an article headlined 'A Political Correctness Roundup', noted that 'an anti-PC backlash is underway, but there are still plenty of cases of institutionalized silliness'. Among the 'silliness' that attracted the magazine's attention was the case of students at the University of Wisconsin-Milwaukee being encouraged 'to go to a toy store and investigate the availability of racially diverse dolls', and of a New York lawyer being censured for calling an adversary in court 'a little lady' and 'little mouse'.[16]

That students should be encouraged to investigate the availability of racially diverse dolls in a racially diverse society seems to me not the least bit silly. Nor does it seem to me unreasonable that a lawyer should be compelled to treat his courtroom adversaries with a certain measure of respect. (I wonder whether the parties at *US News & World Report* might have perceived a need for courtesy had the opposing counsel been a male and the words employed been 'bub' or 'dickhead'.) But that of course is no more than my opinion. And that in turn is the overweening problem with any discussion of bias-free usage, that it is fearfully subjective, a minefield of opinions. What follows are, necessarily and inescapably, mine.

That a subtle and pervasive sexual bias exists in English seems to me unarguable. Consider any number of paired sets of words — *master/mistress, bachelor/spinster, governor/governess, courtier/courtesan* — and you can see in an instant that male words generally denote power and eminence, and that their female counterparts just as generally convey a sense of submissiveness or inconsequence. That many of the conventions of English usage – referring to all humans as *mankind*, using a male pronoun in constructions like 'to each his own' and 'everyone has his own view on the matter' – show a similar tilt towards the male is also, I think, beyond question. The extent of this is not to be underestimated. As Rosalie Maggio points out in her thoughtful *Dictionary of Bias-Free Usage*, when Minnesota expunged gender-specific language from its law-books, it removed 301 feminine references from state statutes, but almost 20,000 references to men.[17] There is no question that English is historically a male-oriented language.

The difficulty, as many critics of political correctness have pointed out, is that the avoidance of gender-specific constructions contorts the language, flouts historical precedent, and deprives us of terms of long-standing utility. People have been using *man, mankind, forefathers, founding fathers, a man's home is his castle,* and other such expressions for centuries. Why should we stop now?

For two reasons. First, because venerability is no defence. Ninety years ago *moron* was an unexceptionable term – indeed, it was a medically precise designation for a particular level of mental acuity. Its loose, and eventually cruel, application banished it from polite society in respect of the subnormal. Dozens of other words that were once unselfconsciously bandied about – *piss, cretin, nigger* – no longer meet the measure of respectability. Just because a word or expression has an antiquity or was once widely used does not confer on it some special immunity.

Moreover, such words are often easily replaced. *People, humanity, human beings, society, civilization* and many others provide the same service as *mankind* without ignoring half the populace. Since 1987 the Roman Catholic Church in the United States has used a text, the *Revised New Testament of the New American Bible,* that is entirely non-sexist. In it, Matthew 4:4 changes from 'Not on bread alone is man to live' to 'One does not live by bread alone.' Matthew 16:23, 'You are not judging by God's standards, but by man's,' becomes instead 'You are thinking not as God does, but as human beings do.'[18] So seamlessly have these changes been incorporated that I daresay few people reading this version of the New Testament would even notice that it is scrupulously non-sexist. Certainly it has not been deprived of any of its beauty or power.

Unfortunately, there remains in English a large body of gender-specific terms – *gamesmanship, busman's holiday, manhole, freshman, fisherman, manslaughter, manmade, first baseman,* and others beyond counting – that are far less susceptible to modification. Maggio notes that many such 'man' words are in fact unexceptionable because their etymology is unconnected to man the male. *Manacle, manicure* and *manufacture,* for example, come from the Latin for *hand,* and thus are only coincidentally 'sexist'.[19] *Tallboy* similarly passes muster because the closing syllable comes from the French for wood, 'bois'. But in many scores of others the link with gender is explicit and irrefutable.

This poses two problems. First there is the consideration that although many gender-based words do admit of alternatives – *mail carrier* for *mailman, flight attendant* for *stewardess* – for many others the suggested replacements are ambiguous, unfamiliar, or clumsy, and often all three. No matter how you approach them, *utility access hole* and *sewer hole* do not offer the immediacy of recognition that *manhole* does. *Gamestership* is not a comfortable replacement for *gamesmanship*. *Frosh, frosher, novice, newcomer, greenhorn, tenderfoot* and the other many proposed variants for *freshman* suffer from either excessive coyness or uncertain comprehensibility.[20]

That is not to say that this must always be so. Twenty years ago, *chair* for *chairman* sounded laughable to most people. *Ms*, if not absurd, was certainly contentious. Most newspapers adopted it only fitfully and over the protests of white-haired men in visors. Today, both appear routinely in publications throughout the English-speaking world and no one thinks anything of it. There is no reason that *gamestership* and *frosh* and *sewer hole* should not equally take up a neutral position in the language. But these things take time. *Ms* was coined as far back as 1949, but most people had never heard of it, much less begun to use it, until some twenty years later.

More pertinently there is the question of whether such words can always be legitimately termed sexist. Surely the notion that one must investigate a word's etymology before deciding whether it is permissible suggests that there is something inadequate in this approach. I would submit (though I concede that I can sometimes feel the ice shifting beneath my feet) that just as 'man' is not sexist in *manipulate* or *mandible* so it is not in any meaningful sense sexist in *manhole* or *Walkman* or *gamesmanship*.

A word that imparts no overt sense of gender – that doesn't say, 'Look, this is a word for guys only' – is effectively neuter. Words after all have only the meanings we give them. *Piss* is infra dig in polite company not because there is something intrinsically shocking in that particular arrangement of letters but because of the associations with which we have endowed the word. Surely it is excessive to regard a word as *ipso facto* objectionable because of the historical background of a syllable embedded in it, particularly when that word does not fire gender-sensitive synapses in most people's minds.

My point becomes somewhat clearer, I hope, when we look at what I think is the greatest weakness of the bias-free usage movement – namely, that often it doesn't know where to stop. The admirable urge to rid the language of its capacity to harm can lead to a zealousness that is little short of patronizing. Maggio, for instance, cautions us not to 'use lefthanded metaphorically; it perpetuates subtle but age-old negative associations for those who are physically lefthanded'. I would submit that a left-handed person (and I speak as one myself) would have to be sensitive to the point of neurosis to feel personally demeaned by a term like 'left-handed compliment'.

Similarly she cautions against using *black* in a general sense – *black humour, black eye, black mark, blacksmith* (though not, oddly, *blackout*) – on the grounds that most *black* words have a negative connotation that subtly reinforces prejudice. Or as she puts it: 'Avoiding words that reinforce negative connotations of black will not do away with racism, but it can lessen the everyday pain these expressions cause readers.' I cannot pretend to speak for black people, but it seems to me unlikely that many can have experienced much 'everyday pain' from knowing that the person who shoes horses is called a blacksmith.

Even 'violent expressions and metaphors' – *to kill two birds with one stone, how does that strike you, to knock someone dead, smash hit, one thing triggers another, to kick around an idea* – are to be excluded from our speech on the grounds that they help to perpetuate a culture sympathetic to violence.

Such assertions, I would submit, are not only an excessive distraction from the main issues, but dangerously counter-productive. They invite ridicule, and, as we have seen, there is no shortage of people who ache to provide it.

A final charge often laid against the bias-free speech movement – that it promotes a bias of its own – is also not always easy to refute. Maggio outlaws many expressions like *a man's home is his castle* (and rightly in my view) but defends *a woman's work is never done* on the grounds that 'this is particularly true and usually more true than/of a man with a paid job and a family'. Just because a sentiment/is true doesn't make it non-sexist. (And anyway it isn't true.) Others take matters much further. When the University of Hawaii proposed a speech code for students and staff, Mari Matsuda, a professor of law, endorsed the idea but added the truly arresting belief that 'Hateful verbal attacks upon dominant group members by victims is permissible.'[21]

With respect, I would suggest that consideration, reasonable-ness and a sense of fairness are qualities that apply to all members of a speech community, not just to those who hold the reins.

III

So where now for America and its distinctive strain of English? One of the few certainties about the future for America is that it will continue to become, far more than any other developed nation, a multiracial society. By the end of this decade, only about half of Americans entering the workforce will be native born and of European stock. By 2020, if present trends continue, the proportion of non-white and Hispanic Americans will have doubled, while the white population will have remained almost unchanged. By 2050 the number of Asian Americans will have quintupled.

Many Americans see this as a threat. They note uneasily that already the most popular radio station in Los Angeles is a Spanish-language one, that Spanish is the mother tongue of about half of the two million inhabitants of greater Miami, that 11 per cent of Americans speak a language other than English at home. Some have even seen in this a kind of conspiracy. The late Senator S. I. Hayakawa expressed his belief in 1987 that 'a very real move is afoot to split the US into a bilingual and bicultural society'.[22] Though he never explained what sinister parties were behind this move, or what they could possibly hope to gain from it, his views found widespread support, and led to the formation of US English, a pressure group dedicated to the notion that English should be the sole official language of the United States.

In fact, there is no reason to suppose that America is any more threatened by immigration today than it was a century ago. To begin with, only 6 per cent of Americans are foreign born, a considerably smaller proportion than in Britain, France, Germany or most other developed countries. Immigration is for the most part concentrated in a few urban centres. Though some residents in those cities may find it vexing that their waitress or taxi-driver does not always speak colloquial English with the assurance of a native-born American, it is also no accident that those cities where immigration is most profound – Miami, Seattle, Los Angeles, San Francisco – are almost always far more vibrant than those places like Detroit, St Louis and Philadelphia where it is not.

Nor is it any accident that immigrants are a disproportionate presence in many of those industries – pharmaceuticals, medical research, entertainment, the computer industry – that are most vital to America's continued prosperity. A third of the engineers in California's silicon valley, for instance, were born in Asia. As one observer has put it: 'America will win because our Asians will beat their Asians.'[23]

Quite apart from the argument that foreign cultures introduce a welcome measure of diversity into American life, no evidence has ever been adduced to show that immigrants today, any more than in the past, persist with their native tongues. A study by the Rand Corporation in 1985 found that 95 per cent of the children of Mexican immigrants in America spoke English, and that half of these spoke *only* English. According to another survey, more than 90 per cent of Hispanics, citizens and non-citizens alike, believe that residents of the United States should learn English.[24]

If history is anything to go by, then three things about

America's immigrants are as certain today as they ever were: that they will learn English, that they will become Americans, and that the country will be richer for it. And if that is not a good thing, I don't know what is.

Notes

1: The Mayflower and Before

1 *American Heritage*, October 1962, pp. 49–55.
2 Flexner, *I Hear America Talking*, p. 271.
3 Heaton, *The Mayflower*, p. 80.
4 Wagenknecht, *Henry Wadsworth Longfellow*, p. 105.
5 Caffrey, *The Mayflower*, p. 141.
6 Blow (ed.), *Abroad in America*, p. 79.
7 Morison, *The Oxford History of the American People*, p. 19
8 Enterline, *Viking America*, p. 10.
9 Morison, op. cit., p. 20.
10 *National Geographic*, November 1964, p. 721.
11 Enterline, op. cit., p. 136.
12 *The Economist*, 29 June 1991, p. 100.
13 *Sydney Morning Herald*, 16 September 1992, p. 8.
14 *The Economist*, 24 October 1992, p. 136.
15 *National Geographic*, June 1979, p. 744.
16 Stewart, *Names on the Land*, p. 23.
17 *American Heritage*, October 1962, p. 50.
18 Caffrey, op. cit., pp. 70–3.

2: Becoming Americans

1 Mencken, *The American Language*, 4th edn., p. 434.
2 Ibid., p. 431.
3 Vallins, *Spelling*, pp. 79–85
4 Krapp, *The English Language in America*, vol. 1, p. 201.
5 Baugh and Cable, *A History of the English Language*, p. 248.
6 Dohan, *Our Own Words*, p. 69.
7 Mencken, op. cit., p. 288.
8 Holt, *Phrase and Word Origins*, p. 55.

9 Fischer, *Albion's Seed*, p. 261.
10 Flexner, *I Hear America Talking*, p. 63, and Mencken, op. cit., p. 139.
11 *American Heritage*, February 1963, pp. 90–6.
12 Craigie, *The Growth of American English*, pp. 209–11.
13 Laird, *Language in America*, pp. 25–6.
14 R. Bailey, *Images of English*, pp. 68–9, and Mencken, op. cit., p. 111.
15 Stewart, *Names on the Land*, p. 63.
16 Holt, op. cit., pp. 49–50.
17 Carver, *A History of English in Its Own Words*, p. 182.
18 R. Bailey, op. cit., p. 67.
19 Krapp, op. cit., p. 175.
20 Quoted in Marckwardt, *American English*, p. 28.
21 *American Heritage*, December 1983, p. 85.
22 Zinn, *A People's History of the United States*, p. 15.
23 *American Heritage*, April 1963, p. 69.
24 *National Geographic*, June 1979, p. 735.
25 Ibid., p. 764.
26 Morison, *The Oxford History of the American People*, p. 41.
27 Lacey, *Sir Walter Ralegh*, p. 90.
28 Jones, *American Immigration*, p. 18.
29 Ibid., p. 22.
30 Morison, op. cit., p. 82.

3: A 'Democratical Phrenzy': America in the Age of Revolution

1 Morison, *The Oxford History of the American People*, p. 172.
2 Fischer, *Albion's Seed*, p. 30.
3 *American Heritage*, June 1970, pp. 54–9.
4 Stephen T. Olsen, 'Patrick Henry's "Liberty or Death" Speech: A Study in Disputed Authorship', in Benson (ed.), *American Rhetoric*, pp. 19–27.
5 Quoted in Cmiel, *Democratic Eloquence*, p. 56.
6 Boorstin, *The Americans: The National Experience*, p. 374.
7 *American Heritage*, December 1973, p. 37.
8 Quoted in Cmiel, op. cit., p. 54.
9 P. Smith, *A People's History of the United States*, vol. 1, p. 271.
10 Letter to William Randolph, June 1776, in Boy (ed.), *The Papers of Thomas Jefferson*, vol. 1, p. 409.
11 P. Smith, op. cit., p. 223.
12 Wills, *Inventing America*, p. 45.
13 Ibid., p. 35.
14 Brodie, *Thomas Jefferson*, p. 103.

15 Fischer, op. cit., p. 6.
16 Ibid., p. 471.
17 Ibid., p. 259.
18 Dillard, *All-American English*, p. 55.
19 Wills, op. cit., p. 36.
20 Quoted in Krapp, *The English Language in America*, vol. 1, p. 46.
21 Flexner, *I Hear America Talking*, p. 7.
22 Cmiel, op. cit., p. 45.
23 Krapp, op. cit., p. 44.
24 Mencken, *The American Language,* 4th edn., p. 539.
25 Dillard, op. cit., p. 53.
26 Hibbert, *Redcoats and Rebels,* pp. 31–5.
27 Stephen E. Lucas, 'Justifying America: The Declaration of Independence as a Rhetorical Document', in Benson (ed.), op. cit., p. 71.
28 Letter to Henry Lee, 8 May 1825.
29 Wills, op. cit., p. xxi.
30 Cmiel, op. cit., p. 83.
31 Boyd (ed.), op. cit., vol. 1, p. 423.
32 Lucas, op. cit., pp. 67–119.
33 Hibbert, op. cit., p. 117.
34 Ibid., p. 117.
35 Safire, *Coming to Terms*, p. 140.
36 Simpson, *The Politics of American English*, p. 23.
37 Boyd (ed.), op. cit., vol. 1, p. 404.
38 Mencken, op. cit., p. 502.
39 Flexner, op. cit., p. 7.
40 Flexner, *Listening to America*, p. 328.
41 Boorstin, op. cit, p. 381.

4: Making a Nation

 1 Mee, *The Genius of the People*, p. 30.
 2 P. Smith, *A People's History of the United States*, vol. 3, p. ix.
 3 Schwarz, *George Washington*, p. 47.
 4 Mee, op. cit., p. 143.
 5 Flexner, *Listening to America*, p. 281.
 6 P. Smith, op. cit., vol. 1, p. 78.
 7 Aldridge, *Benjamin Franklin and Nature's God*, p. 22.
 8 P. Smith, op. cit., vol. 3, p. 397.
 9 Morison, *The Oxford History of the American People*, pp. 308–9.
10 Seavey, *Becoming Benjamin Franklin*, p. 150.
11 E. Wright, *Franklin of Philadelphia*, p. 53.
12 Ibid., p. 54.

13 Granger, *Benjamin Franklin*, p. 66.
14 Willcox (ed.), *The Papers of Benjamin Franklin*, vol. 15, p. 174.
15 Carr, *The Oldest Delegate*, p. 16.
16 Boorstin, *The Americans: The National Experience*, p. 357.
17 Mee, op. cit., p. 90.
18 P. Smith, op. cit., vol. 6, p. 376.
19 Cooke, *Alistair Cooke's America*, p. 140.
20 Mee, op. cit., p. 120.
21 Ibid., p. 237.
22 Boorstin, *Hidden History*, p. 187.
23 Boorstin, *The Americans: The National Experience*, p. 402.
24 Ibid., p. 415.
25 Ernst and Schwartz, *Censorship*, p. 8.
26 Morison, op. cit., p. 311.
27 P. Smith, op. cit., vol. 3, pp. 122–3.
28 *American Heritage,* October 1969, pp. 84–5.
29 *Verbatim*, Summer 1991, p. 6.
30 Flexner, *I Hear America Talking*, p. 9.
31 Simpson, *The Politics of American English*, p. 41.
32 *American Heritage*, December 1963, p. 27.
33 *Journal of American History*, December 1992, pp. 939–40.
34 Quoted in Boorstin, *The Americans: The National Experience*, p. 344.
35 *National Geographic*, July 1976, pp. 92–3.
36, Ibid., p. 97.
37 Mee, op. cit., pp. 33–40.

5: By the Dawn's Early Light: Forging a National Identity

1 Holt, *Phrase and Word Origins*, p. 243.
2 O'Malley, *Keeping Watch*, p. 107.
3 *American Heritage*, October/November 1983, p. 104.
4 O'Malley, op. cit., p. 262.
5 P. Smith, *A People's History of the United States*, vol. 3, p. 757.
6 Flexner, *I Hear America Talking*, p. 124.
7 Morison, *The Oxford History of the American People*, pp. 283–4.
8 Craigie and Hulbert, *A Dictionary of American English on Historical Principles*, vol. 2, p. 397.
9 Carver, *A History of English in Its Own Words*, p. 9.
10 *New Yorker*, 4 September 1989, p. 11.
11 Boorstin, *The Americans: The National Experience*, p. 280.
12 Mencken, *The American Language*, 4th edn., p. 236.
13 Ibid., p. 135,
14 P. Smith, op. cit., vol. 4, p. 252.

15 Ibid., vol. 3, p. 47.
16 Commager, *The American Mind*, p. 16.
17 Cmiel, *Democratic Eloquence*, p. 159.
18 Dillard, *American Talk*, p. xiii.
19 Quoted in Mencken, op. cit., p. 29.
20 Ibid., p. 267.
21 Daniels, *Famous Last Words*, p. 43
22 Mencken, op. cit., p. 77.
23 *Journal of American History*, December 1992, p. 913.
24 Quoted in Mencken, op. cit., p. 87.
25 Marckwardt, *American English*, p. 70.
26 *Journal of American History*, December 1992, p. 928.
27 Quoted in Wortham, *James Russell Lowell's 'The Biglow Papers'*, p. xxii.
28 Dillard, *All-American English*, p. 73.
29 Quoted in Boorstin, *The Americans: The Democratic Experience*, p. 293.
30 Cmiel, op. cit., p. 66.
31 Letter to Lincoln, 25 November 1860, quoted in *Harper Book of American Quotations*, p. 121.
32 Wills, *Lincoln at Gettysburg*, p. 90.
33 Cmiel, op. cit., p. 137.
34 Ibid., p. 144.
35 Wills, *Inventing America*, p. xiv.

6: We're in the Money: The Age of Invention

1 *American Heritage*, August 1964, p. 93.
2 Ibid., August/September 1984, p. 20.
3 Brogan, *The Penguin History of the United States of America*, p. 274.
4 Bursk, Clark and Hidy (eds.), *The World of Business*, vol. 2, p. 1251.
5 Commager, *The American Mind*, p. 5.
6 Daniels, *Famous Last Words*, p. 41.
7 Wylie, *The Self-Made Man in America*, p. 10.
8 Boorstin, *The Americans: The National Experience*, p. 115.
9 Flexner, *Listening to America*, pp. 365–6.
10 *American Heritage*, December 1989, p. 108.
11 Holt, *Phrase and Word Origins*, p. 5.
12 Flexner, op. cit., p. 364.
13 Root and de Rochemont, *Eating in America*, p. 321.
14 Zinn, *A People's History of the United States*, p. 316.
15 *American Heritage*, October 1959, p. 38.

16 Zinn, op. cit., p. 327.
17 Flexner, op. cit., p. 452.
18 Burnam, *The Dictionary of Misinformation*, p. 37.
19 Ibid., p. 60.
20 Keeley, *Making Inventions Pay*, p. 10.
21 Gies and Gies, *The Ingenious Yankees*, pp. 208–10.
22 Barach, *Famous American Trademarks*, p. 75.
23 P. Smith, *A People's History of the United States*, vol. 4,
   pp. 822–3.
24 Carver, *A History of English in Its Own Words*, p. 245.
25 P. Smith, op. cit., vol. 4, pp. 813–17.
26 *American Heritage*, September/October 1990, p. 58.
27 Ibid., April 1965, p. 95.
28 Ibid., p. 96.
29 Barnhart (ed.), *The Barnhart Dictionary of Etymology*, p. 1121.
30 *New York Times*, 26 July, 1992 p. E5.
31 *The Economist*, 13 April 1991, p. 83.
32 *American Heritage*, September/October 1990, p. 48.
33 Carver, op. cit., p. 242.
34 Gies and Gies, op. cit., p. 368.
35 Ibid., p. 311.
36 *American Heritage*, September/October 1990, pp. 48–59.
37 P. Smith, op. cit., vol. 7, p. 858.
38 Ibid.
39 Zinn, op. cit., p. 248.
40 Collins, *The Story of Kodak*, p. 72.
41 Flatow, *They All Laughed*, p. 31.
42 *American Heritage*, November 1979, p. 76.
43 P. Smith, op. cit., vol. 7, p. 858.
44 *American Heritage*, August/September 1978, p. 42.
45 Goldberger, *The Skyscraper*, p. 83.

7: Names

1 Boorstin, *The Americans: The National Experience*, p. 305.
2 Flexner, *I Hear American Talking*, p. 312.
3 Krapp, *The English Language in America*, vol. 1, p. 175.
4 Stewart, *Names on the Land*, p. 64.
5 Ibid., p. 33.
6 Ibid., p. 258.
7 Fischer, *Albion's Seed*, p. 420.
8 Stewart, op. cit., p. 58.
9 Ibid., p. 10.
10 *American Demographics*, February 1992, p. 21.

11 Stewart, op. cit., p. 70.
12 Ibid., p. 223.
13 *Atlantic Monthly*, November 1992, p. 149.
14 Mencken, *The American Language,* 4th edn., p. 649.
15 Dillard, *American Talk*, p. 59.
16 Mencken, *The American Language,* suppl. 2, p. 533.
17 Stewart, op. cit., p. 327.
18 P. Smith, *A People's History of the United States,* vol. 4, pp. 473–4.
19 Fischer, op. cit., p. 654.
20 Rodgers, *Chagrin . . . Whence the Name?*, pp. 1–13.
21 *New Republic*, 29 July 1991, p.8.
22 Mencken, *The American Language,* 4th edn., p. 656.
23 *Atlantic Monthly*, September 1990, p. 20.
24 Stewart, op. cit., p. 344.
25 Ibid., pp. 166–7.
26 Ibid., p. 189.
27 Mencken, *The American Language,* 4th edn., p. 686.
28 Lacey, *Sir Walter Ralegh*, p. 11.
29 Fischer, op. cit., p. 59.
30 Ibid., p. 94.
31 Ibid.
32 Levin, *Cotton Mather*, p. 1.
33 Mencken, *The American Language,* suppl. 2, pp. 577–8.
34 Forbes, *Paul Revere and the World He Lived In*, p. 5.
35 Mencken, *The American Language,* suppl. 2. pp. 579–81.
36 Ibid., p. 585.
37 Sullivan, *Our Times*, vol. 1, p. 250.
38 Mencken, *The American Language,* suppl. 2, p. 597.

8: 'Manifest Destiny': Taming the West

1 Dillon, *Meriwether Lewis*, p. 336.
2 Hart, *The Story of American Roads*, p. 24.
3 Root and de Rochement, *Eating in America*, pp. 110–11.
4 P. Smith, *A People's History of the United States,* vol. 3, p. 534.
5 Moulton, *The Journals of the Lewis and Clark Expedition,* pp. 181–227.
6 Ibid., p 141.
7 Cutright, *Lewis and Clark*, pp. viii-ix.
8 Brogan, *The Penguin History of the United States of America,* p. 263.
9 Tocqueville, *Journey to America*, p. 185.
10 Boorstin, *The Americans: The National Experience*, pp. 91–3

11 Ibid., p. 93.
12 Boorstin, *Hidden History*, p. 200.
13 Boorstin, *The Americans: The National Experience*, p. 121
14 Gies and Gies, *The Ingenious Yankees*, p. 255.
15 Zinn, *A People's History of the United States*, p. 149.
16 *American Heritage*, February 1962, p. 5.
17 *Atlantic Monthly*, November 1992, p. 152.
18 Dillard, *American Talk*, p. xix.
19 Zinn, op. cit., p. 260.
20 P. Smith, op. cit., vol. 3, p. 32.
21 Fischer, *Albion's Seed*, p. 62.
22 Boorstin, *The Americans: The Democratic Experience*, pp. 22–3.
23 Ibid., p. 24.
24 Weston, *The Real American Cowboy*, p. 136.
25 Dillard, op. cit., p. 114.
26 Weston, op. cit., p. 210.
27 Savage, *Cowboy Life*, p. 6
28 *American Heritage*, February 1971, p. 68.
29 Boorstin, *The Americans: The National Experience*, p. 83.
30 Holt, *Phrase and Word Origins*, p. 80.
31 *Washington Post*, 8 December 1989, p. C5.
32 Boorstin, *Hidden History*, p. 288; and Flexner, *I Hear America Talking*, pp. 111–12.
33 Carver, *A History of English in Its Own Words*, p. 199.
34 Harris, *Good to Eat*, p. 117.
35 *The Economist*, 10 August 1991, p. 29.
36 Ibid., 8 June 1991, p. 49.
37 Quoted in *Atlanta Journal*, 17 March 1991, p. A12.

9: The Melting-Pot: Immigration in America

1 Jones, *American Immigration*, pp. 104–5.
2 Ibid., pp. 114, 290.
3 Ibid., p. 107.
4 Ibid., p. 124.
5 Zinn, *A People's History of the United States*, p. 317.
6 Boorstin, *The Americans: The Democratic Experience*, p. 249
7 P. Smith, *A People's History of the United States*, vol. 6, p. 344.
8 Grosvenor (ed.), *Those Inventive Americans*, p. 146.
9 *New Yorker*, 9 April 1990, p. 30.
10 *American Heritage*, April 1992, p. 58.
11 Ibid., p. 62.
12 P. Smith, op. cit., vol. 6, p. 366.
13 *New York Times*, 26 August 1990, p. 6E.

14 Zinn, op. cit., p. 341; and Brogan, *The Penguin History of the United States of America*, p. 413.
15 Jones, op. cit., pp. 140–1.
16 Dillard, *American Talk*, p. 30.
17 Mencken, *The American Language*, 4th edn., p. 90.
18 Dillard, op. cit., p. 82.
19 Marckwardt, *American English*, p. 57; and Boorstin, *The Americans: The National Experience*, p. 287.
20 Carver, *A History of English in Its Own Words*, p. 242.
21 Fischer, *Albion's Seed*, p. 431.
22 Jones, op. cit., pp. 270–1.
23 *American Heritage*, April 1992, p. 62.
24 Ibid., p. 62.
25 Mencken, op. cit., p. 251.
26 *Time*, 13 June 1927, p. 12.
27 Mencken, op. cit., p. 254.
28 *American Heritage*, April 1992, p. 70.
29 Jones, op. cit., p. 298.
30 Mencken, op. cit., p. 253.
31 Beam, *Abridged Pennsylvania German Dictionary*, p. iv.
32 Ibid., pp. viii-ix.
33 Beam, *Pennsylvania German Dictionary*, p. v.
34 Marckwardt, op. cit., p. 59.
35 P. Smith, op. cit., vol. 4, p. 741.
36 Jones, op. cit., pp. 264–5.
37 Quoted in *New York Times*, 14 October 1990, p. 4E.
38 Boorstin, *Hidden History*, pp. 214–15.
39 Jones, op. cit., p. 39.
40 Zinn, op. cit., p. 293.
41 Tannahill, *Sex in History*, p. 400.
42 Jones, op. cit., p. 133.
43 Ibid., p. 312.
44 Johnson, *Modern Times*, p. 204.
45 Quoted in Wills, *Inventing America*, p. xx.
46 *Time*, 13 June 1927, p. 12.
47 *National Geographic*, September 1992, pp. 66–7.
48 Jones, op. cit., pp. 32–5.
49 Fischer, op. cit., p. 305.
50 McPherson, *Battle Cry of Freedom*, p. 18.
51 Zinn, op. cit., pp. 174–5.
52 Ibid., p. 203.
53 P. Smith, op. cit., vol 4, p. 586.
54 Zinn, op. cit., pp. 183–4.
55 Quoted in McDavid, *Varieties of American English*, p. 78.

56 Krapp, *The English Language in America*, vol. 1, pp. 161–2.
57 Dohan, *Our Own Words*, p. 241.
58 Marckwardt, op. cit., p. 66.
59 Ibid., p. 65.
60 Dillard, op. cit., p. 22.
61 Mencken, op. cit., p. 743.

10: When the Going was Good: Travel in America

1 Boorstin, *Hidden History,* p. 60.
2 Hibbert, *Redcoats and Rebels,* p. 335.
3 Root and de Rochement, *Eating in America,* p. 42.
4 Morison, *The Oxford History of the American People,* p. 141.
5 Carver, *A History of English in Its Own Words,* pp. 147–8.
6 Cooke, *Alistair Cooke's America,* p. 77.
7 Boorstin, *The Americans: The National Experience,* p. 394
8 Boyd (ed.), *The Papers of Thomas Jefferson,* vol. 1, p. 408.
9 Wills, *Inventing America,* p. 43.
10 Rae, *The Road and the Car in American Life,* p. 15.
11 *American Heritage,* April 1967, p. 106
12 *American Heritage,* December 1983, p. 91.
13 Davidson, *Life in America,* vol. 1, p. 199.
14 Flexner, *Listening to America,* p. 144.
15 Johnson, *The Birth of the Modern,* p. 171.
16 *American Heritage,* February 1977, p. 16.
17 McPherson, *Battle Cry of Freedom,* p. 12.
18 Patton, *Open Road,* p. 37.
19 Ciardi, *Good Words to You,* pp. 233–4.
20 Barnhart (ed.), *The Barnhart Dictionary of Etymology,* p. 1086.
21 K. Jackson, *Crabgrass Frontier,* pp. 106–7
22 Ibid., p. 105.
23 *The Economist,* 26 October 1991.
24 Nye, *Electrifying America,* p. 93.
25 K. Jackson, op. cit., p. 158.
26 Carver, op. cit., p. 243.
27 P. Smith, *A People's History of the United States,* vol. 7, p. 865.
28 Ibid., p. 866.
29 Flexner, *I Hear America Talking,* p. 330
30 Dohan, *Our Own Words,* p. 266.
31 Flexner, *I Hear America Talking,* p. 333.
32 Hokanson, *The Lincoln Highway,* pp. 6–10; and *American Heritage,* June 1974, pp. 32–7 and 89.
33 Strasser, *Satisfaction Guaranteed,* p. 6.
34 P. Smith, op. cit., vol. 7, p. 868.

35 *American Heritage*, August 1973, p. 11.
36 Ibid., December 1975, p. 66.
37 Liebs, *Main Street to Miracle Mile*, p. 208.
38 Finch, *Highways to Heaven*, p. 162.
39 Liebs, op. cit., p. 177.
40 Barnhart, op. cit., p. 680.
41 Patton, op. cit., p. 199.
42 Rowsome, *The Verse by the Side of the Road*, p. 18.
43 K. Jackson, op. cit., p. 249
44 *The Economist*, 10 August 1991, p. 28.
45 Patton, op. cit., p. 85.

11: What's Cooking?: Eating in America

1 Caffrey, *The Mayflower*, p. 166.
2 Root and de Rochement, *Eating in America*, p. 54.
3 Ibid., p. 29.
4 Ciardi, *A Browser's Dictionary*, p. 212.
5 Mee, *The Genius of the People*, p. 91.
6 Root and de Rochement, op. cit., pp. 94–5.
7 Ibid., p. 162.
8 Boorstin, *The Americans: The Democratic Experience*, p. 324.
9 Carver, *A History of English in Its Own Words*, p. 146.
10 Funk, *Word Origins and Their Romantic Stories*, p. 170.
11 *American Heritage*, December 1989, pp. 123–31.
12 Ibid.
13 Mencken, *The American Language*, 4th edn., p. 264.
14 Ibid., p. 225.
15 Liebs, *Main Street to Miracle Mile*, p. 196.
16 Levenstein, *Revolution at the Table*, p. 189.
17 Ibid., p. 92.
18 Bursk, Clark and Hidy, *The World of Business*, vol. 1, pp. 426–7.
19 Levenstein, op. cit., pp. 198–9.
20 Funk, op. cit., p. 186.
21 Barnhart, Steinmetz and Barnhart, *Third Barnhart Dictionary of New English*, p. 497.
22 Allen, *Only Yesterday*, p. 68.
23 Holt, *Phrase and Word Origins*, p. 59.
24 Boorstin, *The Americans: The National Experience*, p. 287.
25 Dillard, *American Talk*, p. 85.
26 Ibid., p. 84.
27 Ibid., p. 88.
28 Allen, op. cit., p. 205.
29 Root and de Rochement, op. cit., p. 389.

30 Allen, op. cit., p. 209.
31 Bursk, Clark and Hidy, op. cit., pp. 345–7.
32 Dohan, *Our Own Words*, p. 270.

12: Democratizing Luxury: Shopping in America

1 Craigie and Hulbert, *A Dictionary of American English on Historical Principles*, vol. 1, p. 748.
2 Frieden and Sagalyn, *Downtown, Inc.*, p. 8.
3 Goldberger, *The Skyscraper*, p. 42.
4 Strasser, *Satisfaction Guaranteed*, p. 213.
5 Boorstin, *The Americans: The Democratic Experience*, p. 126.
6 Ibid., p. 110.
7 Flexner, *Listening to America*, p. 494; and Liebs, *Main Street to Miracle Mile*, pp. 119–26.
8 Liebs, op. cit., p. 125.
9 *Atlantic Monthly*, June 1992, p. 31.
10 Schrank, *Snap, Crackle, and Popular Taste*, p. 111.
11 Strasser, *Never Done*, p. 276.
12 Kowinski, *The Malling of America*, pp. 104–5.
13 *Business Week*, 17 November 1957, p. 137.
14 Gruen and Smit, *Shopping Town USA*, p. 20
15 *Atlantic Monthly*, May 1993, p. 132.
16 Kowinski, op. cit., p. 112.
17 Frieden and Sagalyn, op. cit., p. 13.
18 Jackson, *Crabgrass Frontier*, p. 261.
19 *American Demographics*, April 1990, p. 38.
20 Schor, *The Overworked American*, p. 107.
21 *Atlantic Monthly*, May 1993, p. 102.
22 *The Economist*, 29 August 1992, p. 37.

13: Domestic Matters

1 Blow (ed.), *Abroad in America*, p. 149.
2 Ibid., p. 139.
3 Ibid., p. 215
4 Garrett, *At Home*, p. 155.
5 Deetz, *In Small Things Forgotten*, p. 123
6 Elias, *The History of Manners*, vol. 1, p. 127.
7 *American Heritage*, December 1989, p. 106.
8 Flexner, *I Hear America Talking*, p. 19.
9 Boorstin, *The Americans: The National Experience*, p. 135.
10 *American Heritage*, August/September 1978, p. 41.
11 Boorstin, op. cit., p. 141.

12 *American Heritage*, December 1989, p. 111.
13 Blow, op. cit., p. 159.
14 Rybczynski, *Home*, p. 139.
15 Ibid., p. 142.
16 Ibid., pp. 148–9.
17 Nye, *Electrifying America*, p.242.
18 Strasser, *Never Done*, p. 76.
19 Nye, op. cit., p. 52.
20 *American Heritage*, November 1979, p. 78.
21 P. Smith, *A People's History of the United States*, vol. 7, p. 856.
22 Johnson, *Modern Times*, p. 224.
23 *American Heritage*, September/October 1990, p. 58.
24 R. Barnhart (ed.), *The Barnhart Dictionary of Etymology*, p. 902.
25 Boorstin, *The Americans: The Democratic Experience*, p. 330.
26 *New York Times*, 1–3 July 1921.
27 Allen, *Only Yesterday*, p. 137.
28 *The Economist*, 28 August 1993, p. 57.
29 Sterling and Kittross, *Stay Tuned*, pp. 61–3.
30 Ibid., p. 60.
31 Schiller, *Mass Communications and American Empire*, p. 25.
32 Udelson, *The Great Television Race*, p. 12.
33 *New York Times*, 8 April 1927.
34 Quoted in Schrank, *Snap, Crackle, and Popular Taste*, p. 17.
35 Castleman and Podrazik, *Watching TV*, p. 16.
36 Ibid., p. 45.
37 Safire, *Coming to Terms*, p. 47.
38 Castleman and Podrazik, op. cit., p. v.
39 *American Heritage*, August/September 1984, p. 25.
40 Flatow, *They All Laughed*, p. 61.
41 Strasser, *Never Done*, p. 289.
42 Schor, *The Overworked American*, p. 8.
43 Rybczynski, *Waiting for the Weekend*, pp. 142–3.
44 Schor, op. cit., p. 22.
45 *Utica* (NY) *Observer*, 4 March 1991.
46 Schor, op. cit., p. 29.
47 Ibid., p. 2.
48 Ibid.

14: The Hard Sell: Advertising in America

1 Collins, *The Story of Kodak*, p. 49.
2 Boorstin, *The Americans: The Democratic Experience*, p. 374.
3 Collins, op. cit., pp. 54–5.
4 Ibid., p. 72.

5 Strasser, *Satisfaction Guaranteed*, pp. 46–7.
6 Flexner, *Listening to America*, p. 17.
7 Ibid., p. 20.
8 Strasser, op. cit., p. 97.
9 *Time*, 13 June 1927, p. 12.
10 *American Heritage*, October 1977, p. 67.
11 Mencken, *The American Language*, 4th edn., p. 218.
12 *American Heritage*, October 1977, pp. 64–9.
13 Ibid., September/October 1990, p. 56.
14 *The Economist*, 7 September 1991, p. 89.
15 Ibid., 14 August 1993, p. 7.
16 *New York Times* magazine, 7 July 1957, p. 14.
17 Diamond, *Trademark Problems and How to Avoid Them*, pp. 188–95.
18 Sterling and Kittross, *Stay Tuned*, p. 71.
19 Castleman and Podrazik, *Watching TV*, p. 70.
20 *New York Times* magazine, 30 September, 1990, p. 76.
21 Schrank, *Snap, Crackle, and Popular Taste*, p. 101.
22 Lutz, *Doublespeak*, p. 82.
23 Ibid., pp. 16–17.
24 Hendon, *Classic Failures in Product Marketing*, p. 169.
25 Ibid., p. 168.

15: The Movies

1 Flexner, *Listening to America*, pp. 374–5.
2 Cook, *A History of Narrative Film*, p. 7.
3 Jowett, *Film*, p. 27.
4 Cook, op. cit., pp. 10–11.
5 Flexner, op. cit., p. 378.
6 Cook, op. cit., p. 12.
7 Ibid., p. 24.
8 Rybczynski, *Waiting for the Weekend*, p. 137.
9 Mencken, *The American Language*, 4th edn., p. 738.
10 Flexner, op. cit., pp. 382–3.
11 P. Smith, *A People's History of the United States*, vol. 7, p. 880.
12 *American Heritage*, December 1983, p. 24; and *New Republic*, 29 July 1991, p. 7.
13 Berg, *Goldwyn*, pp. 140, 214–19, 238, 248–55, 380.
14 *New York Times*, 28 March 1993, p. H15.
15 *The Economist*, 2 October 1993, p. 108.
16 Berg, op. cit., p. 262.
17 Jowett, op. cit., p. 357.
18 Ibid.

16: The Pursuit of Pleasure: Sport and Play

1 Krout, *Annals of American Sport*, p. 11.
2 Fischer, *Albion's Seed*, pp. 146–7.
3 Ibid., p. 6.
4 Ibid., p. 8.
5 Ibid., p. 16.
6 Flexner, *Listening to America*, pp. 504–6.
7 *American Heritage*, December 1967, p. 107.
8 Boorstin, *The Americans: The Democratic Experience*, p. 158.
9 Morison, *The Oxford History of the American People*, p. 88.
10 *American Heritage Dictionary*, 2nd edn., p. xxiii.
11 Fischer, op. cit., p. 737.
12 Dillard, *American Talk*, p. 65.
13 Adams, *Western Words*, p. 109.
14 Dillard, op. cit., pp. 65–71.
15 Holt, *Phrase and Word Origins*, p. 200.
16 Dillard, op. cit., p. 74.
17 Boorstin, op. cit., p. 73.
18 *American Heritage*, June 1972, p. 67.
19 Rae, *The Road and the Car in American Life*, p. 29.
20 Atwan, McQuade and Wright, *Edsels, Luckies and Frigidaires*, pp. 151–2.
21 Liebs, *Main Street to Miracle Mile*, pp. 138–142
22 Allen, *Only Yesterday*, p. 68; and *American Heritage*, June 1972, p. 68.
23 *American Heritage*, February/March 1983, pp. 24–7.
24 Dulles, *America Learns to Play*, p. 185.
25 Flexner, op. cit., p. 33.
26 Fischer, op. cit., p. 151.
27 *American Heritage*, June/July 1983, pp. 65–7.
28 Will, *Men at Work*, p. 102.
29 Voigt, *American Baseball*, p. 30.
30 Ibid, p. 135.
31 *American Heritage*, June/July 1983, p. 74.
32 Mencken, *The American Language*, suppl. 2, p. 737.
33 Krout, op. cit., p. 142.
34 Mencken, op. cit., p. 735; and Flexner, op. cit., p. 39.
35 *Time*, 23 September 1940.
36 P. Smith, *A People's History of the United States*, vol. 6, p. 848.
37 Safire, *On Language*, p. 289.
38 Flexner, op. cit., pp. 48–9.
39 Ibid., pp. 261–80.
40 Jackson, *Crabgrass Frontier*, p. 99.

41 Holt, op. cit., p. 154.
42 *Washington Post*, 21 January 1992, p. D5.
43 *New York Times*, 16 February 1992, p. 1.

17: Of Bombs and Bunkum: Politics and War

1 Holt, *Phrase and Word Origins*, pp. 42 and 129.
2 Mencken, *The American Language*, suppl. 1, pp. 280–3.
3 Mencken, *The American Language*, 4th edn., p. 179.
4 Brogan, *The Penguin History of the United States of America*, p. 274.
5 Carver, *A History of English in Its Own Words*, p. 165.
6 McPherson, *Battle Cry of Freedom*, pp. 111–15.
7 *American Heritage*, December 1975, p. 13.
8 Boorstin, *Hidden History*, p. 263.
9 Mee, *The Genius of the People*, p. 285.
10 P. Smith, *A People's History of the United States*, vol. 3, p. 145.
11 Ibid., vol. 4, p. 126.
12 Brogan, op. cit., p. 312.
13 Flexner, *I Hear America Talking*, p. 161.
14 Allen, *Only Yesterday*, p. 104.
15 Johnson, *Modern Times*, p. 214.
16 *American Heritage*, December 1991.
17 Mencken, *The American Language*, suppl. 2, p. 590.
18 P. Smith, op. cit., vol. 3, pp. 608–9.
19 Flexner, op. cit., p. 405.
20 McPherson, op. cit., pp. 323–5.
21 Flexner, op. cit., p. 450.
22 *American Heritage*, February 1964, pp. 23–96.
23 Ciardi, *A Browser's Dictionary*, p. 227.
24 Barfield, *History in English Words*, p. 76.
25 Holt, op. cit., p. 16.
26 Carver, op. cit., p. 252.
27 Flexner, *Listening to America*, p. 330.
28 Mencken, *The American Language*, 4th edn., p. 759.
29 Ibid., p. 508.
30 Lingeman, *Don't You Know There's a War On?*, pp. 219–21.
31 *The Economist*, 27 February 1993, p. 108.
32 *New York Times*, 2 February 1992, p. 17.
33 *American Speech*, Spring 1992, pp. 86–9.

18: Sex and Other Distractions

1 *Life*, 8 October 1951, pp. 61–2.
2 *American Heritage*, December 1983, p. 86.
3 Fischer, *Albion's Seed*, p. 92.
4 Flexner, *Listening to America*, p. 449.
5 Fischer, op. cit., p. 87.
6 P. Smith, *A People's History of the United States*, vol. 1, p. 69.
7 Hibbert, *Redcoats and Rebels*, p. 7.
8 Fischer, op. cit., p. 681.
9 Flexner, op. cit., p. 492.
10 Ciardi, *Good Words to You*, p. 42.
11 Cmiel, *Democratic Eloquence*, p. 117.
12 Garrett, *At Home*, p. 136.
13 P. Smith, op. cit., vol. 6, p. 264.
14 Tannahill, *Sex in History*, p. 336.
15 Ibid., p. 336.
16 *American Heritage*, October 1974, p. 74.
17 *Observer*, 14 November 1993, Books section, p. 20.
18 *American Heritage*, October 1974, p. 73.
19 Ibid., p. 94.
20 Zinn, *A People's History of the United States*, pp. 109–16.
21 Ibid., pp. 116–17.
22 *American Heritage*, October 1974, p. 43.
23 Cmiel, op. cit., p. 81.
24 Ibid., p. 162.
25 P. Smith, op. cit., vol. 6, p. 264.
26 Ibid., p. 271.
27 Ibid., p. 273.
28 Flexner, op. cit., pp. 452–5.
29 *American Heritage*, October 1973, p. 86.
30 *The Economist*, 14 March 1992, p. 51.
31 Barnett, *Sexual Freedom and the Constitution*, p. 33.
32 Allen, *Only Yesterday*, p. 77.
33 Flexner, op. cit., p. 62.
34 Schumach, *The Face on the Cutting Room Floor*, p. 18.
35 Allen, op. cit., p. 84.
36 *American Heritage*, February/March 1980, p. 17.
37 Mencken, *The American Language*, 4th edn., pp. 360–1.
38 Berg, *Goldwyn*, pp. 266–7.
39 Schumach, op. cit., p. 216.
40 Ibid., p. 222.
41 *American Heritage*, February/March 1980, p. 20.
42 Mencken, *The American Language*, suppl. 1, p. 647.

43 Ibid., p. 646.
44 Castleman and Podrazik, *Watching TV*, p. 14.
45 Ibid., p. 71.
46 Ernst and Schwarz, *Censorship*, p. 95.
47 Sagarin, *The Anatomy of Dirty Words*, p. 167.
48 Safire, *Coming to Terms*, p. 51.
49 *The Economist*, 28 November 1992, p. 35.
50 Safire, op. cit., p. 100.
51 Letter from Allan M. Siegal, 23 July 1993.
52 Funk, *A Hog on Ice and Other Curious Expressions*, p. 88.
53 *Buffalo News*, 20 September 1992.

19: The Road from Kitty Hawk

1 *American Heritage*, June 1970, pp. 61–9.
2 Moolman, *The Road to Kitty Hawk*, p. 124.
3 *American Heritage*, June 1970, pp. 61–9.
4 Moolman, op. cit., p. 117.
5 Ibid., p. 158.
6 *American Heritage*, April 1975, pp. 94–5.
7 Milton, *Loss of Eden*, p. 42.
8 Ibid., p. 116; and *American Heritage*, April 1971, pp. 43–7, 81–4.
9 Milton, op. cit., p. 127.
10 *American Heritage*, December 1975, pp. 23–8.
11 Milton, op. cit., p. 166.
12 Johnson, *Modern Times*, p. 224.
13 *Condé Nast Traveler*, December 1989, pp. 135–78.
14 P. Smith, *A People's History of the United States*, vol. 4, p. 780.
15 *American Heritage*, August 1973, pp. 63–85.

20: Welcome to the Space Age: The 1950s and Beyond

1 Lingeman, *Don't You Know There's a War On?*, p. 374.
2 *Atlantic Monthly*, January 1990, p. 48.
3 *The Economist*, 21 December 1991, p. 72.
4 Oakley, *God's Country*, p. 270.
5 Ibid., pp. 285–6.
6 Kroc, *Grinding It Out*, p. 162.
7 Love, *McDonald's*, p. 5.
8 *Guardian*, 10 May 1993.
9 Binford, *The First Suburbs*, p. 1.
10 *American Heritage*, February/March 1984, pp. 21–37.
11 Mencken, *The American Language*, 4th edn., p. 245.
12 *American Demographics*, May 1993, p. 44.

13 *Independent on Sunday*, 15 November 1992, p. 8.
14 Jackson, *Crabgrass Frontier*, p. 246
15 Ibid., p. 247; and Schrank, *Snap, Crackle, and Popular Taste*, p. 65.
16 Brooks, *Business Adventures*, p. 35.
17 Lacey, *Ford*, p. 489.
18 Brooks, op. cit., p. 31.
19 Rae, *The Road and the Car in American Life*, p. 48.
20 Schrank, op. cit., p. 64.
21. *American Speech*, 66/1 (1991), pp. 105–6.
22 *The Economist*, 26 October 1991, America Survey, pp. 11–12.
23 Boorstin, *The Americans: The Democratic Experience*, pp. 591–2.
24 R. Bailey, *Images of English*, p. 221.
25 Tedlow, *New and Improved*, p. 348.
26 *Life*, 3 March 1961, pp. 109–17.
27 Flatow, *They All Laughed*, p. 181.
28 Carver, *A History of English in Its Own Words*, p. 263.
29 *The Economist*, 9 January 1993, p. 62.
30 *New York Times*, 3 April 1989, p. 1.
31 *Atlanta Journal and Constitution*, 2 August 1992, p. M1.
32 *American Heritage*, June 1970, p. 59.

21: American English Today

1 *Atlantic Monthly*, November 1990, p. 84
2 *New York Times*, 21 January 1992, p. C6.
3 *Atlantic Monthly*, August 1990, pp. 28–33.
4 Ibid., p. 28.
5 *The Economist*, 8 August 1992, p. 41.
6 Ibid., 18 January 1992, p. 80.
7 *Atlantic Monthly*, November 1990, p. 87.
8 Ibid., August 1990, p. 30.
9 Schor, *The Overworked American*, p. 13.
10 *American Heritage*, May/June 1988, p. 10.
11 *The Economist,* 10 October 1992, p. 63.
12 *The Economist*, 18 July 1992, p. 49.
13 *New York Times*, 26 July 1992, p. E5.
14 *Washington Post*, 28 March 1993, p. A15.
15 *Nation*, 12 October 1992, p. 405.
16 *US News & World Report*, 22 June 1992, pp. 29–31.
17 Maggio, *The Dictionary of Bias-Free Usage*, p. 17.
18 *New York Times*, 5 April 1987, p. 1.
19 Maggio, op. cit., p. 173.
20 Ibid., p. 112.

21 *Editor & Publisher*, 6 March 1993, p. 48.
22 *Education Digest*, May 1987.
23 *The Economist*, 18 January 1992, p. 80.
24 Ibid., 26 December 1992, p. 58.

Select Bibliography

Adams, Ramon F., *Western Words: A Dictionary of the American West*, (Norman: University of Oklahoma Press, 1968).

Aldridge, Alfred Owen, *Benjamin Franklin and Nature's God* (Durham, NC: Duke University Press, 1967).

Allen, Frederick Lewis, *Only Yesterday: An Informal History of the 1920s*, (New York: Perennial/Harper & Row, 1964).

—— *The Big Change: America Transforms Itself, 1900–1950* (New York: Harper & Brothers, 1950).

Amis, Kingsley, *The Amis Collection: Selected Non-Fiction, 1954–1990* (London: Penguin Books, 1991).

Atwan, Robert, Donald McQuade and John W. Wright, *Edsels, Luckies and Frigidaires: Advertising the American Way* (New York: Dell Publishing, 1979).

Bailey, Richard W., *Images of English: A Cultural History of the Language* (Ann Arbor: University of Michigan Press, 1991).

Bailey, Thomas A., *Voices of America: The Nation's Story in Slogans, Sayings and Songs* (New York: The Free Press, 1976).

Balio, Tino (ed.), *Hollywood in the Age of Television* (Boston: Unwin Hyman, 1990).

Barach, Arnold B., *Famous American Trademarks* (Washington, DC: Public Affairs Press, 1971).

Barbour, Philip L. (ed.), *The Complete Works of Captain John Smith (1580–1631)*, 3 vols. (Chapel Hill: University of North Carolina Press, 1986).

Barfield, Owen, *History in English Words*, (London: Faber and Faber, 1953).

Barnett, Walter, *Sexual Freedom and the Constitution: An Inquiry into the Constitutionality of Repressive Sex Laws* (Albuquerque: University of New Mexico Press, 1973).

Made in America

Barnhart, David K., *New-Words: A Dictionary of the Newest and Most Unusual Words of Our Times* (New York: Collier Books/ Macmillan Publishing Co., 1991).

Barnhart, Robert K. (ed.), *The Barnhart Dictionary of Etymology* (H. W. Wilson Co., 1988).

—— Sol Steinmetz and Clarence L. Barnhart, *Third Barnhart Dictionary of New English* (H. W. Wilson Co., 1989).

Bartlett, John Russell, *Dictionary of Americanisms: A Glossary of Words and Phrases Usually Regarded as Peculiar to the United States* (Boston: Little, Brown and Co., 1859).

Baugh, Albert C., and Thomas Cable, *A History of the English Language*, 3rd edn. (London: Routledge & Kegan Paul, 1978).

Beam, C. Richard, *Abridged Pennsylvania German Dictionary* (Kaiserslautern, Ger.: Heimatstelle Pfalz, 1970).

—— *Pennsylvania German Dictionary: English to Pennsylvania Dutch* (Lancaster, Pa.: Brookshire Publications, Inc., 1985).

Beard, Henry, and Christopher Cerf, *The Official Politically Correct Dictionary and Handbook* (New York: Villard Books, 1993).

Benson, Thomas W. (ed.), *American Rhetoric: Context and Criticism* (Carbondale: University of Southern Illinois University Press, 1989).

Berg, A. Scott, *Goldwyn: A Biography* (New York: Ballantine Books, 1989).

Binford, Henry C., *The First Suburbs: Residential Communities on the Boston Periphery, 1815–1860* (Chicago: University of Chicago Press, 1985).

Blow, Robert (ed.), *Abroad in America: Literary Discoverers of the New World from the Past 500 Years* (Oxford: Lennard Publishing, 1989).

Boorstin, Daniel, *The Americans: The Colonial Experience* (New York: Vintage Books/Random House, 1974).

—— *The Americans: The Democratic Experience* (New York: Vintage Books/Random House, 1974).

—— *The Americans: The National Experience* (New York: Vintage Books/Random House, 1974).

—— *Hidden History: Exploring Our Secret Past* (New York: Vintage Books/Random House, 1989).

Boyd, Julian P. (ed.), *The Papers of Thomas Jefferson*, 26 vols. (Princeton, N. J.: Princeton University Press, 1950).

Brodie, Fawn M., *Thomas Jefferson: An Intimate History* (New York: W. W. Norton & Co., 1974).

Brogan, Hugh, *The Penguin History of the United States of America* (London: Penguin Books, 1990).

Brooks, John, *Business Adventures* (London: Penguin Books, 1959).

Burnam, Tom, *The Dictionary of Misinformation* (New York: Ballantine Books, 1975).

Bursk, Edward C., Donald T. Clark and Ralph W. Hidy (eds.), *The World of Business*, 2 vols. (New York: Simon and Schuster, 1962).

Caffrey, Kate, *The Mayflower* (London: André Deutsch, 1975).

Calder, Jenni, *There Must Be a Lone Ranger: The American West in Film and Reality* (New York: Taplinger Publishing Co., 1974).

Carr, William G., *The Oldest Delegate: Franklin in the Constitutional Convention* (Newark: University of Delaware Press, 1990).

Carruth, Gorton, and Eugene Ehrlich, *The Harper Book of American Quotations* (New York: Harper & Row, 1988).

Carver, Craig M., *A History of English in Its Own Words* (New York: HarperCollins Publishers, 1991).

Castleman, Harry, and Walter J. Podrazik, *Watching TV: Four Decades of American Television* (New York: McGraw-Hill Book Company, 1982).

Chubb, Michael, and Holly R. Chubb, *One Third of Our Time?: An Introduction to Recreation Behavior and Resources* (New York: John Wiley & Sons, 1981).

Ciardi, John, *A Browser's Dictionary: A Compendium of Curious Expressions & Intriguing Facts* (New York: Harper & Row, 1980).

—— *Good Words to You: An All-New Dictionary and Native's Guide to the Unknown American Language* (New York: Harper & Row, 1987).

Clark, Gregory R., *Words of the Vietnam War* (Jefferson, N. C.: McFarland & Co., 1990).

Clark, Ronald W., *Benjamin Franklin: A Biography* (New York: Random House, 1983).

Clark, Thomas D., *Frontier America* (New York: Charles Scribner's Sons, 1959).

Cleary, David Powers, *Great American Brands: The Success Formulas That Made Them Famous* (New York: Fairchild Publications, 1981).

Cmiel, Kenneth, *Democratic Eloquence: The Fight over Popular Speech in Nineteenth-Century America* (New York: William Morrow and Co., 1990).

Cobbett, William, *A Years [sic] Residence in the United States of America* (New York: Augustus M. Kelley, 1969).

Collins, Douglas, *The Story of Kodak* (New York: Harry N. Abrams, Inc., 1990).

Commager, Henry Steele, *The American Mind: An Interpretation of American Thought and Character Since the 1880's* (New Haven: Yale University Press, 1950).

Cook, David A., *A History of Narrative Film* (New York: W. W. Norton & Co., 1981).

Cooke, Alistair, *Alistair Cooke's America* (New York: Alfred A. Knopf, 1987).

Cottle, Basil, *Names* (London: Thames and Hudson, 1983).

Cowan, Ruth Schwartz, *More Work for Mother: The Ironies of Household Technology from the Open Hearth to the Microwave* (New York: Basic Books, 1983).

Craigie, Sir William A., *The Growth of American English* (Oxford: Oxford University Press, 1940).

—— and James R. Hulbert, *A Dictionary of American English on Historical Principles*, 4 vols. (Chicago: University of Chicago Press, 1940).

Crane, Verner W., *Benjamin Franklin and a Rising People* (Boston: Little, Brown and Co., 1954).

Cummings, Richard Osborn, *The American and His Food* (New York: Arno Press, 1974).

Cutright, Paul Russell, *Lewis and Clark: Pioneering Naturalists* (Urbana: University of Illinois Press, 1969).

Daniels, Harvey A., *Famous Last Words: The American Language Crisis Reconsidered* (Carbondale: Southern Illinois University Press, 1983).

Davidson, Marshall B., *Life in America*, 2 vols. (Boston: Houghton Mifflin Co., 1974).

Deetz, James, *In Small Things Forgotten: The Archaeology of Early American Life* (New York: Anchor Books/Doubleday, 1977).

Deighton, Lee C., *A Comparative Study of Spellings in Four Major Collegiate Dictionaries* (Pleasantville, NY: Hardscrabble Press, 1972).

Diamond, Sidney A., *Trademark Problems and How to Avoid Them* (Chicago: Crain Communications, Inc., 1973).

Dillard, J. L., *All-American English* (New York: Random House: 1975).

—— *American Talk: Where Our Words Come From* (New York: Vintage Books/Random House, 1977).

Dillon, Richard, *Meriwether Lewis: A Biography* (New York: Coward-McCann, Inc., 1965).

Dohan, Mary Helen, *Our Own Words* (Baltimore: Penguin Books, 1974).

Dulles, Foster Rhea, *America Learns to Play: A History of Popular Recreation 1607–1940* (New York: Peter Smith, 1952).

Elias, Norbert, *The History of Manners*, 2 vols. (New York: Pantheon Books, 1978).

Enterline, James Robert, *Viking America: The Norse Crossings and Their Legacy* (Garden City, NY: Doubleday & Co., 1972).

Erens, Patricia, *The Jew in American Cinema* (Bloomington: Indiana University Press, 1984).

Ernst, Morris L., and Alan U. Schwartz, *Censorship: The Search for the Obscene* (London: Collier-Macmillan Ltd., 1964).

Finch, Christopher, *Highways to Heaven: The Auto Biography of America* (New York: HarperCollins, 1992).

Fischer, David Hackett, *Albion's Seed: Four British Folkways in America* (New York: Oxford University Press, 1989).

Flatow, Ira, *They All Laughed . . . From Light Bulbs to Lasers: The Fascinating Stories Behind the Great Inventions That Have Changed Our Lives* (New York: HarperPerennial, 1992).

Flexner, Stuart Berg, *I Hear America Talking: An Illustrated Treasury of American Words and Phrases* (New York: Van Nostrand Rheinhold Co., 1976).

—— *Listening to America: An Illustrated History of Words and Phrases from Our Lively and Splendid Past* (New York: Simon and Schuster, 1982).

Foner, Eric, *Tom Paine and Revolutionary America* (New York: Oxford University Press, 1982).

Forbes, Esther, *Paul Revere and the World He Lived In* (Boston: Houghton Mifflin, Co., 1942).

Friedel, Robert, and Paul Israel, *Edison's Electric Light: Biography of an Invention* (New Brunswick, NJ: Rutgers University Press, 1986).

Frieden, Bernard J., and Lynne B. Sagalyn, *Downtown, Inc.: How America Rebuilds Cities* (Cambridge, Mass.: MIT Press, 1989).

Funk, Charles Earle, *A Hog on Ice and Other Curious Expressions* (New York: Harper & Brothers, 1948).

Funk, Wilfred, *Word Origins and Their Romantic Stories* (New York: Grosset and Dunlap, 1950).

Garrett, Elisabeth Donaghy, *At Home: The American Family, 1750–1870* (New York: Harry N. Abrams, 1990).

Garrison, Webb B., *Why You Say It* (New York: Abingdon Press, 1955).

Gies, Joseph, and Frances Gies, *The Ingenious Yankees* (New York: Thomas Y. Crowell Co., 1976).

Glenn, Robert B., Stewart A. Kingsbury and Zacharias P. Thundyil, *Language and Culture: A Book of Readings* (Marquette: Northern Michigan University Press, 1974).

Goldberger, Paul, *The Skyscraper* (New York: Alfred A. Knopf, 1981).

Gould, Stephen Jay, *Bully for Brontosaurus: Reflections in Natural History* (London: Hutchinson Radius, 1991).

Granger, Bruce Ingham, *Benjamin Franklin: An American Man of Letters* (Norman: University of Oklahoma Press, 1976).

Griffin, Bulkley S. (ed.), *Offbeat History: A Compendium of Lively Americana* (Cleveland: World Publishing, 1967).

Grosvenor, Melville Bell (ed.), *Those Inventive Americans* (Washington: National Geographic Society, 1971).

Grover, Kathryn (ed.), *Dining in America: 1850–1900* (Amherst: University of Massachusetts Press, 1987).

Gruen, Victor, and Larry Smit, *Shopping Town USA: The Planning of Shopping Centers* (New York: Reinhold Publishing Corp., 1960).

Harder, Kelsie B. (ed.), *Illustrated Dictionary of Place Names: United States and Canada* (New York: Van Nostrand Reinhold Co., 1976).

Harris, Marvin, *Good to Eat: Riddles of Food and Culture* (New York: Simon and Schuster, 1985).

Hart, Val, *The Story of American Roads* (New York: William Sloane Associates, 1950).

Hawke, David Freeman, *Paine* (New York: Harper & Row, 1974).

Heaton, Vernon, *The Mayflower* (Exeter: Webb & Bower, 1980).

Hemans, Felicia, *The Poetical Works of Mrs. Felicia Hemans* (Boston: Phillips, Sampson and Co., 1857).

Hendon, Donald W., *Classic Failures in Product Marketing* (New York: Quorum Books, 1989).

Hendrickson, Robert, *The Facts on File Encyclopedia of Word and Phrase Origins* (New York: Facts on File Publications, 1980).

Hibbert, Christopher, *The Court at Windsor: A Domestic History* (London: Penguin Books, 1982).

—— *Redcoats and Rebels: The War for America, 1770–1781* (London: Grafton Books, 1990).

Hokanson, Drake, *The Lincoln Highway: Main Street Across America* (Iowa City: University of Iowa Press, 1988).

Holt, Alfred H., *Phrase and Word Origins* (New York: Dover Publications, Inc., 1961).

Hume, Ivor Noël, *Here Lies Virginia: An Archaeologist's View of Colonial Life and History* (New York: Alfred A. Knopf, 1963).

Hynd, Noel, *The Giants of the Polo Grounds: The Glorious Times of Baseball's New York Giants* (New York: Doubleday, 1988).

Ingstad, Helge, *The Norse Discovery of America*, 2 vols. (Oslo: Norwegian University Press, 1985).

Jackson, Donald, *Among the Sleeping Giants: Occasional Pieces on Lewis and Clark* (Urbana: University of Illinois Press, 1987).

Jackson, Kenneth T., *Crabgrass Frontier: The Suburbanization of the United States* (New York: Oxford University Press, 1985).

James, Sydney V., *Colonial Rhode Island: A History* (New York: Charles Scribner's Sons, 1975).

Johnson, Paul, *Modern Times: The World from the Twenties to the Eighties* (New York: Harper & Row, 1983).

——— *The Birth of the Modern: World Society, 1815–1830* (New York: HarperCollins, 1991).

Jones, Maldwyn Allen, *American Immigration* (Chicago: University of Chicago Press, 1960).

Jordan, Philip D., *The National Road* (Indianapolis: Bobbs-Merrill Co., 1948).

Josephy, jun., Alvin M. (ed.), *The American Heritage Book of Indians* (Boston: American Heritage Publishing Co., 1961).

Jowett, Garth, *Film: The Democratic Art* (Boston: Little, Brown and Co., 1976).

Keeley, Joseph C., *Making Inventions Pay: A Practical Guide to Selling, Protecting, Manufacturing, and Marketing Your Inventions* (New York: McGraw-Hill Book Company, 1950).

Kowinski, William Severini, *The Malling of America: An Inside Look at the Great Consumer Paradise* (New York: William Morrow & Co., 1985).

Krapp, George Philip, *The English Language in America*, 2 vols. (New York: The Century Co., 1925).

Kroc, Ray (with Robert Anderson), *Grinding It Out: The Making of McDonald's* (Chicago: Contemporary Books, 1977).

Krout, John Allen, *Annals of American Sport* (New Haven: Yale University Press, 1929).

Lacey, Robert, *Sir Walter Ralegh* (London: Weidenfeld & Nicolson, 1973).

——— *Ford: The Men and the Machines* (Boston: Little, Brown and Co., 1986).

Laird, Charlton, *Language in America* (New York: The World Publishing Co., 1970).

Levenstein, Harvey A., *Revolution at the Table: The Transformation of the American Diet* (New York: Oxford University Press, 1988).

Levin, David, *Cotton Mather: The Young Life of the Lord's Remembrancer, 1663–1703* (Cambridge, Mass.: Harvard University Press, 1978).

Liebs, Chester H., *Main Street to Miracle Mile: American Roadside Architecture* (Boston: New York Graphic Society/Little, Brown and Co., 1985).

Lingeman, Richard R., *Don't You Know There's a War On?: The American Home Front, 1941–45* (New York: G. P. Putnam's Sons, 1970).

Love, John F., *McDonald's: Behind the Arches* (Toronto: Bantam Books, 1986).

Lowance, jun., Mason I., *Increase Mather* (New York: Twayne Publishers, 1974).

459

Lutz, William, *Doublespeak* (New York: Harper & Row, 1989).

Luxenberg, Stan, *Roadside Empires: How the Chains Franchised America* (New York: Viking Books, 1985).

McAlister, Lyle N., *Spain and Portugal in the New World, 1492–1700* (Minneapolis: University of Minnesota Press, 1984).

McDavid, jun., Raven I., *Varieties of American English* (Stanford: Stanford University Press, 1980).

McPherson, James M., *Battle Cry of Freedom: The American Civil War* (London: Penguin Books/Oxford University Press, 1990).

Madison, James, Alexander Hamilton and John Jay (ed. Isaac Kramnick), *The Federalist Papers* (London: Penguin Books, 1987).

Maggio, Rosalie, *The Dictionary of Bias-Free Usage: A Guide to Nondiscriminatroy Language* (Phoenix, Ariz.: Oryx Press, 1991).

Marckwardt, Albert H. (rev. J. L. Dillard), *American English,* 2nd edn. (New York: Oxford University Press, 1980).

Martineau, Harriet, *Society in America,* 3 vols. (London: Saunders and Otley, 1837).

Mathews, Mitford M. (ed.), *A Dictionary of Americanisms on Historical Principles,* 4 vols. (Chicago: University of Chicago Press, 1951).

Mee, jun., Charles L., *The Genius of the People* (New York: Perennial Library/Harper & Row, 1988).

Mencken, H. L., *The American Language: An Inquiry into the Development of English in the United States,* 4th edn. (New York: Alfred A. Knopf, 1937).

—— *The American Language: An Inquiry into the Development of English in the United States,* suppl. 1 (New York: Alfred A. Knopf, 1945).

—— *The American Language: An Inquiry into the Development of English in the United States,* suppl. 2 (New York: Alfred A. Knopf, 1948).

—— (with new material by Raven I. McDavid, jun.), *The American Language: An Inquiry into the Development of English in the United States,* abridged 4th edn. (New York: Alfred A. Knopf, 1989).

Meyer, Jerome S., *World Book of Great Inventions* (Cleveland OH: The World Publishing Co., 1956).

Milton, Joyce, *Loss of Eden: A Biography of Charles and Anne Morrow Lindbergh* (New York: HarperCollins, 1993).

Moolman, Valerie, *The Road to Kitty Hawk* (Alexandria, Va.: Time-Life Books, 1980).

Morison, Samuel Eliot, *The Oxford History of the American People* (New York: Oxford University Press, 1965).

—— *The European Discovery of America,* 2 vols. (New York: Oxford University Press, 1971).

Moulton, Gary E. (ed.), *Atlas of the Lewis and Clark Expedition* (Lincoln: University of Nebraska Press, 1983).

—— (ed.), *The Journals of the Lewis and Clark Expedition: August 30, 1803–August 24, 1804* (Lincoln: University of Nebraska Press, 1986).

Nye, David E., *Electrifying America: Social Meanings of a New Technology, 1880–1940* (Cambridge, Mass.: MIT Press, 1990).

Oakley, J. Ronald, *God's Country: America in the Fifties* (New York: Dembner Books, 1986).

O'Malley, Michael, *Keeping Watch: A History of American Time* (New York: Viking Penguin, 1990).

Opie, Iona, and Peter Opie, *The Oxford Dictionary of Nursery Rhymes* (Oxford: Clarendon Press, 1951).

Partridge, Eric, and John W. Clark, *British and American English Since 1900* (London: Andrew Dakers Ltd., 1951).

Patton, Phil, *Open Road: A Celebration of the American Highway* (New York: Simon and Schuster, 1986).

Peirce, Neal R., *The New England States* (New York: W. W. Norton & Co., 1976).

Pyles, Thomas, *Words and Ways of American English* (New York: Random House, 1952).

—— *Selected Essays on English Usage* (Gainesville: University Presses of Florida, 1979).

Quinn, David Beers, *Set Fair for Roanoke: Voyages and Colonies, 1584–1606* (Chapel Hill: University of North Carolina Press, 1984).

—— *North America from Earliest Discovery to First Settlements* (New York: Harper & Row, 1985).

Rae, John B., *The Road and the Car in American Life* (Cambridge, Mass.: MIT Press, 1971).

Rodgers, Elizabeth G., *Chagrin . . . Whence the Name?* (Chagrin Falls, OH: pub. privately, 1988).

Root, Waverley, and Richard de Rochemont, *Eating in America: A History* (New York: William Morrow & Co., 1976).

Rosenberg, Bernard, and David Manning White (eds.), *Mass Culture: The Popular Arts in America* (Glencoe, Ill.: The Free Press, 1957).

Rowsome, jun., Frank, *The Verse by the Side of the Road: The Story of the Burma-Shave Signs* (Brattleboro, Vt.: Stephen Greene Press, 1965).

Rybczynski, Witold, *Home: A Short History of an Idea* (New York: Penguin Books, 1987).

—— *Waiting for the Weekend* (New York: Viking Books, 1991).

Safire, William, *On Language* (New York: Avon Books, 1980).

—— *What's the Good Word* (New York: Times Books, 1982).

—— *Take My Word for It* (New York: Times Books, 1986).

—— *Coming to Terms* (New York: Doubleday, 1991).

Sagarin, Edward, *The Anatomy of Dirty Words* (New York: Lyle Stuart, 1968).

Savage, jun., William W. (ed.), *Cowboy Life: Reconstructing an American Myth* (Norman: University of Oklahoma Press, 1975).

Schiller, Herbert I., *Mass Communications and American Empire* (New York: Augustus M. Kelley, 1969).

Schor, Juliet B., *The Overworked American: The Unexpected Decline of Leisure* (New York: Basic Books, 1991).

Schrank, Jeffrey, *Snap, Crackle, and Popular Taste: The Illusion of Free Choice in America* (New York: Delacorte Press, 1977).

Schumach, Murray, *The Face on the Cutting Room Floor: The Story of Movie and Television Censorship* (New York: William Morrow & Co., 1964).

Schwarz, Barry, *George Washington: The Making of an American Symbol* (Ithaca: Cornell University Press, 1987).

Seavey, Ormond, *Becoming Benjamin Franklin: The Autobiography and the Life* (University Park: Pennsylvania State University Press, 1988).

Shearer, Benjamin F., and Barbara S. Shearer, *State Names, Seals, Flags, and Symbols: A Historical Guide* (New York: Greenwood Press, 1987).

Simpson, David, *The Politics of American English, 1776–1850* (New York: Oxford University Press, 1986).

Small, Herbert, *The Library of Congress: Its Architecture and Decoration* (New York: Arthur Ross/W. W. Norton, 1982).

Smith, Elsdon C., *The Story of Our Names* (New York: Harper & Brothers, 1950).

Smith, Page, *A People's History of the United States*, 8 vols. (New York: McGraw-Hill Book Company, 1984).

Stedman, Raymond William, *Shadows of the Indian: Stereotypes in American Culture* (Norman: University of Oklahoma Press, 1982).

Sterling, Christopher H., and Jon M. Kittross, *Stay Tuned: A Concise History of American Broadcasting* (Belmont, Calif.: Wadsworth Publishing Company, 1978).

Stewart, George R., *Names on the Land: A Historical Account of Place-Naming in the United States* (New York: Random House, 1945).

—— *American Place-Names: A Concise and Selective Dictionary for the Continental United States of America* (New York: Oxford University Press, 1970).

Story, G. M., W. J. Kirwin and J. D. A. Widdowson (eds.), *Dictionary of Newfoundland English*, 2nd edn. (Toronto: University of Toronto Press, 1990).

Strasser, Susan, *Never Done: A History of American Housework* (New York: Pantheon Books, 1982).

—— *Satisfaction Guaranteed: The Making of the American Mass Market* (New York: Pantheon Books, 1989).

Sullivan, Mark, *Our Times: The United States, 1900–1925*, 2 vols. (New York: Charles Scribner's Sons, 1926).

Tannahill, Reay, *Sex in History* (London: Abacus/Sphere, 1981).

Tedlow, Richard S., *New and Improved: The Story of Mass Marketing in America* (New York: Basic Books, 1990)

Terrace, Vincent, *The Complete Encyclopedia of Television Programs, 1947–1976*, 2 vols. (South Brunswick, NJ: A. S. Barnes and Company, 1976).

Thomas, Benjamin P., *Abraham Lincoln: A Biography* (New York: The Modern Library, 1968).

Thomas, Charles Kenneth, *An Introduction to the Phonetics of American English* (New York: The Ronald Press Co., 1947).

Thornton, Willis, *History: Fact and Fable* (New York: Barnes & Noble Books, 1993).

Tocqueville, Alexis de (trans. George Lawrence), *Journey to America* (Garden City, NY: Anchor Books/Doubleday, 1971).

Trollope, Frances, *Domestic Manners of the Americans* (New York: Alfred A. Knopf, 1949).

Tulloch, Sarah, *The Oxford Dictionary of New Words: A Popular Guide to Words in the News* (Oxford: Oxford University Press, 1991).

Udelson, Joseph H., *The Great Television Race: A History of the American Television Industry, 1925–1941* (Birmingham, Alabama: University of Alabama Press, 1982).

Vallins, G. H., *Spelling* (London: André Deutsch, 1954).

Van Doren, Carl, *Benjamin Franklin* (New York: The Viking Press, 1938).

—— *The Great Rehearsal: The Story of the Making and Ratifying of the Constitution of the United States* (New York: Viking Press, 1948).

Vieyra, Daniel I., *Fill 'er Up: An Architectural History of America's Gas Stations* (New York: Macmillan Publishing Co., 1979).

Voigt, David Quentin, *American Baseball: From Gentleman's Sport to the Commissioner System* (University Park: Pennsylvania State University Press, 1983).

Wagenknecht, Edward, *Henry Wadsworth Longfellow: His Poetry and Prose* (New York: Ungar, 1986).

Ward, Sir A. W. (ed.), *The Cambridge History of English Literature*, vol. XIV (New York: Macmillan Publishing Co., 1931).

Warren, Louis A., *Lincoln's Gettysburg Declaration* (Fort Wayne, Ind.: Lincoln National Life Foundation, 1964).

Watson, Alice E., *Experimental Studies in the Psychology and Pedagogy of Spelling* (New York: Teachers College/Columbia University, 1935).

Well, J. C., *Accents of English: Beyond the British Isles* (Cambridge: Cambridge University Press, 1982).

Weston, Jack, *The Real American Cowboy* (New York: Schocken Books, 1985).

Will, George F., *Men at Work: The Craft of Baseball* (New York: HarperPerennial, 1991).

Willcox, William B. (ed.), *The Papers of Benjamin Franklin* (New Haven: Yale University Press, 1972).

Wills, Garry, *Inventing America: Jefferson's Declaration of Independence* (Garden City, NY: Doubleday, 1978).

—— *Lincoln at Gettysburg: The Words That Remade America* (New York: Touchstone/Simon & Schuster, 1992).

Wortham, Thomas, *James Russell Lowell's 'The Biglow Papers': A Critical Edition* (DeKalb: Northern Illinois University Press, 1977).

Wright, Esmond, *Franklin of Philadelphia* (Cambridge, Mass.: Belknap Press/Harvard University Press, 1986).

Wright, Frances, *Views of Society and Manners in America* (Cambridge, Mass.: Belknap Press/Harvard University Press, 1963).

Wyllie Irvin G., *The Self-Made Man in America: The Myth of Rags to Riches* (New York: The Free Press, 1954).

Zinn, Howard, *A People's History of the United States* (New York: HarperPerennial, 1990).

Index

Further Non-Fiction Titles Available from Minerva

While every effort is made to keep prices low, it is sometimes necessary to increase prices at short notice. Mandarin Paperbacks reserves the right to show new retail prices on covers which may differ from those previously advertised in the text or elsewhere.

The prices shown below were correct at the time of going to press.

☐ 7493 9815 9	**Neither Here Nor There**		Bill Bryson	£5.99
☐ 7493 9761 6	**The Crystal Desert**		David G. Campbell	£6.99
☐ 7493 9070 0	**Lost in Translation**		Eva Hoffmann	£5.99
☐ 7493 9100 6	**Moscow! Moscow!**		Christopher Hope	£4.99
☐ 7493 9944 9	**Diaries**		Franz Kafka	£9.99
☐ 7493 9881 7	**Blue Highways**		William Least Heat-Moon	£6.99
☐ 7493 9174 X	**The Mirror Maker**		Primo Levi	£5.99
☐ 7493 9906 6	**Between Two Seas**		Charles Lister	£5.99
☐ 7493 9171 5	**The Colossus of Maroussi**		Henri Miller	£5.99
☐ 7493 9920 1	**India**		V. S. Naipaul	£6.99
☐ 7493 9047 6	**Friends of Promise**		Michael Shelden	£6.99
☐ 7493 9707 1	**Race**		Studs Terkel	£6.99

All these books are available at your bookshop or newsagent, or can be ordered direct from the address below. Just tick the titles you want and fill in the form below.

Cash Sales Department, PO Box 5, Rushden, Northants NN10 6YX.
Fax: 01933 414047 : Phone: 01933 414000.

Please send cheque, payable to 'Reed Book Services Ltd.', or postal order for purchase price quoted and allow the following for postage and packing:

£1.00 for the first book, 50p for the second; **FREE POSTAGE AND PACKING FOR THREE BOOKS OR MORE PER ORDER.**

NAME (Block letters) ....

ADDRESS ....

....

☐ I enclose my remittance for ....

☐ I wish to pay by Access/Visa Card Number ☐☐☐☐☐☐☐☐☐☐☐☐☐☐☐☐

Expiry Date ☐☐☐☐

Signature ....

Please quote our reference: MAND